D0771396

Managerial Communication

Strategies and Applications

Managerial Communication

Strategies and Applications Fifth Edition

Geraldine E. Hynes
Sam Houston State University

The McGraw-Hill Companies

McGraw-Hill Irwin

MANAGERIAL COMMUNICATION: STRATEGIES AND APPLICATIONS, FIFTH EDITION

Published by McGraw-Hill, a business unit of The McGraw-Hill Companies, Inc., 1221 Avenue of the Americas, New York, NY 10020. Copyright © 2011 by The McGraw-Hill Companies, Inc. All rights reserved. Previous editions © 2008, 2005, and 2002. No part of this publication may be reproduced or distributed in any form or by any means, or stored in a database or retrieval system, without the prior written consent of The McGraw-Hill Companies, Inc., including, but not limited to, in any network or other electronic storage or transmission, or broadcast for distance learning.

Some ancillaries, including electronic and print components, may not be available to customers outside the United States.

This book is printed on acid-free paper.

1 2 3 4 5 6 7 8 9 0 DOC/DOC 1 0 9 8 7 6 5 4 3 2 1 0

ISBN 978-0-07-337775-9
MHID 0-07-337775-9

Vice President & Editor-in-Chief: *Brent Gordon*
VP EDP/Central Publishing Services: *Kimberly Meriwether David*
Publisher: *Paul Ducham*
Sponsoring Editor: *Laura Hurst Spell*
Editorial Coordinator: *Jane Beck*
Marketing Manager: *Jaime Halteman*
Senior Project Manager: *Lisa A. Bruflodt*
Design Coordinator: *Margarite Reynolds*
USE Cover Image Credit: Left to right: *Corbis/PictureQuest, © Comstock/PunchStock, Digital Vision/Getty Images, Royalty-Free/CORBIS, Stockbyte/Punchstock Images, Digital Vision/Getty Images*
    Background image: *Ken Usami/Getty Images*
Production Supervisor: *Sue Culbertson*
Media Project Manager: *Suresh Babu*
Compositor: *Laserwords Private Limited*
Typeface: *10/12 Times Roman*
Printer: *R.R. Donnelley*

Library of Congress Cataloging-in-Publication Data

Hynes, Geraldine E.
    Managerial communication : strategies and applications/Geraldine E. Hynes.—5th ed.
        p. cm.
    Includes index.
    ISBN-13: 978-0-07-337775-9 (alk. paper)
    ISBN-10: 0-07-337775-9
    1. Communication in management. 2. Business communication. I. Title.
HD30.3.H95 2010
658.4'5—dc22

                                                    2009046355

www.mhhe.com

To Jim, who has been my center for more than 40 years.

About the Author

Geraldine E. Hynes, Ph.D.

is Associate Professor in the College of Business Administration, Sam Houston State University, Huntsville, Texas, USA. She has taught business and managerial communication at both the undergraduate and graduate levels since 1988. She is also a communication consultant and contract trainer for business, government, and nonprofit organizations. Her award-winning research has been published in scholarly journals and books in several countries. She serves her professional association, the Association for Business Communication, as a board member and officer, with a term as President in 2010.

Preface to the Fifth Edition

The roots of this textbook extend back to 1984, when John Wiley and Sons published *Managerial Communication: A Strategic Approach,* by Larry Smeltzer and John Waltman. Their practical, results-oriented examination of managerial communication was groundbreaking at the time. In the Preface, they stated the book's objective: "to develop managers who communicate in a creative manner by understanding and strategically applying appropriate concepts." That objective is still valid.

A second edition added Don Leonard as third author in 1991. I adopted the 1994 edition, authored by Larry Smeltzer and Don Leonard, by then titled *Managerial Communication: Strategies and Applications.* I had been looking for a graduate-level text that presented a balanced approach to workplace communication and that was written for managers and executives.

The strengths that drew me to that early edition were:

- A strategic approach
- A solid research base
- Comprehensive coverage of contemporary issues
- An even-handed examination of oral and written communication channels
- A focus on managerial rather than entry-level competencies

I came onboard as third author with Smeltzer and Leonard for the 2002 edition, and was sole author for the 2008 edition. As I revise yet again, my goal is to ensure that the qualities that made the original book unique and successful are still present in this fifth edition. Truth is truth. It doesn't change with the times. So the task is to bring timeless communication principles into the contemporary workplace. To meet the needs of today's busy manager/student, I updated the chapters, describing current business practices, summarizing relevant research, and providing guidelines for strategic managerial communication.

The reality is that an effective contemporary manager must possess a wide range of skills. While being accountable to an executive board and a customer base, a manager must be able to motivate subordinates and cross-functional teams with diverse backgrounds, interpret complicated rules, foster process improvement, and meet sometimes-unclear organizational expectations. Furthermore, today's manager often must use new technology to accomplish these tasks. Since these advanced abilities don't necessarily come from prior work experience, communication education is a vital component in managerial development.

Working on the fifth edition of this textbook has been both enjoyable and challenging. It has forced me to evaluate the content of the managerial communication course I teach in our MBA program, to sort out what is important and what is no longer important for my students to know and be able to do. I hope that the results of these efforts satisfy other students' professional communication needs as well. After all, we know for sure that effective communication leads to managerial and organizational success. The value of the course is not controversial; the key is to keep the course content fresh.

WHAT'S NEW IN THIS EDITION

Many adopters of the fourth edition of *Managerial Communication: Strategies and Applications* indicated that they especially liked the end-of-chapter cases, the balanced approach to managerial writing and oral communication, and the supplemental materials. Because of their usefulness to instructors and students, these materials have been revised and retained for the fifth edition. Chapters 1, 2, 7, and 8 proved to be very popular with reviewers of the fourth edition, so these chapters were refreshed and updated to address contemporary managerial communication situations. Many additional important changes were made to the remaining chapters to make the fifth edition an even greater resource in the field of managerial communication:

- Chapter 3 ("Technologically Mediated Communication") includes business professionals' uses of the latest technologies, such as corporate blogs and tweets. Emphasis is on the principles and best practices that apply to both emerging technologies and older technologies.
- Chapter 4 ("Contemporary Managerial Writing") introduces the Plain Language movement and provides examples of conversational style in business and government documents.
- Chapter 5 ("Routine Messages") offers guidelines for formatting letters and memos.
- Chapter 6 ("Management Reports and Proposals") takes an in-depth look at special business reports, including proposals and analytical reports.
- Chapter 9 ("Intercultural Managerial Communication") explores cultural differences in meanings of colors, paralanguage, and time, with cases and examples drawn from today's global marketplace.
- Chapter 10 ("Conflict Management") has new material on the impact of power on conflict.
- Chapter 11 ("Managerial Negotiation") includes a major section that describes how networking can increase influence.
- Chapter 12 ("Conducting Interviews") presents guidelines for networking as an employment search tool. It also has a new section explaining legal issues for performance reviews.
- Chapter 13 ("Managing Meetings and Teams") has expanded sections on group members' roles and on project team leadership.
- Chapter 14 ("Making Formal Presentations") explores controversies about PowerPoint as a tool for both oral and written communication in the workplace. In addition, new sections on crisis communication and communicating with the media have been added.

Another major new feature of this edition is the Appendix. In this section, you will find 10 articles composed by graduate business students at Sam Houston State University under the supervision of the author. The articles summarize the latest research on emerging technologies. Each article describes a different technology and how it is applied in U.S. business today. The authors also look to the future and track trends in technologically mediated business communication. Guidelines for best practices relevant to each technology are presented. A list of references and topics for class discussion appears at the end of each article.

Acknowledgments

Most importantly, I wish to acknowledge John Waltman, Larry Smeltzer, and Don Leonard, who pioneered this textbook. I now understand the enormity of the task they undertook. They accomplished it with competence, grace, and professionalism. They have my deepest respect.

Second, I appreciate all the people who helped make this edition a reality. My SHSU Bearkat team included Jennifer Elmi, Darlene Vega, Antonette Harvey, Harini Vemulapati, Matt O'Rourke, Stephen Hunt, and Sara Williamson. They performed all their tasks with diligence and good cheer. I also wish to warmly thank Anna Turri for her excellent contributions. Reviewers of the book also deserve thanks for their insightful feedback: Harvey Lon Addams, Weber State University; Cynthia Barnes, Lamar University–Beaumont; Kathy Hill, Sam Houston State University; Gary Kohut, University of North Carolina at Chapel Hill; Richard Mahee, Delaware State University; Jean Anna Sellers, Fort Hays State University; and Carol White, Georgia State University. Members of the McGraw-Hill team who earned my heartfelt gratitude include Jane Beck, Lisa Bruflodt, and Laura Spell. Their perspicacity, dependability, and professionalism smoothed the way. A special thank you goes to Dave Fosnough, former Irwin/McGraw-Hill field sales supervisor, who started me down this path in 1993. I am where I am today because of his encouragement.

Third, I am grateful to my loving family—Jim, Maureen and Erasmus, Kellie and Bob, and my incandescent grandchildren—who support me unreservedly.

Finally, I salute my students because they are dedicated to improving their managerial communication skills and strategies, and because they believe that I can help them do it. This book is for you.

—*Geraldine E. Hynes*

Brief Contents

Table of Contents

Part **One**

Managing in Contemporary Organizations

Chapter One

The Role of Communication in Contemporary Organizations

Extremists think "communication" means agreeing with them.

—*Leo Rosten, U.S. (Polish-born) author and political scientist*

In the second decade of this century, management communication is both challenging and exciting. It is challenging because organizations are becoming much more complex, and many new forces confront the manager. Greater competitive pressures, shorter product life cycles, increased demands for quality and service, more regulatory constraints, greater concerns for cost containment, heightened awareness of environmental concerns, and renewed emphasis on human rights are just some of the pressures increasing the complexity of the manager's job. But these pressures also make managerial communication exciting. The contemporary manager has a greater opportunity than ever to make a significant difference in the success of the organization and increase the quality of work life for fellow employees. However, this requires effective managerial communication skills, which are becoming more complex, making them more difficult to master.

The workplace is much more diverse and complex than it was just a few decades ago, and it requires more sophisticated management communication skills. At the start of the 20th century, heavy manufacturing was the industrial base of Western countries. Products changed little from year to year, and the work force consisted mainly of white males. Today, however, products and entire management systems change rapidly, and employees must adapt as quickly. In addition, work teams are extremely diverse. At a firm such as the computer chip company Intel, it is not uncommon to have a design engineer from Singapore working with a purchasing manager from Ireland and an accountant from California. This means the manager must have the sophisticated skills required to communicate to a diverse work group in a rapidly changing environment.

cultural challenges

Technology helps with this communication challenge, but it also adds new requirements. Advances in telecommunications have increased our communication capabilities, but we must learn how to best use these capabilities. In addition, the improved communication systems mean we have greater abilities to interact with multiple cultures, which requires that we become better cross-cultural communicators. Furthermore, as technical products and services become more complex, we must be able to communicate about more complicated concepts than in the past.

Effective communication has been shown to be a leading indicator of financial performance. Watson Wyatt Worldwide, a provider of human capital and management consulting services in 30 countries, conducted research on 267 U.S. companies and found that those companies that communicate effectively have a 19.4 percent higher market premium than companies that do not. Other key findings include:

- Shareholder returns for organizations with the most effective communication were over 57 percent higher during the years 2000–2004 than were returns for firms with less effective communication.
- Firms that communicate effectively are 4.5 times more likely to report high levels of employee engagement than firms that communicate less effectively.
- Companies that are highly effective communicators are 20 percent more likely to report lower turnover rates than their peers.
- On average, firms within the financial and retail trade sectors rank among the most effective communicators. Health care, basic materials, telecommunications, and other service companies rank among the least effective communicators.[1]

Communication and its role in the life of an organization will continue to evolve. As a result, we must think about how communication will occur in the future. One way to understand what this will mean for managerial communication behavior is to look at the different stages through which managerial communication has already passed. As you read the following pages and note how managerial communication has changed during the past century, it is interesting and valuable to speculate how it will change during your career. Knowledge of the past will help us prepare for the future.

A BRIEF HISTORICAL OVERVIEW OF MANAGERIAL COMMUNICATION

Managers communicated with subordinates in markedly different ways in the past than they do today. To best understand these changes, it is helpful to review the eras of management as diagrammed in Table 1–1. After an overview of each era, the management communication strategies and techniques appropriate for that era are discussed.

TABLE 1–1
Historical Perspective of Managerial Communication

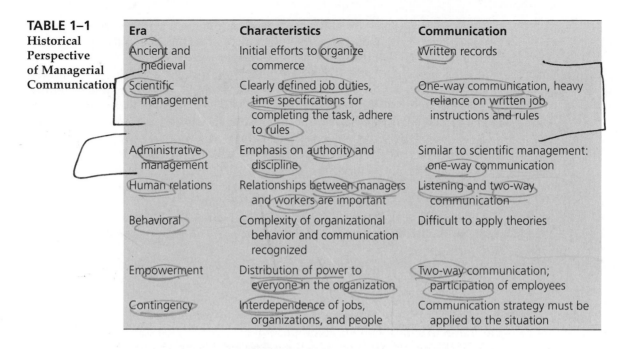

Era	Characteristics	Communication
Ancient and medieval	Initial efforts to organize commerce	Written records
Scientific management	Clearly defined job duties, time specifications for completing the task, adhere to rules	One-way communication, heavy reliance on written job instructions and rules
Administrative management	Emphasis on authority and discipline	Similar to scientific management: one-way communication
Human relations	Relationships between managers and workers are important	Listening and two-way communication
Behavioral	Complexity of organizational behavior and communication recognized	Difficult to apply theories
Empowerment	Distribution of power to everyone in the organization	Two-way communication; participation of employees
Contingency	Interdependence of jobs, organizations, and people	Communication strategy must be applied to the situation

Management Communication in Ancient Times

The earliest known example of managerial communication may be the record-keeping procedure developed by Sumerian priests around 5000 BC. Business transactions were recorded north of the Arabian Gulf as early as 3200 BC. It is interesting to note that these records reflect cross-cultural business transactions. The Egyptians recognized the importance of putting requests in writing—a written code of conduct can be found circa 1750 BC with the Code of Hammurabi. The ancient Romans were the first managers, using commercial languages to negotiate with suppliers, network with customers, and exchange business gifts between 1000 BC and 1 AD. The first committee may have been organized around 325 AD as Alexander the Great organized staff groups. (Do you suppose managers complained about meetings then as much as they do now?)

Venice, Italy, was a major center for merchants and economic exchange during medieval times. Merchants built warehouses and used an inventory system that required periodic reports for the city governing body.[2] These brief examples indicate that since the beginning of commerce, some type of managerial communication has been practiced.

The Industrial Revolution and Scientific Management

Although managerial communication occurred in ancient times, the systematic evolution of managers as communicators began with the Industrial Revolution. The philosophy most generally associated with the early Industrial Revolution is *scientific management*. This philosophy and set of methods and techniques stressed the scientific study and organization of work. During this era, it was believed *def →* that the greatest levels of efficiency could be obtained with extremely precise job instructions and that subordinates should not second-guess the instructions. Thus, managerial authority was not to be questioned.

The background to the scientific management philosophy helps us understand its relationship to communication. Frederick Taylor created scientific management. He was a supervisor at the Philadelphia Midvale Steel Company in the late 1800s when he became interested in ways to improve lathe work. Taylor studied the work of individual lathe workers to discover exactly how they performed their jobs; he identified each aspect of each job and measured anything and everything that could be measured. He believed it was possible to develop a science that could indicate the most efficient and effective manner for performing a task, and then this technique could be written in elaborate job designs and communicated to employees through extensive training. Taylor treated individual employees as another element in the scientific formula.[3]

Several disciples of the scientific management espoused by Taylor developed these concepts further. Frank Gilbreth developed the study of motion to the highest level of perfection. To ensure precision, he invented the microchrometer, a clock with a sweeping second hand that could record time in 1/200 of a minute. Gilbreth's most famous accomplishment was a bricklaying study. After carefully analyzing the procedures followed by bricklayers, he reduced the number of motions from an average of 18 to 4.5 per brick on exterior brick and from 18 to 2 on interior brick.

A second disciple was Harrington Emerson, who developed 12 principles of efficiency for the railroads. One of his most repeated principles was discipline, which included adherence to rules and strict obedience. In other words, he believed management's role was to establish a set of elaborate rules and ensure that employees followed them.[4]

reduce variance Scientific management attempted to systematize the work environment by reducing individual variance. This made the job easier for both managers and the workers because unique situations were eliminated. No deviations from the norm were allowed. The manager was simply required to communicate the job specifications and the related work rules.

Scientific management is most often associated with the manufacturing efficiencies of the Model T Ford. These efficiencies allowed every working person of the day to drive a car. But we also see heavy reliance on the scientific method today in such businesses as McDonald's. Ray Kroc used scientific management techniques to bring quality, service, cleanliness, and value to the fast-food industry. Every employee has a precise job description, each task is to be completed in a specified period, and there is strict adherence to rules. These procedures allow employees to be trained in a short time and reduce the number of unique conditions to which managers must adapt. Only limited strategic managerial communication is required.[5] Rules and job tasks are clearly explained, and employees are expected to follow them. No negotiations or conflict resolution are expected.

TABLE 1–2
Six of Fayol's Principles

1. *Division of work.* Efficiency requires that the total task be broken into small component parts assigned to workers who specialize in these limited tasks.

2. *Authority.* Managers have the formal authority to give orders. However, to be effective leaders, they must also possess personal authority deriving from their skill, experience, and character.

3. *Discipline.* Workers should willfully obey the rules and leaders of the organization.

4. *Unity of command.* Each subordinate should receive orders from only one supervisor.

5. *Subordination of individual interest to general interest.* The company's interest always takes precedence over the individual's interests.

6. *Scalar chain.* An unbroken line of authority runs from the top manager of an enterprise to the lowest levels of the organization. For giving orders and reports, this line should normally be observed.

The Administrative Approach

While scientific management was receiving extensive attention, a second branch of early management thought was developing, called *administrative theory*. Although this approach to management emerged during the same era as scientific management, its focus was quite different. While scientific management was concerned mainly with the individual workers and efficiency at the operational level, administrative theory focused on broader issues facing all managers.

A key figure in developing this theory was Henri Fayol, who developed 14 principles of management.[6] Table 1–2 presents six of these principles of managerial communication. Note that two-way communication between the manager and subordinate is limited; the manager's authority is emphasized. The manager's role is to give orders and maintain discipline; little attention is placed on listening skills. Extensive use of groups and participative decision making are not integral to administrative theory. This approach is reminiscent of the traditional military in which officers were extremely autocratic—no one provided feedback to them, and the officers seldom listened. It is also comparable to the political system used in totalitarian governments.

The sixth principle, scalar chain, has special importance in our discussion of managerial communication. Fayol recognized the traditional organization hierarchy as important in establishing the chain of command. However, he also saw inefficiencies in the system when employees at the same level needed to communicate. Figure 1–1 shows how employee B would communicate with employee J according to prevailing thought at the time. The employee would have to send the message up the organization's chain of command to the top, and then the message would come down through another chain of command. The implications for inefficiency and ineffectiveness are clear to contemporary managers.

To bypass these problems, Fayol developed what is now famously known as the gangplank theory. According to this theory, employee B would be allowed to communicate directly with employee J if each had permission from their

FIGURE 1–1
Following the
Hierarchy

immediate supervisors to do so and they kept the supervisors apprised of the communication. Figure 1–2 diagrams informal networks and horizontal communication. Gangplank theory was the first formal recognition of horizontal communication and acknowledged the importance of informal communication networks, which are now taken for granted in most contemporary organizations. But a strict chain of command is still used in some organizations. Throughout this book, we will discuss how organizations differ and how these differences must be considered when communicating.

The Human Relations Approach

During the early 1900s, the nature of management and the manager's job became the focus of attention. Little was being said about how the manager related to employees. But this began to change in the 1920s and 1930s as the relationships between organizational members began to receive attention.

FIGURE 1–2
Gangplank
Theory

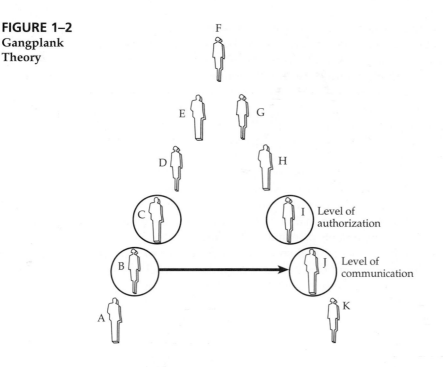

Dale Carnegie

Dale Carnegie was one of the first writers to link communication skill with managerial effectiveness. He wrote extensively about the social and psychological aspects of "winning friends and influencing people."[7]

Carnegie argued that gaining compliance from other people depends on interpersonal dynamics of attraction and influence. He offered his own prescriptions for influencing others by listening, showing an interest in their concerns, and gaining their confidence. Although his primary audience was not managers, his message to them was clear. Obtaining employee commitment to the organization does not depend solely on economic motivators or the authority of a manager's position. Commitment is gained through interpersonal communication skills. This was a radical change to those who previously believed a manager could "buy" commitment.

Before Dale Carnegie's death in 1955, nearly 5 million people had purchased his book, and thousands of managers had flocked to Dale Carnegie seminars.[8] The seminars are still popular throughout the world.

Hawthorne Studies

About the same time that Dale Carnegie was presenting his seminars, a group of Harvard professors, led by Elton Mayo, was conducting a series of studies that became known as the Hawthorne studies.[9] The studies were conducted at Western Electric Company's Hawthorne plant in Illinois, where management followed the scientific management principles in the production of telephones. Little personal communication occurred between managers and employees; job specifications and work rules were spelled out; and the manager's job was to enforce them through authority and discipline.

Originally, a group of industrial engineers designed the Hawthorne studies to show the effect on productivity of increasing the light in work areas. The engineers set out to find the optimum conditions by experimenting with the lighting, but the results of the study defied explanation. Productivity increased regardless of what the researchers did to the lighting. When light was increased, productivity went up. When light was held constant, productivity still went up. Even when the level of light was decreased, productivity continued to increase until workers could no longer see what they were doing.

The results of these illumination studies were disturbing to engineers schooled in scientific management principles. To further study why their principles failed, researchers isolated and studied a small group of workers. These studies included changes in compensation, rest periods, work schedules, and work methods. In general, productivity increased during the studies regardless of changes in the work conditions. The researchers finally concluded the relationship between the researchers and the workers accounted for the results. The researchers had shown a great personal interest in the workers as they consulted with and kept them informed about changes. The relationship established between the researchers and the employees was quite different from that of the managers and employees in other parts of the plant.

Because the results differed from what was expected, the industrial engineers continued to study working conditions. During the next phase, the researchers interviewed thousands of employees to discover their attitudes toward working conditions, managers, and work in general. This was probably the first time extensive interviewing was conducted in the workplace. Traditionally, scientific management advocates simply observed workers as the researchers sought the most efficient way to organize a job. Now the Hawthorne researchers were asking employees about their feelings. Questioning or interviewing became part of the work environment.

The interviews indicated people who work under similar conditions experience these conditions in different ways and assign different meanings to their experiences. The research concluded that employees' attitudes depend on the social organization of the group and their positions in these groups. One of the primary researchers, Elton Mayo, recommended that managers be friendly in their relationships with workers, listen to workers' concerns, and give workers a sense of participation in decisions so they could meet their social needs.[10] In many respects, both Mayo and Carnegie were similar in their advice, and both were in stark contrast to the scientific management philosophy.

Or were they? Did this human relations approach really differ from the scientific management approach? Some would argue that both Mayo and Carnegie were promoting highly manipulative, managerial communication strategies intended only to gain compliance from workers and to promote acceptance of managerial authority. The heart of the human relations approach is that attention to social needs and participation improve morale. In turn, this morale leads to greater compliance with managerial authority. In the human relations approach, managerial communication is seen as a tool for controlling organizational processes.

Although the general orientation of management during that era may have been manipulative, the human relations approach pointed out the importance of interpersonal communication. Because of the human relations approach, managing groups, listening, and interviewing are now all considered integral to managerial communication. In addition, the administrative approach highlighted the importance of organizational structures. Without the administrative and human relations orientations, the only focus of managerial communication would be keeping records, giving orders, and maintaining discipline. But managerial communication goes beyond these functions. Each era approaches communication differently but helps us better understand communication within contemporary organizations and the type of communication that may be appropriate in the future. For instance, the gangplank concept is not totally accepted today in some organizations. Will it be accepted in 2015? What will be the acceptable rule for communicating with other employees?

The Behavioral Approach

The perspectives on managerial communication changed during the 1950s. Managers' behavior, including communication, received extensive attention. Economics, anthropology, psychology, and sociology were all applied to understanding communication on the job. The general orientation was to view organizational members as full human beings, not just as tools used to complete a job. Peter Drucker was among the first management gurus to assert that workers should be treated as assets, not as liabilities. He originated the view of the corporation as a human community built on trust and respect for the worker and not just a profit-making machine.[11]

Many theories emerged during this era, such as McGregor's Theory X and Theory Y, Maslow's hierarchy of needs, Likert's four systems of management, Blake and Mouton's managerial grid, and Herzberg's motivational model. These theories, explained in most comprehensive management textbooks, have valuable information about what is required for effective managerial communication. Unfortunately, the theoretical explanations of managerial behavior became extremely complex, too complex for most managers to understand and apply. Many training programs were developed to help managers apply these theories, but often little benefit resulted.

While theories were being developed about behavior at work, much also was being done in the area of communication theory. For instance, J. L. Austen developed the speech act theory, which maintains that certain communication conventions must be used to be effective, and David Berlo developed a model emphasizing two-way communication.[12] Also, attention was given to social influences on communication but, unfortunately, the social context of managers was given little or no attention.[13]

In addition, the nature of organizational structure received extensive attention. Organizations of the 1950s and 1960s were recognized as being different from the social organizations of the early 1900s. Karl Weick developed a theory of organizing that helped us understand the nature of organizations and how communication operates within them. Weick and others made it clear that organizations are not stable, static entities; rather, they are continually evolving. In addition, both internal and external communication networks are continually evolving, and they must be considered by managers when communicating. For instance, the importance of rumors and informal communication began to receive attention. Also, the types of information managers need were changing from day to day. Earlier, Fayol recognized the importance of communication networks and organization structure when he presented the gangplank concept. Now, entire organizations and their structure were receiving renewed attention.[14]

The nature of managerial and employee behavior, the study of communication, and an analysis of the nature of organizations all had important implications for managers as communicators. But, as mentioned earlier, these studies resulted in a complex body of knowledge that was difficult for managers to use. Out of this behavioral approach, the era of employee empowerment emerged.

Empowerment

The 1990s may be termed the era of empowerment. Empowerment is power sharing, the delegation of power or authority to subordinates in the organization.[15] In the traditional organization, all the power to make decisions was vested in top management, but since the emergence of the behavioral approach, we have seen a major shift away from the centralization of power. Empowerment encourages employees to participate fully in the organization. We then began to see power being given to others in the organization so they could act more freely to accomplish their jobs.

As companies experienced more intense global competition and rapidly developing technology, many top managers believed giving up centralized control would promote faster product development, flexibility, and quality. In a study, 74 percent of the chief executive officers surveyed reported they were more participatory, more consensus-oriented, and relied more on communication than on command. They found less value in being dictatorial, autocratic, or imperial.[16]

The chief executive officer's letter to the General Electric stockholders in the 1990 annual report provides an example of the empowerment philosophy. In this letter, the CEO asserted that managers must learn to delegate, facilitate, listen, and trust. He talked about the sharing of ideas to develop one vision for the huge corporation.

Sharing a vision means sharing information. In the traditional organization, the top managers are frequently the only ones that know the financial condition of the company, but in organizations that attempt to empower employees, information is shared with everyone. For instance, at Springfield Remanufacturing Center Corp. in Springfield, Missouri, workers on the line know—and are taught to understand—almost everything the president knows about costs and revenues, departmental productivity, and strategic priorities.[17]

The empowerment movement can be seen in union–management relations; union members have become more involved in management decisions as management provides more information to them. In fact, information sharing is often part of contract negotiations.[18] Both management and union members can be found on work quality and productivity improvement teams.

But not everything has gone smoothly with attempts at empowerment. Caterpillar Inc., the heavy-equipment manufacturer, made employment involvement a near-religion in the late 1980s; however, when the industry met financial troubles, the employee involvement program became the victim of a bitter battle between the company and the United Auto Workers. An adversarial relationship between union and management returned; accordingly, one-way communication was more frequent than would be expected in an environment of empowerment.

Although efforts to empower employees may run into problems, a number of strategies for empowering employees can be attempted. Such strategies as autonomous work groups, self-leadership, work-out groups, and quality circles should increase employee empowerment. But as mentioned in the discussion of the behavioral approach, some of the theories and programs for empowerment can become so complicated they are difficult to apply and are not suitable for every organization. As a result, the contingency approach has emerged as a management philosophy that makes sense in the early 21st century.[19]

The Contingency Approach

Managers who are effective see the interdependence of the various aspects of jobs, organizations, and communication. The basic idea of the contingency approach is that there is no one best way. The appropriate communication strategy varies from one situation to another. The most effective and efficient strategy depends on a number of factors. Accordingly, a communication method highly effective at one time and place may be ineffective in another situation. The contingency approach recognizes the importance of matching different situations with varying communication strategies. The scientific approach may be more appropriate in one situation, while extensive efforts to empower employees may be better in another setting.

For example, during a crisis, a manager may yell at subordinates and tell them exactly what to do because two-way communication might waste time. But during more tranquil times, discussion between the manager and subordinates may be appropriate. Time allows discussion. Each communication strategy—the direct autocratic approach and the participative approach—is appropriate in different situations.

The contingency approach has grown in popularity recently because of the complexity of organizations. Especially in multinational and multicultural organizations, managers must understand there is no one best way of communicating; effective communication is contingent on the situation. That is not to say, however, that contemporary organizations are managed chaotically. On the contrary, accountability and oversight systems have been emphasized since the meltdown of multinationals such as Enron, Adelphia, and WorldCom in the early 2000s. The Sarbanes-Oxley Act of 2002 (especially Section 404) stresses the need for business control and auditing processes. The point is that, as corporate governance becomes more transparent, information flows more freely, and effective managers adapt to the complexities of each situation when communicating.

In summary, good ideas can be drawn from the scientific, administrative, human relations, behavioral, and empowerment approaches to communication.

Creative analysis is required to ensure that communication strategies adapt to the varying contingencies.

CONTEMPORARY DYNAMICS AFFECTING COMMUNICATION CONTINGENCIES

The nature of communication and a model of managerial communication are presented in Chapter 2. This discussion presents three contingencies that should be considered when developing a strategy for managerial communication. It is impossible to review all contingencies because every manager faces many unique situations. However, it is possible to review the major current events that may influence a manager's environment. The following section reviews major social and business influences that affect managerial communication contingencies, particularly diversity, competition and product quality, and ethics.

Diversity

Today, everyone works with more diverse populations than just a few decades ago. Beginning in the 1960s, the U.S. embraced tolerance and diversity as a strategic mission. However, minimizing cultural bias in the workplace continues to be a challenge for managers. This challenge, which is discussed throughout this text, means managers not only must be able to communicate with a greater variety of audiences, but also must help their employees see diversity as a corporate asset rather than a liability. The contemporary manager should be particularly aware of four types of diversity that are becoming more predominant: gender, culture, age, and education.

Gender Diversity

During the past three decades, much has been written about how men and women communicate differently. Attention has also been given to how women and men communicate with each other. Many questions have been asked: Are men more assertive than women? Do women show more social support and sympathy to colleagues? Do men and women provide different types of feedback? Do leadership styles of men and women differ? Do women convey a different nonverbal message with the same gesture? Do men use space differently with other men than with women? Do men and women use different persuasive strategies?

In many cases, the answers to these and similar questions are not clear; furthermore, there is evidence that the answers evolve as general social changes occur. Sexual harassment is an example of evolving communication between the genders. Janet Andre, who researches women's workplace issues, contends the definition of sexual harassment has been evolving since the early 1980s. As she states, "There are people who haven't realized that behaviors that once were common are no longer acceptable." A management consultant says that when men think of sexual harassment they think of touching. However, to women, sexual harassment can be a tone of voice or other forms of nonverbal behaviors, such as their chest being stared at;[20] the legal definition of harassment is evolving similarly, and broadening to reflect such perceptions.

Because of the evolving nature of communication and the relationship between the genders, definitive answers on gender differences in communication are difficult. But strong arguments for differences have been presented. In her best-selling book, Deborah Tanner makes a case for differences in the communication styles of men and women. In doing so, she also presents interesting reasons men and women have difficulty communicating with each other. These reasons include both inherited traits and learned behavior.[21]

The differences in communication between genders are important because of the increasing gender diversity of the work force. Both men and women will have difficulty succeeding if they cannot successfully communicate with each other. During the Industrial Revolution when scientific management practices prevailed, women had certain types of jobs and men had other types. Women had either mostly routine low-level manufacturing or clerical jobs; if they wanted to be a professional, their choices were teaching and nursing. Most frequently, they were housekeepers. Meanwhile, men had a greater variety of jobs such as management and engineering. Overall, men worked mostly with men, and women worked with other women or children.

But women have greater opportunities today and have access to most professions. Women represented 40 percent of the work force in 1976, and that number grew to 47 percent by 2000.[22] Women are also making their way into management. In 1983, only about a third of managers were women, but by 2002, according to the U.S. Census Bureau, women filled nearly 46 percent of management positions.[23] Furthermore, the number of women serving as corporate officers in the top 10 Fortune 500 companies jumped from 8.7 percent in 1995 to 16.5 percent in 2005. If the current trend continues, women could have equal representation as officers in those firms by 2014.[24]

As mentioned earlier, a strong argument can be made that men and women communicate differently, and men and women have difficulty communicating with each other. Effective managers must be sensitive to gender differences and make special efforts to adjust their communication.

Cultural Diversity

Managers must be able to communicate with those of other cultures. Minorities accounted for over 30 percent of the new entrants in the U.S. work force between 1993 and 2000. Hispanics account for 27.5 percent of this net increase.[25] Furthermore, official population estimates now indicate that the Hispanic community is the nation's largest minority community, with a population of 44.3 million in 2006 (14.8 percent of the population), an increase of nearly 10 percent from the 2000 census. The African-American population is estimated at 40.9 million (13.4 percent of the population), and the Asian-American population is estimated at 13.1 million (4.4 percent of the U.S. total).[26]

The concentration of minorities varies by geographic area. For example, the populations of Mississippi, South Carolina, and Louisiana are more than 30 percent black, while approximately 32 percent of all Asians living in the United States reside in California or Texas, and 35 percent of the population of New Mexico is Hispanic.[27] These trends are important because different cultures possess different work values and communication styles. Managers must learn to communicate with other managers and employees of all cultural backgrounds. By 2010, 33 percent of the U.S. work force will be people of color. By 2050, there will be no majority race in the United States.

Managers must be able to work with diverse cultures both within their own organizations and from other organizations. Communication with employees and managers from other cultures will increase as transportation and telecommunications improve. A graphic demonstration of this development occurred in early 1992 when the CEOs of the three major U.S. auto firms and Japan's big five automakers met to discuss trade relations. They were accused of talking but not communicating on this international problem.[28] Even on a lower level, executives such as purchasing managers must be familiar with cross-cultural communication due to the increase of international business. International purchasing alliances too frequently fail because of poor communication.[29] This may be termed *cross-cultural* or *international communication*, which is discussed in Chapter 9.

Age Diversity

America's population is living longer, and the average employee is getting older. About 6.4 percent of Americans over the age of 75 are working, according to the U.S. Department of Labor. And about 3.4 percent of Americans 80 or older were in the work force last year.[30]

The worker who is 30 years old in 2010 has lived in a much different world from that of the worker who is 60. The 30-year-old, born in 1980, did not experience the national turmoil of the Vietnam War, grew up in an era of relative affluence, and is an avid techie. Social networks are important. The 60-year-old remembers the Vietnam War and the 13 percent inflation of the late 1970s. Economic and national security are major concerns.

These differences in age and experiences may result in even greater communication difficulties than are normally caused by cultural differences. For instance, consider a woman of Korean descent and one of Hispanic descent who are both 30 years old, born and raised in a suburb of Dallas, educated at the University of Texas, and working in Dallas. These two women may have more in common and find it easier to communicate with each other than with either the 60-year-old Hispanic or Asian women they supervise.

Communication across these age differences can be a major challenge in the workplace, a challenge that companies can ill afford. Every generation is different, and generation gaps are natural, but generational tensions seem especially strong between managers and leaders in their 30s and early 40s (called Generation X) and workers in their 20s (called Generation Y). According to Harvard Business School researchers, Gen Xers started working when the economy was slow, and their career paths were rocky. Feeling vulnerable, they made personal and family sacrifices to achieve success. Today, their young employees are less willing to sacrifice their time and their families. They expect to be evaluated for productivity, not hours at their desk, especially when tech tools make their geographic location irrelevant. Their loyalties lie with their social network rather than their job, and they do not fear change.[31] Clearly, when values clash between bosses and their subordinates, effective communication across the generational divide becomes even more important. Managers must consider this contingency because of its implications for employee retention, harmony, and workplace efficiency.

Education Diversity

The education level of the work force is changing also. According to the U.S. Census Bureau's 2002 survey, 84 percent of U.S. residents 25 and older are high-school graduates. The bureau reported record high educational levels for nearly every racial and ethnic group and the nation overall. And approximately 30 percent of the civilian labor force had a college degree, a 16 percent increase from 1970.[32] Greater education levels mean employees will readily question managers. In the scientific management era of Frederick Taylor, a manager could tell an educated employee what to do; however, today's managers can find assistance with problems. About half of the Fortune 500 companies have diversity managers.[33] These managers have a variety of responsibilities, but at such companies as Colgate-Palmolive and General Electric, they provide individual assistance and conduct specialized training programs. Most managers will probably be seeking such assistance with the increased challenges they face.

Competition and the Drive for Quality

In the late 1960s, the French journalist Jean-Jacques Servan-Schreiber received considerable notoriety for his book *The American Challenge*.[34] In this book, he warned Europeans that American industry was well ahead of the industrialized world and the United States was widening its lead. But in 1992, such books as *Quality or Else: The Revolution in World Business* emphasized that quality must be improved if the United States is to remain competitive.[35] Contemporary managers in the United States, as well as in many other parts of the world, are now accepting the idea that business is a globally competitive game and quality is the key to victory. *Competitive advantage* and *quality* are common words in business today. But what do the terms mean?

Competition may be considered as the effort of two or more parties acting independently to secure the business of a third party by offering the most attractive terms. A competitive environment means the organization must produce a product or service in a more efficient and effective manner than its competitors. Also, the service or product must possess greater value at the same or lower price. Little room exists for errors. Defective parts must be minimal, few or no reworked parts can be allowed, few product repairs can be tolerated, and delivery cycles must be short. Continuous efforts are required to find new ways to improve the product or service while reducing costs.

Some of the characteristics an organization needs to gain competitive advantage in today's markets include the ability to do the following:

- Access resources
- Add value
- Develop a good skills base among the work force

- Attract investment
- Develop nonprice characteristics that appeal to other markets
- Be price-competitive
- Be efficient
- Use technology
- Be innovative

As you look over this list of factors, how many directly rely on management's communication competencies? Today's managers must be able to gather information and ideas, share data, and promote and persuade to ensure continuous process improvement.

What does this mean for managerial communication? Managers must be efficient and effective communicators in a fast-paced highly competitive environment. Limited time exists to relax and contemplate communication strategies. For example, Toyota is the number one automaker in America. It relies on manufacturing systems, statistical process control, and other proven methods under a continuous improvement strategy to produce high-quality products that consumers demand. All the elements, including management's communication with dealers, suppliers, and employees, contribute to Toyota's reputation for quality.[36]

To enhance their competitiveness, many organizations use cross-functional work teams in which employees learn a variety of tasks and work together. It is almost the direct opposite of the scientific management approach. When cross-functional work teams are used, managers must understand and coordinate a variety of activities, and must be able to communicate from a variety of perspectives.

In some cases, entire organizational cultures must be changed from one in which quality is of little importance to a culture that says, "Quality is job one." This motto is used frequently by Ford Motor Company, and it represents the corporate culture changes that many companies are attempting. This means managers must be able to communicate a real interest in quality, and they must be willing to listen to employees about quality improvements. In 2003, as Ford celebrated its 100th anniversary, Chairman and Chief Executive Officer Bill Ford said, "Our success always has been driven by our products and our people. . . . We're going to apply fresh thinking and innovative technology to everything we do, from our basic business processes to the products that define who we are as a company." This dedication to quality appears to be paying off. In 2007, Ford received more Initial Quality survey awards from J.D. Power and Associates than any other automaker in the world.

Here's an example of how the organization's quality culture works. A Ford automobile assembly worker believed he had a better way to mount the door mirror. After several discussions with the departmental managers, a better procedure was implemented.[37] If managers are not willing to listen about quality improvements, they will not be successful in implementing the necessary corporate culture.

Ethics

The dangers of unethical behavior have been exemplified in recent years by major scandals in both the political and corporate worlds. Ethics charges filed against the most visible executive officer in the United States—President Bill

Clinton—brought about his impeachment in 1998. A decade later, Rod Blagojevich became the first Illinois governor in history to be impeached after being accused of abuse of power, amid charges that he tried to sell the U.S. Senate seat once held by President Barack Obama.

In the early 21st century, executives at Adelphia, Arthur Andersen, Enron, WorldCom, Martha Stewart Living Omnimedia, HealthSouth, and other corporations were charged with major ethics violations—accounting fraud, stock manipulation, obstructing justice, lying, and so on. In many cases the accused executives were convicted, and in some cases their companies were even destroyed. Such events have triggered renewed concern for ethical standards in business.

Ethical dilemmas and temptations face managers at all levels, not just the political leaders and corporate executives who receive the attention of journalists. Consider the following examples of ethical issues in managerial communication.

- The supervisor of a travel agency was aware his agents could receive large bonuses for booking 100 or more clients each month with an auto rental firm, although clients typically wanted the rental agency selected on the basis of lowest cost. The agents worked on a commission basis. Should the supervisor "warn" his subordinates, or should they be trusted to use their best judgment?

- The executive in charge of a parts distribution facility told employees to tell phone customers that inventory was in stock even if it was not. Replenishing the items took only one to two days; no one was hurt by the delay. Is it ethical for the company to omit this information?

- The project manager for a consulting assignment wondered whether some facts should be left out of a report because the marketing executives paying for the report would look bad if the facts were included. What is the project manager's ethical responsibility?

- A North American manufacturer operating abroad was asked to make cash payments (a bribe) to government officials and was told it was consistent with local customs, despite being illegal in North America. Should the manufacturer make such payments?

Answers to these questions are not easy, and in today's atmosphere of cynicism and mistrust, little room for error exists. Chapter 2 discusses the concept of communication climate and points out that trust is essential to developing a positive communication climate. Unfortunately, managers have difficulty developing trust when so many blatant examples of mistrust surface and individual managers face conflicting ethical demands.

No concrete set of ethical rules exists. There is no law to follow. Many behaviors have not been codified, and managers must be sensitive to emerging norms and values. Sensitivity to the nuances of ethical communication is the only way to maintain employee trust.

Because no universal laws exist, what one person or group considers ethical may be unethical to another. The question of taking bribes is a good example: They are quite ethical in one country but unethical and even illegal in another. Organizations are assisting managers with the many ethical quandaries they face when communicating by providing guidelines, seminars, and workshops. In 2005, companies spent an estimated $6.1 billion on ethics training. This effort is partly in response to the Sarbanes-Oxley Act of 2002, which makes corporate executives responsible for the unethical behavior of their employees—unless they can show that they provided ethical training for them.[38]

Another strategy many companies use to improve communication ethics is to develop a formal code of ethics. The code clarifies company expectations of employee conduct and makes clear that the company expects its personnel to recognize the ethical dimensions of corporate behavior and communication. A code of conduct may be broad or specific and most address managerial communication. For instance, the following is taken from Champion International's statement of corporate values.

> Champion wants to be known as an open truthful company. We are committed to the highest standards of business conduct in our relationships with customers, suppliers, employees, communities, and shareholders. In all our pursuits, we are unequivocal in our support of the laws of the land, and acts of questionable legality will not be tolerated.

Another possibility is an ethics committee or an ethics ombudsperson. With this approach, either one executive or a panel of executives is appointed to oversee the organization's ethics and serve as a consultant to other managers. This provides an opportunity for a manager to go to one person or a group of people to seek advice when confronted with an ethical issue. The importance of such a position is demonstrated by Xerox, where the ombudsperson reports directly to the CEO.

THE TRANSITION

This introductory chapter presents a historical overview of managerial communication, concluding that the contingency approach is the most appropriate, and it reviews three factors that affect contingencies. But organizational management and the corresponding communication are in constant transition. Managers do not communicate today as they did 15 to 20 years ago, and communication styles and strategies will continue to change. Our challenge is to understand management communication and begin to prepare for these changes.

In 1982, John Naisbitt wrote a widely read book titled *Megatrends*.[39] In this book, he presented 10 major predictions. Four of them are particularly pertinent to management communication. First, he stated we would be moving from an industrial society to an informational society. This movement has occurred with the tremendous influence of computer technology and global telecommunications.

The other three trends are highly related: moving from centralized to decentralized decision making; participatory governance replacing representation; and networking becoming more important than traditional hierarchies. Each of these trends implies that both written and managerial communication will become more frequent and intense. Evidence of these trends is increased communication training for managers, more emphasis on work groups, and decision making through governance teams that include all stakeholders. Examples of such governance teams range from the board of directors level to the project level, and they are particularly common in information technology (IT) management.

During the past few years, these trends seem to have grown in importance. Eight years after the original book, Naisbitt and Aburdene wrote a follow-up to the original *Megatrends,* titled *Megatrends 2000.*[40] In this later book, the authors again listed many of the same trends that appeared in the first book. In addition, intercultural communication was emphasized. Not only will managerial communication grow in intensity and importance during the second decade of the twenty-first century, but it also will take on an increased international and intercultural significance. This book discusses the strategies and applications that are required of effective managerial communication. But as mentioned previously, not every contingency can be discussed. Managers must all remain creative and strategic as they communicate in many unique and challenging situations.

Summary

Management communication has gone through a number of changes since ancient and medieval times. Seven separate eras are presented in this chapter: ancient and medieval, scientific management, administrative management, human relations, behavioral, empowerment, and contingency. In each of these models, increasingly more attention has been given to managerial communication.

To better understand managerial situations, several contemporary dynamics affecting communication are presented. Different types of diversity are reviewed: gender, culture, age, and education. The work population will probably become more diverse in the majority of these attributes.

The drive for competitive advantage through improved product and service quality also affects communication. As a result, everything will occur in shorter time cycles, and less room for error will exist as a result of quality demands.

Ethics is another contemporary dynamic that must be considered. Although management ethics can create difficult communication decisions, organizations provide assistance with training programs and codes of ethics. In addition to these dynamics affecting contemporary communication, trends imply that communication will become more frequent, intense, and intercultural as it grows in importance.

Cases for Small Group Discussion

Case 1-1.

A 120-Year Difference

A historian has said this about Gen. George A. Custer: "Generals who led men were rare; generals who won battles were rarer. It is no wonder that he was idolized from President Lincoln down. All the world loves a winner." On June 26, 1874, Custer's 261 soldiers were killed at the Battle of the Little Bighorn. Another historian asks, "Was Custer a hero or a fool?"

On February 27, 1991, the allied coalition forces of Operation Desert Storm led by Gen. H. Norman Schwarzkopf overcame the armies of Iraq's Saddam Hussein in a victory that quickly became known to the world as "The 100-Hour War." Shortly before the war, Schwarzkopf is quoted as saying, "I told my family that during the first month of any military campaign, the guy in charge is a hero, and it's downhill after that."

We don't normally think of military leaders as managers, but they are responsible for the actions of numerous subordinates in critical times. They must be effective communicators to carry out this mission. Generals Custer and Schwarzkopf help demonstrate the differences in managerial communication that have occurred during the past 120 years.

General Custer led his 261 men on horseback in southeastern Montana. Compare this to General Schwarzkopf as you think about him stepping quickly toward the podium in a fourth-floor ballroom at the Hyatt Regency Hotel in Riyadh to address 200 reporters from around the world. No doubt these two managers had different communication support systems, but they also had different responsibilities. General Custer was managing an operation of 261 horse soldiers. Schwarzkopf was coordinating a half-million-strong international military force including the U.S. Air Force, Navy, and Army as well as the first Tank Division of the United Kingdom and corps from Egypt, Saudi Arabia, and France.

What a difference! But in some ways their training was quite similar. Both were educated at West Point, went through army war colleges at Fort Leavenworth, were stationed at Fort Riley, and had frontline battle experience. Both had experienced defeat and victory.

Questions

1. Compare the management communication systems of these two managers. How are the basics similar? What was the role of technology?
2. Which of the two generals had the easier job? Consider this question carefully because Custer had a much smaller group of men, but Schwarzkopf had sophisticated technology and organizational structure.
3. Which of the two managers required more advanced training in management communication? Why?
4. How would you compare these two generals to business managers during the same era?

Case 1-2.

Like Grandfather, Like Granddaughter?

Clarence opened a farm supply store in Montana during the early 1900s. His neighbors in the county were also his customers. Every person who walked into his store felt comfortable. In fact, they would often sit, sip a cup of coffee or shell some peanuts, and solve the world's problems before loading up their purchases. Clarence prided himself on knowing what his customers needed to be successful farmers, and he freely gave them advice about which brand of flea dip would work best on their cattle and which tonic would help a colicky horse. By the time he retired and his son Seth took over, the company had expanded to three stores in three towns and had 14 full-time employees.

As a youth, Seth had attended the state college and earned a degree in agricultural business. He eagerly applied what he had learned to the family business. He was convinced that technology was the key to success, not personal relationships. Over the years, he struggled to convert all his father's old handwritten records to electronic files. Eventually he installed a completely computerized information system that tracked inventory, personnel, and accounts. He sometimes boasted about being an entrepreneur, but Clarence snorted at that term. "Just do what's right for your customers and you'll be doing what's right for yourself," he would retort.

When Seth retired, his daughter Kathy took over the company that now has 23 stores with 228 employees in three states and one wholly owned subsidiary of 18 gas stations. Kathy's vision involves offering a broader range of products than farm supplies. She wants to sell the image of the family farm. Her stores stock western clothing; boots, hats, and jewelry; home furnishings; and even CDs featuring country and western music.

Kathy finds herself traveling extensively from the corporate office to the various stores. Finding time to manage everything is a problem, but she has a staff of 12 professionals in the corporate office to assist her. A computer network, e-mail, and fax machines help tremendously.

Questions

1. How have the communication requirements differed for Clarence in the early 1900s and Kathy in the early 2000s?
2. How do you think the management behaviors differed for Clarence and Kathy?
3. In what ways do you think Clarence and Kathy were alike as company presidents?

Endnotes

1. Watson Wyatt, "Effective Communication: A Leading Indicator of Financial Performance—2005/2006 Communication ROI Study," www.watsonwyatt.com/research/ (retrieved January 11, 2006).
2. C. George, *The History of Management Thought* (Englewood Cliffs, NJ: Prentice Hall, 1972), chaps. 1 and 2.
3. Edwin A. Locke, "The Ideas of Frederick E. Taylor," *Academy of Management Journal,* January 1982, pp. 41–44.
4. William F. Muks, "Worker Participation in the Progressive Era: An Assessment by Harrington Emerson," *Academy of Management Review,* January 1982, p. 101.

5. "McRisky," *BusinessWeek,* October 21, 1991, pp. 114–17.

6. Henri Fayol, *General and Industrial Management* (London: Sir Isaac Pitman and Sons Ltd., 1949), pp. 3–13.

7. M. Richetto, "Organizational Communication Theory and Research: An Overview," in *Communication Yearbook* 1, ed. B. D. Rubin (New Brunswick, NJ: Transaction Books, 1977).

8. Dale Carnegie, *How to Win Friends and Influence People* (New York: Simon & Schuster, 1936).

9. F. L. Roethlisberger and W. Dickson, *Management and the Workers* (New York: John Wiley & Sons, 1939).

10. E. Mayo, *The Human Problems of an Industrial Civilization* (Boston: Harvard Business School, 1947).

11. John A. Byrne, "The Man Who Invented Management: Why Peter Drucker's Ideas Still Matter," *BusinessWeek,* November 28, 2005, pp. 97–106.

12. J. L. Austen, *How to Do Things with Words* (Oxford: Oxford University Press, 1962); and David K. Berlo, "Human Communication: The Basic Proposition," in *Essay on Communication* (East Lansing, MI: Department of Communication, 1971).

13. Larry R. Smeltzer and Gail F. Thomas, "Managers as Writers: Research in Context," *Journal of Business and Technical Communication* 8, no. 2 (April 1994), p. 186.

14. K. Weick, *The Social Psychology of Organizing,* 2nd ed. (Reading, MA: Addison-Wesley, 1979).

15. Edwin P. Hollander and Lynn R. Offermann, "Power and Leadership in Organization," *American Psychologist* 45 (February 1990), pp. 179–89.

16. Thomas A. Stewart, "New Ways to Exercise Power," *Fortune,* November 6, 1989, pp. 52–64.

17. John Case, "The Open-Book Managers," *Inc.,* September 1990, pp. 104–05.

18. Stephenie Overman, "The Union Pitch Has Changed," *HR Magazine,* December 1991, pp. 44–46.

19. Robert L. Rose and Alex Kotlowitz, "Strife Between UAW and Caterpillar Blights Promising Labor Idea," *The Wall Street Journal,* November 23, 1992, p. 1.

20. Susan B. Garland and Troy Segal, "Thomas vs. Hill: The Lessons for Corporate America," *BusinessWeek,* October 21, 1991, p. 32.

21. Deborah Tanner, *You Just Don't Understand* (New York: Ballantine Books, 1990).

22. Howard N. Fullerton, Jr., "New Labor Force Projections, Spanning 1988–2000," *Monthly Labor Review,* November 1989, pp. 3–12.

23. "Women Lag in Highest Salary Levels," *Bryan-College Station Eagle,* March 25, 2003, p. 4B.

24. "Rate of Women's Advancement to Top Corporate Officer Positions Slow, New Catalyst Tenth Anniversary Census Reveals," *Catalyst.org,* July 26, 2006.

25. Fullerton, "New Labor Force Projections," p. 10.

26. B02001. RACE—Universe: TOTAL POPULATION. *2006 American Community Survey.* United States Census Bureau, www.factfinder.census.gov (retrieved January 24, 2008).

27. William Dunn, "Minorities: A Larger Part of the Population," *USA Today,* June 21, 1989, p. 1.

28. "Automakers Talking Past Each Other," *Fortune,* February 10, 1992, p. 90.

29. Michiel R. Leenders, Harold E. Fearon, and Wilbur B. England, *Purchasing and Materials Management*, 10th ed. (Burr Ridge, IL: Richard D. Irwin, 1993), p. 480.

30. John Christoffersen, "More Older Workers Deciding It's Not Time to Clock Out Just Yet," *Houston Chronicle*, August 15, 2007, p. A3.

31. Tammy Erickson, "Ten Reasons Gen Xers Are Unhappy at Work," *Harvard Business Online*, May 15, 2008, www.businessweek.com (retrieved August 20, 2008).

32. *Statistical Abstracts of the United States*, 180th ed. (Washington, DC: National Data Book, U.S. Department of Commerce, Bureau of the Census, 2002), Table 647.

33. Julie Amparano Lopez, "Firms Elevate Heads of Diversity Programs," *The Wall Street Journal*, August 8, 1992, p. B1.

34. Jean-Jacques Servan-Schreiber, *The American Challenge* (New York: Atheneum Publishers, 1968).

35. Lloyd Dolyns and Clare Crawford-Mason, *Quality or Else: The Revolution in World Business* (New York: Houghton-Mifflin, 1992).

36. "'Slow and Steady' Drives Toyota's Growth," *USA Today*, December 21, 2005, USAToday.Money.com (retrieved December 29, 2005).

37. *Netpiper Auto News*, July 6, 2003, www.autoemirates.com/netpiper/news/details.asp?NID=997 (January 16, 2006).

38. William Raspberry, "Straighten the Crooked and White-Collared? Good Luck," *Houston Chronicle*, November 21, 2005, p. B7.

39. John Naisbitt, *Megatrends* (New York: Warner Books, 1982).

40. John Naisbitt and Patricia Aburdene, *Megatrends 2000* (New York: William Morrow and Co., 1990).

Chapter **Two**

The Managerial Communication Process

Today, communication itself is the problem. We have become the world's first overcommunicated society. Each year we send more and receive less.

—*Al Ries, Chairman, Trout & Ries Advertising, Inc.*

Whether working for a hospital, manufacturer, or service firm, more than 75 percent of a manager's time is spent communicating. Considering the amount of information for which a manager has responsibility, this is not surprising. General managers face two fundamental challenges: figuring out what to do as they sort through enormous amounts of information, and getting things done through a diverse group of people.[1] Effective communication is the key to planning, leading, organizing, and controlling the resources of the organization to master these challenges.

Communication—the essential process that managers use to plan, lead, organize, and control—is not easy. Understanding of a manager's message is based on the receiver's perception and message interpretation. The process becomes more complex when communicating to a group of people because of the variety of perceptions and interpretations possible.

In the communication process, symbols, such as words or gestures, comprise messages, and understanding depends on a common meaning or frame of reference for those symbols. When sending a message, a manager may have the meaning of the symbols clearly in mind, but if someone receiving the message attributes a different meaning, the message is misunderstood. The process is made even more complicated because the symbols' meanings not only differ between people but also change as the experiences of the people involved change.

In this chapter, we examine those aspects of developing and exchanging symbols that relate to managerial communication, and we analyze the human factors that aid or hinder understanding. Further, we present a model of the strategic approach to communication that managers follow when developing messages. Finally, we discuss three critical errors that managers must avoid when seeking effective communication.

LEVELS OF MANAGERIAL COMMUNICATION

Managerial communication can usually be thought of as occurring at one of five different levels: intrapersonal, interpersonal, group, organizational, and intercultural.[3] One level is not more important than another. Communication may occur at any or all of these levels simultaneously.

Intrapersonal communication focuses on internal behavior such as observing, listening, and reading. Most of these activities involve the seeking of information; consequently, this communication level is extremely important for managerial decision making and problem solving because effective decisions require accurate information.

The second category is the interpersonal level of communication. At this level, two or more people exchange thoughts. They may be sharing information, providing feedback, or simply maintaining a social relationship.

Group communication is a third level. The most common form of group communication is the meeting, which may be either formal or informal. The various functions of formal meetings are discussed in Chapter 13.

Fourth, the organizational level of communication operates within the networks that link members of a company or other organization. Organizational communication is also concerned with how a group of tasks is linked to complete a job.

Fifth, the intercultural level of communication concerns interactions among people of different cultures. As discussed in the next section of this chapter, intercultural communication is occurring more frequently due to improved telecommunications and transportation.[3] Because of its importance, Chapter 9 is dedicated to intercultural communication.

Communication is a behavior we engage in throughout life and often take for granted. Adults may reach a managerial position yet never deliberately analyze their communication because it has become such common behavior. However, a lack of strategic decision making can cause communication problems for a manager. Just as a complex fiscal transaction triggers many different accounting decisions, a communication situation should trigger strategic communication decision making. The accountant does not intuitively enter a transaction as a debit or credit. She makes a series of analytical decisions to ensure that every transaction is correct. Unfortunately, the same accountant may communicate in a critical situation in a style that seems correct without making a similar strategic analysis.

A STRATEGIC APPROACH

The following discussion analyzes separate elements of a strategic approach to communication. However, these variables do not actually occur separately, nor can they be analyzed separately in the managerial context. They are highly interdependent and affect each other concurrently. For instance, the power of the person sending the message, the intended receiver, the message's purpose, and the organizations involved are all interrelated. Each strategic component is reciprocally interdependent. Although the following discussion considers each of the components separately, remember that each variable is affected by the others.

The strategic approach could be compared to an onion. The strategy is at the very core of the onion, but one must peel away the different layers to get to the core. The outer layer of the onion, which we will examine first, can be compared to the cultural context of the people involved in the communication event.

The First Layer

The first layer consists of communication climate and culture, both of which are discussed in the following subsections.

Communication Climate

Past communication, such as whether employees and managers have been trusting and open or closed and defensive, has a cumulative effect.[4] A trusting open climate makes it much easier to communicate in an organization. And there seems to be a positive correlation between communication openness and trust. Major events in an organization's life cycle can affect the communication climate. For example, often when a company is restructuring, or a merger is planned, managers reduce the amount of information flowing through the formal channels. The result of this information "vacuum" is employee anxiety and distrust. In such a climate, employees turn to each other, relying on the rumor mill to learn about impending changes and layoffs. Not surprisingly, productivity drops off.

On the other hand, success breeds success. Effective communicating results in trust and openness, which generally improve job performance.[5] In turn, future effective communication will get easier because of the trust and openness that has developed. A positive climate is fragile, however. After only one or two critical errors, a positive environment can quickly change to one of distrust and closed communication, making future communication more difficult. This is why the skills and principles discussed in the following chapters are so critical—managers must avoid communication errors that may result in a negative climate.

Cultural Context

All communication occurs within a culture. Culture is the social glue that binds members of nations and organizations together through shared values, symbols, and social ideals. Culture generally remains below the threshold of conscious awareness because it involves taken-for-granted assumptions about how one should perceive, think, and feel. But it is ubiquitous.

To a large extent, national culture determines how we communicate. Obviously, language differs among cultures, but managers need to be aware of many more subtle conventions. For example, an American manager may perceive his British associates as reserved but his Italian connections as outgoing. Autocratic management is acceptable in India in businesses, while a more participative approach is expected in the United States. Chapter 9 discusses more thoroughly how national culture affects business communication.

Organizational culture also affects how managers communicate. In some organizations, a communication value may be to use e-mail for every request or suggestion, whereas in another organization oral communication is the norm. But an organization's culture affects more than preferences for a particular

FIGURE 2–1
The First Layer of the Model

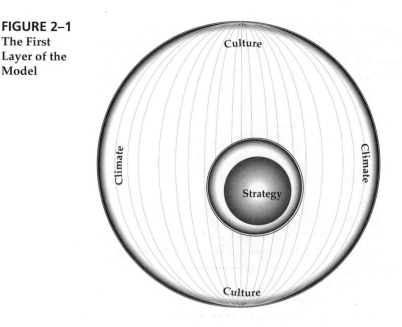

layout of areas [handwritten note]

communication channel. The culture, as reflected in an organization's physical space, can encourage or discourage information flow. Office design can consist of closed doors, long empty hallways, surveillance cameras, and sparse furniture. How many casual conversations are likely to take place among employees who work in such a culture? Or office design can consist of a large open space free of walls, with lots of seating, music, food, live plants, a waterfall, and employees' workspaces all visible to one another. In such an environment the organization's cultural values regarding open communication are clear. A cultural analysis does not provide definitive answers, but it gives an understanding of generally accepted values. These values must be related to communication. For instance, if independence is valued, a persuasive approach rather than a demanding approach may be required. If formality is valued, a formal typed memo rather than a telephone call may be necessary. If extensive technical details are part of the organizational culture, all reports may require technical elaboration.

Because culture and climate provide generally accepted patterns of communication, they are depicted as the outer layer of our analysis. Or, to use our analogy, they constitute the outer layer of the onion, as depicted in Figure 2–1. This layer must be analyzed as we develop the communication strategy.

The Second Layer

In addition to reviewing the climate and cultural aspects of the communication context, managers should consider the sender, receiver, and the purpose of the communication. Figure 2–2 shows these three variables as the second layer of the onion. Note that the relationship of the three variables is circular rather than linear. Each affects the other concurrently; one does not necessarily come before the other. To simplify our discussions, the manager will be considered the encoder.

FIGURE 2–2
**The Second
Layer of the
Model**

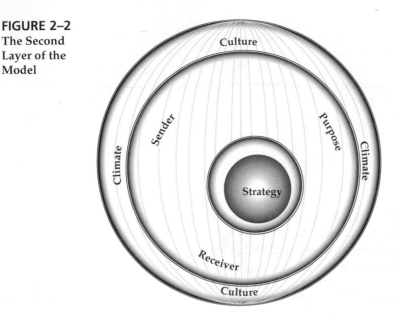

Sender (Encoder)

The manager encodes a message's meaning depending on his or her personality and experiences. Managers must analyze their own frames of reference and communication preferences to determine how they will affect the outcome of the communication.[6] Thus, self-awareness is critical for effective communication.

For instance, what strategy is best when persuading a work group to accept a new procedure? A manager may have realized he is most comfortable talking with just one person rather than a group, has trouble with grammar but can usually find the right words, is a patient listener, and holds a company position that makes it difficult to place demands on others.

Consequently, the manager decides it would be best to meet with employees individually in a face-to-face setting to persuade them to accept the new procedure. The manager thus has strategically analyzed his own frame of reference and his role in the communication situation.

Receiver (Decoder)

Now we can add the second element to this layer: the receiver, or decoder. Managers must continually adapt communication to different receivers to be effective.

Several characteristics of the receiver require analysis: personal relationship of the receiver to the sender, status, interest in the message, feelings toward the message, knowledge about the subject of the message, and the communication skills of the receiver. Together, these characteristics may cause distortions to the intended message. They are sometimes referred to as "internal noise." A review of these items indicates the types of strategic communication decisions a manager must make relative to the receiver.

Relationship   Participants in a friendly relationship tolerate error and initial misunderstanding more than do those in a neutral or hostile relationship.[7] Friendly participants need less time and concentration when communicating than is required in a hostile relationship. For instance, suppose a manager discussing a report with a colleague finds a certain table difficult to read. A friendly colleague will be more tolerant and more willing to ask for clarification than will a hostile one who might criticize the report but seek clarification or provide constructive criticism.

Status Difference   Status differences between senders and receivers deserve attention. Status may require that certain customers or traditions be integrated into the communication. For example, the manager may need to refer to certain people as sir, Mr., Ms., doctor, or chief in some organizations to avoid offending the receiver. Also, the manager may need to stand when addressing a person of higher status, but it may be appropriate to sit down with a person of equal or lower status. People of different status levels may easily interpret words and gestures differently.[8] Suppose a manager says, "Can I meet with you for a few minutes?" This simple statement may be a request or a demand, depending on the receiver's status. Obviously, verbal emphasis needs to be adapted to different audiences.

Receiver's Interest   A third type of "noise" is caused by the interest level of the receiver. Thus, managers may have to make another strategic consideration.[9] If the receiver has low interest, some persuasive elements may be appropriate to get the person's attention even when the ultimate goal of the message is to inform. The audience's interest level may affect the objective of the communication. Managers must adapt the nature of the message to fit the interests of the receiver rather than just the managers' personal interest.

Receiver's Emotional State   The receiver's emotional state at the time of communication may affect how the message is received. A receiver upset about something requires a different communication strategy than that used with a relaxed person. When a receiver is upset, the sender needs to deal first with the person's feelings and attempt to relax the individual so they're more receptive to the main message. In addition, strategic analysis of the possible emotional reaction to a message makes it possible to be on guard without getting caught up in the emotion.

Receiver's Knowledge   Remember that technical words and examples are appropriate in a message only if everyone understands them. Unfortunately, technical concepts may add confusion if receivers do not understand them. Would it be appropriate to ask "Have you checked the FAR on the VOR at LAX?" How many technical terms may one use with this particular reader or listener? Will certain concepts need explaining? Incorrectly assuming the receiver has considerable knowledge may result in a communication breakdown. But assuming too low a level of knowledge may waste time and insult the receiver. A receiver's level of knowledge can be gauged quickly by asking questions and getting feedback. The answer given to an open-ended question on a specific topic is often the best indication of a receiver's level of knowledge.

Receiver's Communication Skills The receiver, as well as the sender, must be a competent communicator.[10] Can the receiver communicate clearly? Does the receiver get nervous in communication situations? If the receiver cannot express concepts clearly or gets nervous when communicating, a manager needs to exercise patience and assist or even relax the person as much as possible.

In summary, a manager should consider six characteristics of the receiver before communicating: personal relationship, status, interest in the message, feelings, knowledge, and communication skills. Knowing one's audience is a critical strategy. Next, the manager needs to analyze the purpose of the message for effective communication in critical situations.

Purpose of the Message

Unless managers analyze their goals, the resulting communication may waste time and effort. Before reviewing the purpose of a communication, managers should first determine whether it is best to verbalize a message at all.

A manager has four major reasons for choosing to communicate. First, the mere act of communicating with a fellow worker may be enjoyable. Communication does not always have to mean business, although one should not confuse working with socializing. At work, some socializing by managers can boost employee morale.

Second, managers communicate to present information, and, third, to gain information. Ironically, not all managers distinguish between gaining and presenting information. Many managers tend to do all the talking when they are trying to gain information. While it seems to be human nature to tell others everything one knows, managers must resist this tendency if they wish to gain information.

Fourth, managers communicate to persuade.[11] Managers with persuasion as a goal must develop an appropriate persuasive strategy. Would a rational-logical approach be best, or should it be an emotional appeal? This question of goals can become complicated because goals may be combined. For instance, a goal may be to inform a subordinate of a new procedure while also persuading her to accept the procedure. In these situations, managers need to identify goals clearly and develop appropriate strategies; otherwise, they may achieve neither goal.

The communication goal or purpose often defines the strategy appropriate for a given situation. Consequently, effective managers are keenly aware of their communication goals. Subsequent chapters explain how this strategy relates to the audience and the goal and present several examples. For instance, in our discussion on memos and letters, we explain why a deductive rather than an inductive approach should be used in certain situations.

The Third Layer

Managers must consider four more elements in determining an effective communication strategy:

- The specific content of the message
- The message's channel
- The physical environment in which it occurs
- The time the communication occurs

FIGURE 2–3
The Complete Model

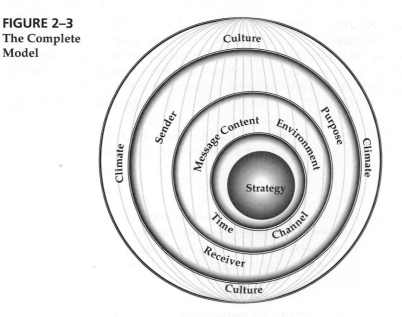

Figure 2–3 presents the complete strategic managerial communication model. These four elements appear on the most inner layer because they depend on the sender, receiver, and purpose of the message, as well as the culture and climate. For purposes of discussion, we review each component separately. But again, remember that in reality a manager needs to consider all interrelationships when developing a communication strategy. Neglecting any one component when analyzing a critical situation may result in a communication failure.

Message Content

We can simplify our discussion by classifying the content of a message according to four factors.

First, will the receiver perceive the message as *positive, negative,* or *neutral?* When the message is positive, the best strategy is to present the good news immediately; however, with a negative message it is best to present neutral information before the negative news.[12] To determine whether the message is positive or negative, consider the receiver's perspective. What may seem positive to a manager may be negative to the receiver.

For example, the manager of an accounting firm was ecstatic as she announced a new contract with a growing firm. But staff members were unhappy with the news because they all felt overworked.

Second, does the message deal with *fact* or *opinion?* A fact may be established with concrete information, but opinion is largely based on assumption. The manager should critically analyze the objective basis of his message because he may feel so sure about his opinion he will present it as fact. When the manager presents opinions as facts, the receivers may be deceived.

Third, to what extent is the message *important* to the receiver? If the message is important to the manager, but not to the receiver, the manager has to emphasize attention-getting techniques. She would structure such a message according to the needs of the receiver rather than those of the sender. A manager needs to determine how to make the content of the message important to the receiver and then integrate that importance into the information. For instance, an announcement of a staff meeting to be held at 2 p.m. may not capture an employee's interest; however, if the notice states one of the items on the agenda is a possible new incentive program, employees are more apt to pay attention.

Fourth, to what extent is the message *controversial?* A controversial message calls for neutral words that can reduce the emotional response. In these situations, phrases such as "Surely you realize . . . ," "Everyone else believes . . . ," "Can't you see . . . ," or "You have to understand . . ." can make the receiver defensive and create conflict.

Effective managerial communication requires analysis of these content factors—negative versus positive messages, fact versus opinion, importance to the receiver, and level of controversy. Consider these factors simultaneously with the sender, receiver, and purpose, because they all affect one another when developing strategic managerial communication.

Channel of the Message

With the advent of sophisticated telecommunications and overnight delivery, the question of how the message is to be sent becomes increasingly complicated. Habits further complicate channel selection. Managers find ways of communicating that are comfortable for them and continue to use the same methods, even when they are inappropriate.

Which channel is appropriate for which message? Written communication (memos, letters, reports) provides the opportunity for permanent records and may be precise and clear; however, it usually does not provide the opportunity for immediate feedback. Electronic mail is less permanent and is often hastily written, but it has the advantages of immediacy and speed. Oral communication is often more persuasive than a written message. The telephone can be quick, but it generally provides no permanent record of the conversation. Also, while it provides oral feedback, the participants can observe few nonverbal messages. Since so many factors are involved, it is difficult to declare one channel invariably preferable to another.

The question becomes one of minimizing costs while maximizing communication effectiveness. Consider just these basic options: (1) oral, (2) written, (3) oral and written, and (4) visual. Now subdivide these further into formal and informal approaches. Table 2–1 presents some of these options. But let's complicate the options even further by adding technologically mediated communications such as video teleconferences, electronic mail, and fax. It quickly becomes apparent that the correct channel choice is not simple. This is why Chapter 3 presents an extensive discussion of communication channels mediated by some form of technology.

Should the message be presented to one individual at a time or to a group? While individual communication allows the manager to adapt the message to each person, group communication is quicker and cheaper. The manager needs

TABLE 2–1
Channels of
Communication

	Informal	Formal
Oral	Personal contacts	Staff meetings
	Interviews and counseling	Public address system
	Telecommunication	Conferences
	Employee plant tours (orientation)	Order giving and instructions
		Briefing
Written	Bulletin boards	Company policy manuals
	Daily news digests	Management newsletters
	Electronic mail	Company intranets
		Company reports
		Company website
Both oral and written	Face-to-face contact between superior and subordinate where written information is exchanged	Company meetings where reports and data are presented
Visual	Sound-action exhibits	Motion pictures
	Closed-circuit TV	Slides; PowerPoint slide shows
	Satellite downlinks	Chart talks

to decide if individual adaptation is necessary or if the time saved with group communication is more important. The chapter on meetings will detail this later.

The question of individual versus group is a key to persuasive communication. In some situations, it may be easy to persuade a group of people; however, in other situations, one-to-one communication may be more effective. The manager must strategically analyze all the factors to determine which would be best in a given situation.

Not surprisingly, cost affects all questions regarding channel selection. A letter requires time for drafting and typing. A group meeting requires many individuals to commit their time, and that pooled time can be expensive. These costs must be balanced with the fact that groups allow for input and feedback from different employees. A telephone call may be quick, but long-distance rates can add up. A formal report may be extremely time-consuming to put together, but others may refer to it again later, whereas an oral report is temporary. Thus, managers balance cost and time factors when selecting the appropriate channel for their communication.

Physical Environment

The environment in which communication occurs has a clear effect. Just as receiver characteristics may cause "internal noise," so elements of the physical environment may cause "external noise," resulting in message distortion.

Ask four questions when you analyze the environment factors in strategic communication:

1. Is it a public or private situation?
2. Does it involve a formal or informal setting?
3. What is the physical distance between the sender and the receiver?
4. Is it a familiar or unfamiliar environment?

The answers to each of these questions can significantly affect the communication strategy.

Privacy   A congratulatory comment may be best in a public forum, while a sensitive question is best asked in a private setting. Some choices between public and private settings are obvious, but others are more difficult. For instance, should a team's performance problem be discussed with each person individually, or should the discussion be held with all members of the team in a public forum? In the past, managers were advised to "praise in public, punish in private." But this simplistic approach to employee feedback can backfire. Singling out subordinates for special attention can result in other employees ostracizing them as the "boss's pet." The outer layer of the onion model reminds us to consider culture and climate when deciding whether privacy is important as a communication strategy.

Formality   The formality of the setting affects the wording of the message as well as the opportunity for feedback. Thus, while official titles may be appropriate when presenting a formal oral report, they may restrict communication in an informal group discussion. Also, feedback is often more difficult to obtain in a formal setting because questions may seem inappropriate or the questioner may be shy. Finally, people are generally more reserved in their nonverbal behavior in a formal setting, which makes their feedback more difficult to read.

Physical Distance   A third variable to consider is the physical distance between the sender and receiver. In oral communication, physical distance mutes the variations in the voice's tone and loudness and in the participants' gestures and posture. Thus, it is less effective to use these strategies for emphasis when distance is great. Proximity, on the other hand, makes messages compelling. In written communication, distance also affects feedback and time. The quality of feedback for a report mailed from Ohio to California may be less timely (and, consequently, less useful) than it is for a report exchanged in one building. A manager can expect less comprehensive feedback as distances increase. Distance also makes persuasion more difficult because opposing arguments cannot be answered immediately. A manager may have to decide if it is better to wait until a face-to-face opportunity is available or if the persuasive efforts should occur over a greater distance for the sake of timeliness.

Familiarity   The final factor to consider when discussing environment is its familiarity. This concept needs to be analyzed from the perspective of the manager as well as the receiver. A familiar environment allows the participants to be relaxed, which is important when controversies or feelings are involved. When communicating in an unfamiliar environment, a manager should anticipate the distractions that may occur. Distractions that we might be accustomed to in our own environment can be unnerving when we encounter them in unfamiliar surroundings. Something as seemingly simple as heavy traffic outside an office window can be a distraction when we aren't used to it.

In summary, managers must strategically analyze privacy, formality, distance, and familiarity when considering the environment of a communication event.

Time

Time affects all elements of management, and it has a ubiquitous effect on communication. Clearly, the adage that "time is money" is appropriate here. Managers need to consider the amount of time spent in preparing to communicate and the amount of time spent in the process. Consider the time of both managers and receivers to obtain cost and communication efficiency. Thus, while a meeting may at first seem advisable because it allows for questions and feedback, it may not be efficient because of the time required to assemble people. Consequently, an e-mail may be more efficient in certain situations. This effort is the type of strategic time decision a manager must make.

Remember also that time is power and time is status. People with busy schedules are perceived as more important than those whom you can approach at any time. Also, while the subordinate must make an appointment to see the manager, the manager, who has higher status, can drop in on the employee without notice. Status is also communicated by the amount of time a person is kept waiting.

The actual timing of the communication is another important consideration. Communication behavior appropriate at one time may be inappropriate or even detrimental at a different time. It is not appropriate to try to get the attention of someone immediately before an important meeting. Also, it is highly unlikely that a report will receive much attention if it arrives late on a Friday afternoon. As another example, consider the timing of an announcement made at a large urban hospital consisting of several buildings. For several years, landscaping improvements were being installed to improve water runoff. The grounds were beautiful on completion. But as the project was completed, layoffs of hospital staff were announced. It appeared the landscaping was done at the expense of jobs. Understandably, many employees were bitter about the allocation of funds.

FEEDBACK AND MEASURES OF EFFECTIVENESS

Integral to a strategic management communication approach are feedback and measures of effectiveness. These variables are not included in the onion model (Figure 2–3) because they are so pervasive. They are inherent in each variable and cannot be separated. Feedback is important in two ways. First, it should be continually obtained to determine how changing events may affect the overall strategy. For instance, a manager determines that a memo about a new procedure was not as clear as he thought because many questions were being asked. Based on this feedback, he quickly calls a meeting to clarify the procedure. In this case, the channel is changed to improve the communication strategy.

Second, feedback may be obtained to determine if the strategy was effective even though it may be too late to change it. Unfortunately, many managers may avoid this feedback because they believe nothing can be done about it. For example, an advertising agency submits a proposal for an ad campaign. When the contract is given to another agency, the tendency is not to evaluate the effectiveness of the written proposal. After all, nothing can be done about it now. But this is the opportunity to thoroughly evaluate all aspects of the proposal, including such items as an analysis of the receiver, writing style, and timing. Lessons thus learned should be applied to the next proposal. Postmortems, while unpleasant and often avoided, are valuable tools for organizational improvement.

Obtaining feedback and measuring effectiveness may be extremely difficult. In one case, a regional insurance manager is disappointed in sales. She writes a number of letters, makes phone calls, and personally meets with her independent sales agents to motivate them, yet sales continue to slide. She contracts a management consultant to determine how she can improve her motivational strategies. However, it cannot be determined if poor sales were the result of communication with the sales agents or the insurance products themselves. Managerial communication is so interrelated with other factors that it is often difficult to determine effectiveness.

CRITICAL ERRORS IN COMMUNICATION

Despite consideration of all the foregoing elements, managers make communication errors. The communication process depends on the personalities of those involved and the environment in which they operate. This process creates a dynamic interaction, and as the onion model shows, this interaction is not perfect.

Even when people believe they are communicating what is real, they are communicating only what is reality in their own minds. No perfect correspondence exists between what is real in the world and the reality perceived by the mind because of the mental filters. This imperfect correspondence is manifested in a person's attempt to communicate real events of the world. These critical but common errors arise from problems in our mental filters: the assumption-observation error, the failure to discriminate error, and the allness error.[13]

The Assumption-Observation Error

An assumption occurs when people accept something as valid without requiring proof. Every day we must act on assumptions. For example, we assume the food in the cafeteria is not toxic (despite our persistent jokes to the contrary), the ceiling in the office will not fall, and numbers being used in a report are valid. Assumptions are essential and desirable in analyzing materials, solving problems, and planning.

When we drop a letter in the mailbox, we assume it will reach its destination in a reasonable time. But is this assumption completely accurate or safe? Evidence suggests the letter may be lost, delayed, or even destroyed. Nevertheless, we take a calculated risk, and the act seems to be relatively safe. But if the same envelope contains something valuable, we insure the envelope's contents.

At what point is insurance necessary? That is, when is an assumption safe and when is it a risk? Strategic communication continually addresses this question. Strategic communicators must avoid assumptions that may be incorrect and unreliable and that result in miscommunication. Consider the following example.

The manager of the quality control department noticed that Bill, a new chemist, was extremely conscientious. Bill remained after work at least a half-hour every night to check all the figures. The manager was so impressed with Bill's commitment that she wrote a special commendation letter for his personal file. Later, the manager discovered Bill was really having a lot of difficulty with the tests and was remaining late to correct the many errors he normally made.

To avoid the assumption-observation error, a manager should ask "What are the facts?" We must determine the extent of risk that a statement is true for a specific situation. Once done, the resultant communication should be stated as either a fact or an assumption. For instance, "I see we got a shipment of copper [fact]." On the other hand, expressions such as "In my opinion," "It looks to me as if," and "I am assuming" can help us differentiate between fact and assumption. Just as these phrases can help managers clarify in their own minds when they are using assumptions, they also give the receiver a clearer understanding of the message.

The Failure to Discriminate

The failure to discriminate is the failure to perceive and communicate significant differences among individuals or changes in situations. This failure to make clear distinctions or to differentiate can lead to the neglect of differences and the overemphasis of similarities. One of the consequences of the failure to discriminate is what William Haney calls "hardening of the categories." A leading researcher in the field of interpersonal communication and organizational behavior, Haney observed:

> Most of us have a penchant for categorizing—for classifying. Show someone something he has never seen before and one of his first questions is likely to be: "What kind is it?" We meet a new person and we are uneasy until we can pigeonhole: What is she? How is she classified? Is she a salesperson, plumber, farmer, teacher, painter? Is she Protestant, Catholic, Jew, atheist? Democrat, Republican, independent? Lower, middle, upper "class"?[14]

This hardening of categories can result in stereotypes because people may apply their set image of the group to any individual in the group. Consequently, inappropriate labels may be applied. One common example concerns managers who are interviewing job applicants. An applicant may have attended a school whose graduates the interviewer categorizes as undesirable. Therefore, the interviewer does not fully listen to the applicant. The hardening of categories can also cause a person to communicate in terms of general categories rather than specifics and thus lose valuable information. For example, "Joyce is a union member" omits the fact she is the most qualified inspector in the department.

The potential danger is that those who put everything into a category are usually not aware they are doing it. This blindness makes failure to discriminate an extremely difficult tendency to overcome. However, Haney provides two valuable suggestions.[15] The first is to internalize the premise of uniqueness—that is, to develop a sensitivity to all the differences in the world. No two things have ever been found to be exactly the same. A second technique is to index evaluations. This means each person, thing, or situation should be indexed according to some unique characteristic. This can soon lead to the conclusion that everything and everyone is unique and, in turn, provides sensitivity to differences.

Polarization is a special form of discrimination involving "either-or" thinking. Some situations are true dichotomies that can be stated in terms of either-or: an employee is either absent or present; a person is either male or female. However, we cannot accurately describe many situations in either-or terms: a product is neither good nor bad; a person works neither fast nor slow. Polarization occurs when a person deals with a situation involving gradations and middle ground in strict either-or terms. Thus, someone may state he will either succeed or fail in a job and may truly believe that no middle ground or success exists. Conversely, if a person is told the only options are either success or failure, the person may begin to believe that in-between possibilities do not exist. When managers are wary of either-or statements, they can more accurately distinguish the degree of differences between two items and more accurately perceive the world.

Frozen evaluation is another failure to discriminate. It occurs when people disregard possible changes in persons, places, or things. Because everything in the world changes, evaluations cannot remain static. However, while it is easy to say that change is a major aspect of business, it is often difficult to adapt to that continuous change. Frozen evaluation can result in an inaccurate perception of the world, and management errors may result.

The key to avoiding frozen evaluations is to remember that all things change. The manager who continually asks when and what has changed avoids assuming that events are static, thus preventing a common communication error. A simple question a manager may ask is "What labels have I applied to this situation?"

Allness and the Process of Abstraction

Another error a manager must conscientiously avoid is that of allness. People commit this error when they structure communications as if all there is to know about a subject is being stated. The astute person understands that reality is too complex for anyone to know all there is to know about something. However, the error is still made. Haney states that allness is the result of two false beliefs: (1) it is possible to know and say everything about something, and (2) what I am saying (or writing or thinking) includes all that is important about the subject.[16] Normal communication patterns contribute to the problem of allness because people abstract as they speak. Abstracting is the process of focusing on some details and omitting others. When communicating, we need to select some details and omit others. The very process of abstracting, however, can conceal that we have selectively omitted certain data. As a result, the listener, and in some instances the speaker, has no warning that certain information is being left out. Sometimes the more that is omitted, the harder it is to recognize that one has left out anything.

As Herta Murphy and Charles Peck state in their classic business communication textbook:

> A conspicuous example is that of the high school sophomore chatting with a man who (unknown to the student) was a distinguished scientist devoting his lifetime to studying botany. The smug sophomore commented, "Oh botany? I finished studying all about that stuff last semester." As Bertrand Russell stated, "One's certainty varies inversely with one's knowledge."[17]

Almost everything we do involves some level of abstraction, so the solution to the allness error is not simply to omit abstraction. Rather, it is important to be aware of the level of abstraction occurring. Once the person is aware of the level of abstraction, the message can be phrased accordingly: "as far as I know," "according to the information I have," "this is what I consider to be the critical information." To help overcome the allness error when listening, ask "What has been omitted?" or simply "What else?" Also, if it is possible to put the phrase *et cetera* at the end of a sentence, ask what that would include.

The foregoing critical errors—assumption-observation, failure to discriminate, and allness—were discussed largely from the perspective of the intrapersonal and interpersonal levels of communication. However, management communication seldom operates at just the intra- or interpersonal levels. The process may grow more complex as more people become involved. In a meeting, the three communication errors discussed exist, and specialized problems inherent in groups must also be considered. When a manager of one department communicates with a group in another department, organization-level dynamics become involved. In both of these cases, the basic errors presented in this chapter can occur, and specialized types of potential errors must be considered also. More is said about group and organizational levels of communication in Chapter 13, which is dedicated to meetings and group dynamics, while Chapter 9 addresses intercultural communication.

Summary

Managerial communication occurs at five levels: intrapersonal, interpersonal, group, organizational, and intercultural. Each of these levels is considered in this text.

This chapter also presents a model for strategic managerial communication that may help managers reduce errors in critical situations. While it is not possible to present concrete rules that will serve in every instance, we explored factors the manager should review before communicating.

These factors are presented as three layers of an onion model. The first layer includes climate and culture. The communication strategy must be consistent with the context of national and organizational cultures. The second layer involves the sender, receiver, and purpose of the message. The third layer includes the message, channel, environment, and time of communication. The appropriate strategic implementation of these factors—the model's core—depends highly on these three layers of variables.

Considering these elements during the development phase, however, is insufficient to ensure communication success. Managers must also seek feedback and measures of effectiveness to ensure continuous improvement of their interaction skills.

Finally, this chapter examined critical errors in the communication process. The most common are (1) the assumption-observation error, (2) the failure to discriminate, and (3) the allness error. The assumption-observation error results when a manager communicates something as real when no observable evidence is present. The failure to discriminate is the failure to perceive and communicate changes in events or significant differences between things. The error of allness occurs when a person structures communication as if it states all there is to know about a subject. Managers need to consider all these factors and human foibles when communicating.

Cases for Small Group Discussion

Case 2-1.

Developing a Brochure

Mitch Finley, a 29-year-old with a degree in finance, began working as a loan officer at a bank two years ago. Later, he began consulting for other businesses in financial planning. His career goal has been to start his own business.

Recently, Finley opened The Suite Thing, a development company using one of his original business ideas—the construction of two large hotel-like buildings containing suites (living room, bedroom, kitchen) rather than single rooms.

The hotels are located in two cities that are important regional centers for the oil industry. Instead of renting the suites, he is selling them to large oil companies to meet entertainment and tax planning needs.

Finley had been using a brochure his architects put together, but he was not pleased with its presentation. He had collected other company brochures that he liked and decided to call an advertising firm to design a new brochure and logo for his company.

In the initial meeting, Finley told the advertising representative he needed a new company logo and a brochure folder that would hold his leaflets. Most important, the logo and kit had to be completed as soon as possible, because time was money to him.

The advertising representative (very new on the job) acknowledged that his company could do logo and brochure layouts. The representative then asked Finley a few general questions about his two projects—what they involved, where they were located, and their surroundings. The agency rep said he would return within one week with his ideas.

Two-and-one-half weeks later, Finley called the advertising agency and wanted to know if it had developed the materials. The representative came by later that afternoon with his idea. The agency's approach centered on a hard-sell theme of "Beat the Hotel Game with the Suite Thing." Finley, frustrated by the response delay and the inconsistency between the advertising agency's offering and his own image of the project, said, "No, that's not at all what I want."

The advertising representative, taken aback, sat in silence for a time before responding in a frustrated voice, "Well, what do you see your project as being?" and reminded him of the time constraints Finley had given. Finley said he did not see hotels as his competitors, and he wanted a brochure and logo that used soft sell to introduce his idea to top-level executives as an investment.

The next day the advertising representative returned with a more conservative soft-sell piece. Finley said, "That's *kind of* what I want, but not really."

Finley cannot understand why he did not get what he wanted the first time because "that's their business and they should know how to do it."

Questions

1. What are some possible causes of Finley's communication problem? Of the advertising representative's?
2. Identify how assumptions caused communication problems in this case.
3. What actions would you recommend to the advertising representative to ensure this does not happen again?
4. Do you believe there is a communication deadlock? If so, what should the participants do to resolve it?

Case 2-2.

Why Is Jones Changing?

The Finance Investment Company is located in Houston, Texas. The company is only two years old, but it has made the headlines in regional magazines as "the company to watch." It is staffed with three investment analysts and four secretaries. The firm occupies a fairly small space with the secretaries in the front office and the analysts' offices adjacent to the front office.

Mr. Jones, a top-notch analyst, is very unfriendly. He runs the company with an iron fist. Jones is the first one at work and the last one to leave. Promptness is his motto.

The women working in the office think the middle-aged Jones is attractive. One secretary commented to another, "I wonder what it's like to be married to him. He's so good looking, but he's such a geek. He couldn't be that much fun to be married to." Jones never talked to them; it seemed as if business was the only thing on his mind.

Recently, Jones began coming in late, taking long lunch hours, and leaving earlier. One of the secretaries commented, "Wow, what a change in Mr. Jones. I wonder what's going on?" Another secretary replied, "You're right; I've noticed a change in him also. He started all this about the time that new woman began working here."

The secretaries did not like the new woman in the office. She was tall, blonde, and beautiful. She talked little, could hardly type, and knew little about computers. The other secretaries wrote her off as a "dumb blonde." One secretary commented to another, "Old Jonesey is not only coming in from lunch late, but lately he's been in the best moods. He even talked to me today!" Another said, "I noticed that, and I also saw his secretary coming in the door right after he did. And a woman calls about 6 p.m. every afternoon for Mr. Jones, but he has been leaving the office at 4:30 and cannot take the call." The other secretary said, "Well, I can put two and two together. Can't you?"

Questions

Evaluate each of the following statements as true (T), false (F), or questionable (?). Do not reread the story before evaluating the statements, and do not change any of your answers.

1. Financial Investment Company is located in Houston, Texas.
2. Financial Investment Company is the fastest-growing company in Houston.
3. The building has four offices.
4. Jones is unfriendly.
5. Jones is very prompt.
6. Jones owns the company.
7. Jones has an iron fist.
8. Jones is about 45 years old.
9. Jones is married.
10. Jones hired a new secretary.
11. The new secretary is a gorgeous blonde.
12. The new woman types well.
13. Jones returns to the office in a good mood.
14. The secretaries in the office think Jones is having an affair with the gorgeous blonde.
15. Jones is having lunch with his secretary.
16. Jones is not going home after work.
17. A woman calls Jones every day at 6 p.m.
18. Jones's wife is probably looking for him.
19. Jones is going through a midlife crisis.

What critical communication error is demonstrated with this exercise? Explain.

Case 2-3.

Resigning from the TV Station

Jane Rye is a student of advertising at State University and will graduate at the end of the next term. She has a part-time job in the sales department at a local television station. When hired, Rye thought she was very lucky to have a job there, not only for the money but also for the work experience.

Pat Trent, the sales manager who hired her, was Rye's immediate supervisor. Rye was doing a very good job and received considerable support from Trent. In fact, the sales manager had nothing but praise for Rye's work when reporting to top management. Trent often told her subordinate that her work was exceptional and Trent would like to hire her on a permanent basis after graduation to head a new media research department for the station. The job seemed to promise a challenging and rewarding career.

While Rye was flattered by the offer, she was not interested in the position because she found her present job unsatisfying. However, she never told Trent her feelings about the job or the possible appointment. Because Trent had trained Rye and had promoted her to everyone, Rye had become very loyal and grateful to her sales manager. Thus, Rye thought she would betray Trent if she refused the job. After six weeks, however, Rye decided to quit and work part-time at the university, but she did not know how to approach her boss.

Rye, feeling unable to say anything unpleasant to Trent, let time pass until the day she was ready to quit to start her new job. When Rye got to work that day, the sales manager was scheduled to leave town later that morning. Rye was forced to go into Trent's office while two other people were there discussing another matter. Trent asked Rye what she wanted, and Rye replied, "I am resigning." The sales manager was taken completely by surprise, asked Rye why she was resigning, and wondered what was to be done with the project Rye was handling. Rye apologized for such short notice. Rye explained that she was taking a part-time job at the school starting tomorrow. Trent, very disappointed in her subordinate, said, "If you had told me sooner, I could have phased out the project to someone else—now I'm in a bind."

Questions

1. How should Rye have handled her resignation?
2. Where, when, and how do you think Rye should have resigned? Do you think Trent would have understood under different circumstances?
3. How did Trent foster Rye's reluctance to communicate?
4. What are some possible long-term repercussions of the way Rye handled her resignation?

Endnotes

1. John P. Kotter, "What Effective General Managers Really Do," *Harvard Business Review* 77, no. 2 (1999), pp. 145–58. For a list of key managerial skills, see the American Management Association's "2001 Managerial Skills and Competencies Survey" results, available online at http://www.amanet.org/research/archive_2001_1999.htm.
2. Lee Thayer, *Communication and Communication Systems* (Burr Ridge, IL: Richard D. Irwin, 1968).
3. Harry C. Triandis and Rosita D. Albert, "Cross-Cultural Perspectives," in *Handbook of Organizational Communication*, eds. F. Jablin, L. Putnam, K. Roberts, and L. Porter (Newbury Park, CA: Sage Publications, 1987), pp. 264–95.

4. M. S. Poole, "Communication and Organizational Climate: Review, Critique, and a New Perspective," in *Organizational Communication Traditional Themes and New Directions*, eds. R. D. McPhee and P. K. Tompkins (Beverly Hills, CA: Sage Publications, 1985), pp. 79–108.

5. Raymond L. Falcione, Lyle Sussman, and Richard P. Herden, "Communications Climate in Organizations," in *Handbook of Organizational Communication,* eds. F. Jablin, L. Putnam, K. Roberts, and L. Porter (Newbury Park, CA: Sage Publications, 1987), pp. 195–227.

6. John Petit, Jr., and Bobby C. Vaught, "Self-Actualization and Interpersonal Capability in Organizations," *Journal of Business Communication* 21, no. 3 (1984), pp. 33–40.

7. Joseph N. Cappella, "Interpersonal Communication: Definitions and Fundamental Questions," in *Handbook of Communication Science*, eds. C. R. Berger and S. H. Chaffee (Newbury Park, CA: Sage Publications, 1987), pp. 184–238.

8. C. L. Hale and J. G. Delia, "Cognitive Complexity and Social Perspective-Taking," *Communication Monographs* 43 (1976), pp. 195–203.

9. Kitty O. Locker, "Theoretical Justifications for Using Reader Benefits," *Journal of Business Communication* 19, no. 3 (1982), pp. 51–66.

10. Gary F. Soldow, "A Study of the Linguistic Dimensions of Information Processing as a Function of Cognitive Complexity," *Journal of Business Communication* 19, no. 1 (1982), pp. 55–70.

11. Mohan R. Limaye, "The Syntax of Persuasion: Two Business Letters of Request," *Journal of Business Communication* 20, no. 2 (1983), pp. 17–30.

12. ———, "Buffers in Bad News Messages and Recipient Perceptions," *Management Communication Quarterly* 2, no. 1 (1988), pp. 90–101.

13. Much of this discussion is drawn from William V. Haney, *Communication and Interpersonal Relations: Text and Cases*, 6th ed. (Burr Ridge, IL: Richard D. Irwin, 1992).

14. *Ibid.*, pp. 359–81.

15. *Ibid.*, p. 368.

16. *Ibid.*, pp. 320–57.

17. Herta A. Murphy and Charles E. Peck, *Effective Business Communication*, 3rd ed. (New York: McGraw-Hill, 1980), p. 20.

Chapter **Three**

Technologically Mediated Communication

Men are going to have to learn to be managers in a world where the organization will come close to consisting of all chiefs and one Indian. The Indian, of course, is the computer.

—*Thomas L. Whisler, Professor of Business, University of Chicago*

If you spend as much time as most managers do creating and responding to e-mail, texting your staff, blogging, participating in podcasts or netmeetings, and compulsively grabbing your BlackBerry at stoplights, you may well assume that developments in technology will determine the future of business communication. Where does a discussion of technologically mediated communication begin? Technology is changing so quickly that it sometimes seems impossible to get a focus on the topic. Forty-five years ago, a communication theorist stated, "Communication is essentially a social affair . . . but life in the modern world is coming to depend, more and more, upon technical means of communication, telephone and telegraph, radio and printing."[1]

Think about all the technology that has developed in the past 45 years. Only a couple of generations ago, the communication revolution meant the long-distance telephone. Thirty years ago, the discussion of telecommunication included the definition of "floppy disk" and what was meant by a personal computer. Twenty-five years ago, many textbooks like the one you are reading would have dedicated much space to an explanation of the difference between hardware and software, the purpose of a modem, and how word processing could soon replace the electric typewriter. Ten years ago managers didn't routinely look at a candidate's Facebook page as a step in the hiring process. And just five years ago businesses were unaware of the power of corporate blogs for reaching out to their market.

Today, electronic communication channels are an integral part of our everyday lives. But given the speed with which the business communication environment changes, it is unrealistic to assume that this chapter will accurately reflect what's going on both when I wrote it and when you read it. So instead of describing "current" practices, the chapter focuses on time-honored principles for using technology in the workplace. Reading it will help you develop a framework for making strategic decisions in the use of whatever technologically mediated communication tools are available at that time. Information about emerging practices, trends in technologies, and contemporary issues is presented in a series of research articles in the Appendix of this book. Each article explores a new business technology or a new application of technology and offers guidelines for best practices.

A FRAMEWORK FOR USING TECHNOLOGICALLY MEDIATED COMMUNICATION

The decision to use a telephone, e-mail, text message, or teleconference can be complicated because of the many variables involved. To understand these variables, refer to Chapter 2 and the discussion on strategy. With technologically mediated communication, a technological channel transmits the communication. Thus, the main difference is in the channel. However, every other variable is also affected by the technology. Four concepts help us understand the use of mediated communication: bandwidth, perceived personal closeness, feedback, and the symbolic interactionist perspective.[2]

Bandwidth

Communication occurs along five sensory channels: visual, auditory, tactile, gustatory, and olfactory.[3] Bandwidth is the information transmission capacity of the available sensory channels. Face-to-face communication between two people within an arm's length of each other has a wide bandwidth because it can use all five channels. When a manager first meets a job applicant, the two people usually shake hands. They are concurrently sharing visual, auditory, tactile, and olfactory cues, so this communication has a wide bandwidth.

Mediated communication generally omits one or more of the channels. For instance, a videoconference omits tactile and olfactory channels or cues, while the telephone omits tactile, olfactory, and visual cues.

How many messages sent via different channels can the mind comprehend at one time? This theoretical question has plagued communication researchers for centuries, but it remains a relevant question when considering technologically mediated communication. To help understand this question, imagine a Y. Assume that each communication message or bit is a ball that approaches our brain—the base of the Y—along an arm of the Y. The arms of the Y are different communication channels. What happens if both balls approach the intersection of the Y concurrently, but there is room for only one ball? Information jamming will occur. In terms of information theory, selective attention results, so the receiver pays attention to only one of the information bits while ignoring the others. In other words, the mind decides which ball can proceed to the base of the Y. This process is diagrammed in Figure 3–1.

The goal is to have as much information as possible processed in the central nervous system without jamming. How many cues from different sources can be processed simultaneously?[4] This leads to the concept of between channel

FIGURE 3–1
Information
Processing

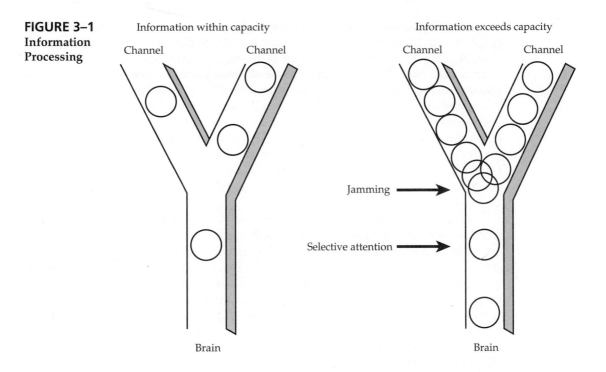

redundancy (BCR). BCR results in multichannel communication when information is shared among auditory, olfactory, tactile, gustatory, or visual channels.

Consider meeting a job applicant. When auditory and visual channels transmit identical information, BCR is complete. This would occur when the person dresses neatly and speaks in an articulate, precise manner. Both of these cues are complementary because they signal that the person is a professional. BCR is mixed or incomplete when different channels transmit conflicting or incongruous information. BCR is zero when each channel transmits completely different or contradictory information. Other things being equal, information transfer is theoretically most effective when BCR is complete. Interference is highest when BCR is zero.

Information theory has not been able to totally determine what information humans process or how they process it. However, several conclusions can be stated. First, we can process only a limited amount of information. Second, certain types of information overpower other types of information.[5] Both of these conclusions have powerful implications for strategic managerial communication. Managers must determine how much information can be valuable in various situations. Only valuable information—cues—should be provided so a person's information-processing capabilities are not overpowered with useless cues.

The choice between videonetworking, videoconferencing, and audioconferencing indicates why this is important for technologically mediated communication. Management may be tempted to use videonetworking because it provides real-time interactive video, audio, and data sharing via the Internet. Videoconferencing provides visual cues in addition to audio cues. But the cost of setting up online collaboration tools and videoconferences is much higher and it may not be justifiable. Sharing data and files in real-time during a meeting may not be important. Even visual cues may be of little value or even distract from the critical audio message that can be provided with a simple, audio-only teleconference.

On the other hand, managers typically should not choose communication channels with narrow bandwidths for emotional messages. Text messaging an employee that she has been terminated or e-mailing an expression of sympathy for the loss of a loved one are "tech-etiquette" blunders that are becoming all too common. And the broadest bandwidth channel, face-to-face, may be crucial for effectively communicating with key clients, especially in certain cultural contexts, as discussed in Chapter 9.

If circumstances require the use of a narrow bandwidth channel to transmit a sensitive message, managers should do their best to offset the consequences. A recent example was provided by a major corporation that used e-mail to notify 400 employees of layoffs. While initial reactions to that channel choice for termination notices may be critical, a closer look shows that the company chose e-mail because it was efficient and practical for the mass announcement. In addition, company officials had held a series of meetings (a broad bandwidth channel) during which they explained the method they would use. Employees also could use the company intranet site to get answers to their questions.[6] Thus, managers should consider using multiple channels of varying bandwidth for important emotional messages.

In addition to the concept of bandwidth, the theory of electronic propinquity, or perceived personal closeness, provides a framework for understanding technologically mediated communication.

Perceived Personal Closeness

Participants in the communication process can feel either attached or removed from each other. Two people in the same room may feel miles apart, while those on different continents may feel close to each other. Many factors, such as the history of the two people as communication partners, can affect this feeling of closeness. Of particular concern here is how media affect the feeling of closeness, or propinquity.

Much research indicates electronic media affect the extent to which people feel close to each other. For instance, some people are much more apprehensive about leaving voicemail messages than others and feel uncomfortable even when making a simple call.[7] When this apprehension exists, telephone conversations will not help a person feel psychologically close to another. Indeed, the psychological distance could be increased because of the accompanying apprehension. Some suggest it is the inability of the communicator to read nonverbal communication that causes this apprehension.[8] Others, however, may prefer and enjoy some form of technology over face-to-face communication. Some people actually warm up to the technology. An example is young people's reliance on the cell phone for friendly interactions. When a person feels warm to the technology, psychological distance may be decreased.

Telecommunications may actually increase a person's sense of closeness. One study found that participants in certain situations enjoyed group meetings more when mediated by technology than when everyone was physically present.[9] Another example of preference for technology as an interpersonal communication tool is the use of text messaging. Instant Messaging (IM) has become the long-distance communication medium of choice for young adults. More similar to an electronic conversation than e-mail, IM is used by nearly three-quarters of teens online, and most use it every time they log on.[10] More relevant to this discussion is the fact that about a third of today's 200 million IM users worldwide are doing it at work.[11] Text messaging is also popular among business professionals. Personal digital assistants (PDAs) such as the BlackBerry are wireless handheld communication devices that add keyboards to cell phones. They allow remote e-mail access and Web browsing. Some managers prefer texting co-workers rather than e-mailing or leaving voicemail messages, because they ensure quick brief responses, especially when they are in the field rather than in their offices.

Interestingly, voicemail is becoming obsolete as an interpersonal communication tool. While a human voice may seem to convey personal closeness more successfully than text, the number of steps required for dialing in and checking voicemail messages, recording the phone numbers, redialing, and leaving a return call may be more trouble than it's worth. Research shows that employees take longer to reply to voice messages than other types of technology—more than 30 percent of voice messages are not retrieved after three days. By contrast, 91 percent of people under 30 respond to text messages within an hour, according to a 2008 study. But substituting text for talk is not just a generational phenomenon. Even adults over 30 are twice as likely to respond within minutes to a text than to a voicemail message.[12]

In summary, the impact of electronic media on feelings of personal closeness has not yet been adequately determined. But there does not seem to be a simple inverse relationship between technology use and closeness. Managers need to determine the extent to which perceived personal closeness is important in different situations. Also, to what extent do various types of technology affect this closeness between the sender and receiver? If this question is not addressed, inappropriately used technology designed to enhance managerial communication may be destructive rather than constructive.

In addition to bandwidth and electronic propinquity, we should consider feedback when discussing technologically mediated communication.

Feedback

Feedback binds the sender and receiver together so they truly communicate with each other. Feedback is always present if it is sought. To understand fully the implications of this statement in relationship to mediated communication, it is important to consider both bandwidth and perceived personal closeness.

Mediated communication may reduce channels for obtaining feedback. When using the telephone, we do not see the facial expression of our communication partner. Thus, feedback is reduced. Also, when managers are not totally comfortable with a particular medium, they may ignore potential feedback cues. Consider a conference call involving five people at five locations. Such a call requires a different set of skills than a normal conversation, and the manager may not be totally comfortable with the situation. Not only are different skills required to monitor feedback, but the manager's anxiety may also reduce attention to feedback.

Time is related to feedback. The feedback cycle can be dramatically shortened with technology. For example, an Arco purchasing manager sent a rather long contract via fax to a vendor. The manager used fax because the contract was long and complex—too long to send via e-mail. Immediately after sending the contract, the sender went to another person's office for a meeting. On returning, the manager checked the voicemail system and found that the receiver of the contract called to indicate it had arrived and was being reviewed. About two hours later, the purchasing manager received an e-mail indicating how the vendor wanted the second paragraph changed. This was all done in a matter of a few hours even though the transaction occurred in two cities a thousand miles apart. Also, no busy telephone lines interrupted the process and no secretaries were required to draft letters.

Videoconferencing affects feedback in several ways. First, although visual feedback is present, it is reduced. Also, it is not possible to make eye-to-eye contact. However, the time required to arrange for the communication is greatly reduced. The major advantage, and a reason that many companies use videoconferencing, is that travel time for meetings is reduced.[13] A meeting with participants miles apart can be arranged without accounting for travel time, an important consideration for geographically dispersed members of an organization.

At the same time, the reduced time for feedback can cause problems. According to information theory discussed earlier, we have limited capabilities to process information. However, managers may be pressured to decipher information and respond quickly just because the technology allows it. Imagine a manager who receives about 200 e-mails and text messages daily. These media represent speed and responsiveness. But constant interruptions such as e-mail alerts may result in stress and overload. Recent research examining the effects of interruption overload and continuous partial attention is alarming. Higher cognitive functions, starting with decision making, can be impaired. Fragmentation of attention also appears to impede creativity.[14] Multitasking, rather than a step toward efficiency, apparently prevents us from focusing on anything in a significant way.[15] Managers need to be aware that continuous availability for feedback may have damaging consequences on their thought processes. The impression that a manager must respond quickly is related to our next discussion.

A Symbolic Interactionist Perspective

Symbolic interactionism is a theoretical framework that can be used to explain sociological and psychological phenomena. In the imagery of symbolic interactionism, we view society as a dynamic web of communication. Thus, society and every organization in which managers function is an interaction. An interaction is symbolic because, through their interactions, people assign meaning to things and events. Over time, many symbols evolve within the organization and take on an agreed upon meaning.[16]

The media that managers choose to use for communication may be based partially on symbolic reasons. Some argue that managerial communication behavior represents ritualistic responses to the need to appear competent, intelligent, legitimate, and rational.[17] For example, a face-to-face medium may symbolize concern or caring. Conversely, the manager who congratulates a subordinate on 25 years of service with an e-mail message may unintentionally communicate a lack of personal concern. A handwritten note or a special card would symbolize more personal warmth to some people.

A comprehensive study of managers and their communication media indicates that channel choice was highly symbolic.[18] Managers interviewed in this study said they choose the face-to-face channel to signal a desire for teamwork, to build trust or goodwill, or to convey informality. Both face-to-face and telephone communication symbolized urgency, showed personal concern, and signaled deference to the receiver who preferred that medium. By contrast, written media were thought to show authority, make a strong impression, and be legitimate and official. Written media were also used to get attention and to comply with protocol.

The results of this study indicate that managers should not simply rely on the channel they feel most comfortable with when communicating; they should consider its symbolism. Here is a true story that demonstrates this principle. There once was an accounting department manager who relied solely on sticky notes for communicating within his department, to the extent that he would silently tack the note onto a subordinate's computer monitor, even while the subordinate was sitting right in front of it. How do you think the employee felt about the manager and his message?

In summary, managers should consider four factors when deciding on the most effective and efficient use of mediated communication: bandwidth, perceived closeness, feedback, and symbolism. The choice of technology becomes rather complicated, and it is difficult to generalize from one situation to another. But certain general conclusions can be stated.

MATCHING TECHNOLOGY AND THE MESSAGE

The discussion so far has emphasized how the channel may vary when communication is mediated by technology. Now consider matching the message and the technology. Not all technology is appropriate for all types of messages. To facilitate this discussion, messages are categorized along these continuums: sensitivity, negativity, complexity, and persuasiveness (as diagrammed in Figure 3–2).[19] The challenge is to consider the message and how it fits into the various categories, and then match it with the appropriate technology.

FIGURE 3–2
Message
Types

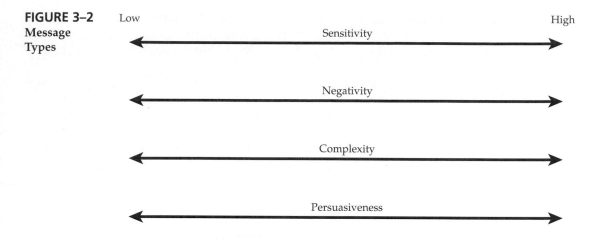

Message Sensitivity

When considering technology, managers must determine the extent to which the message is sensitive. A sensitive message is one that evokes an emotional reaction from the receiver. Neutral messages convey information that readers process and respond to intellectually but not emotionally. Receivers will not become upset with neutral messages, but neither will they become ecstatic or pleased.

Sensitive messages should usually be communicated in face-to-face settings to increase the personal element. An extreme example is when a U.S. soldier is killed in battle. A military representative first informs relatives in a personal meeting. Telephone calls are not considered an option. An example at the other end of the continuum is that a meeting agenda could be circulated by e-mail, and a meeting reminder could be posted on employees' calendars using Microsoft Outlook.

What if it is not possible to communicate a sensitive message face-to-face? Here the technology with the widest bandwidth should be used. Also, an interactive system with an opportunity for feedback should be supplementally used if possible. Symbolically, this may indicate a high level of concern. For instance, a company with offices in several states was forced to restructure. The grapevine was rampant with concerns about layoffs, loss of benefits, and forced relocations. It was not possible for the CEO to visit all the locations in a timely manner. The company chose to announce the general plan for the restructuring via an interactive video teleconference. All the employees met in various conference rooms and lunchrooms throughout the company. After the CEO announced the restructuring, the telephone lines were opened for questions.

This technology had one distinct advantage even though it may not have been as personal. It allowed the message to be sent throughout the company concurrently so all the employees received the same message at the same time, thus controlling rumors and minimizing anxiety. This is an advantage that would not have been possible without the technology.

Message Negativity

Messages extend along a continuum from positive to negative. When sending a negative message, managers should generally be sensitive to the receiver. Consequently, the extent to which a message is negative and the extent to which it is sensitive are highly related. Some of the same generalities exist for the other categories.

Another important consideration exists when communicating negative messages via technology, however. A person receiving bad news via a technological channel may believe the manager was hiding behind the technology rather than facing the receiver directly. Or it may appear that the manager did not want to be responsible for the message.

Almost everyone has complained to a company about poor service or an incorrect billing. Frequently, the response to the complaint is an impersonal form letter. The reaction was probably increased frustration and even hostility. In short, technology often depersonalizes. Contemporary organizations are making efforts to balance "high tech" with "high touch." Addressing customers by name in mass mailings (a process made possible by technology) is one example. Other strategies for softening the blow when sending negative messages are presented in Chapter 5. Managers can successfully influence receivers' reactions to bad news.

Message Complexity

Guidelines for using technology are somewhat clearer when considering message complexity. As the complexity of the message increases, managers should attempt to use (1) wider bandwidth, (2) the medium that will add to psychological closeness, (3) the technology that provides for the greatest amount of feedback, and (4) symbolism consistent with the complexity.

Discussion of a complex team project schedule involving a series of dates and figures provides an example. Assume seven managers at four locations are a "virtual team." A number of viable solutions exist for communicating complex messages, without getting everyone together face-to-face. Fax, e-mail attachments, shared databases, and conference software are the norm for electronic communication. A relatively wide bandwidth is used; feedback is provided, and the sophisticated technology symbolizes the seriousness of the task.

Research shows the communication of complex, detailed information is not necessarily improved by face-to-face interaction.[20] An explanation of a complex engineering formula, for instance, can be just as effective with audio and graphic communication as when the person doing the explanation is physically present. Interactive computer conferencing via local area networks (LANs) can facilitate the communication of complex messages because it may stimulate better concentration from the receiver.

Message Persuasiveness

Persuasive messages involve an effort to induce a receiver to take a particular action. Persuasion is not an effort to coerce, fool, seduce, or manipulate the receiver. Rather, it is an attempt to get employees to comply with behaviors that will meet the goals of the organization. When thinking of persuasion, salespeople probably come to mind; however, managers frequently use persuasion, influence tactics, or compliance-gaining strategies to affect employees' performance. Efforts to introduce new work procedures, increase teamwork, or change corporate culture require persuasive communication. Suggestions for delivering persuasive business presentations are found in Chapter 14.

The topic of persuasion has been of interest since Aristotle's time. But a leading researcher more recently wrote: "Despite the vast number of pages written and the countless studies undertaken about persuasion, it is difficult to shake the uneasy feeling that we have precious little reliable, socially relevant knowledge about it."[21] Our understanding of persuasion is further complicated when considering mediated communication. Little research has been conducted in this area; consequently, it is necessary to generalize about what we know from nonmediated communication.

A popular book, *Influence: The New Psychology of Modern Persuasion*, presents three conclusions about persuasion that are particularly pertinent to our discussion.[22] First, managers can more easily persuade those who like them. Second, people are more easily persuaded when they perceive the persuader as an authority. Third, it is easier for managers to persuade others as they get psychologically and physically closer to them.

Persuaded by the One You Like

Few would be surprised to learn that we most prefer to say yes to the requests of someone we know and like. In addition, we like people with whom we spend more time, even if we are forced to spend this time together.

This research finding is important to our discussion because the quality of the time we spend with people via technology is generally not the same as if the person were physically present. In other words, no matter how much time we spend with people in teleconferences, it cannot substitute for personal presence.

Persuaded by the One You Believe

The second principle is not overly surprising either. We listen and are persuaded by those who appear to be authorities on the topic. This point is important among television executives. The newsperson or the special reporter must be believable. Whether it is Jim Lehrer or Anderson Cooper, they succeed partly because they look and sound like authorities.

But what about average managers who must use video or telephonic technology in an attempt to persuade? It would seem they are at a disadvantage. Again, these technologies should be used for persuasion only when necessary due to time or cost restrictions.

Another point adds to this caveat: It is more difficult to say no when looking a person directly in the eye. Even when we like a person or believe she is an authority, it is easier to say no from a distance. This is one reason sales professionals try to get a person to say yes in their presence.

Persuaded by the One Who Is Close

Much sophisticated work has gone into preparing persuasive audiovisual presentations. But these presentations are not as effective as personal exposure of the one attempting the persuasion. If possible, it is best to have the person physically present. When physical presence of an authority is not possible, a well-organized presentation by a somewhat less credible source may be a good substitute. Often, the PowerPoint slide show is sent electronically to audience members. What is the balance between physical presence and credibility? These questions must be addressed. When considering persuasive managerial communication, however, one principle must always be considered. A person physically present is more persuasive than one who is present only via technologically mediated communication. That is why, despite the recent dramatic increase in online automobile sales, dealers continue to make an effort to lure online shoppers into their showrooms. And a test drive remains the best way to close a sale.

A LOOK TO THE FUTURE

E-mail, faxes, audio and video teleconferencing, intranets, PDAs—all of these systems are with us today and are being used more and more frequently in the workplace. If one were to speculate about what developments would affect managerial communication in the future, any number of possibilities would exist. However, several safe projections can be made. The first is that technology will simply be used more. Second, decision making will be affected; third, job and organizational design will be altered; fourth, mediated collaborative writing will be common. These trends are discussed next.

Technology Proliferation

This chapter has described the advantages and disadvantages of technology for communication in organizations. Problems with technology include the danger of sensory overload with useless cues (jamming), narrow bandwidth, diminished feelings of personal closeness, and reduced opportunities for feedback. Despite these disadvantages, however, networked organizations are the norm. The strategic decision for managers, therefore, is not *whether* to use technological media but *which* electronic medium will best suit the situation and *how* to maximize its capabilities.

An estimated 247 billion e-mails are sent each day worldwide, with the number expected to increase to 294 billion by 2010.[23] According to a recent White Collar Productivity Index survey of time spent in the workplace, the average U.S. executive receives 200 e-mails per day after spam is extracted. Administrative and newer staff receive an average of 50 e-mails per day.[24] Nearly 1 in 10 workers say they would need two or more days to catch up on e-mail if they went on a two-week vacation.[25] E-mail's influence has likewise grown. Fifty-six percent of workers surveyed by *USA Today* believe that e-mail increases their productivity. And one-third of chief information officers say losing an e-mail system for a week would be more traumatic than getting divorced, according to a survey by computer storage company Veritas.[26]

The risk of sensory overload, rather than motivating managers to ignore technological media, has stimulated managers to develop a variety of coping skills.

They may use an assistant to sort and redirect the crush of messages. Features in most e-mail programs also are useful for coding and filtering messages according to sender or topic. Some companies try to help their managers cope with e-mail overload by enforcing "e-mail-free Fridays" or at least banning the use of the "reply all" feature. But managers most often are turning to Instant Messaging and text messaging to avoid the crush of e-mail. That strategy, described earlier in this chapter, cuts e-mail traffic but does not diminish the amount of time spent interacting with technology or the level of resultant anxiety.

There are exceptions to today's technology-oriented executives. John Scully, the former CEO of Apple Computer, was infamous for not allowing employees to send him e-mail messages. Colleen Barrett, President Emeritus of Southwest Airlines, is proud that as president until 2008 she did not have an e-mail address, didn't use a PDA or surf the Web, and only recently acquired a cell phone. She thinks e-mail is "very impersonal . . . a horrible way to communicate."[27] These examples of managerial nonuse of technology are the obverse of executives and employees in a company such as Colruyt, the Belgian discount food chain. Colruyt uses technology to maximize both vertical and horizontal information sharing. Secrecy is minimized, empowerment for decision making is maximized, and power no longer equates with access to information in such postmodern organizations.[28]

In networked organizations, the hierarchical culture is dissolved. Rank does not matter as much to workers who are on the network and who know what everyone is doing. Today's managers no longer manage information; they manage networks of people. Teams use groupware and Group Decision Support Systems (GDSSs) to collaborate despite geographic distances among team members. In addition to increasing efficiency, the technology reduces groupthink, defuses emotional issues, and enhances the creativity of decisions. Clearly, these advantages outweigh the risks and costs of using technology for workplace communication.

Decision Making

Managerial decision making may be defined as the process of identifying and solving problems. Decision making requires that managers scan for pertinent information. Most discussions on this topic generally contain two major stages. One is the problem identification stage. Information about relevant conditions is monitored both to determine if performance is meeting expectations and to diagnose the cause of any shortcomings. The other stage involves solution identification. Alternative actions are considered, and one alternative is selected and implemented. A more thorough explanation of the rational problem solving process is presented in Chapters 10 and 13. In both stages of the process, the more information available, the greater the probability that effective decisions will be made. And more and more information is available with increased technologies.

Burger King provides an example of the effect of communication technology on decision making. Each Burger King store is networked via computer to a central office where each sale is transmitted and recorded. When one store is running low on a product, without even placing a phone call, the central facility is aware of the shortage and can send supplies. This is comparable to e-mail except the messages are automatically prepared and transmitted. Stage one in the decision process, the problem identification stage, is more easily accomplished because of communication technology.

As organizations become larger and as more sophisticated information systems are available, the probability is greater that technological communication systems may be used in many situations. For instance, Intel, the world's largest microchip maker, has several manufacturing and research facilities in Arizona and northern California. Attempts to resolve complex technological problems frequently require input from various experts. Assume that highly technical information is needed for a unique problem. This information may be available only in the Science Library at Arizona State University. An engineer in California can access the information through a special terminal in her office that is connected to the library in Tempe, Arizona. A copy of the document can be available to the engineer within seconds.

This quick access to information has three apparent implications. First, anyone who wants to remain competitive must know where and how to access the information.

Second, managers who are bombarded with masses of information find the odds of making an effective decision greatly decreased. If managers receive large quantities of both relevant and irrelevant information, the important facts and figures may be overlooked and can create problems. The human mind can process only so much data. As noted earlier in Figure 3–1, a point develops at which the mind blocks out any additional, though valuable, information. As technology allows for rapid acquisition of greater amounts of information, poorer rather than better decisions may result.

Third, communication technology allows managers to quickly change their decisions. Say a manager writes an analytical report comparing the acquisitions of two pieces of property for a retail outlet. The report's recommendation is finalized and ready for submission to an executive committee. At the last minute, new information is made available through a database to which the company subscribes. This allows the manager to alter the report's recommendation at the last minute. As presented in Chapter 2, the manager's challenge is to know where to get information, when and how to present it to others, and how and when to use it. In some ways, information technology makes the decision-making process easier, but in other ways it becomes more complex.

Job and Organizational Design

Increasing communication technology will allow managers to monitor more closely the standards expected from a job performance. Take a simple example of a sales representative responsible for calling on furniture stores. The objective is to obtain cooperation in setting up a special display within the stores. The standard of performance is to make two calls per day and obtain three displays per 10 calls. The formal agreement is to report the day's activities to the central office at the end of each day. This is done via phone or laptop. The salesperson may leave questions in the voice mailbox, and managers may send instructions via Push-to-Talk or PDA. E-mail messages can be exchanged continuously.

In the past, this level of interaction would not have been possible. It would have been necessary to mail reports to the central office, so feedback may not have been obtained for several days. Interaction via technologically mediated communication allows the manager to maintain control.

In addition to improved control of specific jobs, organizational relationships may change with mediated communication. We generally think of jobs being connected by means of either horizontal or vertical integration. Horizontal communication or integration occurs between people at the same hierarchical level. Managers may meet horizontally to coordinate activities, solve problems, resolve conflicts, or just share information. Regardless of the purpose, more horizontal communication can occur as a result of technology. Assume the board of directors of a hospital system with eight locations directed the human resources managers to implement a safety training program in each hospital. The managers would probably want to share ideas with each other on the most efficient way to implement the program. Travel would not be necessary for a meeting—a video teleconference, satellite downlink, or a conference call could meet the purpose. In this case, technology would allow for greater integration at lower expense.

Vertical integration is the coordination among higher and lower levels within the hierarchy. Unfortunately, it often seems that different levels of the organization typically do not communicate well with each other.[29] But as noted when discussing formalization, mediated communication should assist this process. Managers and subordinates are more accessible with technology. Distance and time are less troublesome.

This improved vertical and horizontal integration is resulting in dramatically different job and organizational structures. Several reports have indicated that, in an effort to create competitive advantage, managers' jobs have become more information-oriented, while the number of layers of managers has decreased.[30]

Collaboration

Picture five managers, each sitting at a computer in five different locations around the country. Special software allows the managers to edit the same document simultaneously. Any changes made to the document are visible to all members as changes occur. Furthermore, protocols built into the software allow group members to alter or even delete each other's work.

Most business documents require more than one person to be involved in the writing process. Examples include proposals, reports to regulatory agencies, annual reports to shareholders, policy manuals, operating procedures, newsletters, directives, user manuals, training materials, mission/vision and strategic goal statements, progress reports, and personnel reports. Technology allows collaborative writing of such documents to be performed concurrently, not just sequentially. Unfortunately, collaborative writing too often means one person writes part of the report and then sends it to another person for revision. This person then passes it on to another and so forth. This is extremely time-consuming, and coordination is difficult.

Today's technology allows managers to do more than relay documents; it lets them develop synergy that accompanies true collaboration. Groupware is a family of software that supports group tasks in various levels of shared electronic environments. Groupware provides computer-mediated communication systems, allowing different viewpoints and ideas to be compared and discussed in real time. As versions of the text are compared, a better product results without bruising egos. Because collaborative writing is becoming so important, it is discussed more extensively in Chapter 4.

Group Decision Support Systems (GDSSs) are software and associated processes that have been designed to advance coordination of group projects. The fundamental goal of a GDSS is to support collaborative work activities such as idea creation, message exchange, project planning, document creation, copyediting, and joint decision making.[31] Group Decision Support Systems exist for groups whose members are dispersed, working in their separate offices, homes, or client locations. Other systems support face-to-face meetings that occur in one physical setting, such as a conference or boardroom. With these, it is possible to instantaneously display ideas on large screens, vote on individual preferences, compile the anonymous input of ideas and preferences, and electronically exchange ideas between members. GDSS programs include various quantitative analysis techniques. The most sophisticated systems include expert advice in the selecting and arranging of rules to be applied during interpersonal communication.[32]

THE MANAGEMENT CHALLENGE

What does all this mean for managers? It means they must become sensitive to the correct type of communication channel to use in different situations. It means managers must learn to use these new technologies. It means another dimension has been added to managerial communication.

Let us expand on each of these points. Several studies have indicated a strong correlation exists between a manager's media sensitivity and managerial performance. When a task involved complex information or was highly emotional, for instance, effective managers were more inclined to use communication channels with a broad bandwidth.[33]

A whole new dimension has been added to the manager's job: understanding and selecting the correct communication technology. A corollary to this requirement is that managers must guide their subordinates in the proper, ethical use of the technology. For instance, Instant Messaging is an official corporate communication tool for approximately 26 percent of U.S. companies. Employees use IM on their own in another 44 percent of companies, sometimes for personal as well as business-related use. Yet 35 percent of companies don't have an official IM policy, risking breaches of confidentiality, viruses, and copyright infringement.[34] New alternatives are constantly becoming available, requiring strategic decisions. It is clear that U.S. business is committed to technology. Companies will be expecting their managers to make this investment pay off.

The technology payoff could be increased if managers had a table summarizing when the technology is best used, but such a table is not possible. Too many contingencies must be considered to say which technology should be used when.

FIGURE 3–3
Technology
Choice
Contingencies

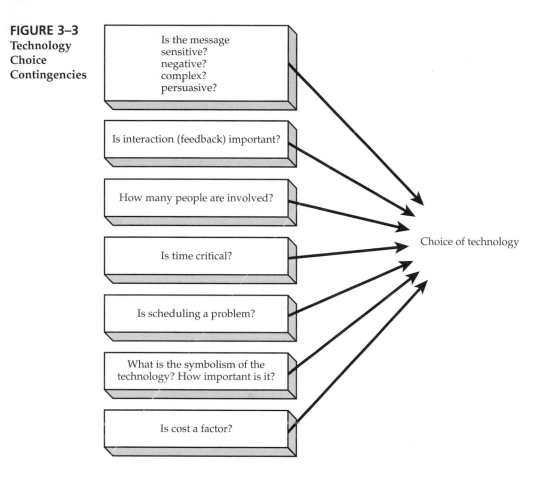

Figure 3–3 demonstrates some of the questions that must be addressed when selecting a technology.

Summary

To understand better how technology affects managerial communication, four concepts are discussed. First, bandwidth is affected because one channel is generally omitted when technologically mediated communication is used. Perceived closeness, or propinquity, is a consideration because electronic media affect the extent to which people feel close to each other. The feedback cycle is much shorter with technology, so this is also a consideration. Finally, the symbolic interactionist perspective is considered because the use of various communication channels has different symbolic values.

When matching technology to the message, four message factors are considered. First is message sensitivity: Greater bandwidth should generally be used with sensitive messages. The second category is message negativity. Managers must be careful not to hide behind technology when presenting negative messages. The third category is message complexity. Two ways to effectively transmit relatively complex messages are teleconferencing and computer conferencing. The fourth category is message persuasiveness. The extent to which the receiver likes the sender and the extent to which the sender is perceived as an authority must be considered. In general, persuasion is less effective when the communication is mediated by technology.

Going forward, technology will continue to proliferate, affecting managerial communication in decision making, job and organizational design, and collaborative writing. All these technologies will challenge future managers as they make strategic decisions and as they monitor and guide their employees' technologically mediated communication.

For articles on contemporary issues in technologically mediated communication, current practices, and the latest business trends, see the Appendix.

Cases for Small Group Discussion

Case 3-1.

The Potential for Technology

Bill Emory is the operations vice president of a banking firm in California that has 48 branch operations. These operations vary from drive-in facilities with 10 employees to larger facilities employing as many as 150 people. Employee turnover has always been a major problem in these branches, and no employment strategy has been effective in reducing this problem. The high turnover has made employee training a special problem.

The human resources department is responsible for employee training, but HR charges branch operations for the expenses incurred. The recent expansion in training due to ever-changing services offered by the bank has become extremely costly. Emory has decided it is time to attempt to reduce these costs by implementing some new training strategies. He believes that many of the new communication technologies could be used to save training expenses. In particular, savings could be realized for the branches that are more than 400 miles from the corporate office. (In the past, the training representatives would travel to the branch site, stay overnight, present a one- or two-day training session, and then return. Emory would like to reduce these travel and lodging expenses.) Emory has casually asked the HR manager, Joan Tyson, to investigate communication technology possibilities in training, but no action has been taken; consequently, Emory has decided to write a persuasive letter to Tyson encouraging Tyson's staff to investigate this subject.

Project

Write a memo to the HR manager, Joan Tyson, which could be used for this purpose. Include one or two specific technologies that might be appropriate, their advantages, and the communication impact that could be expected. Special attention should be given to training for the tellers. For instance, the procedures for recording the various transactions and customer communications should be part of the training.

Case 3-2.

Improvements at ServeNow

ServeNow is a grocery store chain that has seven stores in the southeastern United States. ServeNow's strategy is to target smaller towns (under 50,000 population) so it can become the dominant store in the area. The chain is headquartered in the largest town (population 75,000) in which it has a store. Each store is at least 50 miles from another store within the network.

The owner of the stores, Edward Bushley, has found that it is extremely difficult to monitor store activities because of travel logistics. As a result, the manager of each store has traditionally had a lot of latitude. Many of the pricing and inventory decisions are made at the individual locations. However, most purchasing is made through a central purchasing office in the headquarters city.

But during the past two weeks, three managers left ServeNow to start an online grocery brokerage service. This took Bushley by surprise, but being an entrepreneur himself, he understands their desire to start their own business. In addition, another manager is nearing retirement. Bushley has found that it is extremely difficult to find qualified replacements for these energetic, creative managers.

Bushley had hoped that potential managers would be available among his present employees, but he discovered the company is weak in its succession planning. Current staff members do not seem to have the capabilities or desire to become store managers. It has become obvious that managers have to be found outside of the present staff.

Bushley has retained a small-business consultant, Solange DePeres, who specializes in personnel problems. DePeres agreed that no potential managers were on the present staff. The assistant store managers would be able to manage during the transition, but ultimately new personnel would have to be hired. She stated that Bushley would have to hire managers who were not familiar with the stores' operations and simply spend more time with them than he had with the previous managers. In particular, Bushley would have to spend time training them and answering operational questions.

Bushley asks DePeres, "How can I possibly spend more time at the individual stores? It seems that I am already too busy to maintain a balanced lifestyle."

Project

Assume you are the small-business consultant, Solange DePeres, and make several recommendations to help Bushley stay in touch with his stores and develop his managerial force. Consider especially the technological communication tools on the market. Explain your recommendations.

Endnotes

1. C. Cherry, *On Human Communication* (New York: John Wiley & Sons, 1961).

2. Selection of these variables is partially based on C. Heeter, "Classifying Mediated Communication Systems," in *Communication Yearbook,* vol. 12, ed. James A. Anderson (Newbury Park, CA: Sage Publications, 1988), pp. 477–86.

3. Felipe Korzenny and Connie Bauer, "Testing the Theory of Electronic Propinquity," *Communication Research* 8, no. 4 (1981), pp. 479–98.

4. For further discussion, see Larry R. Smeltzer and Charles M. Vance, "An Analysis of Graphics Use in Audio-Graphic Teleconferences," *Journal of Business Communication* 26, no. 2 (1989), pp. 123–42.

5. Steven H. Chaffee and Charles R. Berger, "What Communication Scientists Do," in *Handbook of Communication Science,* eds. C. Berger and S. Chaffee (Newbury Park, CA: Sage Publications, 1987), pp. 99–123.

6. "Radio Shack Uses E-Mail to Fire 400 Employees," *Huntsville Item*, September 1, 2006, p. 1.

7. N. L. Reinsch, Cam Monroe Steele, Philip V. Lewis, Michael Stano, and Raymond W. Beswick, "Measuring Telephone Apprehension," *Management Communication Quarterly* 4, no. 2 (1990), pp. 198–221.

8. N. L. Reinsch, Jr., and Raymond W. Beswick, "Voice Mail versus Conventional Channels: A Cost Minimization Analysis of Individuals' Preferences," *Academy of Management Journal* 23, no. 4 (1990), pp. 801–16.

9. Larry R. Smeltzer, "An Analysis of Receivers' Reactions to Electronically Mediated Communication," *Journal of Business Communication* 23, no. 4 (1986), pp. 37–54.

10. Jim Louderback, "IM's: No Longer Just a Teen Thing," *USA Weekend*, January 3, 2003, p. 4.

11. Jennifer Tanaka, "You Pinging Me? IM Has Already Arrived at the Office," *Newsweek*, May 12, 2003, p. E12.

12. Jill Colvin, "You've Got Voice Mail, but Do You Care?" *Houston Chronicle*, April 5, 2009, p. G6.

13. Earl C. Gottschalk, Jr., "Firms Are Cool to Meetings by Television," *The Wall Street Journal,* July 26, 1983, p. 1.

14. Sharon Begley, "Will the BlackBerry Sink the Presidency?" *Newsweek*, February 16, 2009, pp. 37–38. See also Gail Thomas and Cindy King, "Reconceptualizing Email Overload," *Journal of Business and Technical Communication,* vol. 20 (2006), pp. 252–87.

15. Maggie Jackson, *Distracted: The Erosion of Attention and the Coming Dark Age* (Amherst, NY: Prometheus Books, 2008).

16. R. L. Daft and K. E. Weick, "Toward a Model of Organizations as Interpretation Systems," *Academy of Management Review* 9, no. 2 (1984), pp. 284–95.

17. M. S. Feldman and J. G. March, "Information in Organizations as Signal and Symbol," *Administrative Science Quarterly* 26, no. 1 (1981), pp. 171–86.

18. R. L. Daft, R. H. Lengel, and L. K. Trevino, "Message Equivocality, Media Selection, and Manager Performance: Implications for Information Systems," *MIS Quarterly* 11, no. 2 (1987), pp. 355–66.

19. This categorization was largely drawn from Ronald E. Dulek and John S. Fielden, *Principles of Business Communication* (New York: Macmillan, 1990).

20. R. E. Rice, "Evaluating New Media Systems," in *Evaluating the New Information Technologies: New Directions for Program Evaluation*, ed. J. Johnson (San Francisco: Jossey-Bass, 1984), pp. 53–71.

21. Gerald R. Miller, "Persuasion," in *Handbook of Communication Science,* eds. C. Berger and S. Chaffee (Newbury Park, CA: Sage Publications, 1987), pp. 446–83.

22. Robert B. Cialdini, *Influence: The New Psychology of Modern Persuasion* (New York: Quill, 1984).

23. Yuki Noguchi, "Make It Stop! Crushed by Too Many E-Mails," www.npr.org (retrieved June 16, 2008).

24. Bary C. Sherman, "More Proof That E-Mail Wastes Time and Money," *BusinessWeek,* December 19, 2005.

25. Kevin Maney, "How the Big Names Tame E-Mail," *USA Today,* July 24, 2003, p. 1A.

26. "She Hates E-Mail," *Newsweek,* May 12, 2003, p. E18.

27. Maney, "How the Big Names Tame E-Mail," p. 2A.

28. Dubravka Cecez-Kecmanovic, Marius Janson, and Ann Brown, "The Rationality Framework for a Critical Study of Information Systems," *Journal of Information Technology* 17, no. 4 (December 2002), pp. 215–27.

29. Gerald M. Goldhaber, *Organizational Communication* (Dubuque, IA: Wm. C. Brown, 1983), p. 156.

30. Jeffrey Pfeffer, "Producing Sustainable Competitive Advantage Through the Effective Management of People," *The Academy of Management Executive* 19, no. 4 (2005), pp. 95–108.

31. Paul Benjamin Lowry, Aaron Curtis, and Michelle Rene Lowry, "Building a Taxonomy and Nomenclature of Collaborative Writing to Improve Interdisciplinary Research and Practice," *Journal of Business Communication* 41, no. 1 (January 2004), pp. 66–99.

32. Marshall Scott Poole and Geraldine DeSanctis, "Understand the Use of Group Decision Support Systems: The Theory of Adaptive Structuration," in *Organizations and Communication Technology,* eds. J. Fulk and C. Steinfield (Newbury Park, CA: Sage Publications, 1990), pp. 173–93; and "Smart Programs Go to Work," *BusinessWeek,* March 2, 1992, pp. 97–105.

33. Gail S. Russ, Richard L. Daft, and Robert H. Lengel, "Media Selection and Managerial Characteristics in Organizational Communications," *Management Communication Quarterly* 4, no. 2 (November 1990), pp. 151–75.

34. "The Present (and Future) of Business Communications," Accounting Web (n.d.), www.accountingweb.com (July 25, 2005).

Part **Two**

Managerial Writing Strategies

Chapter **Four**

Contemporary Managerial Writing

If writing must be a precise form of communication, it should be treated like a precision instrument. It should be sharpened, and it should not be used carelessly.

—*Theodore M. Bernstein, editor, The New York Times*

Managers spend about 75 percent of their time communicating,[1] and the higher managers go in their organizations, the more time they spend communicating. While much of this communication involves oral, face-to-face interaction, some requires writing e-mails, memos, letters, and reports. All have the potential to play a critical part in the success of the manager and the organization.

Given the time and effort required to put things in writing, readers may wonder why managers would prefer to write a message rather than communicate it orally. Written managerial communication offers several strategic advantages: economy, efficiency, accuracy, and official permanence.

Writing is usually more economical than long-distance phone calls and much more economical than long-distance travel. Furthermore, it provides immediacy, in that the manager can write the message whether or not the receiver is immediately available to receive it.

Writing is efficient because the manager can work independently and use words selectively. Additionally, e-mail allows receivers to read messages at their convenience and thus avoids the time wasted in telephone tag.

Accuracy is another advantage of writing; writing permits greater control of words and message organization than does oral communication. Accuracy, in turn, often eliminates confusion, ensures clarity, and further contributes to economy and efficiency.

Finally, writing provides an official record that can be retained for recall and review. In our increasingly litigious society, the importance of documentation cannot be overstressed. Managers must understand that all documents generated by their organization are "discoverable." That is, attorneys can compel their disclosure as part of pretrial procedures. This fact implies that all official records must be accurate and clear, and able to stand up to scrutiny. The difference between a legal judgment for or against organizations and their managers is becoming more often a matter of adequate documentation.

Once a manager has decided to capitalize on the benefits of writing as a communication channel, the manager should consider two unique characteristics of writing in a business context: collaboration and the uniqueness of managerial writing. Collaboration and the unique roles of business writing are examined in the next sections of this chapter.

COLLABORATIVE WRITING

A major development in the modern corporate world is the emergence of collaborative writing. It is becoming more prevalent because of the increased emphasis on teamwork. Also, these teams frequently consist of people with unique specialties that they bring to bear toward the successful completion of major projects.

Though it may assume any of many forms, collaborative writing is entrenched in contemporary professional writing. In personal interviews with 200 businesspeople in two states, one team of researchers found that 73.5 percent of respondents routinely collaborate with at least one other person in writing.[2] Another research team found that 87 percent of respondents sometimes wrote as members of a team or group.[3] At America West Airlines, most of the reports are collaboratively written. The same is true at Accenture.

Collaborative writing comes in a number of different guises. Sometimes a supervisor has a staff member research and write a document, after which the supervisor edits it. Sometimes the collaboration comes in the planning of the document, which is composed and revised by an individual. Other times, an individual does the planning and composing of work that is revised collaboratively. Peers often critique one another's work. And there are times when the collaboration pervades the entire writing process from start to finish.[4] Recent research indicates that a typical document cycles through three to five revisions before it is sent to the intended readers.

Advantages of Collaborative Writing

Collaborative writing is becoming more popular largely because of the advantages of group decision making. It often works better than an individual effort because of the additional minds and perspectives being applied to creating the document. Furthermore, the understanding of, and the motivation to carry out, the directives of the document are greater among those who actually contributed to its development.

Collaborative writing is also thought to be particularly advantageous when the size of the task and/or time limits call for the labor of more than one person, when the scope of the job calls for more than one area of expertise, or when one of the task goals is the melding of divergent opinions.[5]

Gebhardt notes that the theoretical underpinnings of collaborative writing are "the rhetorical sense of audience; the psychological power of peer influence;

the transfer-of-learning principle by which (people) gain insights into their own writing as they comment on the works of others; and the principle of feedback through which (people) sense how well their writing is communicating."[6]

Terry Bacon has found that collaborative writing socializes employees in several fundamental ways. It helps to acculturate newcomers by teaching writers about the corporation's capabilities and history and by modeling the corporation's values and attitudes in the actions of the experienced members. It also helps break down functional barriers, and it fosters the informal chains of communication and authority through which the corporation accomplishes its work.[7]

Finally, and perhaps most importantly, collaboration can improve writing quality.[8] People, without outside direction, can respond to each other's drafts with sharply focused and relevant comments.[9] Recent developments in technology facilitate collaborative writing. Use of software such as New Aspects and Lotus Notes has been shown to not only result in better documents, but also avoid emotional conflict among collaborators.

Disadvantages of Collaborative Writing

Some disadvantages of collaborative writing are also those associated with group decision making. Some members do not do their fair share. Coordinating schedules for meetings can be complicated and vexing. Personality conflicts can all but stall the group's progress. And some people believe that one person acting alone could probably complete the chore in much less time than it takes a group to do so. Finally, though one person may do a poor job on part of the project, everyone is held responsible for the entire end result.

Respondents in one study noted that the two major costs of collaboration were time and ego. One commented that in collaboration you had to "check your ego at the door," you had to be "confident in your own abilities and yet able to take criticism."[10]

Another surveyed group of professional writers cited several problems associated with collaborative writing. They spoke of difficulty in resolving style differences; the additional time required to work with a group; the inequitable division of tasks; and the loss of personal satisfaction, ownership, or sense of creativity.[11]

Probably the most serious problem associated with collaborative writing is ineffectively dealing with conflicts that arise. Some people see all conflicts as bad and try to ignore them or sweep them under the carpet. They do not realize that some conflicts are functional and can help the group to come to a more creative resolution of its problem.

Guidelines for Effective Collaborative Writing

In their extensive research into the collaborative writing of people in a number of professions, Lisa Ede and Andrea Lunsford came up with the following profile of effective collaborative writers:

> They are flexible; respectful of others; attentive and analytical listeners; able to speak and write clearly and articulately; dependable and able to meet deadlines; able to designate and share responsibility, to lead and to follow; open to criticism but confident in their own abilities; ready to engage in creative conflict.[12]

Generally, this profile depicts people who are able to work with others, people who are going to be in greater demand as collaboration becomes more the norm than the exception.

In addition to the advice implicit in the preceding characterization of effective collaborative writers and groups, there are other ways to achieve successful collaborative writing experiences. One basic guideline is to make sure the work is divided equitably among group members. Nothing is surer to destroy a person's morale than to begin feeling overworked compared to others in the group.

Second, writing teams should use electronic technology for collaboration; the media appear to buffer emotions while increasing efficiency.

Third, all collaborative writing groups should have a team leader, even though the person may not have any formal authority. The leader should be responsible for coordinating the team's collaborative efforts, shaping the team's vision, and resolving conflicts among individuals and functional departments. The latter task usually requires good interpersonal skills if the leader has no formal authority.[13]

Though no one can guarantee that all collaborative writing experiences will be problem-free, we are confident that anyone who follows the preceding guidelines will encounter fewer insurmountable problems and will attain greater success in group writing projects.

THE UNIQUE ROLE OF MANAGERIAL WRITING

In recent years, the various fields addressing composition have given much attention to discourse communities. A *discourse community* is a group of people who think in similar ways about how to communicate subjects to be dealt with and how to approach them, as well as what makes up legitimate knowledge. These communities may be large or small, and any organization may contain a number of discourse communities.

Managers serve in sufficiently common roles and work in sufficiently common contexts to make them members of a unique discourse community. Managers are people who plan the organization's objectives, organize the functions of the organization, lead people in the accomplishment of those objectives, and control activities to make sure they are proceeding in the right direction.

Equally important in defining the discourse community of managerial writers is the context in which they do their work. Context may be the most powerful variable affecting what writers in organizations do, and how these writers perceive, interpret, and value their own activity. The following paragraphs examine several aspects of the unique context in which managerial writing occurs.

One of the most critical aspects of the context of managerial writing is the fragmented nature of a manager's workday. Most people think of managers, especially higher-level executives, as having meticulously organized days overseen and protected by assistants. Henry Mintzberg found the opposite to be true. As he and colleagues recorded the activities of a number of managers, he found their days to be filled with interruptions. On average they had a full half hour of uninterrupted time only once every four days.[14] More recently, Gloria Mark observed employees at two high-tech firms and found that the average worker spends only 11 minutes on any given project before being interrupted. IT workers have it worse, getting interrupted every three minutes.[15] Most people faced with a writing task like to go somewhere quiet and work in sizable blocks of time. Such luxury is rarely available to managers.

Another aspect of the managerial writing context is the extent of collaboration and delegation that occurs. As was noted earlier, collaboration is becoming more common in business and requires managers who can work well with others. Additionally, managers have the option of delegating some of their more routine writing chores.[16] This delegation, however, presupposes the manager's knowledge of various subordinates' abilities and willingness to handle the assignment.

The size and culture of the organization are also important elements of the context of managerial communication. Small companies can communicate many things orally, but the larger a company gets, the greater is the need to put things in writing for the record. With size also comes a tendency for greater formality in many written documents. With regard to culture, bureaucracies thrive on formality, while more participative organizations lean toward informality.

Authority and politics play a significant role in the context of managerial writing. Max Weber described three types of authority as traditional, charismatic, and legal.[17] How managers communicate messages is greatly influenced by the type of authority they are perceived to have. Also, business organizations must be viewed as political systems.[18] Managers who forget to consider the political forces at work in the company may soon find they no longer work at the company.

In our increasingly litigious society and given the ever-increasing role of government in business, legal concerns represent another important element of the managerial writing context. Managers are considered legal agents of the organization in many types of writing they do. They must be conscious of such things as libel, slander, privacy, and equal opportunity.

For managers, the phenomenon of a discourse community means they face a unique writing environment. They must carefully analyze the organizational culture in which they work, they must find the best time and place to write, and they must always remember that writing has a unique role in the manager's job (see Table 4–1).

A manager who has committed to using the written communication channel and who has considered the unique characteristics of writing in an organizational

TABLE 4–1

Elements of a Manager's Discourse Community
Fragmented workday
Extensive collaboration
Option to delegate
Organization's size and culture
Lines of authority
Political forces
Legal concerns

environment, as described in the previous sections of this chapter, is now ready to begin the writing process. This process consists of three stages: planning, composing, and revising. If the manager follows this process, the resulting document is more likely to be successful in reaching its goal.

STAGE ONE: PLANNING

The planning process for a managerial writer is a lot like the one journalists are trained to use. The parallel is logical since both might be characterized as professional writers. Both spend a significant amount of time writing at work and both write for readers who are in a hurry. Thus, both might be expected to determine the five Ws—what, why, who, when, where—and how.

What?

The "what" question deals with the nature of the message. A manager should have a fairly clear idea of what needs to be communicated early in the planning stages. Does he need certain information? Is she granting or rejecting a request? Is he informing subordinates of a policy change? Is she trying to secure the cooperation of workers in implementing certain procedures?

Any time readers see a message that seems to bounce from one side of an issue to another, any time readers are forced to wade through a message that rambles on endlessly and incoherently, any time readers wonder, "What is this person trying to say?" the chances are good that the writer *didn't know* exactly what he was trying to say or what purpose he was trying to accomplish.

Why?

The answer to the "why" question is probably just as important as the answer to the "what" question. Furthermore, the answer should be just as clear to the reader as it is to the writer. Unfortunately, many miscommunications occur because the sender does not know why a message is being sent or does not bother to share with the reader the reason for the message.

Many corporate policies, procedures, and rules, for example, are imposed on employees without any accompanying justification. Personnel would probably be much more receptive to these directives if they understood why the directives were necessary. Humans are complex creatures who like to deal with cause and effect. When an effect is imposed and the cause is withheld, one likely result is resistance.

Who?

One of the most important elements of the planning that should precede any managerial communication is the answer to the "who" question—who is receiving the message?

Demographic characteristics such as age, sex, education, political affiliations, and job title may provide some indication as to how the reader will interpret a message. Within an organizational setting, however, these characteristics fall short of telling us about the writer-reader relationship and about the characteristics of the organization and the department that may be pertinent to successful message transmission.

To engage in a truly thorough reader analysis and to be fully attuned to the reader's likely reception of a message, a writer should consider the following points:

- The relative power position between the writer and the reader.
- The communication requirements the organization exerts on the reader and the writer.
- The business functions the writer and reader work in.
- The frequency of communication between the writer and the reader.
- The reader's reaction to past messages from the writer.
- The relative sensitivity of the message.

The time spent on reader analysis may vary with the relative importance of the message. For very important messages, a writer may scrutinize all the information available to determine the best wording, the most appropriate organization, the right medium, the best timing, and the best source and destination for the message. However, even routine messages will improve as a result of audience analysis and adaptation.

When?

The importance of the answer to the "when" question may vary according to how routine the information being conveyed is. Many routine messages, such as sales reports, are distributed periodically. No actual decision must be made as to when they are sent because dates have already been set. Likewise, trivial information is likely to be received in the same way regardless of timing.

For a nonroutine message, however, the decision on when to send it may directly affect how the message is received. For example, the managers of a textile mill had to tell employees they were not going to get a pay raise even though the company had shown a profit the preceding quarter. Management chose to convey this message in letter form just before the employees went on vacation. Not only did this timing likely ruin the vacations of many employees, but it also probably encouraged a number of them to spend their vacations looking for another job.

On the subject of timing, managers need to keep in mind that it is possible to send messages too early as well as too late. For example, the agenda for a meeting and supporting material could be sent so early that the recipients forget the meeting by the time it is scheduled to occur. But if the material is sent too late, participants might not have time to get fully prepared for the meeting. Two to five days' notice is a generally safe range; but the longer the meeting and the greater the amount of supporting material to be distributed, the longer the lead time needed.

Where?

The "where" question sometimes has to be addressed at both ends of the communication spectrum: From where should the message come and to where should it be directed? Should the message come from a manager at a particular level, or should it come from a person higher in the organization, so as to carry the additional weight of authority?

At the other end of the spectrum, we may have to decide where the reader should be while receiving the message. To illustrate, some companies have grappled with the problem of newsletter distribution: whether to send it to employees' homes or distribute it at work. Sending it to the homes might get the families interested, but it might also be viewed as an infringement of employee privacy or personal time.

How?

The "how" question is largely a matter of media selection. Even when managers decide to put it in writing, they are still faced with a number of written media options: letter, memo, report, e-mail, brochure, newsletter, manual, or even bulletin board. The choice of medium is determined at least in part by how personal the message needs to be, how widespread its distribution, and how quickly it needs to reach the audience.

Additionally, managers should remember a rule of thumb that applies to media selection in general. Specifically, if a manager regularly uses one particular medium, the choice of a different medium might communicate a sense of urgency or importance. For example, if a manager regularly communicates with subordinates in person, a memo might suggest something unusual and worthy of extra attention.

Though the preceding planning concerns were discussed separately and in a particular order, they are all interdependent and should not be treated in isolation. The good managerial communicator learns to see the interrelationships and to treat the five Ws and H as a decision package.

STAGE TWO: COMPOSING

Once the planning stage has been carried out satisfactorily, the manager is ready to begin building the message that will accomplish the purpose to be served. More specifically, the manager must compose a message. Words need to be chosen with care and organized in a clear, comprehensive, and coherent fashion. The manager should follow the guidelines described next when selecting words and composing them into sentences and paragraphs. The result is a document written in contemporary style.

Selecting Words

Words are symbols that define the content of a message; thus, words should be carefully selected so the overall content will accomplish the communication's goal. Each word carries the potential for contributing to the effectiveness of the message, and each carries the potential for causing misunderstanding. Great care should be taken to ensure message effectiveness and avoid misunderstanding. The following principles will help writers accomplish their goals.

Principle One: Choose Words Precisely

While some business documents (contracts, job offer letters, performance appraisals) may call for high levels of precision, managers would be wise to exercise care in choosing words in all their writing. And as they strive for this precision, they should remember that words can have both denotative and connotative meanings.

Denotative meanings are objective; they point to; they describe. Most people think of dictionary definitions as denotative meanings because these definitions are compiled from the common usages associated with a word. Most people agree on the denotative definitions of terms—that is, they agree as long as there are no words similar in sound or appearance to confuse the issue. For example, can you pick out the correct word in each of the following sentences?

- The advertising agency that we just bought should profitably (complement, compliment) our manufacturing and distribution interests.
- My computer printer has operated (continually, continuously) for the last five years.
- The manager assured us that he had (appraised, apprised) his superior of the shipping problem.
- The secretary made an (illusion, allusion) to what had taken place in the cafeteria.
- To persuade upper management to take this action, we will need the testimony of an expert who is completely (uninterested, disinterested).

Along the same lines, consider the following excerpts from letters written to a government agency.

- "I am very much annoyed to find that you have branded my son illiterate. This is a dirty lie as I was married a week before he was born."
- "Unless I get my husband's money pretty soon, I will be forced to lead an immortal life."

In business writing, wrong word choices can produce embarrassing humor at best and considerable confusion at worst. Neither is likely to provide a boost to a manager's career.

Connotative meanings, on the other hand, are subjective. They can be different for different people because they are determined largely by a person's previous experiences or associations with a word and its referent.

Though connotations are subjective, people can manipulate the language to bring forth either positive or negative connotations. An expression with intended positive connotations is called a *euphemism*. The words *slim* and *slender* are much more euphemistic than are words such as *skinny* and *scrawny*.

As advertisers and other interested parties try to portray life in the most pleasant way possible, euphemisms have become a part of American life. When, however, euphemisms are used in an effort to veil or gloss over major human and environmental tragedies, we must recognize the language abuse and the feeble cover-up. When "collateral damage" is used to describe the deaths of innocent civilians in war, for example, we must wonder at the value assessed to human lives by the people using these descriptions.

Managers, as well as people in other careers, bear a responsibility to their audiences to use the language as accurately as possible. Managers should strive to communicate precisely and honestly and to avoid insulting the reader's intelligence. Additionally, they should try to act as responsibly as they can in using words as control tools and instruments of change.[19]

Principle Two: Use Short Rather than Long Words

Winston Churchill once said, "Big men use little words and little men use big words." People who are genuinely secure generally feel quite comfortable using simple words that are easy to understand. Short words are usually less confusing than long words. Long words, especially when strung out with several other long words, can produce a communication barrier between writer and reader.

Written business communications should be economical and efficient. The following lists provide alternatives for some of the many longer words used and abused in business writing.

Instead of Using	Use
advise	tell
ameliorate	improve
approbation	approval
commence	begin
demonstrate	show
encounter	meet
expectancy	hope
explicate	explain
locality	place
modification	change
perspicacity	sense
subsequent to	after
terminate	end
usage	use
utilize	use

We are not suggesting that the use of any words in the left-hand column will condemn a message to ambiguity and obscurity. The caution here refers to the unnecessary use of long difficult words. When overused, they tax a reader's understanding—and patience—and create a barrier to effective communication.

The U.S. Congress has recognized the importance of "plain language" in government forms, benefits applications, reports, regulations, and other documents. In recent years, they have considered bills mandating that government agencies use language that is clear and well-organized, and that follows best practices of writing. The Plain Language in Government Communications Bill of 2007 (S.2291), cosponsored by 10 senators (including then-Senator Barack Obama), failed by just one vote in the fall 2008 session. Utah's Senator Robert Bennett expressed concern that such legislation would cause legal terms to become lost in translation, though he agreed that the measure would improve Americans' access to their government. The Plain Language Act of 2009 (HR 946), introduced in February 2009, calls for enhanced "citizen access to Government information and services by establishing that Government documents issued to the public must be written clearly." At the time of this writing, the status of the bill is "in Committee." At the state level, over 22 states now have Plain Language statutes on their books, notably New York, Connecticut, Pennsylvania, Florida, Minnesota, California, Oregon, and Washington.

FIGURE 4–1
Abstraction
Ladders

Levels of Abstraction	High ↑	transportation surface transport vehicle truck 18 wheeler	environment resource wood writing device pencil
	Low ↓		

Principle Three: Use Concrete Rather than Abstract Words

In discussing a topic, a writer can choose from a range of words. This range, or continuum, might be thought of as a ladder that the writer can climb. This ladder moves from concrete (specific) words on the lowest rungs to the more abstract (general) words on the highest rungs.

Concrete words tend to be specific; they create clear pictures in the reader's mind. Abstract words are less specific and produce wider, more general interpretations of meanings. The ladder moves from something easily visualized to something that is more abstract, even vague, as shown by the examples in Figure 4–1.

The level of abstraction or concreteness depends in part on the reader's background, needs, and expectations. Abstract words and phrases threaten some readers and generate mistrust and confusion. They give rise to questions that the text may or may not answer: When? How many? Who? How much? Which one? Notice the differing amount of information in the following pairs of expressions:

Abstract	Concrete
She was a good student.	She earned the highest semester total in a class of 68 students.
in the near future	by Friday, June 19
a significant profit	a 28 percent markup
a noteworthy savings	50 percent off the normal price
at your earliest convenience	by the close of business this Friday

Concrete words and phrases frequently create sharp vivid images and stimulate reader interest. Forming concrete phrases may take more time and thought, but they are more efficient and stay with the reader longer than abstract phrases.[20] Additionally, concrete writing takes less time to read, produces better message comprehension, and is less likely to need rereading than abstract writing.[21]

Principle Four: Economize on Words

The scientist Pascal wrote a 20-page letter to a friend in 1656. In a postscript, he apologized for the letter's length, saying, "I hope you will pardon me for writing such a long letter, but I did not have time to write you a shorter one." Pascal was testifying to the fact that conciseness, or economy of word choice, takes time and effort.

A practical bottom-line reason exists to write concisely. Wordiness costs companies money. Unnecessary words take valuable time to compose and read; they waste paper and resources. Consider the following two versions of a business message:

- Enclosed please find a check in the amount of $82.56. In the event that you find the amount to be neither correct nor valid, subsequent to an examination of your records, please inform us of your findings at your earliest convenience.
- Enclosed is a check for $82.56. If this amount is incorrect, please let us know.

The second version takes 15 words to say the same thing said by the first version in 41 words—a reduction of over 63 percent.

Why do people in business continue to be wordy when such reductions are possible? Two likely reasons stand out. One is that writers often use wordy phrases out of habits that developed when they had to write long essays in school. In evaluating students' work, quantity is sometimes as important as quality to teachers.

The other reason is that untrained business writers often look to the files for a model when faced with a writing assignment on the job. When the files are filled with jargon and wordy expressions and when the novices mimic these writing patterns, the tradition of verbal waste continues. Note in the examples that follow how the wordy/redundant expressions on the left can be replaced by the more economical alternatives on the right.

Wordy/Redundant Phrases	Alternatives
due to the fact that	because
for the purpose of	for
for the reason that	since, because
in order to	to
in the event that	if
with reference to	about
pursuant to your request	as requested
subsequent to	after
along the lines of	like
true facts	facts
necessary steps required	requirements
basic principles	principles
enclosed herein please find	here is
look forward with anticipation	anticipate
consensus of opinion	consensus
from the point of view of	from
inasmuch as	since, because
in accordance with	as
on the grounds that	because
at a later time	later (or a time)
within a period of one year	within one year
take into consideration	consider
a check in the amount of	a check for
for which there was no use	useless
that could not be collected	uncollectible
notwithstanding the fact that	although

If today's emphasis on controlling costs is to be applied to business writing, the expressions illustrated in the left-hand column will have to be replaced by the alternatives in the right-hand column.[22] Though writing concisely is time-consuming at first, it eventually becomes a relatively easy habit.

A good example of economy in writing is text messaging. Students and workers alike have learned to extract main ideas from chunks of information and experiences and to communicate these ideas in cryptic messages. As discussed in Chapter 3, texting has replaced e-mail in many organizations as the channel of choice because of its simplicity and immediacy. Living in the era of information overload, readers ask, "What do we need to know? And why do we need to know it?" And texters limit their messages accordingly.

One might argue that economy in writing necessarily causes meaning to be lost. However, Larry Smith and Rachel Fershleiser have shown that messages can be short on words while deep in meaning. Founders of the online magazine SMITH, they asked the world to send in six-word memoirs. They used Ernest Hemingway's example as a model. According to legend, when asked to write a novel in only six words, Hemingway came up with "For sale: baby shoes, never worn." Over 15,000 people responded to the challenge. Some notable examples posted on SMITH include these:

- "My second-grade teacher was right." —Janelle Brown
- "Secret of life: Marry an Italian." —Nora Ephron
- "Took scenic route, got in late." —Will Blythe
- "Became my mother. Please shoot me." —Cynthia Kaplan
- "It's pretty high. You go first." —Alan Eagle[23]

Principle Five: Avoid Clichés and Jargon

Trite expressions or clichés have an accepted meaning; however, these words yield dull messages that lack creativity. Readers may understand what is written, but the message appears impersonal since the writer has injected nothing original into it.

Additionally, trite phrases often go out of style quickly, so the writing (and writer) may seem timeworn. The following list presents some overused phrases to avoid, and their alternatives:

Overused Phrases	Alternatives
white as a sheet	pale
busy as a bee	busy, working
smart as a whip	intelligent
follow in the footsteps of	pursue the same career
get it all together	get organized, resolve the problem
stretches the truth	exaggerates, lies
clean as a whistle	sanitary, clean
rock of Gibraltar	reliable, dependable
really down to earth	realistic, honest, sincere
as luck would have it	unfortunately, luckily

The last of the preceding examples illustrates a significant shortcoming in the use of these hackneyed phrases. They can have more than one meaning. Furthermore, sometimes they are simply vague, and sometimes their logic can be questioned. These weaknesses are illustrated in the following examples:

"... at an early date" or "... at your earliest convenience"

Such phrases usually follow a request for information or for a favor of some sort. They are normally used by people who do not want to appear pushy. Such people don't realize two things. One is that the reader's "earliest convenience" may end up being something quite different from what the writer had in mind. The second is that businesspeople deal with deadlines all the time. They are not likely to take offense when asked for something within a range of time if the writer concisely and courteously states the reason for the time range, as in the following example:

"So that we may fill your order as quickly as possible, please send us this information by March 21."

Two other clichés some readers interpret as presumptuous are

"Thanking you in advance ..." and "Permit me to say ..."

Besides being timeworn, mechanical, and impersonal, the first expression seems to say, "I expect you to comply with my request, but I don't want to have to take the time to thank you later, so I'll do it now." The second expression seems to seek permission, but the writer says what he or she wants to say before getting that permission. The second expression should be dropped and the first might be replaced by:

"I appreciate any help you can give me in the matter."

Jargon is the technical language or specified terms that become part of the everyday vocabulary of an organization or discipline. Insiders know what the words mean, but outsiders/customers may not. Jargon includes technical terms, acronyms, and terms used in special ways. When writing to readers outside the organization, managers should avoid using jargon. Rather, they should choose the layperson's version whenever possible to reduce the likelihood that the reader will misunderstand the message.[24] Additionally, some organizations are so large that the people in one functional unit may not understand the jargon of other units. The following list illustrates how some jargon used in business might be simplified:

Jargon	Layperson's Version
TQM	Total Quality Management
accounts receivable	firms or people owing money to the company
amounts payable	amounts owed by the company
HVI bonus	extra pay for selling high-volume machines
maturity date	date that final payment is due
feedstock	raw materials used for manufacturing in the petrochemical industry

Jargon	Layperson's Version
duplexing	photocopyist's term meaning copying on both sides of a sheet of paper
FAA	Federal Aviation Administration
abstract	history of the property
per diem	daily
assessed valuation	value of the property for tax purposes
current ratio	ratio of current assets to current liabilities
CRM	Customer Relations Management

With only one exception, the descriptions on the right are wordier than the jargon on the left. If these wordier versions ensure understanding and prevent inquiries aimed at clarification, then the extra effort and words used will have been worthwhile. This is a decision managers must make when writing.

Acronyms can be particularly troublesome. In some situations, an acronym may be perfectly appropriate, while in other situations, it may cause a problem. For instance, in one division of Exxon, DHR is the director of human resources, but in other divisions it is a by-product of the chemical scrubbing process.

Finally, a word of caution about *business-ese.* Expressions and terms can quickly become popular in business circles, and then become obsolete just as quickly. A Texas entrepreneur, Ron Sturgeon, captured 1,200 examples of "biz jargon" in his book, *Green Weenies and Due Diligence.* Some are funny and colorful ("herding cats," "circling the drain," "mouse milking"), while some are more sober ("dilution," "FTE," "synergy").[25] When deciding whether to use business-ese in your message, be guided by your receiver's expectations, the communication climate, and the cultural context (see Chapter 2).

Principle Six: Use Positive Words That Convey Courtesy

As stated earlier, written communications present stimuli and generate responses. Generally, the more positive the stimuli, the more positive the response. Conversely, the more negative the stimuli, the more negative the response. Behavioral scientists, for example, tell us that subordinates will live either up or down to the expectations communicated by their managers.[26]

Whether a manager is dealing with subordinates, superiors, peers, customers, suppliers, or others, she is likely to want her message to be well received. The positive wording of a request, of information, or even of bad news should increase the probability of a positive or at least neutral reaction by the receiver.

The difference between positive and negative wording is not a matter of content, but of emphasis. Negative messages emphasize the least desirable aspects of a situation. As such, they are likely to arouse defensive or antagonistic responses from the reader.

The sender of an effective communication must establish credibility and goodwill with the receiver, and positiveness and courtesy aid the manager in developing these aspects. The following examples illustrate the different impacts that can be generated by positive and negative wordings of messages:

I cannot have the report ready by tomorrow morning.
I can have the report completed by 3:30 p.m. Wednesday.

You should not use Form A to file the weekly sales report.
Form B is the weekly sales report form.

We regret to inform you that we must deny your request for a promotion because you haven't earned enough continuing education credits.
As soon as you earn six more continuing education credits, we can process your request for a promotion.

In each of the alternative statements in the preceding examples, the writer states what can be done or what has been done rather than what cannot be done or what has not been done.

Let's look at a real-life example. In the hospitality management industry, theft of hotel-room amenities is a major cost of doing business. Guests routinely steal towels, pens, even furniture from their hotel rooms. Instead of posting warnings or threats, Holiday Inn Express takes a positive approach. A notice placed on the bathroom countertop reads:

Dear Guest,

Due to the popularity of our guest room Amenities, our Housekeeping Department now offers these items for sale:

    Irons: $40.00
    Ironing Boards: $30.00
    Blow Dryer: $30.00
    Bath towels: $15.00
    Hand Towels: $10.00

Each Guest Room attendant is responsible for maintaining the guest room items. Should you decide to take these articles from your room, instead of obtaining them from the Executive Housekeeper, we will assume you approve a corresponding charge to your account. Thank You.

[handwritten margin note: positive & courteous climate]

Some phrases, because they seem discourteous, are likely to irritate readers. Avoid them to ensure a positive and courteous climate. Although we should not totally avoid negatives, we can minimize them. Words and phrases like "inexcusable," "you claim that," "your insinuation," "you failed to," and "obviously you overlooked" should be avoided if possible. The next chapter on messages will explain this point further.

Being positive and conveying courtesy in word choice also involves using gender-neutral language. Rarely is it necessary for writers to identify people as male or female.

Today we use gender-neutral terms to describe jobs. Also, pronouns and nouns that refer to one sex when both are being described (*manpower*) are unacceptable. Likewise, expressions that belittle the behavior or qualities of one gender should be avoided. The following listings present unacceptable and acceptable terms.

Terms to Avoid

man (when referring to the species)	man-hours
man-made	steward, stewardess
manpower	homemaker
grow to manhood	fairer sex
businessman	weaker sex
cameraman	old man, breadwinner
fireman	career woman
foreman	lady doctor/lawyer/realtor
salesman	workman's compensation

Acceptable Terms

business executive	work hours
state career (e.g., doctor, lawyer, editor)	camera operator
	firefighter
humanity, human beings, humans, people	supervisor
human power, human energy	sales representative, salesperson, salesclerk
workers, work force, employee	flight attendant
	workers' compensation

On the subject of sexism in writing, one particularly thorny problem is the generic or universal pronoun *he.* Until about 30 years ago, the standard practice had been to use *he* in impersonal constructions where both sexes were to be included: "Each person has his own problems to resolve." Authorities have noted that such constructions can make women feel ignored in the business world.

Fortunately, managers have several options available for avoiding such pronoun use. One is the use of plural nouns and pronouns. Instead of "A manager should motivate his employees," one could write "Managers should motivate their employees."

Another option is the use of "he and she," "his or her," "s/he," or "his/her." Though not entirely graceful, this option is considered acceptable. Writers should be careful, however, not to use this option too often, for it could hinder style and readability.

they
their
not
"he"

Another technique, one used widely in this book, is to alternate masculine and feminine pronouns. One paragraph may use *she* as the generic pronoun, while the next might use *he*. While this technique avoids the generic *he*, it does not sacrifice style the way *he or she* sometimes does. Furthermore, traditional usage is spared, at least in part.

A fourth nonsexist technique is one that is not satisfactory to strict grammarians. It uses plural pronouns for traditionally singular antecedent references such as *each, every, everyone, everybody,* or *anybody*. For example, "Everyone has their problems to resolve." This technique legitimizes popular use.

The last, and best, suggestion is to replace third-person pronouns *(he/she)* with second person *(you)*. Not only does this avoid the gender issue; it directly engages the reader. Thus, "If you are going to be late, call your supervisor" is better than "If an employee is going to be late, he/she should call his/her supervisor."

Principle Seven: Use a Conversational Style

Sentences communicate effectively when they use everyday language; that is, when the words are those that would be used in face-to-face communication. A conversational style involves writing with words from a person's speaking vocabulary. Usually, the words should not include colloquialisms, slang, or jargon; they should be the language most people would use in conducting everyday business.

The most successful business professional who exemplifies writing in a conversational style is billionaire investor Warren Buffett, chairman of Berkshire Hathaway, Inc. In 2005, the National Commission on Writing honored Buffett's folksy annual report. "No annual report has had a greater impact on American business," said Bob Kerrey, the commission's chair and president of New School University in New York.[27]

Buffett's 2008 annual letter to shareholders, while maintaining his trademark style, communicated the bad news that his holding company was reporting a 62 percent drop in net income. With characteristic candor, Buffett took the blame for some of the decline, stating that he "did some dumb things." Commenting about the U.S. economic crisis, Buffett explained the danger of derivatives, writing, "Participants seeking to dodge troubles face the same problem as someone seeking to avoid venereal disease. It's not just whom you sleep with, but also whom they are sleeping with."[28]

Buffett's conversational writing style is not an aberration. Other successful executives, such as Bill Gates, openly admire it. In an interview with Maria Bartiromo in February 2009, Gates admitted that writing an annual letter about his foundation's activities was Buffett's idea, and that Gates "ran a few drafts by him . . . . His advice is very helpful."[29]

A conversational style is particularly important in business letters since it aids in developing the "you viewpoint." The you viewpoint involves consideration of the reader's point of view. It helps a writer personalize letters, something most readers appreciate in business correspondence.[30]

Before writing, the sender identifies who will receive the information; the reader's need for the information; and as much as possible, her knowledge, expertise, interests, culture, and value system.

Even form paragraphs and letters can be written with a category of reader in mind, people who might have certain common concerns that have to be addressed. Form paragraphs and letters can be written in a conversational style, as though they were composed by a human being rather than a jargon-stuffed computer. And technology makes it easier than it has ever been to personalize a form paragraph or letter.

These first seven principles have focused on the selection of words. Since each word can influence the total message, each word deserves attention. The manager also needs to analyze the combination and organization of words strategically to ensure effective communication. The remaining principles will address the ways in which words might be grouped for best effect.

Organizing Words for Effect

The next four principles discuss organizational guidelines for putting words together to convey a message. Comprehension is largely determined by the extent to which the writer uses these principles.

Principle Eight: Keep Sentences Short

We sometimes encounter long-winded sentences in business writing. These seemingly never-ending constructions stem from several possible causes. One cause mentioned earlier is the need to impress. Consider the following example from a government report:

> It is obvious from the difference in elevation with relation to the short depth of the field that the contour is such as to preclude any reasonable development potential for economic utilization.

One would have to study the preceding message long and hard to figure out that the writer was, in fact, saying:

> The field is too steep to plow.

On the other hand, some people write these lengthy roundabout sentences to avoid appearing forward or pushy, as in the following example:

> During the past two weeks, we have been wondering if you have as yet found yourself in a position to give us an indication of whether or not you have been able to come to a decision on our offer.

Most businesspeople who face deadlines daily would not be offended if they were asked a question more to the point:

> Have you decided on the offer we made you two weeks ago?

Another possible cause for unnecessarily long sentences is the need to say everything that can be said about a topic in one sentence. Note the confusion created by the following example and the improvement in the alternative version.

> Although 17 people from our department (purchasing) attended the workshop, 9 of them, including Jerry Stoves, had no background for the topic of the workshop (advanced negotiating technique) offered by the Purchasing Association of Chicago.

Last week 17 people from our purchasing department attended a workshop on advanced negotiating techniques. The Purchasing Association of Chicago offered the workshop. Of the 17 who attended, Jerry Stoves and 8 others lacked the necessary background.

One way to shorten sentences is to avoid expletive constructions: "It . . . that" and "There is . . ." or "There are . . ." An expletive has no grammatical antecedent in a sentence, and it often diffuses the focus of the message by displacing or even eliminating people in the sentence. For example, in the sentence, "It is thought that interest rates will fall," the word *it* has no antecedent, yet *it* gets the main emphasis. The person who holds this opinion is unknown. A better wording would be, "I think that interest rates will fall." Instead of "It is suggested that you rewrite this proposal," say, "Please rewrite the proposal." Generally, "there is" and "there are" constructions merely add length and waste time. Rather than saying, "There are three options from which you can choose," say "You can choose from three options."

Unnecessarily long sentences require readers to spend too much time trying to understand the message. And the more time and patience required to understand a message, the less likely the reader will understand its purpose.

Effective writing is easy and quick to read. Studies show that good business sentences are 15 to 20 words long. They also use no more than 10 long (three-or-more-syllable) words in every 100 words.

Effective sentences express one main point. Any connected phrases or clauses should explain that point. When we place two or more important ideas in the same sentence, we reduce the importance of each and often confuse the reader.

Principle Nine: Prefer the Active to the Passive Voice

The active voice presents the parts of a sentence in the normal order expected by English-speaking people. The subject of the sentence is the actor, who is acting in a way portrayed by the verb, and the action is directed toward the object. The following sentences illustrate the active voice.

- David Lopez directed the meeting.
- Donna Hebert enforced the policy.
- Ridley Gros promoted the university.

The passive voice reverses the order of the parts so that the subject is being acted on by the object in a way depicted by the verb.

- The meeting was directed by David Lopez.
- The policy was enforced by Donna Hebert.
- The university was promoted by Ridley Gros.

Besides the reversed order and the slight additional length, the passive voice weakens the sentence construction by making the doer of the action the object of the "by" phrase. Furthermore, the passive voice carries the hazard of luring the writer into longer, more roundabout expressions.[31] For example, instead of writing,

The new president reorganized the administration.

we see:

A reorganization of the administration was effected by the new president.

Though managerial writers should favor the active voice in the majority of the sentences they construct, they may occasionally prefer the passive voice.

The passive voice is more diplomatic. Notice that by eliminating the "by" phrase from a passive-voice sentence, we eliminate the doer of the action. In sensitive matters, or when addressing people of higher authority, this may be appropriate. Note the following diplomatic transformation.

Active: The director of purchasing has been soliciting bids from unauthorized vendors.

Passive: Bids from unauthorized vendors have been solicited by the director of purchasing.

Passive minus the "by" phrase: Bids from unauthorized vendors have been solicited.

Principle Ten: Organize Paragraphs Logically

Paragraphs bring separate thoughts together and arrange them to convey a single important idea. A paragraph is a device to combine sentences to form messages. Alone, these sentences might seem illogical and would not make the same point.

Five guidelines can help writers develop effective paragraphs (see Table 4–2). First, present one major idea in a paragraph, along with whatever support is necessary for the development of that idea.[32] This paragraph quality is called *unity.*

Second, determine if a deductive or an inductive pattern is appropriate. Deductive paragraphs present the main idea in the first sentence and the supporting ideas in the sentences that follow. Inductive paragraphs begin with the details or the support and end with the main idea. The deductive pattern is the most commonly used, but the inductive pattern is useful for persuasion.

persuasion

Third, use a variety of sentence structures in a paragraph. A paragraph that contains all simple sentences can be tedious; interest builds when a combination of sentence structures is used.

Fourth, structure paragraphs to emphasize important points. Emphasis can be accomplished in a variety of ways:

- Repeat key concepts.
- Use attention-getting words such as action verbs and the personal pronoun "you."
- Use mechanical devices such as bullets, text boxes, italics, boldface, or numbers.

TABLE 4–2 Developing Effective Paragraphs	1. Present one major idea in a paragraph. 2. Decide if a deductive or an inductive pattern is appropriate. 3. Use a variety of sentence structures in a paragraph. 4. Structure paragraphs to emphasize important points. 5. Keep paragraphs relatively short.

Be sure that bulleted lists, repeated phrases, and compound structures are in *parallel* form. That is, sentence elements that are alike in function should also be alike in construction.[33] Look at the following examples:

Parallel: The company has *a* mission statement and *a* code of ethics.

Not parallel: Citizens are concerned whether the president *has lied* under oath or *looking* directly into the cameras.

Excellent examples of parallel structure can be found in the words of great orators. Look at this excerpt from the Rev. Dr. Martin Luther King, Jr.'s famous I Have a Dream speech: "So let freedom ring from the prodigious hilltops of New Hampshire. Let freedom ring from the mighty mountains of New York. Let freedom ring from the heightening Alleghenies of Pennsylvania. Let freedom ring from the snowcapped Rockies of Colorado." Notice how the repetition and parallel structure of these sentences add rhythm, balance, and a build-up of emotion.

Fifth, keep paragraphs relatively short. Short paragraphs are easy to read and give more emphasis to the information they contain. Readers need visual and mental breaks so they can assimilate the message; short paragraphs help to achieve these breaks. In business letters and short memos, paragraphs usually average four to six lines in length; in reports, they average eight to ten lines. Exceptions, however, will sometimes be justified by the need for emphasis (shorter paragraphs) or by the complexity of the material (longer paragraphs).

These guidelines for composing short, strong, clear messages are followed by prominent leaders in fields other than business. One example is Lieutenant General Gus Pagonis, who was the officer in charge of logistics during the Persian Gulf War of 1991. His book, *Moving Mountains: Lessons in Leadership and Logistics from the Gulf War,* tells how he delivered meals, fuel, ammunition, and other supplies to 541,000 U.S. military forces in Kuwait during the 100-hour lightning ground war. Pagonis wrote that his operating principle was KISS—Keep It Simple Stupid. An important application of that principle was his communication patterns. He limited paperwork to an amazing 3- × 5-inch index card per report. Furthermore, he limited all e-mail messages to just six lines. Apparently no one could take time to scroll. Under harrowing wartime conditions, Pagonis's insistence on good writing contributed to his success.

Principle Eleven: Be Coherent

With coherent writing, the relationship between sentences is clear. Sentences flow from one to another easily and smoothly. This movement from one thought to another is accomplished through transition, which is sometimes described as a bridge that connects thoughts. Transitions may be natural or mechanical.

Natural transition occurs when the content of the thoughts is such that the second flows naturally and smoothly from the first. Note the smooth movement from the first thought to the second in the following opening paragraph to a job application letter.

Now that the Dillon Pharmaceutical Company is expanding its Western region, won't you need trained and experienced sales representatives to call on accounts in the new territory? With a degree in marketing and eight successful years in pharmaceutical sales, I believe I am well qualified to be one of those representatives.

The first sentence introduces the ideas of training and experience, and the second sentence builds on that introduction.

Often, however, a writer cannot rely on the content of thoughts to show a clear connection between them. The writer may have to show that connection with mechanical *transitions*. A writer can (1) repeat key words to show the reader that the same subject is still being addressed, (2) use pronouns and synonyms to avoid being too repetitious, or (3) use transition words, words that are used to connect thoughts and show a particular type of relationship between them. Table 4–3 lists some frequently used transition words.

In addition to making sure the thoughts within a paragraph flow smoothly, writers should be concerned that this quality of coherence pervades entire documents. More specifically, paragraphs, like sentences, need to be clearly related. Sometimes this relationship is shown through the use of transition devices such as those previously discussed. At other times, an entire sentence at the beginning or end of a paragraph will be used to show the relationship of that paragraph to the one that precedes or follows it.

As we move into longer and more complex documents such as reports, the task of ensuring coherence becomes more involved. For example, a 5-page section of a 25-page report may need an introductory paragraph to show what is included in that section. It may also need a concluding paragraph to tie up the section and show how it relates to the larger purpose of the report. A simpler kind of transition device is a "Janus statement," named for the Roman god with two faces—one looking backward and one looking ahead. The writer can accomplish both a review and a preview with a Janus statement such as "Now that we have described X, let us turn our attention to Y."

A final way to build coherence in long documents is by using headings and subheadings. Chapter 6 addresses report and proposal writing in more detail, including heading use.

Before we leave the subject of coherence, a word of caution may be in order. Though the transition devices discussed here can show relationships to readers, logical organization is the foundation of coherent writing. Writers must clearly understand why information is being arranged in a certain way. They must have a logical plan of presentation, for transitional devices cannot show relationships that don't exist.

TABLE 4–3
Frequently Used Transition Words

but	accordingly	even so
next	again	on the other hand
thus	consequently	furthermore
then	otherwise	in summary
finally	besides	similarly
hence	conversely	as a result
still	to illustrate	in contrast
also	in addition	subsequently
and	however	for example

STAGE THREE: REVISING

The third stage, revising and editing, is perhaps the most important to practice. Few writers possess the skill to write clear copy in one sitting.[34] The multitude of writing principles, approaches, and grammatical rules requires all writers to check their work. Revising is a service to the reader. Thus, the writer should begin stage three by shifting perspective, distancing himself from the writing, and assuming the role of the reader. It is difficult to objectively examine the message from the reader's viewpoint; however, the following questions can help systematize the revision process:

- What is my purpose?
- Have I included all the information the reader wants or needs to know to understand my message?
- Does my message answer all the reader's questions?
- Is there any information nonessential to the reader that I can delete?
- Have I included reader benefits?

Next, revising involves (1) reading what has been written for clarity, concreteness, and conversational tone; (2) determining factual accuracy; (3) organizing to ensure coherence;[35] (4) rewording awkward sentences and phrases; (5) rearranging content and adding illustrations and transitions. Writers should not assume their prose is satisfactory after only one or two drafts. Few people write that well.[36]

The final step is to edit the document for correctness. Running a spell checker and grammar checker will catch most surface errors. However, these devices are insufficient since (so far) they do not always predict intended meanings. An amusing well-known case where punctuation significantly changes a sentence's meaning is the following:

A woman, without her man, is nothing.

A woman: without her, man is nothing.[37]

The amount of revising and editing necessary will depend on the individual writer's skill. However, all good writers rewrite. They even sometimes have someone else read their work before finalizing it. Others can often detect errors or confusing statements that writers miss because writers read into their messages what they want to communicate. At the very least, a writer should set aside a draft and let it "cool off" for a while before revising. When e-mailing, a writer can queue messages to be reread rather than composing and immediately clicking the Send button. Hastily sent e-mails can be embarrassingly incomplete or inaccurate.

Though revising and editing may seem time-consuming and tedious, the results are worth the effort. By making the message clearer and easier to understand, revising benefits the reader and reduces the likelihood of requests for later clarification. In the long run, it saves time and money while enhancing the writer's image.

When revising and editing, an easy way to keep your goal in sight is to remember the "7 C's" of good business writing. Table 4–4 presents these guidelines.

TABLE 4-4
The 7 C's of Good Business Writing

Completeness	Answer all reader questions Include the five W's and H
Conciseness	Shorten or delete wordy expressions Avoid repetition
Consideration	Focus on "you" the reader Show reader benefits or interests Emphasize the positive
Concreteness	Use specific facts and data Use active, not passive, voice Rely on vivid image-building words
Clarity	Use short familiar words Avoid jargon Follow a logical sequence of points
Courtesy	Be tactful and appreciative Avoid discriminatory language Respond promptly
Correctness	Maintain accurate writing mechanics Avoid "wrong word" errors

Summary

Written managerial communication has several strategic advantages: economy, efficiency, accuracy, and official permanence.

In addition, managerial writing has two unique characteristics: (1) collaboration is used quite often when creating documents, and (2) managers work in an environment that makes special demands on their documents. First, collaboration is a fact of modern organizational life. In addition to the advantages of group decision making, it also socializes employees in several ways and can improve the quality of the writing. In addition to the disadvantages associated with group decision making (e.g., domination and reluctant contributors), time, potential ego damage, style differences, and conflicts can work against effective collaboration.

Despite the potential pitfalls, we can identify effective collaborative writers. Good writers are flexible, respectful, attentive, articulate, responsible, and confident people who work well with others.

Guidelines for effective collaboration include dividing the work equitably among members. Conflict should be viewed as potentially constructive. The group's leader should coordinate efforts, shape the team's vision, and resolve conflicts.

Second, managers are members of a discourse community. Among the aspects of their managerial writing context are the fragmented nature of their time at work, the extent of collaboration and delegation, the size and culture of the organization, the authority and politics they must deal with, and the legal considerations of which they must remain aware as they write.

Once a manager recognizes these unique aspects, she is ready to write. The writing process consists of three stages: planning, composing, and revising. In the planning stage, the manager identifies what, why, who, when, where, and how. In the composing stage, the writer selects words and arranges them for proper effect, keeping certain strategic concerns in mind. The following principles guide the selection and arrangement of words for message clarity, comprehension, and coherence:

Selecting Words:

1. Choose words precisely.
2. Use short rather than long words.
3. Use concrete rather than abstract words.
4. Economize on words.
5. Avoid clichés and jargon.
6. Use positive words that convey courtesy.
7. Use a conversational style.

Organizing Words:

1. Keep sentences relatively short.
2. Prefer the active to the passive voice.
3. Develop logically organized paragraphs.
4. Be coherent.

In the revising stage, the writer examines the message for ways to improve on these 11 principles. Additionally, the manager edits for correctness of expression. Surface errors affect the success of a document in reaching its goals and also can damage the reader-writer relationship.

Case for Small Group Discussion

Back to School

Because you are known to be a good writer, the director of human resources has asked you to put together a seminar on written communication for employees in your company who need help. The seminar would cover basic principles of written communication, letters, memos, and formal business reports. Managers have complained to the HR director that their employees don't write well. They produce as evidence sloppily proofread e-mails. The employees, on the other hand, are grumbling that having to attend a writing seminar would be like going back to high school, where a fussy old English teacher berates them over minor punctuation concerns.

Questions

1. How would you determine who should attend the seminar?
2. How would you market it so that participants of the seminar would attend willingly rather than through coercion?
3. How would you organize the seminar? What materials would you use?
4. What topics would you address in the seminar?

Exercises for Small Groups

A. Rewrite the following sentences to eliminate long confusing words.

1. Bill received excessive remuneration for his promulgated work according to his professional colleagues.
2. What form of personal conveyance shall we solicit between the airport and the hotel?
3. The best operative unit for this interaction is the computer-assisted storage system.
4. Extel, the computer company, has an inordinate influence on your purchasing agent.
5. The company terminated its contract with the city as a consequence of its ineffectual payment procedures.
6. The audience was demonstrating engrossment with the audio-visually mediated presentation.
7. We received approbation from the executive committee.
8. This antiquated procedure could be liquidated with a new word processing system.
9. Last year's profits were exorbitant in that division.
10. Our assets cannot be utilized to the maximum due to the unavailability of trained human resources.

B. Rewrite the following sentences using concrete words.

1. We received a lot of responses to our survey.
2. The personnel department has expanded in the last several years.
3. Profits are up throughout the industry.
4. If we don't receive the order pretty soon, we will have to cancel it.
5. Please send your reply as soon as possible.
6. We would like to receive as many bids as possible.
7. We need the shipment by sometime next month.
8. Extel is a large company.
9. Is it possible to meet next week?
10. We are expecting a rapid rate of inflation.

C. Reduce the length of the following sentences.

1. Record sales were set by the top division, from $48.2 million to $51.4 million; the home appliance division decreased from $67.2 million to $58.4; the big shock was in the electronic division, which saw a drop from $17.2 million to $14.9 million; but all in all top management were generally pleased.
2. Management attributed the decline to several significant business environment economic factor conditions including higher borrowing interest rates.
3. At this point in time pursuant to your request we find it difficult to meet your stated requests as made in your letter.

4. The task force has been given the special responsibilities to accomplish the goals as stated in the letter sent yesterday by the executive vice president to the task force chairperson who was assigned the position.

5. On the grounds that this action could be completely finished in a period of one year, it was not seen as a totally practical action to take.

6. The past history of the new innovations indicates that the product innovation department should be terminated and ended.

7. We received your recent inquiry of last week regarding our new products we just came out with.

8. For the reason that all the information was not completely available, no immediate decision could be made then.

D. Rewrite the following sentences to eliminate trite expressions and improve clarity.

1. Enclosed please find a check in the amount of $40.

2. Please be advised that your order will be shipped within a short period of time.

3. I enclose herewith an order to which you will please give your earliest attention and forward, with as little delay as possible, as per shipping instructions attached.

4. Your letter dated July 25 has been duly received and noted.

5. Referring to your letter of the fifth, we wish to state that there has been an error in your statement.

6. With reference to your letter of the tenth, permit me to state that there will be no interference with the affairs of your department.

E. Change the negative tone and use more courteous words in the following sentences.

1. We cannot deliver all 100 units by Friday, March 6.

2. We don't provide second mortgages.

3. We are sorry that your total deposit on the trip cannot be refunded.

4. No. An extension will not be permitted.

5. We do not feel that you qualify for the excessive request that you made.

6. You are not qualified for this position.

7. The competition provided a much more favorable bid, and they have a reputation for fine service.

8. Sorry, but the product you requested is no longer available.

F. Clarify the following message by using paragraphs and transitions, and by generally following the guidelines presented in this chapter.

Most managers would agree that there are advantages to both the telephone and letters. Letters are more effective in some situations, whereas the use of the telephone is best in others. So now the question is, "What are the advantages of each?" The telephone's advantages are speed, immediate feedback, lesser cost, and it consumes less time. An advantage of the business letter is that a hard copy is available. Also, future reference can be made to it for legal reference, and enclosures can be included. One of the disadvantages of the telephone is that the conversation cannot be filed for future reference. Another advantage of the letter is that it can be circulated to other people who may be involved with the topic involved. Another disadvantage of the telephone is that you may not know if you are disturbing the receiver at a busy time during the day. The letter can be read when the receiver is ready to read it. All of these advantages and disadvantages must be considered when strategically determining the most effective communication tool. The greatest mistake may be to communicate via the most "convenient" media without considering the alternatives. Analysis of the situations is required to ensure that the most effective technique is used.

Endnotes

1. Henry Mintzberg, *The Nature of Managerial Work* (Englewood Cliffs, NJ: Prentice Hall, 1980), pp. 38–39.
2. Lester Faigley and Thomas P. Miller, "What We Learn from Writing on the Job," *College English* 44, no. 6 (October 1982), p. 567.
3. Lisa Ede and Andrea Lunsford, *Singular Texts/Plural Authors* (Carbondale, IL: Southern Illinois University Press, 1990), p. 60.
4. Nancy Allen, Dianne Atkinson, Meg Morgan, Teresa Moore, and Craig Snow, "What Experienced Collaborators Say about Collaborative Writing," *Journal of Business and Technical Communication* 1, no. 2 (September 1987), p. 71.
5. *Ibid.*, p. 85.
6. R. Gebhardt, "Teamwork and Feedback: Broadening the Base of Collaborative Writing," *College English* 42, no. 1 (September 1980), p. 69.
7. Terry R. Bacon, "Collaboration in a Pressure Cooker," *The Bulletin*, June 1990, p. 4.
8. A. M. O'Donnell, D. F. Dansereau, T. R. Rocklin, C. O. Larson, V. I. Hythecker, M. D. Young, and J. G. Labiotee, "Effects of Cooperative and Individual Rewriting on an Instruction Writing Task," *Written Communication* 4 (1987), pp. 90–99.
9. Rebecca Burnett, "Benefits of Collaborative Planning in the Business Communication Classroom," *The Bulletin*, June 1990, p. 10.
10. Allen *et al.*, "What Experienced Collaborators Say about Collaborative Writing," pp. 82–83.
11. Ede and Lunsford, *Single Tests/Plural Authors*, p. 62.
12. *Ibid.*, p. 66.
13. Bacon, "Collaboration in a Pressure Cooker," p. 5.
14. Henry Mintzberg, *Mintzberg on Management: Inside Our Strange World of Organizations* (New York: Collier Macmillan, 1989), p. 8.
15. Sharon Begley, "Will the BlackBerry Sink the Presidency?" *Newsweek*, February 16, 2009, p. 37.
16. Marie Flatley, "A Comparative Analysis of the Written Communication of Managers at Various Organizational Levels in the Private Business Sector," *Journal of Business Communication* 19, no. 3 (Summer 1982), p. 40.

17. Max Weber, *The Theory of Social and Economic Organization,* translators A. M. Henderson and Talcott Parsons, and ed. Talcott Parsons (New York: The Free Press, 1947), pp. 324–86.

18. James G. March, "The Business Firm as a Political Coalition," *Journal of Politics* 24, (1980), pp. 662–78.

19. Barbara Czarniawska-Joerges and Bernward Joerges, "How to Control Things with Words: Organizational Talk and Control," *Management Communication Quarterly* 2, no. 2 (November 1988), pp. 170–93.

20. Sarah Ellen Ransdell and Ira Fischler, "Effects of Concreteness and Task Context on Recall of Prose among Bilingual and Monolingual Speakers," *Journal of Memory and Language* 28, no. 3 (June 1989), pp. 278–79.

21. James Suchan and Robert Colucci, "An Analysis of Communication Efficiency Between High-Impact Writing and Bureaucratic Written Communication," *Management Communication Quarterly* 2, no. 4 (May 1989), pp. 454–84.

22. "Weak Writers," *The Wall Street Journal,* June 14, 1985, p. 1.

23. Larry Smith and Rachel Fershleiser, "Not Quite What I Was Planning: Six-Word Memoirs by Writers Famous & Obscure," www.smithmag.net (retrieved February 11, 2008).

24. Peter Crow, "Plain English: What Counts Besides Readability," *Journal of Business Communication* 25, no. 1 (Winter 1988), pp. 87–95.

25. Ron Sturgeon, *Green Weenies and Due Diligence: Insider Business Jargon* (Mike French Publishing, 2005).

26. Sterling Livingston, "Pygmalion in Management," *Harvard Business Review,* September–October 1988, pp. 121–30.

27. "Billionaire Buffett Gets an Award—for Writing," http://msnbc.msn.com/id/6913932/print/1/displaymode/1098/ (retrieved February 8, 2005).

28. Berkshire Hathaway, Inc. *2008 Annual Report,* www.berkshirehathaway.com/2008ar/ (retrieved March 12, 2009).

29. Maria Bartiromo, "Facetime: Melinda and Bill Gates on Making a Difference." *BusinessWeek,* February 16, 2009, pp. 21–22.

30. Kitty Locker, "Theoretical Justification for Using Reader Benefits," *Journal of Business Communication* 19, no. 3 (Summer 1982), pp. 51–65.

31. Pamela Layton and Adrian J. Simpson, "Deep Structure in Sentence Comprehension," *Journal of Verbal Learning and Verbal Behavior* 14 (1975), pp. 658–64.

32. Thomas L. Kent, "Paragraph Production and the Given-New Contract," *Journal of Business Communication* 21, no. 4 (Fall 1984), pp. 45–66.

33. For a comprehensive explanation of parallel structure, see Gerald J. Alred, Charles T. Brusaw, and Walter E. Oliu, *The Business Writer's Handbook,* 8th ed. (New York: Bedford/St. Martin's Press, 2006).

34. Larry Smeltzer and Jeanette Gilsdorf, "How to Use Your Time Efficiently When Writing," *Business Horizons,* November–December 1990, pp. 61–64.

35. ———, "Revise Reports Rapidly," *Personnel Journal,* October 1990, pp. 39–44.

36. Jeanne W. Halpern, "What Should We Be Teaching Students in Business Writing?" *Journal of Business Communication* 18, no. 3 (Summer 1981), pp. 39–53.

37. Lynne Truss, *Eats, Shoots & Leaves: The Zero Tolerance Approach to Punctuation* (New York: Gotham Books/Penguin Group USA, 2003).

Chapter **Five**

Routine Messages

And, of course, you have the commercials where savvy business-people get ahead by using their Macintosh computers to create the ultimate American business product: a really sharp-looking memo.
—*Dave Barry, humorist and columnist*

As earlier chapters have emphasized, written communication is an important part of a manager's job. One study of 837 business school graduates with varying years of experience found that they spent over one-fourth of their time at work writing.[1] And of all the different types of writing they do, e-mail, letters, and memos are certainly the workhorses of written managerial communication.[2] Another study (of 188 participants in a writing seminar) revealed that 63.1 percent of the managers surveyed wrote letters daily and 76.3 percent wrote memos daily.[3]

E-mail, letters, and memorandums are probably the forms of written communication that benefit most from the strategic considerations we discuss in this text. The conciseness of these messages and the relatively detached atmosphere in which managers usually write them can help ensure that the principles of reader adaptation and strategic analysis are used.

Unfortunately, too many managers take routine writing tasks for granted. Perhaps because managers write so many of them, e-mails, letters, and memos frequently can become impersonal things that convey information in a lifeless manner. Rather than being responses to a specific communication situation, many messages merely respond to types of situations. Thus, some managers write stock answers to claims and ignore, or at least discount, the factors making the claim unique and calling for adaptation.

Additionally, because e-mails, letters, and memos are such common and relatively informal media, managers often become lax regarding the quality of their messages. One study of correspondence in 13 industries found punctuation errors in 43.7 percent of the correspondence surveyed, word usage errors in 52.2 percent, and sentence construction mistakes in 45.3 percent.[4]

Perhaps because routine correspondence is so bound by conventions of format, the language used in it poses another problem. These media can easily become choked with stock phrases and clichés that turn the message into a ritual utterance: "as per your request," "reference your letter," "herewith acknowledge receipt," and "please do not hesitate to contact me." Such documents often communicate very little except a negative impression of a stuffy, impersonal author.

This chapter takes a strategic approach to e-mail, letter, and memo writing, emphasizing ways in which a writer can adapt correspondence to fit as nearly as possible to the needs of the intended reader. The chapter also offers two general patterns for correspondence situations you are likely to face as a manager, and specific types you can use for guidance in certain cases. Of course, use these models as a foundation only—as suggested in Chapter 2, each message a manager writes needs to be adapted to fit the audience and the situation.

AUDIENCE ADAPTATION

In many writing situations, a writer may not know the reader of the message very well. Indeed, the writer may not know the reader at all. Thus, managers must carefully consider the strategies of messages they send in order to achieve the maximum benefit. Fortunately, we can recognize some writing strategies that suit most correspondence situations.

The "you" attitude is the basis for the organizational strategies this chapter details. Writers who have this attitude prepare messages matching their readers' interests. They do this by putting themselves in the reader's place. A writer with the you attitude begins by asking herself, "How would I feel if I were this person in this situation? What would I want to read in this message?"

The you attitude requires empathy, the ability to understand another's feelings. We show empathy when we say to a colleague who is having trouble solving a problem, "I know what you mean" or "I know what you're going through."

Basis of the You Attitude

The great American film director Billy Wilder said, "An audience is never wrong." Furthermore, every audience is unique. Just as you wouldn't give the same birthday gift to every member of your family, you shouldn't give the same message to every employee. Audiences want to know that you understand their specific needs and concerns, so you must address them personally.

The you attitude, which is reader-oriented, grew out of an awareness that most people, especially when they are involved in business matters, are likely to be looking after their own interests. In reading a message, they want to know how they can gain, or at least how they can minimize a loss. Thus, when communicating in a positive situation, good writers seek to increase the positive impact of the news. In a negative situation, writers seek to reduce negative impact while stressing reader benefits.

Few people have trouble using the you attitude in positive situations, but some balk at using it in negative ones, fearing that the you attitude shows weakness. This view is a misperception.

Anticipating Questions

To be effective, writers should anticipate the questions a reader might have. Thus, as they write, they ask themselves just what the reader might be uncertain about and then answer the uncertainties so no additional correspondence is needed. Remember the five Ws: who, what, when, where, and why.

Stressing Reader Benefits

Arguably, the most likely audience question is "What's in it for me?" or WII-FM. With the you attitude, the writer always strives to show the reader how she benefits. This is not to say that the writer gives in to the reader. Rather, the writer designs the message to either capitalize on or overcome the reader's attitudes about the writer as well as the issue at hand. Thus, a businessperson trying to collect on a past-due account might stress that the reader needs to pay the account balance to retain credit privileges at the store as well as an overall good credit rating. The potential for success in this case is far greater than if the credit manager had stressed only the company's interest by writing of its need to receive payment.

Avoiding Negatives

A writer should avoid negatives and words with negative connotations, especially in negative situations. These words have a way of jumping off the page and putting the reader on the defensive. Watch, especially, words such as *unfortunately, claim, allege, problem, damage,* and *regret.* A negative word can affect a reader's perceptions so much that he won't be able to read the rest of the message objectively. Stressing the positive, on the other hand, will improve the writer-reader relationship and make it more likely that the writer's goal will be reached.

An easy way to find positive words for a negative message is to say what *will* happen rather than what *won't* happen. So instead of telling a customer, "Unfortunately we can't meet Friday's deadline," one could say, "Your shipment will arrive on Monday." Recall the Holiday Inn Express example in Chapter 4. Instead of warning guests not to steal the towels (a negative message), hotel management offers towels and other room amenities for sale, with a price list that includes positive terms such as "approve" and "popularity."

Nonverbal Elements and the You Attitude

The you attitude shows itself in a variety of ways, some more obvious than others. One of these ways is metacommunication. Without reading a word, an individual receiving a message can tell a lot about the sender and the sender's attitude toward the reader.

Both the stationery chosen for correspondence and the keying job send messages to readers. A positive letter marred by smeared or pale print, typos, stains, or hand corrections or a cheap grade of paper creates static in the communication channel. While the written message says the writer cares, the physical elements of the medium suggest indifference at best. On the other hand, error-free letters with crisp black print on white high-rag-content bond paper suggest professionalism and concern for the reader's feelings.

Similarly, the nonverbal elements of e-mail can make a positive or negative impression on the reader. A writer implementing the you attitude will send concise e-mails. How concise? Most readers prefer them limited to one screen in length so they don't have to scroll. Brief paragraphs with spaces between them improve readability. If the e-mail is a reply, or the latest in a series of exchanges, the writer should delete all but the most recent message being responded to. Formatting is often lost when a reader opens an external e-mail, so the writer should limit the use of tabs and other design and formatting elements.

Diction

The you attitude also influences a message's wording. If the reader's interest is of central concern, show this by making the reader central as well. If the reader is asking "What's in it for me?" she will have a hard time determining this if you write exclusively about yourself, using *I, me, mine,* or *we, us, our, ours.* A better focus is on *you, your, yours.* Thus, rather than saying "We are sending the samples of the ads we worked up for Reality Industry's new pump," a writer should substitute "You will soon receive three samples of the magazine ads for your new pumps." The revision makes the reader rather than the writer the focus of attention.

STRATEGIES

Thus far, we have looked at a variety of ways in which a manager can personalize messages to make them better understood and received by readers. However, one key element remains: overall strategy. The suggestions given so far for signaling concern for the reader will fall short if you do not organize the message in a manner that anticipates reader reaction. Let's look then at two basic strategies that, when used properly, can appropriately address reader reaction. The strategies deliver the message while promoting a positive image of the writer.

Direct Strategy

The direct strategy is used for messages conveying good news or neutral information. Someone receiving good news is pleased after reading it and appreciates having the good news as quickly as possible. However, if the message's main idea is buried in the middle or is located near the end, the reader, who probably began with some enthusiasm, loses interest and becomes frustrated at wasting valuable time searching for the main point. This frustration can affect the reader's attitude toward the writer: "Why can't she come right to the point?" Thus, such a message in a positive situation with lots of potential for building goodwill can instead weaken and even destroy the positive impact.

Opening

A better strategy is to put the main point first. A brief introduction might be needed to orient the reader, but this introduction should not delay the presentation of the main point. An easy way to remember this principle is the acronym BIF, or Big Idea First.

Body

A message using the direct strategy next provides the necessary supporting details: the reasons for the decision, background or history, specifics about the situation, or the procedures the reader needs to follow. Of course, these details promote the writer or the company she represents, especially when the message grants a favor.

Close

A direct message has a positive ending. Among the choices can be an offer to help, a statement of gratitude, or a call for any further action the reader needs to take.

Indirect Strategy

Unfortunately, not all messages communicate good news or even neutral information. Often, requests are denied, proposals are rejected, and job applications are turned down. The readers are naturally not pleased, but the documents need to be written. The effective bad news message conveys its information while creating a minimum of resentment. If possible, it should help build goodwill for the company since the reader may be desirable as a customer, client, or future employee.

A good strategy for negative situations is the indirect one. Using this strategy, a writer leads the reader logically to the bad news. Successfully developed, the message minimizes the reader's negative reactions and builds goodwill. A comparison between the direct and the indirect approaches is presented in Table 5–1. Not all indirect messages convey bad news. The persuasive message is a specialized type of indirect message that will be detailed later in the chapter.

Opening

Instead of BIF (Big Idea First), the writer should use the BILL formula—Big Idea a Little Later. The indirect message begins with a buffer, some neutral or positive statement that clearly relates to the purpose that both reader and writer agree on. The beginning might be agreement with the reader; it might express appreciation for the reader's candor in writing; or it might be a compliment.

A good opening begins to let the reader down gently. Ideally, it would subtly set up the explanation that follows in the body of the message. As we saw with the good news strategy, the reader expects things to go his way. When the indirect beginning fails to reinforce that expectation, the stage is set for the denial or bad news to follow.

Body

Next, the message analyzes the circumstances or provides details about the facts that led to the bad news being conveyed. The challenge here is to be convincing. The tone of this part is cooperative. The writer does not have to say "Let's look at the facts," but the reader should have that feeling. A large body of research

TABLE 5–1
The Direct
Approach
Compared to
the Indirect
Approach

Direct	Indirect
Opening	Opening
Main point	Neutral buffer
Body	Body
Supporting information	Explanation and negative news
Close	Close
Positive statement	Goodwill building

summarized by Professor Kitty O. Locker of Ohio State University shows that you can improve the reader's response to the bad news when you (1) offer a reason for the outcome, and (2) provide an alternative or a compromise whenever possible.[5]

Next, one implies or directly expresses the negative information in as positive a tone as possible. Naturally, a writer should not be so subtle in implying the negative news that the reader is left hanging. But any direct statement should be tactful and not blunt. The best approach is to subordinate the actual point where the bad news is stated in the middle of a paragraph, rather than allow it to appear at the beginning or end.

Close

The next step is important: At the end, strive to rebuild goodwill. Depending on the situation, several options are available. One is to suggest another course of action open to the reader. In response to claims for goods, suggest others that are more durable or appropriate for the reader's use. A letter rejecting a proposal, for example, might give another outlet for the idea.

Close the indirect message on a positive, friendly note. Often, the effort at building goodwill is enough. Sometimes a little more is necessary. A manager might want to offer services or information. For example, a letter written to an old customer might have a catalog enclosed and end by looking forward to the reader's next order.

Handling Negatives

Since an indirect message conveys bad news, it is potentially very negative. To minimize the damage to a company's goodwill, good writers generally avoid negative words. Although the task is a challenge, avoiding negatives pays off in the long run because the practice helps keep the overall tone positive. The following three rules hold the key:

- Place negative information at points of low emphasis.
- Avoid *no* or *not* when possible.
- Avoid words with negative connotations.

De-emphasize negative facts by placing them in a subordinate structure (a dependent clause, a parenthetic expression, or a modifier) rather than in a main clause or a sentence. In a paragraph, negative information should not be placed in a prominent position. Compare the following two short paragraphs telling a job applicant that the company has no job openings in his area.

> We do not anticipate any openings in the Baytown Company anytime soon since we have been laying off people in your field. You might apply at Rumfield and Company or Bennington, Inc., since they are adding to their staffs.

The writer could easily have softened the negatives by placing them in a less prominent position.

Please consider applying for one of the engineering positions now open at Rumfield and Company or at Bennington, Inc. rather than at Baytown Company. Currently Baytown's personnel needs are in other areas.

The second suggestion for avoiding negative writing (avoiding *no* and *not*) is easier to follow than it seems at first. In the revisions in the following example, the writer emphasizes what she *can* do, not what she *cannot* do.

We cannot fill your order until you tell us what size grill your restaurant currently uses.

- We can fill your order as soon as you let us have your restaurant's grill size.
- Please specify your grill size so we may fill your order as quickly as possible.

The third suggestion (avoiding words with negative connotations) is one of the most important. Whereas *claim* and *state* might have very similar denotations, their connotations are widely separated. Writing to a person and saying "You next claim that . . ." makes it sound as if the reader is wrong. Numerous words are likely to irritate or even inflame when they appear in bad news messages:

allege	argue
failure	mistake
claim	damage
regret	error
careless	broken

SPECIFIC TYPES: DIRECT MESSAGES

The direct and indirect strategies are useful for most writing situations managers face. Nevertheless, because some situations are so frequent (for example, the inquiry) and because some are so sensitive (for example, negative responses to claims), several specialized versions of the direct and indirect patterns have developed. Table 5–2 lists seven specific versions reviewed here.

The patterns suggested here are not absolute. After strategic analysis, a manager may determine that a different approach is appropriate. That kind of adaptation is to be encouraged because it helps to prevent following a mechanical pattern. First, we look at correspondence using the direct pattern, and then we consider those following the indirect. Remember to use a direct approach for good news and neutral informative messages.

TABLE 5–2
Types of Direct and Indirect Messages

Direct	Indirect
Inquiries and requests	Negative responses to inquiries and requests
Positive responses to inquiries and requests	Refused claims
Claims	Persuasive messages
Positive responses to claims	

Inquiries and Requests

Perhaps the most common direct correspondence is the inquiry. Managers in all areas of business routinely need information to conduct their affairs. A manager might need to know about the performance of a product; another might want credit information about a client or wish to know about the qualifications of a job applicant. Since most readers see these requests as routine and reasonable, they are likely to respond to them willingly.

If you project yourself into the position of a reader receiving an inquiry, you'll see why the direct approach is so appropriate. You are probably busy with other matters and need to know quickly what is required of you. When you receive an inquiry, you appreciate the reader's efforts to be direct and to let you know from the start what she wants.

Opening

Make the inquiry clear from the start. One effective method is to begin with a question that summarizes the writer's objective. For example, an inquiry about a potential employee could begin with "Would you please comment on Mary Keynes's qualifications to become a management intern? We at Infovend are considering her for the position, and she has given your name as a reference." The question beginning the inquiry makes the purpose immediately clear.

Body

In many cases, the next step in the inquiry is an explanation of the inquiry's purpose. In the example just given, you quickly made it clear that you are considering Keynes for a job. The amount of information a writer gives depends on the situation. In an inquiry about the potential employee, you also probably would want to assure the reader that her response will be kept confidential.[6]

The body of the inquiry needs to be efficiently organized; it cannot simply be a "fishing expedition" for information. Even after the purpose is clear, the reader usually needs guidance to answer the inquiry satisfactorily. Given as much of the sample letter about Mary Keynes as we have so far, it might be answered several ways depending on how the reader projected your needs—or it might not be detailed at all. Thus, the next part of the inquiry should set out the areas requiring information, plus any necessary additional information. Numbering the questions may also help the reader respond.

Close

The close of the inquiry is friendly and builds goodwill. In some cases, it is appropriate to offer similar services. In situations where a purchase might follow, you might ask for a speedy reply.

Let's look at the complete inquiry about Mary Keynes. Note that in this inquiry about a person, you have emphasized confidentiality, an advisable practice in this kind of correspondence.

Dear Professor Renton:

Would you please comment on Mary Keynes's qualifications as a management intern? Infovend is considering her for the position, and she has given your name as a reference. Of course, whatever information you give us will be held in confidence.

1. How well does Keynes manage time? Is her work punctual?
2. Did you have a chance to observe her under pressure? If so, does she manage well or does pressure adversely affect her performance?
3. How well does she relate to her peers? Please comment on her relationship with them: Is she a leader or a follower, gregarious or shy, and so on?

I look forward to hearing your comments on Keynes's qualifications and appreciate whatever insights you can share with us.

Sincerely,

Tim Inman
Human Resources Manager

Positive Responses to Inquiries and Requests

Inquiries naturally need answers. The favorable response to an inquiry is a direct one, as the reader is pleased to get the requested information or item.

Opening

You begin by identifying the request you are responding to. This identification appears in the first sentence of the message. The opening also makes it clear the reader's request is being granted.

- I found Mary Keynes, the subject of your June 5 inquiry, to be one of the most promising students I have ever taught.
- As-Best-As Filing Cabinets have all the features you mentioned in your March 4 letter and several more you might be interested in knowing about.
- Here is my response to your September 14 inquiry about our experiences with the M-102 Security System.

You can begin by directly answering the most general of the questions originally asked (as in the first two examples) or by agreeing to respond to the question originally posed (as in the third example).

Body

The way in which you organize the body of the message varies depending on the original inquiry. For an inquiry that asked one question, the details in response appear in order of importance. If you are responding to a series of questions, normally answer them in the order asked. If the original is really a request (for example, "May we use your facilities for a club meeting?"), the body gives necessary conditions for use.

Not all responses to inquiries are completely good or bad news. Thus, although a manager is willing to answer most questions, some topics are confidential. In these cases, the denial is subordinated and appears after the writer explains why. For example, the response to the inquiry about a company's experiences with the M-102 Security System may withhold some details for security reasons.

Close

The positive response to an inquiry continues to be positive in the close. Note the following closes to the messages whose beginnings we gave earlier.

- If I can help you with any other information about Mary, please contact me.
- If you need any other information on how As-Best-As Filing Cabinets can meet your storage needs, please let me know.
- I'd be delighted to answer any further questions about our experiences with the M-102 Security System. I think you'll be pleased with the system.

Claims

A third type of direct message is the claim. Usually, a dissatisfied customer writes about a problem and requests a solution or claim. Project yourself as manager and consider how you would feel receiving a claim letter. Customer dissatisfaction not only leads to a loss of goodwill and revenue, but also reflects badly on your ability as a manager. Naturally, you would want to find out quickly what the problem is and resolve it.

Opening

Even though the claim deals with something negative, it is written directly. From your perspective, directness strengthens the claim. In fact, some readers may interpret indirectness as a lack of confidence in the claim being made. Indirectness would thus be a strategic error.

Early in the claim, you should include details about the faulty product, service, or sale. Which details to incorporate depend on the situation, but they may include invoice numbers, dates, and the product identification or serial number.

Another good tactic that makes the message convincing is to include the significance of the problem to you or your business. For example, a warehouse manager whose new intercom system failed might write:

The new intercom system you sent us (Invoice #16789) has broken, thus considerably slowing the processing of orders in our company warehouse.

Body

The next step is logical: The facts of the case need detailing. In the intercom example, you discuss how the system broke down and the possible cause. Naturally, you do not need to be an expert analyst, but the more facts you include, the more convincing your argument. If appropriate, you may also wish to detail the damage that resulted.

Of course, detailing the problem requires tact and forbearance. You feel justified in writing about the problem, but you don't attack the person who sold or installed the product or its manufacturer. Name-calling or accusations do little, if any, good and may create reader resentment, which usually precludes a favorable settlement. Abusive messages are best left unsent.

The next part of the letter states what you want: What will set things right? Unfortunately, some letters end before this point. An unhappy writer complains and then forgets to say what he wants. Specifying the action or amount of money needed for satisfaction is usually preferable. Occasionally, the settlement can be left up to the reader if the situation is routine.

You may also wish to include a deadline for action on the matter. Naturally, a deadline needs something to back it up. One authority recommends that the writer make a threat or ultimatum that she is willing and able to carry out if the situation is not resolved.[7] Weigh threats carefully. They can be counterproductive.

Close

Once again, avoid negativity in the close. If you threaten to take your business elsewhere, the reader may lose any motivation for cooperation. End by expressing confidence in the good faith of the reader or by expressing intended gratitude for the early resolution of the problem.

Let's look at the rest of the claim about the faulty intercom and see how it illustrates these points.

Dear Mr. Packard:

The new intercom system you sent us (Invoice #16789) has broken, thus considerably slowing the processing of orders in our company warehouse.

Although the system worked fine immediately after installation, we began to notice problems with it during stormy weather. When it rained, static garbled many of the messages. Finally, during one heavy downpour, the main transmitter stopped working and began smoking.

We are shipping the transmitter to you via Brown Express. We would like it either repaired or replaced. Your prompt attention will help our warehouse return to normal.

Sincerely,

Patricia Muranka

Purchasing Manager

In this message, the manager detailed the problem her department faced, yet she resisted accusatory language. She set out her experience with the system and provided enough information for the manufacturer to diagnose the problem. The ending is positive, yet assertive.

Positive Responses to Claims

The fourth type of direct message is the positive response to a claim. While use of the direct order is unquestionable, this type still challenges the writer who is aware of the unpleasantness the reader experienced. The reader may have lost sales or may have been uncomfortable or inconvenienced. The challenge here is to rebuild goodwill and, in many cases, restore faith in the product. The reader who does not believe in the product will buy elsewhere next time. Occasionally, especially when dealing with angry customers, you respond to a very unpleasant or accusatory letter. You must not rise to the bait.

Opening

Begin the adjustment grant with the good news. The reader needs a reminder to recall the situation, but this reminding should be done quickly. Thus, the letter responding to the claim about the faulty intercom might begin in the following manner:

> Your transmitter is now in working order and should arrive in Cedar Rapids by truck in the next few days.

Body

After the good news, the development of the body depends on the situation. Routine cases need little explanation. In many cases, however, the reader needs more. It is usually necessary to explain what went wrong, and it is often a good idea to stress that the problem is corrected and will not recur.

Occasionally, you will need to explain the proper use of the product to a reader who unintentionally misused the product. In such cases, the reader's goodwill is worth the cost. This explanation needs to be tactful and is most effective when presented impersonally, as in the second example that follows:

- You left the valves open on the unit. As a result, your heater was on constantly and wore out.
- The valves leading out to the unit must be kept tightly closed to reduce the demand on the heating unit.

In the explanatory material and the close, keep the tone positive. Common courtesy seems to dictate an apology, but it often serves to open old wounds. Instead, look to the future with a confident positive approach:

> You can expect many more years of trouble-free service from your transmitter.

Close

The closing of an adjustment grant is positive. It anticipates continued good relations with the customer and may include information on other products or services the company offers. You build goodwill by discussing the advantages of the product. You also refrain from stating the fault was the electrician's rather than the manufacturer's, although you have taken steps to protect the equipment in the future.

Dear Ms. Muranka:

Your transmitter is now in working order and should arrive in Cedar Rapids by truck in the next few days. Please call your electrician when it arrives so his installation will protect the warranty.

You reported that the system had static in it during rainstorms and that it smoked when the system stopped working. I've checked the new patented fusible ground lead and found that it had melted, as it was designed to do, and protected the transmitter and you from electrical shock.

When your electrician installs the transmitter, have him check the unit's grounding. At present, when it rains, the unit is shorting out because of incomplete grounding.

You might be interested in our new security alarm system that hooks into the existing intercom system. The enclosed pamphlet gives you the details. We will be glad to discuss its installation with you.

Sincerely,

Robert Packard
Customer Service Manager

SPECIFIC TYPES: INDIRECT MESSAGES

Most managers cannot comply with all the requests made of them. In those situations, the response is best organized according to the indirect plan.

Negative Responses to Inquiries

The strategy for constructing negative responses to inquiries requires thought and planning. When requests need denying, use a bad news strategy. Reasons appear first, followed by the refusal.

Opening

The opening should remind the reader of the request. This initial statement should also serve as a buffer that does not imply either a positive or negative answer. Furthermore, the opening should lead logically into the body.

Suppose, for example, you received a letter from a researcher inquiring into the population sample used to determine your company's marketing strategies. Since such questions deal with proprietary information that the company keeps confidential, you must deny the request. At the same time, you do not want to refuse directly. Your request might begin with one of the following buffers:

- Thank you for your inquiry about our marketing research and strategies.
- The results of your study of population samples should prove interesting.

This introduction gives no false hope for a positive reply, yet it does not deny the request yet. However, it lays the basis for that rejection. The rest of the letter develops the approach.

Body

From this beginning, you move into a discussion of why the request cannot be granted. You consider the reader and choose examples or reasoning likely to convince the reader that yours is the only viable solution. For example, in the preceding letter, you could appeal to the reader's own experience as a researcher who has spent hours developing ideas. Similarly, after great expense, your company had developed ideas that it applies to its own needs.

Once you have given the reasoning, you can state the refusal. Occasionally, writers refuse requests so vaguely that the reader still sees hope for the request. The well-written refusal reasons the reader out of the original request. However, the reasoning does not suggest the original request was ill advised or misdirected.

Close

Close positively to build goodwill. The close can look to the future, such as a wish for success in the reader's work or a suggestion for some other sources of information the reader could use.

In the letter refusing the request for information on marketing strategies, note how you imply the refusal rather than state it. Note also that you make no apology for refusing.

Dear Ms. Leeper:

The results of your study of population samples should prove interesting, as most companies protect these data because they are so central to their marketing strategies.

At Flo-Sheen Fabrics, we develop our marketing strategies only after our test market has had a chance to examine our new fabrics. As a researcher, you can surely appreciate the countless hours that go into any marketing campaign.

We keep the population sample used for our marketing analysis confidential both to protect their privacy and to help us keep our competitive edge. Our competition would have an unfair advantage over us if they were able to know in advance what products we planned to introduce or what strategies we would use.

You might look into any text on statistical sampling to learn the considerations managers must take in selecting population samples.

Sincerely,

Sheila Hebert
Vice President

Refused Claims

A greater challenge than the negative response to an inquiry is the refused claim. In most cases, the person making the claim believes she is justified; her interests have been damaged by what she sees as bad products or services. However, for whatever reason, you have determined that you must reject the claim.

In doing so you must maintain a positive tone and build goodwill. The key is empathy. Imagine how you would want to be treated in this situation—probably reasonably. To respond in an authoritarian or a condescending fashion would be foolish. The language must be positive and selective. Most likely, the reader will be sensitive to any possible nuances.

Opening

The claim refusal must begin as most negative messages would: with a buffer. This buffer can refer to the reader's original claim as its subject, or it can be an expression of appreciation—some opening that brings the reader and writer together neutrally.

The effective opening also indicates the line of reasoning to be followed. Take, for example, the opening sentence, "Whitlow Co. does guarantee its sump pumps for 18 months in normal operation under normal circumstances." The reader is reminded of the original claim and is introduced to the line of reasoning in "normal operation" and "normal circumstances." Another opening might be the following:

> Your recent letter shows you are a person who appreciates being treated fairly and openly. You will be interested in what we have found in our investigation into your questions.

Body

The body details your findings. This explanation should be objective and convincing, but it should avoid a my-side/your-side dichotomy. One effective tactic in some situations is to describe the effort that went into investigating the matter. For example, a negative response to a warranty claim may emphasize the laboratory tests made on the broken part. This detail is useful because it projects a caring image; the decision made is not just some automatic response.

Give the refusal once the reasons are clear. Of course, the refusal should appear at a point of low emphasis. If the refusal is based on company policy, the policy should be clearly explained. But remember that customers generally resent managers "hiding behind" company policy. Use logic whenever possible instead.

Close

Most claim refusals close with an effort at resale. If the customer has been treated fairly in a reasonable manner, she may stay with the product since the company was not at fault. Frequently, it is a good idea to get off the immediate topic by mentioning an upcoming sale or by sending a recent catalog.

Dear Ms. Clark:

Whitlow Co. does guarantee its sump pumps for 18 months in normal operation under normal circumstances. After your recent letter, we looked closely into the questions you raised.

Our laboratory examined the returned pump and found that the entire unit had been submerged for some time. This submersion was in keeping with the newspaper accounts of heavy flooding in your town last month. Apparently the area where your unit was located was also inundated. While the pump is designed to take care of normal seepage, it is mounted at least 18 inches above the basement floor to protect the housing and pump. Like most motor-driven appliances, the pump must be kept totally dry, as it is in normal circumstances.

You might be interested in another model pump we offer, the SubMerso. Its water-proof housing withstands even prolonged immersion. The enclosed pamphlet details its capacities. We'll be glad to answer any questions you might have on it.

Sincerely,

Lionel Naquin
Customer Service Representative

Apologies

When composing a bad news message such as a negative response to an inquiry or a refusal to a claim, you may be tempted to include an apology. This decision is controversial. Corporate attorneys have traditionally warned against apologizing because it implies responsibility for wrongdoing and even guilt, inviting legal action against the writer and her organization. Public relations professionals agree that apologies can be interpreted as an admission of error or carelessness, damaging a company's image. In a 1997 study titled "Liability Means Never Being Able to Say You're Sorry," the author concluded that our present legal system discourages apologies.[8]

Recently, however, the trend has been changing due to evidence that an apology can help rather than hurt, in terms of both image and legal judgments. In the field of medicine, malpractice-reform advocates say an apology can help doctors avoid being sued and can reduce settlements. The hospitals in the University of Michigan Health System have been encouraging doctors since 2002 to apologize for mistakes. The system's annual attorney fees have since dropped by two-thirds, and malpractice lawsuits have fallen by half.[9]

The U.S. has witnessed a remarkable rise in the number of public corporate apologies. During the 2000 "summer of apologies," company executives begged pardon for unreliable flights, bad phone service, and tire blowouts. Since then, the pattern has continued. Southwest Airlines mailed more than 26,000 individual letters of apology last year, most of them with vouchers for free or discounted flights. Colleen Barrett, President Emeritus, said, "We've never been afraid to say we're sorry."[10] CEOs have even apologized for sins to which they had no connection, as in 2005, when Ken Thompson, CEO of Wachovia, announced that two of its acquired companies had owned slaves. He stated, "On behalf of Wachovia Corporation, I apologize to all Americans."[11]

If a manager makes the strategic decision to apologize, either individually or on behalf of the organization, what are some guidelines? A good apology is genuine and timely. It should consist of four parts:

- An acknowledgment of the mistake or wrongdoing
- The acceptance of responsibility
- An expression of regret
- A promise that the offense will not be repeated[12]

Perhaps the most critical issue is acceptance of responsibility or fault. A partial apology, where the manager expresses sympathy or regret without admitting guilt, softens the blow and may be wise when there is significant damage or injury. Partial apologies can also resolve disputes when the extent of fault is unclear or difficult to establish. In other circumstances, when a manager or company has clearly committed an egregious act, a more complete apology may be appropriate. In either situation, the focus should be on the future and on making amends.[13]

An excellent example of a corporate apology occurred in February 2006. Hallmark's Web site crashed under the volume of traffic on Valentine's Day. An e-mail went out the next day to all customers who had attempted to send an eGreeting. It began, "We owe you an apology." It continued with a description of what had happened and its consequences—"We cringe at the disappointment we caused." It ended with a positive look to the future: "We are now challenging our team to reevaluate every step."

Persuasive Messages

The indirect strategy is appropriate for persuasive messages. A manager uses the indirect persuasive strategy when trying to persuade others to do things they might not ordinarily wish to do. You might need to write a persuasive letter to convince a reluctant client to pay his bill. Or you might write a persuasive e-mail to gain a colleague's support on a project.

Opening

The persuasive message opens by catching the reader's interest.[14] One effective way of doing this is to show the reader that her goals are your goals. The best way to show this identity of goals is to show her that the message deals with matters she is interested in. At the same time, since the message must catch the reader's interest, the opening must be brief.

Body

The body consists of several parts. First, it must set out the problem that you and the reader share. Then, it must reveal the solution to the problem—the solution you want the reader to embrace. This section reflects careful strategy since the reader's possible objections must be anticipated and answered. In this section (which can consist of several paragraphs), you must stress the benefit accruing to the reader as a result of the solution.[15]

Close

The ending is important. The effective persuasive message does not end after the proposed answer is revealed. At the end, after the reader's interest has been aroused, the interest must be channeled into action. Otherwise, interest will decline, with nothing resolved. The action item should be specific: a meeting, an order, a payment, an interview, a change in procedure. An action must be prompt. Delay only lessens the probability of action.[16]

The following job application letter illustrates the implementation of the persuasive strategy.

Dear Mr. Harris:

Now that Lynch's is about to open its third department store in Jonesboro, won't you need a sufficient staff of part-time employees to supplement your full-time workers? I believe I have the background and motivation necessary to become one of your most productive part-time workers.

As a junior marketing major at State University, I am currently taking marketing courses. I could apply what I learn over the next two years to my sales work at Lynch's. The job references listed on the attached résumé will all attest to the fact that I am very energetic and enthusiastic about my work.

Another reason I think I would make a good part-time employee for you is that I am very interested in pursuing a career with Lynch's after graduation. I would see these two years as a testing period to prove myself, and you would have the two years to decide whether or not you would be equally interested in me.

If I have described the kind of part-time salesperson you want at Lynch's, may I have an interview to further discuss the position? I can be reached at 992-8403, and I can be available at a time convenient to you.

Sincerely,

John Morris

LETTER FORMATS

Thus far we have discussed strategies for organizing routine messages sent to external audiences such as customers, clients, regulatory agencies, and other stakeholders. Typically, these messages are in letter or e-mail format. Good writers know that the appearance of a document can affect the reader's reaction to its content, much the same way a speaker's appearance affects the listeners' response to her message. A word about contemporary letter format is therefore appropriate.

Many routine business messages are sent electronically, either as e-mails or as e-mail attachments. Formatting elements such as tabs (indents) and centering can change or even disappear according to the technology used to open the message. So the appearance of a message should be simple, plain, and as easy to read as possible. A standard contemporary style is to begin every part of a business letter at the left margin (left-justified).

Reliance on the concept of white space makes sense, too. Standard business letter style calls for single spacing within paragraphs, and double spacing between paragraphs and between elements of the letter. Keeping paragraphs short, as discussed in Chapter 4, also builds white space. The persuasive letter in Figure 5–1 exemplifies excellent strategies for both content and format.

INTERNAL CORRESPONDENCE

While letters are the most frequently used medium of communication between firms, memos and e-mail are the most frequently used within an organization.[17] The memo is an efficient straightforward kind of communication. Often, memos are sent electronically, as e-mails. E-mail is becoming more commonly used for routine external communication as well. A hybrid format is a business letter or memo sent as an e-mail attachment, a practice that allows the sender to stabilize design and format elements when the document is opened.

Because the reader of a memo is human, the writer needs to adapt strategically. This is especially true when one is writing to employees at a different level within the organization, or who possess a less specialized knowledge of the subject, or when the memo deals with sensitive matters. While internal messages are often routine informal exchanges of information, they should be composed carefully.

Memo Format

Memo formats differ from one another in minor details, but they generally have four standard headings: *To, From, Subject,* and *Date.* In e-mails, these headings are automatically provided. The "From" line offers few problems. However, if needed, a writer can add to her authority by including her job title after her name. She can add the names of others here as well—assuming she has their agreement.

The "Subject" line has obvious value in directing the reader's attention. Be specific about your topic and purpose. For instance, "Subject: Request for Vacation Schedules" is more likely to stimulate reader response than the vaguer "Subject: Schedules." Using key words in the "Subject" line will often aid in the memo's later retrieval from computer files as well.

Just as with face-to-face interactions, memos sent within an organization typically have a set protocol one should respect. This means paying attention to the format generally used, as well as noting any subtleties related to whom the memorandum or its copies are sent to.[18] Often, by noting at the "cc:" line that the memo is being sent to a boss, one sends the message that one has easy access to that boss. Similarly, be sure you copy your immediate supervisor when contacting his bosses. In general, copy your supervisor to keep him aware of what

FIGURE 5–1   Sample Persuasive Letter

LaSalle Senior Center
1111 N. Wells St., Suite 500 Chicago, IL 60610
312-573-8840 Fax 312-787-1219

Gerry Hynes
3780 Copperfield Dr. Unit 1018
Bryan, TX 77802

Dear Gerry,

As the year moves to an end, I think about two of our seniors who died this year. They were each exceptional in their own way; each had a key role at the LaSalle Senior Center and each benefited from the services we offered just as we benefited from their gifts. They were like many of the seniors we work with, both a client and a volunteer.

Marc Stuart was a regular volunteer at both the Wednesday and Sunday meals. Having management experience, he was inclined to supervise both clients and volunteers. He was part of the fabric of the Senior Center and showed his support by his presence and by his care for other seniors. The Senior Center provided Marc with a place to serve and live out his faith. He told me on several occasions that his first priority was LaSalle Street Church followed by the Senior Center.

Allene Hales was exceptional by any standard. With little formal education, very modest means, and compromised health, she brought people together at the Senior Center and in her community. She knew everyone. And she was always helping others, offering a kind word, sharing money or food. The Senior Center recognized her for her gifts and provided her some real help with day-to-day matters.

Marc and Allene found a home at the Senior Center. They found a place that offered them help, a place where they could serve and a place to belong. Thanks to your support, the LaSalle Senior Center continues to be that place for over 200 local seniors every month.

Please consider making a gift* to help continue our ministry to our neighborhood's older friends.

Sincerely,

Keith Chase-Ziolek
Director

*A generous donor will match the first $5000 in gifts.

is going on. Even in cases where that individual is not immediately involved, he appreciates knowing about events. However, the proliferation of e-mail "copies" and "Reply to All" in most organizations is a caution not to flood people with excessive messages that are merely "FYI" ("For your information").

Another format element to note is the need for either your initials or signed name on the "From" line of the paper memo. This authenticates the document just as a signature does on a letter. However, adding your name at the end of a memo or e-mail is redundant—it appears on the "From" line. Pithy quotations, illustrations, and similar "signature" elements at the bottom of e-mails add clutter and can be annoying distractions to business readers. Remember that short simple messages have the most impact.

Finally, remember that design elements such as tabs and bullets may not be preserved in e-mail at the receiving end. Instead, rely on double spacing between sections to frame your paragraphs with white space.

E-Mail Format

Standard e-mail format varies from organization to organization, and often from writer to writer. You have probably noticed differences in the following style categories:

- Forms of address—greetings and sign-offs
- Linguistic novelties—emoticons, jargon, and acronyms
- Punctuation and capitalization
- Spelling—conventional or "IM shorthand"
- Endings—thought of the day, slogans, images

Rules have emerged for e-mail style, or "netiquette," but they are often ignored. For instance, some writers begin an e-mail with a salutation or "Dear" line, despite the "To" line at the top. *Dear* was born about a thousand years ago, meaning "honorable, worthy," and took on the sense of "esteemed, valued" and "beloved." In the age of the quill pen, according to William Safire, an American book author and columnist who wrote about language use, *Dear* was used as a polite form of address for anyone—friends, business acquaintances, or strangers. Today's e-mails are as likely to begin with "Good afternoon," "Hello!" or "Hi—" as "Dear." Occasionally managers address multiple audiences as "All" or even "Folks."

Judith Martin, author of *Miss Manners' Guide to Excruciatingly Correct Behavior, Freshly Updated,* suggests that you may begin an e-mail "with almost anything civil. Or even nothing, because an e-mail is like a memo and doesn't require a salutation . . . . But that is presuming informality is understood not to be a euphemism for rudeness or sloppiness."[19] Good advice for e-mail writers, then, is to be courteous but concise. Overly formal formatting is as inappropriate as overly casual formatting.

Memo and E-Mail Uses

Memos and e-mails serve a variety of uses within an organization. We have listed the most common in the following subsections. You may see other practices where you work as well.

Communicating to Groups

Managers find memos and e-mail useful for communicating the same information to several individuals at once. The memo or e-mail not only saves time over talking, but it also ensures that each person has the same information.

Fixing Responsibility

The memo or e-mail can be a valuable management tool in other ways. For example, it can fix responsibility for actions. A manager who uses memos for giving assignments has a written record if questions of responsibility arise later.

Communicating with Opponents

Managers quickly learn to appreciate the memo and e-mail as a way of communicating with those they cannot get along with. Personal dislikes crop up in any organization from time to time, but memos and e-mails bridge the gaps that may ensue. The message gets delivered without bringing the two factions together. However, it is never appropriate to "flame" a reader with an emotion-packed e-mail. Remember the permanency of all memos, whether paper or electronic. Never write something you could not defend in a meeting or courtroom.

Communicating with the Inaccessible

Memos and e-mails are handy for dealing with people (especially supervisors) who are hard to reach. Those who are busy or absent can be reached by memo or e-mail, or increasingly by text message. A series of memos can also be proof of past attempts to contact a boss if problems arise.[20]

An example of a clear, concise, informative memo follows.

MEMORANDUM

TO: All Salaried Employees

FROM: Alan Reynolds, Director of Human Resources

DATE: October 3, 2010

SUBJECT: Changes in Payroll Practices

We've made a couple of changes in the payroll procedures to alleviate some of the bottlenecks that have delayed paychecks in the past few months.

1. Paychecks will no longer be mailed out. You will receive your check for the month on the last working day of that month. Direct deposits will still be made to your checking or savings account provided you use direct deposit for only one account.
2. All travel and expense reimbursements received before the 20th of each month will be included in that monthly paycheck. Requests for reimbursement will no longer be paid by individual checks as in the past. Of course, these expense reimbursements are not taxed.

These changes in payroll should help guarantee timely paychecks.

Types of Internal Correspondence

Memos and e-mails tend to fall into two groups: announcements and requests. Both these general types can be directed to large groups within a firm (especially announcements), and both can be directed to individuals.

Announcements

Announcements concern policy changes, meetings and conferences, new procedures, and personnel changes (including promotions). By nature, they are informative messages and follow the direct order strategy. Other types of notifications include status reports, such as progress and periodic reports. The informative memo appearing in the previous section is an example of an announcement.

The good-bye e-mail announcement has recently emerged as a new genre, due to massive layoffs. In 2008, more than 45 million Americans lost their jobs. Rather than notify colleagues by phone or memo, workers are sending blast e-mails. Some are understandably sad, angry, or bitter in tone, but experts warn that negativity in these permanent messages could hurt a job search. Donna Flagg, a New York business and management consultant, suggests staying professional and upbeat, simply announcing you're leaving and how to reach you. A good-bye e-mail can even help with the job search.[21]

Requests for Action

The nature of the request-for-action memo dictates its organization. When a manager requests action that typically falls under her jurisdiction, direct order is appropriate and the memo or e-mail begins with a clear subject line. When the requested action may meet with resistance, a less specific subject line and a more persuasive strategy (indirect order) are appropriate. Direct or indirect, these memos and e-mails often require listing steps and careful wording for successful action. Remember, concrete language is always preferable to vague expressions such as "please give your attention to this matter" and "reply at your earliest convenience" when requesting behavior change (see Chapter 4).

Political Uses in Business

Recall from the previous chapter that managers belong to a "discourse community" with unique characteristics and uses for their writing. The memo and e-mail are an example of a strategic tool for managers. In fulfilling their ostensible task of communicating announcements and requests for action within an organization, they are often put to other strategic uses. The uses are detailed next.

One political device is the copy list. Managers can protect themselves, publicize alliances, and show favor by including—and not including—certain people as a "cc:".

Another practice that is widely used is to write a memo or e-mail summarizing a meeting. While the message is ostensibly "for the record," its recording of the meeting or conversation can affect perceptions. The meeting minutes become the reality and may, for example, prove ownership of an idea.

Still another political tactic is to attach a cover memo to that of a colleague. If the original memo reflects poorly on the writer, the practice serves to offer another viewpoint.

Managers sometimes use memos to shape employees' opinions. A prominent example is Donald Rumsfeld. As secretary of defense from 2002 until his resignation in 2006, he composed some 20,000 memos and e-mails to his staff. That averages out to 20–60 per day. Rumsfeld poured out his thoughts about the Iraq War in the memos, often referred to as "snowflakes." He argued the need to "keep elevating the threat," "link Iraq to Iran," and develop "bumper sticker statements" to rally public support for the increasingly unpopular war.[22]

A valuable lesson for managers is that putting anything in writing makes it permanent. Think twice about how you commit yourself to paper or e-mail in controversial situations. "Routine" documents can have an important impact on a manager's effectiveness.

Summary

Letters, e-mails, and memos can benefit greatly from strategic considerations. However, they are frequently mere impersonal messages written automatically. One key consideration for audience adaptation in routine messages is the you attitude. The writer with this attitude projects himself into the reader's position and prepares messages to suit that reader.

The you attitude also influences the organization of ideas: Direct order is appropriate for good news and neutral information; indirect is for bad news messages and persuasive messages. Direct order places the main point first; indirect, later.

Common types of direct messages are the inquiry, the positive response to an inquiry, the claim, and the positive response to a claim.

Indirect messages include the negative response to an inquiry, the refused claim, and the persuasive message.

Negatives must be handled carefully in correspondence. A writer should de-emphasize the negative by using subordination, by avoiding terms such as *no* and *not*, and by avoiding negative wording or words with negative connotations. Apologies are a strategy that can improve a manager's and organization's image. They can also create the impression of guilt and liability.

Memos and their electronic equivalent, e-mails, are the most frequently used internal written communication. E-mails and memos are efficient, straightforward messages that require some strategic considerations in their writing. They have several uses for a manager, including communicating to groups, fixing responsibility, communicating with opponents, and communicating with the inaccessible. They fall into two categories: announcements and requests for action.

Memos and e-mails are frequently used in office politics.

Cases for Small Group Discussion

Case 5-1.

Claim Refusal Letter

You are the sales manager for a furniture manufacturer and have just received a strongly worded claim letter from Hyram Blalock, who owns a large hotel in a nearby city. Blalock has been refurbishing his hotel and had placed a special order with you for 115 headboards to fit specifications he sent.

He ordered headboards an inch and a half narrower than for conventional king-size beds. He also specified a finish different from that normally used in this grade of headboard. Finally, he wanted his hotel's logo imprinted on each headboard. You completed this order and shipped it to him about a week ago.

He ordered the mattresses directly from a manufacturer that has since gone out of business. They did, however, deliver his mattresses before going bankrupt, just a week before your headboards arrived. The problem is that all these mattresses were manufactured in the conventional dimensions, rather than the narrower ones for which the headboards were designed.

Blalock is asking you to take back the current shipment and either change the dimensions to fit the conventional mattresses or send a different set (which would, of course, have the finish he specified and his hotel's logo on them).

Obviously, you cannot comply with his request. Write an appropriate strategic claim refusal. The facts are on your side—he ordered the headboards in the size and finish that he received. However, the challenge is to tell him so without lecturing or using negatives. If you do choose to alter the headboards in the original order, feel free to do so—but be sure to charge him. Most importantly, you want to keep Blalock as a customer.

Case Note

This case tempts the writer to respond to Blalock with the same kind of letter he sent. Those using the appropriate indirect negative response will avoid lecturing to the reader as they remind him of his role in the problem. The suggested option (remodeling the headboards) is one strategy, but it should not be presented as if the writer feels guilty. If the letter suggests guilt, then the writer can expect more problems.

Case 5-2.

Inquiry Letter

You are the assistant human resource manager for an insurance company whose territory includes your state and three surrounding states. Your company has recently revamped its retirement and employment benefits packages, and you have been assigned the task of communicating these changes to all employees.

Since some of the changes are complex, you will be traveling to four sites in your region to meet with the company's agents and their personnel. You need to arrange hotel accommodations for the personnel at each of the sites, and you will need a meeting room with a screen and equipment for projecting your PowerPoint slide show. Since the company has had a very good year, management wants the employees to enjoy their stay at the hotels. So, you also need to inquire into the recreational and banquet facilities available.

Write a letter of inquiry to the Hotel Beacon in a major city in one of your surrounding states. The letter should elicit the information you will need to decide if the hotel is the right one for your meeting. Make it clear that you will be looking at other hotels, seeking the best rate for services required.

Case Note

The most common pitfall in this case will be the lack of clarity. The letter is actually more complex than it seems. The temptation for some will be to write a brief letter, which the hotel marketing manager will be unable to answer in proper detail. In addition to being thorough, the letter should also build goodwill, since the writer may be interested in doing more business in the future with the reader.

Case 5-3.

Request Refusal Letter

You are the administrative assistant to R. D. Spenser, president of Flo-Sheen Fabrics. Flo-Sheen employs over 300 people in its mill and corporate offices. Each year, these employees contribute generously to the city's annual fund-raising drive. Spenser also has developed a volunteer program that allows some employees to work on charitable projects on company time.

On your desk today, you found a letter that was sent to Spenser from a statewide youth organization requesting permission to conduct a fund-raising drive in your plant for a new project it is developing. The organization wants to establish a scholarship fund for its brightest members.

Spenser jotted a note at the bottom of the letter asking you to deny the request. Do so, but build up goodwill. Be positive, yet assertive; do not leave the organization wondering if the request is denied.

Case Note

Since the letter must build goodwill, the writer must use tact in denying the request. One option would be holding out the possibility of putting the youth organization on next year's list. But do not leave the reader feeling that another letter might get the results that the first one missed. The letter also needs to explain why the president of the company is not responding.

Endnotes

1. Gilbert C. Storms, "What Business School Graduates Say about the Writing They Do at Work," *Bulletin of the Association for Business Communication* XLVI, no. 4 (December 1983), pp. 13–18.
2. JoAnne Yates, "The Emergence of the Memo as a Managerial Genre," *Management Communication Quarterly* 2, no. 4 (May 1989), p. 486.
3. Mary K. Kirtz and Diana C. Reep, "A Survey of the Frequency, Types, and Importance of Writing Tasks in Four Career Areas," *Bulletin of the Association for Business Communication* 53, no. 4 (December 1990), pp. 3–4.

4. Edward Goodin and Skip Swerdlow, "The Current Quality of Written Correspondence: A Statistical Analysis of the Performance of 13 Industry and Organizational Categories," *Bulletin of the Association for Business Communication* L, no. 1 (March 1987), pp. 12–16.

5. Kitty O. Locker, "Factors in Reader Responses to Negative Letters: Experimental Evidence for Changing What We Teach," *Journal of Business and Technical Communication* 13, no. 1 (January 1999), pp. 5–48.

6. Stephen B. Knouse, "Confidentiality and the Letter of Recommendation," *Bulletin of the Association for Business Communication* L, no. 3 (September 1987), pp. 6–8.

7. Marlys Harris, "Gaining Through Complaining," *Money,* May 1982, pp. 174–75.

8. Lisa Tyler, "Liability Means Never Being Able to Say You're Sorry: Corporate Guilt, Legal Constraints, and Defensiveness in Corporate Communication," *Management Communication Quarterly* 11, no. 1 (August 1997), pp. 51–73.

9. Lindsey Tanner, "Doctor's 'Sorry' a Novel Approach in Healing Process," *Houston Chronicle,* November 12, 2004, p. A10.

10. Loren Steffy, "Southwest Shows Industry Importance of Sincerity," *Houston Chronicle,* April 6, 2007, pp. D1, D4.

11. Barbara Kellerman, "When Should a Leader Apologize—and When Not?" *Harvard Business Review,* April 2006, pp. 73–81.

12. *Ibid.,* p. 76.

13. Ameeta Patel and Lamar Reinsch, "Companies Can Apologize: Corporate Apologies and Legal Liability," *Business Communication Quarterly* 66, no. 1 (March 2003), pp. 9–25.

14. Mohan R. Limaye, "The Syntax of Persuasion: Two Business Letters of Request," *Journal of Business Communication* 20, no. 2 (Spring 1983), pp. 17–30.

15. Chadwick B. Hilton, William H. Motes, and John S. Fielden, "An Experimental Study of the Effects of Style and Organization on Reader Perceptions of Text," *Journal of Business Communication* 26, no. 3 (Summer 1989), pp. 255–70.

16. Jeanette Gilsdorf, "Write Me Your Best Case For . . .," *Bulletin of the Association for Business Communication* LIV, no. 1 (March 1991), pp. 7–12.

17. Marie E. Flatley, "A Comparative Analysis of the Written Communication of Managers at Various Organizational Levels in the Private Business Sector," *Journal of Business Communication* 19, no. 3 (Summer 1982), pp. 35–50.

18. Gerald J. Alred, Charles T. Brusaw, and Walter E. Oliu, *Business Writer's Handbook,* 8th ed. (New York: St. Martin's Press, 2006), p. 327.

19. William Safire, "To Whom It May Concern: Here's How to Address E-Mail," *Houston Chronicle,* October 22, 2006, p. E6.

20. Max Rose, "A Memorandum about Memos," *Supervisory Magazine,* March 1980, pp. 6–8.

21. Kelly Dinardo, "Laid-Off Workers Let E-Mails Fly," *Houston Chronicle,* March 6, 2009, p. A11.

22. Robin Wright, "Rumsfeld's Blunt Style on Display in 'Snowflakes,'" *Houston Chronicle,* November 1, 2007, p. A17.

Chapter **Six**

Management Reports and Proposals

No one who has read official documents needs to be told how easy it is to conceal the essential truth under the apparently candid and all-disclosing phrases of a voluminous and particularizing report.

—*Woodrow Wilson, 28th U.S. president*

Reports are among an organization's most important communication tools. They appear in a variety of forms, carry out a number of functions, and ensure the efficient transfer of data. Data transfer takes place within an organization and between an organization and its stakeholders. Managerial reports should be well organized and objective. They carry verifiable information that addresses some purpose or problem.

Evidence indicates the importance of reports in business is not likely to diminish soon. In one study of recent business graduates, 65.6 percent of respondents noted that they frequently wrote informational reports, while 31.3 percent replied that they sometimes wrote these reports. In the same study, 40.6 percent responded that they frequently wrote analytical reports and 43.8 percent replied that they sometimes wrote these reports.[1]

In another, larger study of recent business graduates (837 respondents), 74 percent either sometimes, often, or very often wrote short reports. In that same study, 42 percent of the respondents either sometimes, often, or very often wrote long reports.[2] Another researcher found that report writing in private-sector firms differed by level—middle-level managers write a bit less than lower-level managers, and upper-level managers write less than middle-level managers.[3]

Report audiences can be both internal and external to the organization. In their role as report writers, managers appreciate how internal reports can contribute to the management functions. Reports are essential to managers' ability to control organizational actions. Managers are required to plan, organize, execute, evaluate, and improve, and they need some medium for carrying out these tasks.

Internal reports are a means to those ends. While some internal reports depict current status or progress toward a goal, others convey the results of previous management decisions. Still others relay a manager's evaluation of results and performance and give suggestions (or orders) for change in current policies and procedures to bring about greater effectiveness and efficiency.

Managers also write reports to external audiences. For example, corporate annual reports are read by shareholders and other stakeholders. Government regulatory agencies often require companies to file reports periodically. Common to all these diverse report writing settings is that managers must have the know-how to approach problems, solve them, and communicate the findings to internal and external readers.

THE REPORT WRITING PROCESS

Typically, managers write reports for one of three reasons. The most common is simply that someone has asked them to. A higher-level manager who sees an area where information is lacking or a problem that needs solving will ask a subordinate to fill that gap or solve that problem. A report may also be part of a company's regular business. Thus, writing progress or periodic reports may be one of a manager's regular duties. Finally, a manager may write reports spontaneously, perhaps to fill gaps he has found on his own or to share information with the rest of the staff or to propose changes.

Groundwork

Of course, managers do not just sit down and write reports one after another. Typically, they must lay the groundwork for the report. The prewriting process mirrors "Stage One: Planning" of routine documents that is discussed in Chapter 4. This preliminary effort often takes more time than actually writing the report and can intimidate some writers.[4]

Defining the Problem or Objective

After accepting a report writing assignment, a manager must make sure the process leading up to the report will yield optimum results. The writer's time is valuable not only to the company but to the writer as well. Valuable hours spent following blind leads waste personal energy and resources.

First, the report writer must determine the problem under study or the objective. What does the person who authorized this report want from her effort? The problem may be nothing more than an information gap—someone needs data or demographics on sales, for example. The problem may also be one requiring analysis. Thus, the report writer must choose from among several options and recommend a plan of action.

Developing Recommendations

Once the problem and purpose have been determined, the next step before gathering data is to develop solutions or action items. The manager must analyze the need for change and determine the best plan for improvement. For example, productivity in a plant has dropped and a manager needs to determine the cause (or causes) and propose a solution. Possible causes might be raw material shortages, equipment malfunctions, abuse of sick leave, or a host of combinations.

Once these causes are analyzed, the researcher develops solutions and considers constraints such as resources and time frames in identifying the most reasonable plan.

Seeking Data

Once the manager has done the problem analysis and determined the information needed for the report, she gathers data to support her ideas. Most of the data needed for business reports are primary data—that is, data the writer collects from interviews, surveys, experiments, and observation. Occasionally, writers draw from secondary research data—in other words, material already published.

The next step is to gather and analyze the data. Finally, the manager transforms the results into a format that will clearly and easily be understood by the report readers. Supporting data must be carefully selected and described so they enhance the writer's purpose.

Classification of Reports

Knowing what form the final report will assume helps writers gauge the effort needed to prepare the report and thus helps in the budgeting of time and resources.

Various systems exist for cataloging groups of reports. Probably the most effective classification system is according to level of *formality*. This continuum starts with the most informal routine reports, which may resemble forms. The manager simply fills in several blank spaces and, in some cases, provides a brief narrative or description. Examples are the trip report, the expense report, and the attendance report.

Next on the formality continuum is the letter or memo report. Either of these may be several pages long (10-page letter reports are not unheard of). As explained in the preceding chapter, letter reports are addressed to external audiences, while memo reports go to internal audiences. Detailed descriptions of letter and memo reports are presented later in this chapter.

Next on the continuum, the report becomes more formal, and front matter appears. For example, the writer may precede a report with a transmittal document, title page, and table of contents. Back matter such as appendixes and glossaries may be added as well. Later in the chapter, we describe what goes into those elements of a formal report.

Another useful classification system for reports is according to their frequency. *Regularly scheduled* reports must be written at certain stages of a project or as the calendar dictates. Thus, a corporation produces annual reports, quarterly reports, monthly reports, even daily reports that are read by various audiences. On the other hand, a manager may perceive a unique need for a document. In these cases, one-time-only paperwork, known as *special* reports, might need to be composed. Problem analysis reports, proposals, and evaluations are the most common special reports that fall under the one-time-only umbrella. Problem analysis reports can be crucial for a company and are necessary when an issue becomes more complex and requires objective, unbiased facts. The goal is to define or clarify a problem and explore solutions.[5] Proposals suggest changes in organizational policies or procedures. They can be directed to internal or external audiences. Evaluations present assessments of how well or how poorly a current policy or procedure is working. Evaluation reports may trigger proposal reports.

Companies may classify special reports according to their level of formality. For example, an informal proposal might recommend staff changes, new product ideas or methods, and procedural or departmental changes. When proposals are more complex, and involve more time and money, a more formal approach is in order. Formal proposals are typically directed toward senior management and other companies. Although the key analysis and solution components of informal and formal proposals are similar, a few noticeable differences exist. Table 6-1 lists parts of the informal proposal and the formal proposal.[6]

As you can see from Table 6-1, the core parts of proposals are an analysis of the problem, a description of the solution, and a list of advantages or benefits of the proposed solution. As extra details or parts are added to the proposal, its classification evolves from informal to formal.

STRATEGIC CONSIDERATIONS

As with all other communications undertaken by managers, reports should reflect careful strategic decisions. These decisions fall into a number of areas, many of which are subtle but important.

Format

The format of a report is one of the report writer's careful strategic decisions. As we discussed in the previous section, generally the more significant the contents of the report, the more formal it is. Length also corresponds to formality, with

TABLE 6–1
Proposal
Formats

Informal	Formal
1. Introduction	1. Letter of transmittal
a. Problem	2. Title page
b. Solution	3. Executive summary/abstract
2. Analysis	4. Table of contents
a. Background	5. Body
b. Causes	a. Statement of problem
c. Scope, significance, implications	b. Proposed solution
3. Detailed solution	c. Facilities/equipment
a. Work and management	d. Personnel
b. Drawbacks	e. Schedule
c. Benefits	f. Costs
4. Action stimulus	g. Advantages/disadvantages
	6. Supporting materials

longer reports having a formal appearance. Several other factors that determine format are discussed next.

Audience

A report's intended audience guides, at least partially, the format and degree of formality. A manager preparing a report recommending the purchase of one component over another might choose memo form for the company controller but a short report form (with a title page) if the same report is to go to the chief executive officer. Just as we might dress more formally for an interview with the CEO than we might for subordinates, our reports similarly get more or less dressed up to match their readers.

Effort

Another significant factor in determining the report format is the amount of time spent researching and preparing the report. Usually related is the actual size of the report, which often reflects the effort expended. The report that requires a couple of phone calls and a half hour for the writing calls for less dressing up than does one resulting from several weeks of careful planning, the administration and evaluation of testing instruments, and several days of writing. The extra effort merits more formality.

Significance

We also must consider the value of the findings the report shares. Some findings are more important than others. For example, a report on options for a new janitorial service might conceivably reflect as much effort as one recommending a new product line. However, the significance of the second calls for a dressier treatment than that of the former.

The Original Assignment

A report writer should use any clues given in the initial assignment. It might be unwise to prepare a formal report if the original assignment from your manager was to "shoot me an e-mail when you've found the answer." If on another assignment that same manager indicated a different report might be forwarded to top management, you might give it a more formal treatment.

Precedent

Precedent is also relevant to the format a report will assume. A new manager is advised to learn what format is traditional for certain types of assignments. Many companies, such as ExxonMobil, Honeywell, and Accenture, specify guidelines. Precedent is especially relevant with periodic reports, which are expected to look like previous periodic reports.

Recently, some companies and government agencies have begun using graphics software such as MS PowerPoint as a report format. Considered by some managers to be simpler and more user-friendly than word processing software such as MS Word, graphics software will produce "decks" or "flipbooks" that include more text, data tables, and illustrations than are seen on traditional presentation slides and that can stand alone. On the other hand, this report format is more concise than traditional narrative reports because of space limitations. Best practices for PowerPoint report formats have yet to emerge, but they seem to fill the gap between sparse bulleted lists on presentation slides and long formal corporate reports.[7]

Arrangement of Points

Another strategic decision that report writers must make is the order of the information appearing in the report.

Direct Order

As the previous chapter showed, direct order puts the main point first, followed by the details. In routine messages conveying good news or neutral information, direct order is appropriate. Similarly, with short reports, when the reader is likely to agree with the writer's main point, direct order is often best.

Most readers receive reports neutrally, and since recommendations are needed for deciding on actions to take, the sooner a reader gets to them, the better. Direct order is especially appropriate when the reader trusts the writer's work. If the reader needs to check on any point, the specifics are in the text.

Indirect Order

Indirect order is often favored for long reports and proposals. The traditional inductive organizational pattern of introduction, body, and conclusion described in Chapter 5 is common for such reports. The indirect approach is unquestionably called for when a reader is likely to interpret the conclusions as bad news. Then, too, in analytic reports, proposals, or persuasive reports, when readers might disagree with the conclusions, the writer must lead the readers logically to the conclusions using indirect order.

Organization of the Body

Whether a writer uses direct or indirect order to arrange the ideas, the body of the report also needs organization. The body, the part that gives the reasons for the conclusions and recommendations, needs unifying elements to ensure that the material is in its clearest, most useful form.

The organizational plan chosen is situational and depends on the problem under study, the nature of the information being reported, and the reader's needs. The most common organizational plans are by time, place, quantity, and criteria (or factors). The plan chosen should be the one that moves the reader smoothly from the body's beginning to its end through a series of clearly interrelated parts.[8]

Time

Time organization is obviously appropriate for chronologically sequenced material. Any report that narrates events uses this pattern. For example, a quarterly report might have main divisions for each of the three months covered. Chronological organization works to the advantage of the writer since she can work either forward or backward through the time period being detailed. Once the writer chooses this order, questions about what comes next are easily resolved.

Place

Organization by place is more complex than is organization by time. This pattern would be appropriate for an activity report dealing with simultaneous but separate events (for example, a monthly report on the activities of several branch offices of a company). It is also appropriate for descriptive reports. Using spatial organization in complex reports dictates some order in which to proceed. Regions of the United States, for example, could be covered in a clockwise fashion.

Quantity/Size

Organization by quantity or size is another option that is relevant when the data lend themselves to quantification. For example, a report discussing a city's household characteristics might be best organized by the number of individuals per household or by the incomes of the household heads. A writer discussing cities might organize by population ranges. And sales reports might give information about the best-selling product first.

Criteria or Factors

The final category, organization by criteria or factors, is a catchall. It is also the most useful since it is so broad. Here, the report's body is organized by the relevant factors that led to the conclusions. In an informational report, these factors are the categories into which the information falls. For example, a report discussing the characteristics of a sales market that is largely homogeneous might deal with the income, age, education, and tastes of the market.

In an evaluative report, the conclusions and recommendations are based on a set of criteria or reasons on which a decision is based. For example, a writer may prepare a personnel report recommending the selection of a job candidate. He might divide the report by the optimum characteristics of an employee filling the position. Thus, an office assistant might be evaluated in terms of keyboarding skills, communication skills, and competence in office procedures.

Recommendation reports may also be organized by the alternative solutions available. Each major section of the proposal would describe an option in detail. For example, a report recommending the fleet purchase of a particular car might begin with an overview of criteria used, such as safety, comfort, financial considerations, and dependability. Then, each of three or four car models under consideration might be described. Finally, the features the reader needs to compare would be presented in one place. For example, the purchase prices would probably be presented on one page of the report. The report would conclude with a recommendation for the fleet purchase.

Headings

All business reports (not just formal ones) benefit from the use of headings. Headings indicate to the reader the relative degree of significance of the material that follows. Headings are also useful signposts to guide the reader through the report. They make the structure of the report explicit. And headings provide white space in reports, which contributes appreciably to their visual appeal, as mentioned in the preceding chapter. The following paragraphs offer guidelines for developing report headings.

Content

Write headings with the reader in mind. They should be descriptive of the content to follow but relatively short. Generally, seven words (or fewer) are appropriate for first-level headings, and even fewer than seven are usually needed for lower-level headings. Although single words and phrases are typical content headings, occasionally a question can serve as a heading. This format works especially well when the report is a response to an inquiry or a Request for Proposal (RFP) that included questions.

The report writer can choose from a variety of heading systems. The heading system described next and shown in Figure 6–1 is suitable for most needs.

First-Level Headings

The first-level heading is used for all major divisions of the report, including headings for some prefatory parts (executive summary, table of contents), the introduction, the major divisions of the body of the report, and the closing sections. To indicate its major importance, it may be centered, bold, in a larger font, or all uppercase. When reports are double-spaced, first-level headings will sometimes be triple-spaced from the text. The writer may choose any variation but must apply it consistently throughout the report.

Second-Level Headings

The second-level heading indicates material subordinate to the main divisions of the report. These headings are often left-justified, bold, and in upper- and lowercase. The text begins one or two spaces below the heading. The sample report at the end of this chapter provides examples of first- and second-level headings.

FIGURE 6–1
Report
Headings
Style Sample

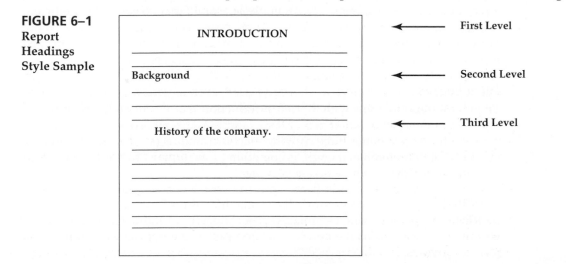

Third-Level Headings

Generally, the third-level heading is as far as a report needs to be divided. The writer might indent the heading, bold it, and capitalize the initial letter of only the first word (unless proper nouns appear in the heading). Often, the writer will follow the heading by a period and continue the text on the same line after skipping two spaces.

Transitions

Use other transitional devices besides headings. In moving from one major section to another, a writer should summarize the previous section and preview the next to show the change. In moving from one subsection to another, a brief sentence should signal the shift and help the reader see the flow of ideas. A good rule for judging transitions is to see if the text reads well without the headings. If it does, then the reader is not likely to become lost or confused in working through the text.

Now that we have discussed strategic decisions on format, arrangement of points, organization, headings, and transitions, we are ready to talk about the content of some of the more common types of business reports: memo reports, letter reports, and formal reports.

MEMO AND LETTER REPORTS

The first specific types of reports we examine are memo and letter reports. They fall toward the informal side of the formal-to-informal continuum for business reports. More and more often short reports are delivered electronically, perhaps as e-mail attachments, rather than as paper documents. Whether hard copy or electronic, they should follow these guidelines.

Memo Reports

In addition to being the most informal type of report used within an organization, memos are efficient and suggest a no-nonsense approach. They invariably have some form of headings—*To, From, Subject,* and *Date*—at the top for efficient routing and a quick understanding of purpose. The comments made about *Subject* lines in the previous chapter apply here as well. In an indirectly ordered report, the *Subject* line should not give away the conclusions.

Introduction

The memo report begins with a brief introduction that usually tells the purpose of the report and who authorized it. For example, "This report, which you authorized on June 8, evaluates three copying machines and recommends the purchase of one." Often preferable, though, is something less formal: "Recently, you asked me to look into the purchase of a new copier."

It is also appropriate to indicate how the writer derived the information: "I called sales representatives from three manufacturers," or "I examined sales materials supplied by three companies." A statement of the scope—that is, how widely the research into the problem ranged—is appropriate as well, although it is often obvious.

Close to the beginning, a direct report indicates the conclusions and/or recommendations reached in the report. In the example on copiers, the writer using direct order might end the first paragraph with her choice of copier.

Body

Whether the overall report uses direct or indirect order, the body of a memo report details the findings that led the writer to the conclusions the report makes. For the sake of efficiency, headings often set off this material. Either centered or left-justified, these headings guide the reader through the contents; he can tell at a glance what a given section discusses.

The list is another highly appropriate organizational tool in the memo report. The writer must introduce the list, but that introduction is often no more than a sentence. Lists help to cut down on prose, and their simplicity can improve reader comprehension and retention of the material. To maximize reader comprehension, lists should be constructed in parallel grammatical form. For example, in the report on copiers, the writer might state the following:

My evaluation of the copiers sought to determine four things about each unit:

- Use of energy
- Cost of operation
- Speed of operation
- Frequency of repairs

Writers must be careful not to let the memo degenerate into a mere catalog of lists. The report needs to be efficient without being an outline or series of phrases.

In a memo report, a manager may also choose to use visual aids (discussed later in this chapter) to help the reader identify key ideas and supporting material.

Closing

The end of a memo report needs planning. If the report uses indirect order, the last paragraph will give the conclusions and recommendations reached. On the other hand, a report using direct order easily ends on the last point. The writer might wish to introduce the last paragraph with some transitional device that indicates the approaching end: "Finally, I evaluated the ease of operation of the copiers. I found . . ." Often this transition is enough to signal the end.

Letter Reports

The letter report is similar to the memo report, but three essential differences exist: form, tone, and audience.

The differences in form are products of necessity (the inside address, for example) and convention (the salutation and complimentary close). The inside address is necessary because the report is to be sent to someone outside the organization (as opposed to the memo, which is delivered within the organization).

A more subtle difference between the two is tone. Since the letter report goes to a reader outside the organization, it is a tool for building goodwill, and goodwill means increased business. Thus, the letter report stresses reader benefits more than the memo report and is likely to close with a goodwill statement that promises continued cooperation.

Organization

The letter report may use direct or indirect order, although most prefer indirect order because the reader's reaction might be difficult to gauge at a distance. When the findings are unquestionably positive, direct order is advisable. In these cases, a clear *Subject* line can orient the reader to the nature of the problem and solution addressed in the letter report.

Introduction

Like the memo report, the letter report needs a brief introduction. The opening acquaints the reader with the purpose. Often, the purpose and authorization (or reference to the request being granted) can appear in a single sentence. For example, "As you requested in your letter last week, here is a report on our experiences with Ace Maintenance Service." If appropriate, the scope of the report and the methodology used for developing the details can be included, although these may be clear from the discussion.

Body

The letter report has no set length, and it is not unheard of for such a report to reach eight to ten pages.

Headings are appropriate in a letter report, especially a long report, since they quickly guide the reader to whatever sections might be of special interest. Since managers write some letter reports in response to a series of questions submitted by the reader, the headings can reflect those questions. As with memo reports, bulleted lists are appropriate for the letter report.

Closing

If conclusions and recommendations are reserved for the end of the report, they precede the last short paragraph. The last paragraph of a letter report is a statement of goodwill. Readers appreciate the writer's personal involvement, and writers appreciate an opportunity to close on a positive note, procuring the likelihood of future business transactions.

The final type of report to be examined here is the formal report. Though we will review all the elements of long, formal reports, not every element will appear in every report. Remember that as reports get longer, they tend to pick up the trappings of formality.

ELEMENTS OF THE FORMAL REPORT

Though you may not often write long, formal reports, when the situation arises, you'll want the report to look right. Formal reports are delivered as paper documents more often than in electronic form, whether sent to internal or external audiences. In the next sections, we will first discuss front matter, then review parts of the report proper, and finally describe back matter. (See Table 6–2.)

TABLE 6–2
Formal Report Elements

Front Matter	Report Proper	Back Matter
Title page	Introduction	References
Transmittal document	Body	Bibliography
Table of contents	Summary	Appendixes
List of illustrations	Conclusions	
Executive summary	Recommendations	

Front Matter

These parts come before the report itself. They tend to be directly associated with report length and formality. The longer and more formal a report is, the more front matter it is likely to have. Each element appears on a separate page.

Title Page

The title page is the first page for most formal reports. Generally, it consists of four main components: the title, the complete identifications of the reader and the writer, and the date. In constructing the report title, the writer should strive to make it a concise but complete description of the report's purpose and topic. Because of their charge of completeness, titles of business reports tend to be longer than titles of other literary works.

The complete identification of the reader and writer includes the person's name, position, organization, city, state, and (if needed) country. The identifying blocks of information are generally preceded by expressions such as "presented to" or "prepared for" and "prepared by." If the organization and/or location are the same for the reader and writer (internal reports), they may be omitted. These blocks of information should be spaced evenly down the page and laterally centered. See the sample report at the end of this chapter for a model title page.

Transmittal Document

The transmittal memo or letter is the next item found in most formal reports (although some writers actually clip it to the cover of the report). Internal reports get a transmittal memo; external reports get a transmittal letter. Generally, it replaces the conversation the writer would have with the reader if the report were being handed over in person.

The first paragraph serves three purposes. First, it announces the accompanying report with wording like "Here is the report . . ." It also briefly states the nature of the report and mentions authorization details. Note that all three purposes might be accomplished in one sentence, as in "Here is the report on cost-cutting options you requested in your memo of July 10."

The content of the transmittal's body may vary with the circumstances. Generally, it is viewed as an opportunity to motivate the reader to read, interpret, and use the report. Also, the writer might wish to acknowledge people who helped her do the research and compile the report. To keep the transmittal short, do not summarize the report here. That function is served by the executive summary.

Typically, the transmittal closes with a call to action ("After reading the report, please call me") and a goodwill gesture. It thanks the recipient for the assignment and looks forward to continued service. To some, the idea of thanking someone for giving them work might sound strange. Such skeptics should remember that report writing assignments present chances to showcase analytical abilities and communication skills—abilities and skills that might be carefully viewed and valued when promotional opportunities arise.

Table of Contents

The table of contents follows the transmittal document. Contemporary word processing software has a feature that allows automatic creation of the table of contents, following the order of headings and subheadings in the text. The real value of the table of contents is that it displays all the report sections at a glance and refers the reader to the page number of a section of particular interest.

If you must create the table of contents by hand, be sure the entries use wording identical to that in the text. Also, to connect an entry to its page number, use leader dots (made by alternating periods and spaces on the line, aligned for all the entries). The page numbers should have their right digits aligned.

List of Illustrations

The list of tables and figures is an optional feature appropriate to a report with five or more visual aids, such as a technical report. If needed, and if there is room, the list begins several spaces below the end of the table of contents. It is titled "List of Illustrations" and is set up like the table of contents. Most report writers divide the list into tables and figures. The table or figure number is followed by its title and is separated from its page number by leader dots.

Executive Summary

The next prefatory element found in formal reports is the executive summary. Also called the epitome, abstract, brief, digest, or synopsis, it provides a quick overview of the report.[9] Managers are often interested only in a report's highlights. They will use the executive summary as a replacement for the report. The challenge is to shrink the report down to its major facts, analyses, and conclusions, including everything that is key, while keeping it to about one-tenth the length of the report. The easiest way to accomplish this task is to first write the entire report; then go through it and highlight the key statements, generalizations, and topic sentences. Typically, they appear at the beginning of each section and paragraph. Then, just transfer the key statements to a fresh file or page, in the same order that they appear in the report. After polishing, this list of the report's highlights turns into the executive summary. See the sample report at the end of this chapter for a model executive summary.

The Report Proper

The report proper begins with an introduction, presents all the information, and ends with the conclusions and/or recommendations. The following paragraphs detail the content of the various parts of the report proper.

Introduction—Required Elements

The first page of the body of the formal report contains the introduction, which should be identified as such with a first-level heading. The introduction contains a number of elements, some of which are required and some of which are optional. No rule sets the order in which the elements may occur, although the order in which they are discussed in the paragraphs that follow is appropriate for most circumstances.

Every introduction should include the purpose of the report. Generally, the purpose statement indicates the problem addressed in the report.[10] You can state the purpose as simply as "The purpose of this report is to . . ." or "This report recommends a new procedure for . . ."

Another element necessary to most reports is the authorization. It can usually be stated quite simply, as in "This report, which you requested on December 10, is . . ." or "This report, which Mr. Bruce Ferrin authorized on March 5, shows why . . ." The authorization is valuable because it establishes a clear chain of responsibility. The authorization justifies the time, effort, and resources that went into the preparation of the report. The only time it is not needed is when the writer developed the report on her own.

A statement of methodology must be included in report introductions. Readers want to know how a writer found the data because knowing that may indicate the degree of authority the contents possess. If the material was previously published, it is called secondary research. But if the data were the result of primary research, the writer should describe the technique used (surveys, interviews, observations) in sufficient detail to allow the reader to judge the quality of the research.

The last necessary item, and almost always the last item in an introduction, is the plan of development in which the writer tells the reader how the body of the report is organized. This invaluable element of the introduction signals a major transition and sets the order of the report's ideas firmly in the reader's mind. The plan of development is usually quite simply written: "This report first . . . then . . . and finally . . ." The report then must follow the precise order set out in the plan of development.

Introduction—Optional Elements

The introduction also might include other elements, depending on the reader's and writer's needs. For example, a statement of limitations details external factors that may have limited the range of exploration in developing the report. The most typical constraint is fiscal; report writers often work on limited budgets that prohibit extensive travel or detailed samplings of populations. Time is another common limitation. Deadlines often limit the depth in which you might research a problem.

Another optional element of the introduction is the scope. In preparing a scope statement, a writer might ask herself what the reader might reasonably expect in such a report. If any inconsistency exists between these expectations and the report content, the writer would delineate briefly those areas that are and are not covered. For example, in the scope statement for a report recommending a new plant site, the writer might note that the report covers only the top four sites and that architectural and engineering details are available elsewhere.

Definitions are another element required in some introductions. If several key terms used throughout the report are unfamiliar to the reader, they should be defined in the introduction. On the other hand, if only a few unfamiliar words are used a few times, they should be defined the first time they appear in the text. If numerous terms need defining, a glossary should be used.

Sometimes circumstances call for a brief statement about the background of the report problem. Some writers detail background in the introduction; others put it into the report. A short background statement fits better as part of the introduction than as a main section of the body.

Body

The body of the report follows the introduction. Since most proposals are set up using indirect order, the conclusions and recommendations appear at the very end of the report proper (but before any appendixes). If the report is informational or nonsensitive, it is written using direct order; those conclusions and recommendations will appear right after the introduction.

The information in the body of a formal report is usually set off using some sort of heading system, either that described earlier in this chapter or some other. Remember that a heading is not usually enough of a transition. If necessary, repeat the information in the heading as part of the transition into that section.

The body of the report should be clearly organized, using one or more of the bases of organization discussed earlier. It should also be coherent, allowing the reader to move smoothly from one part to another. Appropriate transitions will connect the major and minor parts of the report.

The report body should employ the right degree of objectivity. Generally, persuasive reports, such as proposals to potential clients, are not as coldly objective as informational and analytical reports. In all reports, however, writers need to distinguish between facts and inferences. Assumptions and inferences need to be recognized with words like "Assuming that . . ." and "The figures suggest that . . ." One assumption or inference treated as a fact could jeopardize the credibility of the entire report.

The report body should also use the correct time perspective. The time perspective deals with the tense used in presenting the report's findings and in making cross-references to other parts of the report. Present tense is suitable when the data are current, as in the case of a recent survey. The finding might be presented as follows: "Fully 68 percent of our employees *believe* that their benefits are adequate." Using this perspective, a writer would also use the present tense to cross-reference other parts of the report: "Table II, in the previous (or next) section, *presents* the responses to questions 4, 5, and 6 of the questionnaire."

When the data are not current, as in the case of secondary research referencing studies that are years old, the past tense is appropriate. For example, "In the Gifford study, 51 percent of the respondents *reported* dissatisfaction with their benefits." For consistency, the writer uses the past tense in referring to earlier parts of the report and the future tense in referring to parts of the report yet to come.

informational=
summary

analytical=
conclusion

Summary, Conclusions, and/or Recommendations

The final elements in most formal reports are the summary, conclusions, and/or recommendations. An informational report ends with just a *summary* of the main points in the report body. An analytical report might end with a conclusion or with a conclusions and recommendations section. A proposal ends with a separate recommendations section.

The *conclusions* section does nothing more than list the results of the writer's analysis. If he were researching alternative sites for a new plant, he might conclude that site A is the least expensive and the most accessible, whereas site B is the largest, closest, and safest for the company's needs.

Recommendations move a step beyond. To prepare recommendations, the writer must make a decision about the problem. Occasionally, the person authorizing the report may want conclusions but not recommendations—that is, she may want to know the results of the investigation, but she may want to reserve the decision making for herself.

The conclusions should not introduce any new material; the report body should support all conclusions. Of course, the recommendations will be new material, but they should arise from the conclusions. The evidence should not point in one direction while the conclusions point in the other.

The direct order formal report contains the conclusions and recommendations at the beginning of the report. A summary is an appropriate ending for this kind of report, or one might begin the final section with some kind of statement that makes it clear it is the last section of the report.

Back Matter

Back matter is optional. Many formal reports are complete without attachments at the end. However, under certain circumstances the writer may choose to add one or more of the parts described next.

References/Bibliography

If secondary research was used to compose the report, and if intended readers may want to trace back the information to its original sources, then a references list may be called for. Sometimes labeled "Works Cited," the references section lists just that. Further, the writer may add a bibliography of relevant sources that the reader may find useful. A standard bibliographic format should be followed for both lists. The key for determining how much information to include in a citation is that the source must be recoverable.

Appendixes

Supplemental material should be added to formal reports as appendixes. Examples of such material are tables of financial data, graphs, work samples, pictures, interview transcriptions, survey results, and mockups. In short, if the writer feels that a reader may want to look at more information, but that information does not fit into the report proper because it is too lengthy or detailed or would disrupt the continuity, then this information should be presented in appendixes.

Appendix format conventions are as follows: Each table, chart, or other type of information should appear as a separate appendix, numbered and titled, on a separate page. Page numbering for the report proper should continue through the appendixes. If the report has a table of contents, the appendixes should be included in it.

The sample report at the end of this chapter provides a model of the parts discussed thus far. The last section of this chapter reviews the common types of visual aids found in business reports and guidelines for their most effective use.

VISUAL AIDS

Visual aids are a common, very effective means of clarifying trends and relationships that are not easily understood in verbal form. The great majority of the research done on visual aids shows that tables and graphics can boost the comprehension of material.[11]

Visual aids can appear in a report of any length or level of formality, but they are most likely to be used in formal reports. They can be incorporated into the report proper or attached as back matter. Visual aids take a number of forms including tables, line graphs, bar charts, pie charts, and pictographs. The choice a report writer makes depends on the nature of the material under discussion and on the audience.

Audience adaptation can best be explained by placing visuals on a continuum that ranges from dramatic to informational. In general, less sophisticated audiences and those not familiar with the workings of a business will appreciate dramatic visual aids. Thus, a pictograph might be effective in an annual report comparing a company's production figures for the past three years. A glass company might use small drawings of bottles to represent millions of units produced. While such a dramatic visual aid gives a clear idea of any significant rise or fall in production, it may not accurately portray smaller changes. The fractions of a bottle needed to represent fractions of a million are difficult to interpret precisely. The exact quantities or percentages can be added to the side to increase the informational impact.

On the other hand, a formal report submitted to upper-level management would use visual aids fitting the readers' need for precise data. For example, a comparison of several years of production figures broken down by products might appear in a table. A table, while providing large quantities of information, has very little dramatic impact. The reader has to analyze the data and even after that may see little that is dramatic.

Midway on the continuum between dramatic and informative visual aids is the line graph, which can emphatically show trends. Using this graphic aid, readers can easily determine what specific production rate, interest rate, or income the graph is charting. They simply read across to the scale representing the amount.

General Rules

Several general rules apply to all visual aids. By following them, report writers create visual aids that are clear and strategically suited to their readers.

Appropriateness

First, visual aids should add value to the section of the report in which they appear. The data they contain or symbolize should complement the text without duplicating it. The visual aid that merely repeats what the text has shown belongs in an appendix rather than in the report proper, which it merely clutters. Additionally, the type of visual aid chosen should be suited to the data being portrayed.

Reference and Placement

Second, when using visual aids, writers should always refer to them in the text. The best approach is to refer to the visual aid just before it appears. This reference can be as simple as "see Table 1" in parentheses. Keep the visual as close as possible to the relevant narrative. If the writer decides to put the visual into an appendix, the reference will be "see Appendix 3" or something similar.

Content

Third, the content of the visual aid needs to relate closely to the current discussion. Do not try to pack too much data into a single chart or graph. Some of the data may apply to later sections of the report and may be used more appropriately at two or more points in the report.

Related to the need for relevancy is the need for simplicity. Strive to keep visuals—especially bar graphs, pie charts, and line drawings—simple. The content should unambiguously reflect the discussion. The use of abbreviations and standard symbols is also advisable for simplifying complex visuals. While symbols are usually not appropriate in the text, the need for compactness in visual aids calls for such special references. A writer needs to make sure, however, that the reader understands the symbols and abbreviations used by including a legend.

Conventions

Several conventions apply to visual aids. For one, writers have traditionally distinguished between tables and figures in reports, with figures being considered all types of visual aids other than a table. A related convention has tables and figures being counted as two separate series in a report. Thus, a report containing three tables and four figures would label them as follows: Table 1, Figure 1, Table 2, Table 3, Figure 2, Figure 3, Figure 4.

A third convention calls for the titles of tables and figures to reflect the data included. In constructing the titles of visual aids, writers should keep two goals in mind: conciseness and completeness. In as few words as possible, a title should describe the information the visual conveys. Thus, a line graph comparing employees' level of job satisfaction to length of time on the job would be titled "Satisfaction by longevity."

The following paragraphs examine the visuals most commonly used in business reports: pie charts, bar charts, line graphs, and tables.

Pie Charts

Pie charts are useful for showing proportional amounts of a unit. Their division into wedges representing the proportions makes a dramatic impact on a reader, but only when the differences are great enough to visibly affect the sizes of the divisions. The wedges represent percentages, so the "pie" must add up to 100 percent. In business reports, pie charts are properly used to illustrate the distribution of a budget or sources of income for a fiscal year. But they will not show trends or groupings that represent less than the entire population of interest. Figure 6–2 illustrates a typical pie chart. The sample report at the end of this chapter also includes a pie chart.

Bar Charts

The pie chart is very useful for symbolizing parts of one whole, but it is not good for comparing one total and/or its components with another. With the naked eye, it is difficult to judge the relative size of two more circles and/or their wedges placed side by side. The bar chart is more suited to that need.

The bar chart, in its simplest form, is useful for comparing units at one point in time. The bar chart should be constructed with the bars positioned either horizontally or vertically (generally the latter). The axis from which the bars rise identifies the units, and the opposite axis measures quantity.

The more complex stacked bar chart can compare totals as well as components of totals. The stacked bar chart is one in which each bar (which represents a total) is subdivided into its component parts. This graph is handy for comparing totals and subparts of totals.

To show the composition of new car sales for a given year, a writer could draw one bar representing the total new car sales, and then divide it with each division representing one company. Clearly, this visual aid is preferable to a pie chart for comparisons. The total differences would be easier to judge from a bar than from a circle, and components would be easier to compare as rectangles than as slices of pies. Figure 6–3 illustrates a typical stacked bar chart.

FIGURE 6–2
A Sample Pie Chart

Distribution of 2010 Sales Income XYZ Corporation

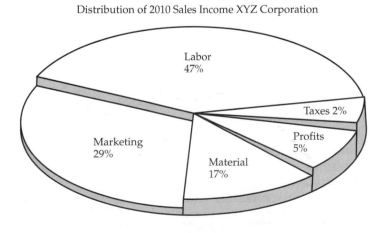

FIGURE 6–3
Sample
Stacked Bar
Chart

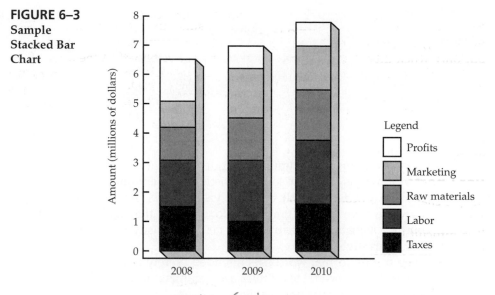

Line Graphs Δ over time

The line graph represents a balance between informational and dramatic impact. It conveys change over time, including overall changes and specific dates and amounts. The line graph also allows the reader to compare changes of several factors. You can plot several lines (up to four) within a single graph with each representing a different product or factor. Line graphs must represent information accurately. The scales chosen for a graph should be consistent. Graphs should not be manipulated to skew the facts. For example, a line graph showing yearly sales must not change the scale from years to months at a given point in order to de-emphasize a decline. (See Figure 6–4 for a typical multiple line graph.)

FIGURE 6–4
Sample Line
Graph

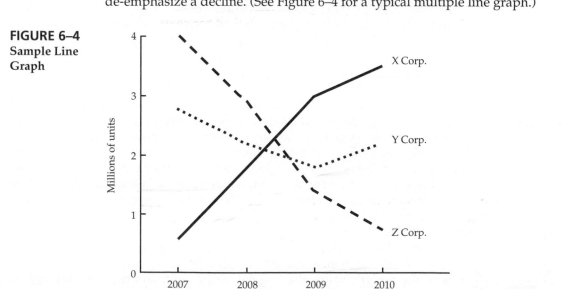

TABLE 6–3
Sample Table

Product	Year		
	2008	2009	2010
Heaters	632	716	805
Bread makers	231	367	592
Indoor grills	114	298	613

Tables

Tables are very useful visual communication devices that arrange data in a concise manner to allow easy comparison of statistics. As mentioned earlier, they are informational and not as dramatic as other visual aids. They do not showcase trends or carry the credibility of graphs.[12] Nonetheless, they assist the reader in grasping complex statistical or factual data far more easily than if the material appeared in the narrative.

Tables range from informal word lists intended merely to aid comprehension, to complex formal reference tables. Tables are organized into columns and rows. Several rules apply to constructing a table:

- Identify each reference table with a title and number (and source notation, if appropriate).
- Use the left-hand vertical column, the stub, to list items detailed in the horizontal rows to the right. This row head defines its subject.
- Use the column headings (listed horizontally across the top) to indicate the material in each vertical column below them.
- Use rulings if necessary to set off column heads and stubs, but not so many that the table is cluttered.
- Use abbreviations and symbols where appropriate.
- Align figures on the decimal points; right-align figures with no decimals.
- Keep the tables as simple and uncluttered as possible, leaving adequate white space.

Table 6–3 illustrates a typical table.

Summary

Reports are among an organization's most important communications and help managers plan, organize, execute, evaluate, and improve an organization. They can address internal or external audiences. Managers write these reports because they have been assigned to do so or because they themselves see a need for one. In preparing to write a report, a writer must first define the problem to be addressed. Then, if the report is analytical, he must conduct research and determine a likely solution.

Reports can be classified according to their level of formality or according to their frequency. How formal or informal a report is depends on several strategic considerations: the audience, the effort expended on researching and writing the report, the report's value, the original assignment, and the company policy.

Reports can also be classified as regular (occurring every so often) or one-time-only (under special circumstances). Examples of special reports include analysis reports, proposals, and evaluations.

The order of ideas chosen for a report is significant. Direct order is appropriate for good news or neutral information. It places the main conclusions and recommendations at the beginning of the report. Indirect order, best for reports delivering bad news and proposals, puts the main points last. The material within the body may be organized by time, place, quantity, and factors.

Headings guide the reader through the report. The appearance and placement of the headings indicate the relative significance of the material they cover. Transitions such as internal summaries are another tool for broadcasting a report's structure.

The memo report is the most common informal report within an organization. The contents can be set off using headings, as necessary. Letter reports are similar but are intended for audiences outside the organization. They also usually attempt to build goodwill, a characteristic that is not as significant with memo reports.

The formal report, whether sent to internal or external audiences, typically consists of front matter, the report proper, and back matter. Front matter may include the title page, transmittal document, table of contents, list of illustrations, and executive summary. Usually, the longer and more formal the report, the more front matter it includes. The report proper includes the introduction, the major subdivisions that make up the report body, and the closing sections made up of summary, conclusions, and/or recommendations. Back matter contains supplemental information that does not readily fit into the report proper—usually a list of references and/or appendixes.

Visual aids may appear in the report proper or as appendixes. They exist on a continuum ranging from dramatic to informational. The choice of visual aids depends on the audience. The visual aids should be appropriate to the text and placed close to the first reference or as an attachment. Pie charts are useful for showing parts of a whole. Although largely dramatic, their informational impact can be enhanced. Bar charts are also dramatic, but they can clearly represent information as well. The stacked bar chart is particularly useful for making proportional comparisons between (or among) different units. The line graph shows change over time. It is both informational and dramatic, but it must be constructed with care to be accurate. Tables are not as dramatic as other visual aids, but they still make their content much easier to understand than the same information presented in narrative form.

COMMUNICATION AUDIT REPORT

Prepared for
Jeff Walters, Executive Vice President

Prepared by
Kim Jacko, Senior Vice President

November 4, 2009

EXECUTIVE SUMMARY

During October 2009, I conducted a survey on communication effectiveness between the district managers and the regional managers of our company. The survey was designed to identify areas that are lacking and gather input on improvements.

District managers throughout the state were invited to participate in the survey. Secondary data regarding effective communication were obtained from business articles and books.

My research revealed the following:

- E-mail is the communication method preferred by regional operations managers and regional sales managers.
- Meetings with both regional managers are harmed by tardiness, repetitive conversation, and lack of planning/agendas.

The frequency of face-to-face meetings between district managers and their regional managers needs to be increased.

Recommendations for improvement are:

- Do not use e-mail as a substitute for face-to-face communication.
- Provide regional managers with periodic business communication training.
- Require formal agendas and time constraints to be set to enhance meeting productivity.
- Require more frequent face-to-face meetings.
- Make the regional managers accountable for correcting miscommunications.
- Develop standards for what must be communicated to both regional managers and what can be reported to one.
- Expect regional managers to report pertinent information to each other.

INTRODUCTION

The quality and consistency of communication of supervisors with their direct reports is vital to the success of any organization. In the case of our company, district managers must communicate with two supervisors and the two supervisors must routinely communicate with one another. Each of the supervisors has a different focus. Efficiency and clarity of communication often suffer in this environment.

You are very familiar with the difficulties our organizational structure poses in regard to communication. This report evaluates the current model and includes my recommendations to improve communication between regional operations and sales manager partners and their district manager direct reports.

My primary data were collected via an electronic survey of 18 district managers statewide. I also incorporated my personal observations from my prior role as a regional manager and my current role supervising the regional operations managers. I used an Internet article and a book as secondary resources.

In the report, you will find general information about the benefits and pitfalls of current communication practices, including e-mail usage, various meeting forms, phone calls, and text messages. Finally, you will note my recommendations for improvement to overall communication.

E-MAIL

Regional managers and district managers employ various types of communication vehicles, but e-mail is used most frequently. While this is an efficient way to communicate to multiple parties, it is not always the right choice.

From Regional Manager to District Manager

E-mail is overwhelmingly the mode of communication used between regional and district managers. When asked, it was the district managers' preferred method to receive information from their regional managers. Although the district managers do not have a dedicated work computer, they have access to Webmail and centralized district manager workstations. Many reported their Treo phone/multimedia equipment has been very useful.

Most messages are sent via e-mail in the interest of time and dual notification to individual district managers. Messages are easier to deliver to two busy people via e-mail. The "courtesy copy" to a regional partner is standard practice. Communicating with two busy people verbally by phone or in person is generally more complicated. However, the nonroutine or time-sensitive messages would often be better delivered face-to-face or by phone.

The district managers also receive information as regional groups from their regional managers. The nonroutine nature of some of these e-mails has the same complications as e-mails received individually. "When your message is sensitive or contains an emotional component, no communication channel is superior to being there" (Deep & Sussman, 1995, p. 70).

Providing the regional managers with periodic training on the importance of choosing the appropriate communication method would keep their perspective fresh and improve the quality of communication received by the district managers.

From District Manager to Regional Manager

The district managers' preference to receive communication by e-mail matches their preference to use e-mail to communicate upward. The same underlying reasons apply—time and dual notification.

District managers often use e-mail to clarify conflicting directives they receive. If one boss tells them something contradictory to the other, e-mail is an effective way to ask both simultaneously for a consistent answer. The responsibility of sorting out the conflict then rests on the regional manager team.

MEETINGS

Meetings can be an extremely effective way to communicate goals, disseminate information, and solve problems. The district managers attend various types of meetings involving their regional managers: conference calls, face-to-face with their region's team, and individual meetings with each boss or both bosses. These meetings are discussed in the following.

Conference Calls

Regional managers generally meet with their district manager groups on conference calls. Some of them meet weekly and some bimonthly. While these meetings are seen as necessary and generally productive, improvement is possible.

These meetings are reportedly plagued by tardiness, repetitive topics, and a lack of proper planning. This creates "wasted time and deflated energy for the participants, not to mention a culture of meeting-dread" (Walters, 2003, January). Therefore, corrective action should be taken. Primarily, setting an agenda and following it would alleviate most of these shortcomings. The agenda would establish a time frame, ensure relevant topics are covered, and encourage preparedness, if published in advance.

Regional Meetings

These meetings have some of the same challenges as the conference calls. Formalized agendas would have the greatest positive impact.

The frequency of these meetings is another area to be considered. Most district managers surveyed felt they needed more face-to-face interaction with their direct superiors. The majority felt that monthly face-to-face meetings would be helpful. Instituting a monthly standard for all regional managers to follow would aid all of the regional teams.

Interpersonal Managerial Communication

District managers meet with one boss or with both depending on what is needed. Many district managers felt they would benefit from increased contact with regional management.

Any time there is communication with one regional manager without the other present, an additional burden is placed on the district manager to tell any issues discussed to the absent regional manager. The district managers need to be able to report issues to one manager without fear of conflict with the other regional manager. The regional managers should communicate with one another to reduce the bureaucracy their more hands-on direct reports shoulder now.

Additionally, standards of "who to tell what" could be instituted. If a district manager is meeting with his operations manager, there should be certain topics that are clearly her responsibility—for example, teller outages. The regional operations manager could then be responsible for notifying the regional sales manager, if necessary.

PHONE CALLS

Phone communication is typically used when there is a time-sensitive issue. Some regional managers call their district managers individually each day to stay connected. The phone is a vital communication link for regional teams who are all geographically divided.

One Regional Manager with One District Manager

The phone provides a quick answer to many questions. Most calls from district manager to regional manager are to report issues and get answers. Reporting issues involves two conversations under current guidelines, unless the district manager is able to get both regional managers on a conference call.

Instituting standards of "who to tell what," as mentioned with face-to-face meetings, would alleviate this reporting burden from the district managers. The added stress of having two bosses was viewed as somewhat to very difficult by over 50 percent of respondents, as shown in the following figure.

Figure: Two-boss difficulty rating by district managers.

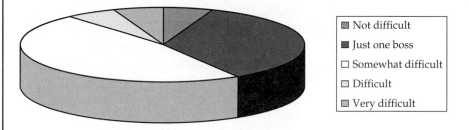

- ■ Not difficult
- ■ Just one boss
- □ Somewhat difficult
- □ Difficult
- ■ Very difficult

Both Regional Manager Partners with One District Manager

While this communication is unencumbered by an extra communication to the missing party, it can be complicated by logistics. However, the speed and unity of three-party phone calls are helpful to the district manager.

TEXT MESSAGES

Text messages are used frequently to communicate quick information by both regional and district managers. The reliance on pages as a replacement for phone calls speeds the work flow. Text messages are often used when an immediate phone call response is needed or to indicate that someone was sent a high-priority e-mail. The new Treo phones have decreased text message use for full informational purposes due to a 120-character limitation on messages and more difficult keyboarding than prior pager hardware.

SUMMARY

To summarize, our organizational structure creates barriers to clear communication at the regional and district manager level. While varying forms of communication used all have value, each has its own impediments. The main mode of communication between regional and district managers is e-mail, which is generally efficient, but has limitations when nonroutine information is included. Alternatively, meetings that include the district and regional managers are handicapped by a lack of planning. The district managers want to increase the frequency of interpersonal communication. Phone calls are a good tool, but may not include all parties affected. This can lead to misunderstandings, just as other forms can, due to dual reporting responsibilities. Text messages are a useful supplemental form of communication.

RECOMMENDATIONS

The following recommendations are thoughtfully submitted to help our company eliminate obstacles that hamper the success of the regional and district managers.

- Do not use e-mail as a substitute for face-to-face communication.
- Provide regional managers with periodic business communication training.
- Require formal agendas and time constraints to be set to enhance meeting productivity.
- Require more frequent face-to-face meetings.
- Make the regional managers accountable for correcting miscommunications.
- Develop standards for what must be communicated to both regional managers and what can be reported to one.
- Expect regional managers to report pertinent information to each other.

REFERENCES

Deep, S., and Sussman, L. (1995). *Smart moves for people in charge.* Cambridge, MA: Basic Books.

Walters, J. (2003, January). Meetings 101: Was that a good meeting, or a bad one? *Ivy Sea, Inc.* Retrieved October 29, 2005 from http://www.inc.com.

Cases for Small Group Discussion

Case 6-1.

Recommendation Report

You are a middle-level marketing manager in a large wholesale organization. This morning, your boss called you into her office and informed you that 126 cars in the company's sales fleet were ready for replacement. She asked you to do the research and write a report that would recommend a purchase to replace the cars about to be retired.

Pick four cars that are comparable—for example, the Ford Fusion, the Honda Accord, the Chevrolet Malibu, and the Toyota Camry. In selecting a particular type of car, you might want to make some assumptions about the products handled by your salespeople and whether they carry bulky samples. For the purposes of this report, we will assume you considered other similar cars but the four you chose are the top contenders.

Your next task is to identify the criteria to be used in selecting the car to be purchased. Remember that the quality of your research and report will hinge largely on how thoroughly you identify the relevant criteria to be weighed. Once you have identified the criteria to be used and all subfactors of those criteria, you are ready to begin your research. You will probably find *Consumer Reports* and websites such as cars.com to be invaluable sources of information, but don't overlook other less obvious sources such as dealerships.

After collecting and organizing your information, you will be ready to write your report. What format should that report take? Which strategic aspects ought to be considered in determining that format? If you choose to use a formal report format, which prefatory parts should you include? Which subsections should you include in the introduction? How should the body of the report be organized? What will the ending sections of the report proper contain?

Case Note

This type of report should use a direct, formal format since it is being written for superiors and contains neutral information. Prefatory parts must include a transmittal memo reflecting the authorization of the senior management official who originally assigned the writer responsibility for this report. The introduction should include the research method used, as well as the purpose and scope of the report. The report should be organized to include all of the automobiles considered and tables that report the necessary statistics on each auto to the deciding committee. Conclusions should be presented that will lead management to the same outcome outlined in the writer's report, as specified in the recommendation section.

Case 6-2.

Informational Report

Develop a questionnaire containing at least 10 statements about typical ethical dilemmas faced by businesspeople. Use "strongly agree—agree—undecided—disagree—strongly disagree" as response options. Possibilities might include "It is acceptable for an American businessperson in a foreign country to bribe a public official if that practice is accepted and expected in that country." Another possibility might include "It is acceptable to give a poorly performing employee a good reference to get rid of him or her."

At the end of the questionnaire, ask for some demographic information that might make the analyses of your findings more interesting. You might ask for gender, employment status, age, marital status, years of work experience, educational level, and so on.

Next, circulate the questionnaire randomly on campus. Try to get at least 100 respondents. Remember that the larger your sample, the better your findings will be statistically. You might consider having a ballot-like box with you to ensure confidentiality.

After you have collected your data and analyzed your findings, you will be ready to put your information into a report to be presented to your instructor.

What format will that report assume? What factors should you consider in determining that format? What parts will the report contain? Will you use the direct or indirect order? On what basis will the body of the report be organized?

An interesting twist on this report might be to circulate the questionnaire to businesspeople. If it were possible for you to circulate the questionnaire to people on campus *and* to businesspeople, you might then be able to compare the results overall.

Case Note

If addressing a business executive in this report, your results should be presented both informally and indirectly, since the findings and conclusions may not be welcomed.

Endnotes

1. Anita S. Bednar and Robert J. Olney, "Communication Needs of Recent Graduates," *Bulletin of the Association for Business Communication* 50, no. 4 (December 1987), pp. 22–23.

2. C. Gilbert Storms, "What Business School Graduates Say about the Writing They Do at Work: Implications for the Business Communications Course," *Bulletin of the Association for Business Communication* 46, no. 4 (December 1983), pp. 13–18.

3. Marie Flatley, "A Comparative Analysis of the Written Communication of Managers at Various Organizational Levels in the Private Business Sector," *Journal of Business Communication* 19, no. 3 (Summer 1982), pp. 35–50.

4. Patricia Dorazio, "Preparing Technical Proposals: Planning and Prewriting Considerations," *Bulletin of the Association for Business Communication* 55, no. 3 (September 1992), pp. 49–52.

5. Steven H. Gale and Mark Garrison, *Strategies for Managerial Writing* (South-Western, 2006), p. 209.

6. Maris Roze, *Technical Communication: The Practical Craft* (Prentice-Hall, 1997), pp. 107–111.

7. David K. Farkas, "Toward a Better Understanding of PowerPoint Deck Design," *Information Design Journal + Document Design* 14, no. 2 (August 2006), pp. 162–71.

8. James Van Oosting, "The 'Well-Made' Report," *Bulletin of the Association for Business Communication* 45, no. 4 (December 1982), pp. 9–10.

9. Frank Weightman, "The Executive Summary: An Indispensable Management Tool," *Bulletin of the Association for Business Communication* 45, no. 4 (December 1982), pp. 3–5.

10. F. Stanford Wayne and Jolene D. Scriven, "Problem and Purpose Statements: Are They Synonymous Terms in Writing Business Reports?" *Bulletin of the Association for Business Communication* 54, no. 1 (March 1991), pp. 30–37.

11. Becky K. Peterson, "Tables and Graphs Improve Reader Performance and Reader Reaction," *Journal of Business Communication* 20, no. 2 (Spring 1983), pp. 47–56.

12. Jeremiah J. Sullivan, "Financial Presentation Format and Managerial Decision Making: Tables versus Graphs," *Management Communication Quarterly* 2, no. 2 (November 1988), pp. 194–216.

Part **Three**

Strategies for Understanding Messages

Chapter Seven

Managerial Listening

To listen is an effort, and just to hear is no merit. A duck hears also.

—*Igor Stravinsky, Russian composer*

During the past several decades, the essential role of listening in business and management has received increased attention. Over 35 studies reveal that listening is the form of communication that is:

- Most important for entry-level positions
- Most critical in distinguishing effective from ineffective subordinates
- Most critical for managerial competency

Yet many of these studies report that listening skills are seriously lacking in subordinates and managers.[1] Listening is not just hearing, and the effective manager differentiates between the two. Hearing is mechanical, an automatic sort of thing often difficult to avoid. A horn blaring, heavy construction equipment groaning, children shouting in a playground—all these sounds, plus others, may be heard even though they are not listened to actively. Hearing usually requires little special physical or mental effort.

By contrast, listening results from a concentrated effort; it requires both physical and mental effort. Listening requires a special effort because physical and psychological factors work against the process. In this chapter, we review those physical and psychological barriers to listening and then analyze techniques to reduce these barriers. But first we examine why listening well is worth the effort.

BENEFITS OF LISTENING

A number of essential managerial skills involve listening. First, much of the data necessary for decision making comes through listening to employees, and poor listeners miss important information. Second, listening makes a person more dependable. People who listen well follow directions better, make fewer errors, say foolish things less often, and generally become the kinds of people others will ask for advice or direction. Third, good listeners are more respected and liked by those they work with. Managers who listen compliment those they listen to, in effect telling them they are worthy people.[2] This trait can lead to harmonious labor relations since employees generally trust and support managers who "listen them out."[3]

Fourth, better listening enables a manager to be better informed overall. We learn about the world around us from listening, not talking. Fifth, good listening spares a person many embarrassments. In many situations, people may miss a name because of poor listening, or they may need to have critical information repeated because of daydreaming. Worse yet, a direct question may be unanswered because of inept listening. Such embarrassing situations can quickly label a manager as unconcerned or even apathetic.

Ultimately, the major reason for developing effective listening is to build relationships between people. All people need to be heard for their own emotional well-being and to create understanding among each other. Mutual understanding leads to trusting relationships, which are required in any work group.

Several successful organizations provide models for including listening in the list of key managerial skills. Harley-Davidson has survived and grown over the past 100 years to be one of the world's leading motorcycle manufacturers. CEO Jeffrey Bleustein attributes its success to respecting customers' wishes. "Other companies talk about customer loyalty, but we have a loyalty that goes beyond most businesses," he says. Further, Bleustein is known for listening to his employees. "He gets out and visits with his dealers and really promotes a strong team atmosphere in the company," according to one retailer.[4]

Another corporation that understands the power of managerial listening is Procter & Gamble. A recent profile in the *Harvard Business Review* describes how the company has developed an elaborate system for surveying employees, customers, and other stakeholders to gain new ideas for improving products, processes, and services.[5]

Furthermore, managers' listening behavior has been shown to factor into complex issues such as employee retention. A recent study by Harris Interactive showed that 40 percent of workers plan to find a new job within the next year, while their employers predict just 14 percent turnover in the same time period.[6] This disconnect between employees and managers could be prevented in an environment that promotes strong communication, trust, and work relationships.

BARRIERS TO LISTENING

Communication doesn't occur in discrete units and the term *barrier* may remind us of something mechanical rather than an interactive dynamic process like listening. As a result, the title *listening barrier* may misrepresent listening somewhat; however, dynamic interactive processes are easier to discuss when categorized and put in a list. Table 7–1 lists the listening barriers presented here.

One of the greatest barriers to listening arises from our own *physical limitations*. People speak approximately 25 percent as fast as they think. Thus, while most Americans speak at a rate of about 125 words per minute, they are able to think at least four times as fast. This barrier is known as the 25–75 problem.[7] As a result, instead of listening carefully, some people think about other things and

TABLE 7–1
Barriers to Listening

1.	Listening–speaking differential (25–75 problem)
2.	Motivation
3.	Willingness
4.	Internal and external noise
5.	Detouring
6.	Debate
7.	Time

devote only a fraction of their capacity to taking in what is said. They become impatient with the slow rate of the spoken word and begin to think about topics other than the words being spoken; consequently, our inability to speak more rapidly becomes a physical barrier in listening situations. The listening–speaking differential, or the 25–75 problem, is listed first because our wandering attention partially causes many of the other listening barriers.

A lack of *motivation* is another barrier to listening. Many people find maintaining the continuous motivation required for listening to be a challenge. Managers who should be listening may be daydreaming, making private plans, or even focusing on an emotional problem. During that 75 percent void, many things can overpower the 25 percent listening.

Researchers have long known that motivation or incentive is a prevalent problem in the listening process. Research completed almost 30 years ago demonstrated that people score better on listening achievement tests when they know in advance they are going to be tested than when they think they are just supposed to listen.[8] More recent research has also indicated that scores on listening tests rise as the incentive to listen increases. Since listening is hard work, we can expect greater effort when the goal is known and listeners can observe a positive outcome of the effort. This is why the listening goal discussed later is so important.

A barrier related to motivation is lack of *willingness*. A manager may not *want* to listen. Before listening is even required, he may have lost any desire to listen. Since we have already discussed motivation as a barrier to listening, we must differentiate willingness from motivation. These concepts are closely related, but for this discussion, assume that a lack of willingness develops *before* listening even begins. This is why it may supersede all other barriers. If a person consciously or unconsciously decides not to listen, listening skills are of no advantage. Manny Steil, who does extensive listening training for companies such as Honeywell, often refers to the LAW of listening—Listening equals *Ability* plus *Willingness*.

Why would a manager lack the willingness to listen? Several reasons explain this attitude. First, most people would rather talk than listen, and even when they ask a question, they often interrupt the first sentence of the response.[10] Second, the listener may quickly stereotype the speaker as one who has little to contribute and is not worth listening to. Third, a listener may lack willingness because she may not want to receive negative information. For the speaker who bears "bad tidings," what incentive is there to listen? Defensive behavior works against listening. Some managers consider the slightest attack on one of their opinions as an attack on them personally; consequently, they will rise to the defense. This defense often involves verbal attacks that preclude the possibility for listening.

Internal noise that cannot be ignored is another barrier. Our autonomic nervous system involuntarily pays attention to certain events such as a headache, sore feet, or an empty stomach. It is difficult to divide attention between these internal involuntary distractions and concentrated listening. *External environmental noise* that may compete with the main topic of interest is also a barrier. It is hard to listen to a subordinate who speaks softly in a noisy foundry or to a phone conversation mixed with static on the phone line. In these situations, separating the speaker's voice from all the surrounding noise can be exhausting.

Another barrier may be termed *detouring*. The listener may become distracted by a phrase or concept and detour toward the distraction. This distraction then stimulates thought on another subtopic more interesting than the central point of the message; consequently, thoughts detour to the more interesting topics. Detouring is closely related to bias. For instance, a listener's negative bias toward a mannerism can distract from the content of the message. If a speaker places her hands over her mouth while speaking, or continually plays with a pencil, or looks away from the listener, such mannerisms can distract and get in the way of messages.

The *debate* represents a sixth type of barrier. A listener may suddenly find herself disagreeing with the speaker and begin to plan her rebuttal. As she plans the rebuttal, she blocks out the speaker and misses his message. For instance, a manager listening to complaints from another department might prepare a rebuttal as the other person explains the incident. As a result, the manager creates a defensive climate and misses the most important information.

Finally, *time*, an important factor in every manager's day, can also be a barrier to listening. "I just don't have time to listen to this" is a common reaction for managers. Time seems to drag when people have to listen to something in which they have no interest. When listening appears to take too much time, managers tend to stop listening. One way some terminate listening is by making a hasty conclusion. This time pressure may lead to the tendency to judge, evaluate, approve or disapprove a person's statement too hastily. To achieve real communication, it is important to resist the temptation to form hasty conclusions.

The preceding review is only a summary of the many barriers to listening. All those personal factors mentioned in Chapter 2—knowledge, culture, status, attitudes, emotions, communication skills—can also create potential barriers to listening. Nevertheless, research indicates we can improve listening skills. When managers strategically analyze the critical components of communication and apply the techniques suggested in the following section, their listening skills and effectiveness as managers will improve.[11]

GENERAL TECHNIQUES FOR LISTENING

Let us first identify two different types of listening so we can adapt techniques to the appropriate situation: active and interactive.

TABLE 7–2
Examples of Listening Situations

	Active Situation	Interactive Situation
Casual	Radio program	Social conversation
Factual	Informative presentation	Conference
Empathic	Sermon	Counseling session

For the purposes of this discussion, active listening occurs in situations in which a manager has little or no opportunity to directly respond to the speaker. People in a large audience use active listening as do those listening to a recorded message or reviewing an audiovisual replay. People use interactive listening when they have the opportunity to interact verbally with the speaker by asking questions or summarizing. Interactive listening occurs when a manager is involved in a conversation with another individual or in a meeting with many people.

Our commitment to listening is often determined by the relevance, the importance, or the significance of the information involved. Listening basically has three levels of intensity—casual, factual, and empathic. Table 7–2 shows examples of listening occasions for each intensity level. Casual or marginal listening is used when the specific or technical information being discussed is not critical. Because no goal for specific information is established, a manager need not be as alert as in other situations. For example, casual listening occurs in social conversations or when listening to the radio. Although it is not as intense as many types of listening, it is nonetheless important. A manager can indicate social support by simply listening to an employee talk about a special event in her life. By listening, the manager is saying, "You are important as a person."[12]

A note of caution is important here. What one person considers casual another may consider critical information. The importance of the information is not inherent in the information itself. Therefore, in the same situation, different people could be listening with different intensities.

The next level of intensity, factual listening, is necessary when specific information needs to be obtained. Probably the most common type of listening in business meetings and conferences, factual listening is the level that most people probably think of when they consider the topic of listening. At this level, the listener should ask questions and receive feedback to ensure effective communication.

A manager uses the empathic level of listening when she wants to understand another person from that person's own internal frame of reference rather than from the manager's own frame of reference. The empathic listener tries to get inside the speaker's thoughts and feelings. The listener expresses empathy when she verbally and nonverbally communicates such messages as "I follow you," "I'm with you," or "I understand." The empathic level of listening is not easy to achieve because we naturally tend to advise, tell, agree, or disagree based on our own view. It is well worth the effort to become an empathic listener, however. A speaker who sees that a manager is really trying to understand his meaning will trust the manager and be more willing to talk and explore problems. Empathic listening can be such a powerful form of listening that, even when it is only partially attained, the mere attempt can be enough to open communication.

To summarize, when listening, a manager should first determine the level of listening he needs to achieve—casual, factual, or empathic. He can accomplish this by establishing a "listening goal," a specific statement of the purpose for listening. In the give-and-take of most communications, the need to adjust one's listening goal arises as the interchange develops.

But this is not always easy. Consider Andy Wilson, who is a regional vice president of Walmart. He visits a different Walmart store at least every week where he wanders around talking to customers, stock clerks, and store managers. One minute he may be listening to someone describe the weather in Salem, Oregon, and the next minute he may be discussing the drop in sales of bedding items. Soon after that, he may be listening to a manager describe why she is so frustrated with her work. Within five minutes, each of the different types of listening intensities is required, so Andy Wilson must be quick to adjust.[13]

Once the manager has established the level of listening, it is important to prepare physically and psychologically to listen. He should complete the following steps during the preparation stage.

1. Pick the best possible place. While it is not always possible to change the place, the manager should not overlook better facilities when available.
2. Pick the best possible time. As with place, it is not always possible to change the time. However, the astute manager must be careful not to eliminate more favorable opportunities.
3. Think about personal biases that may be present.
4. Review the listening objectives.

A brief review of these four steps shows why they are important in reducing the barriers to effective listening discussed earlier. First, selecting the best time and place helps one reduce internal and external noise. In addition, because time influences the psychological barriers of motivation, emotion, and willingness, the choice of time may significantly alter the outcome of the conversation.

Is it polite to tell another that you cannot listen at the moment? In a survey of more than 200 managers, respondents indicated they would not be offended if someone asked them to wait before discussing something for fear that important information might be missed. Of course, if time cannot be changed, it is important that the parties be aware of the barriers present and make a special effort to concentrate on the listening process.

A manager's personal biases may also have a drastic effect on the outcome of the communication. A manager unaware of personal bias may become selective and hear only what he wants to hear. The person may deal only with preconceived notions and even debate the speaker on points of disagreement. For example, a manager who believes that young adults are unreliable may disregard any information indicating that a particular young adult *is* reliable. To control this psychological barrier of bias, first be aware of it, and then recognize the burden it places on the speaker–listener relationship.

Emotional words or phrases can also trigger listener bias. Such phrases as "typical humorless accountant," "it really isn't my job," "we tried that before, and it didn't work," or "all engineers think alike" can lead to emotional responses. The danger in such phrases is that they cause a listener to attend (or not to attend) to different parts of a message. The listener should be aware of the possible emotional responses and not let them distract from the message.

Finally, it is important to review and be aware of the listening objective. Without the objective in mind, a manager may use casual listening when factual listening is required, or factual listening when empathic listening would be more effective. The person who can state in one sentence the specific goal and the type of listening involved is well aware of the listening objective.

Thus far we have examined some general listening strategies. The manager who is physically and psychologically prepared to listen should use additional, more specific techniques to improve listening. Let us next look at techniques that are appropriate for active and interactive listening.

SPECIFIC TECHNIQUES FOR ACTIVE LISTENING

A person uses active listening in situations where direct response to the speaker is difficult or impossible. For example, a person who is sitting in a large audience or listening to a recording cannot interact with the speaker. If asking questions is not possible, a listener needs to have a clear and complete understanding of the message the first time. An active listener should implement the following techniques.

Identifying the Main and Supporting Points

A message usually has one or two main points followed by supporting information (examples, figures, or descriptions). One good clue to main points is the non-verbal techniques the speaker uses when giving them; she might raise her voice, speak faster, repeat key words, or use gestures. Later we will detail nonverbal aspects that can be invaluable when identifying the main and supporting points. In the following example of a president speaking at an annual meeting, note the emphasis on main and supporting points in a speech:

> The electronic division was pleased with the successful introduction of *four new products* (raised voice) in the last year. All four of these products sold at a better rate than projected. We were especially pleased with the temperature sensor that sold 14 percent above projections. This small sensor, which has many applications and is easy to install, should do as well or better next year.
>
> Besides introducing four new products (pause), we expanded the Western division's sales force by adding 16 high-quality salespeople. These salespeople were recruited from all over the United States, and we're confident of their ability to help us expand in the West. They all have a thorough understanding of the product and the changing nature of our industry.
>
> No immediate changes are seen in the home implement division (lowered voice). It will be necessary to wait and see what happens with the entire housing industry. We're stable here since garage openers, intercom systems, and burglar protection

devices are all holding their own. We developed a new burglar protection system that can be programmed by means of a digital device. This has been an interesting project to watch as it developed.

The main points in this example are the four new products, expansion of the Western division's sales force, and a stable home implement market; the remainder of the message is supporting information. Separation of main and supporting points helps the listeners retain the critical information.

Organizing the Message

Often, a speaker has some type of organization pattern that a listener uses to understand the message. For instance, a speaker may organize the message by pros and cons, advantages and disadvantages, likes and dislikes, similarities and differences, chronological events, or functional duties. Just as it is easier to remember the basic structure of a chapter rather than every word in it, it is easier to recall the structure of a spoken message rather than all the specifics.

Summarizing the Message

Another active listening technique is the summary, which can take the form of a mental picture of the main points. The summary need not contain elaborate sentences and details; simple words or sentence fragments may suffice. Furthermore, summarization does not have to wait until the end of the message; it may be more efficient at major transition points. The president's speech, shown earlier, could be summarized in three phrases: (1) four new products in electronics, (2) 16 new salespeople in the Western region, and (3) a stable home implement market.

The three techniques tested so far—differentiating between the main and supporting points, organizing, and summarizing—operate together for accurate listening. The effective use of a fourth technique assists in the development of the others.

Visualizing the Message

A fourth strategy for active listening, putting the message into a picture, will help keep the listener's mind on the message. The beauty of this technique is that it allows a person to use some of that 75 percent of her mental capacity not required to keep up with the message. Consequently, a manager can commit more effort to listening, thus reducing the possibility of missing a major part of the message. Finally, retention of the message improves because a picture can now be associated with it. In the annual meeting described earlier, a manager might imagine the 16 new sales personnel in the Western region as 16 little people running from different points of a U.S. wall map to California. Absurd as the device might seem, these 16 little people running across a wall map will help the manager remember one of the main points of the message.

Related to visualization is mnemonics. One mnemonic device is the acronym, a combination of letters, each of which is the first letter of a group of words essential to the message. For instance, suppose a person is presenting his main objection to taking additional training in computer programming. The objection may stem from the cost, the individual's ability, and the time involved.

The mnemonic CAT—cost, ability, time—can be used to record these main ideas whenever the speaker refers to them. Mnemonics in general, and acronyms specifically, may be considered a type of visualization because it is easier to see and recall the acronym. Other types of memory games such as word association and riddles are also beneficial.

Personalizing the Message

Effective listeners are those who search a message for information that has special meaning for the listener. A topic is naturally more interesting and easier to concentrate on if it personally relates to the listener. In fact, those who relate the message to personal experiences ensure that two key elements of listening—willingness and motivation—are present. The managers listening to the president in the previous example may also personalize the message by asking questions of themselves: "How will these four products affect my job?" "Will continued expansion of the electronic group affect me?" "Will those 16 new salespeople increase my workload for the Western region?" "How will the stable market in the home implement group affect our division?" In answering these questions, the managers find how the message personally relates to them. Then, their incentive to listen to the message increases.

Taking Notes

All these techniques are strengthened when the listener takes notes. College students understand the importance of notes, but they may lose this good habit once they leave the classroom. A listener can easily make short notes to help organize, visualize, and personalize a message. Not only do notes provide a written record of the communication, but they can also provide valuable feedback that tells the listener just how well she is listening. If the notes are not well organized with main and supporting points, the listener probably has not mentally organized the message. If a quick review indicates no notes have been taken for some time, the listener may find that his attention has been wandering.

Notes also benefit a listener by keeping her physically involved. Listening is a predominantly mental activity. Consequently, people who are accustomed to being physically active get restless or impatient when listening for long periods.

Of course, note taking can be a problem for people who overdo it. One can concentrate on the notes to the extent that major components of the message are missed. Instead, jot down just key words and phrases in outline form using abbreviations when possible.

A final thought on notes: The listener who takes notes indicates a sincere interest in both the message and the speaker. The speaker will have a greater degree of confidence that note-taking listeners are paying attention to the message. The fact that it is important to demonstrate effective listening is discussed in more detail later.

Each of these techniques—identifying the main points, organizing, summarizing, visualizing, personalizing, and note taking—is useful in both active and interactive listening. However, the techniques are especially critical in situations where the ability to ask questions and observe nonverbal messages is limited.

When questions are possible, the ideal is to ask questions of the speaker for clarity, in addition to the six techniques just discussed. The next section discusses situations in which is it easy to ask questions. We refer to this as interactive listening.

SPECIFIC TECHNIQUES FOR INTERACTIVE LISTENING

Table 7–3 summarizes techniques to use in active and interactive listening situations. When managers are engaged in two-way communication, they can improve their listening effectiveness by paraphrasing and asking questions.

Paraphrasing

Paraphrasing is commonly thought of as simply repeating what a speaker has *said*. However, a true paraphrase reflects what the listener thinks the speaker *intended to say*. The listener uses different words to express the speaker's meaning, thereby checking understanding. Further, a paraphrase reflects the underlying attitudes or emotional tone of the message. While many people are reluctant to paraphrase for fear of sounding like a parrot, paraphrasing is an excellent listening technique for two reasons. When properly done, a paraphrase not only allows the listener to be sure she has received the message as the speaker intended; it also strengthens the relationship between speaker and listener. When a listener paraphrases, she indicates effort, commitment, and good intentions, thereby increasing the likelihood that the speaker will respond in kind.

Questioning

The skillful use of questions adds immensely to a manager's ability to listen. This book recommends several areas when questioning techniques are appropriate: listening, interviewing, resolving conflict, and coaching. Questions are important because they provide the two-way process of communication that Chapter 2 discusses. Without the use of questions, feedback and mutual understanding are severely curbed.

In an interactive situation when the meaning of a message is either unclear or incomplete, a listener should ask questions. When key words, phrases, or concepts are vague or when inconsistencies or contradictions appear, questions help to develop clarity. Questions may also help a speaker clarify his thoughts. When questioned, the speaker may be forced to reanalyze his message to the listener's benefit.

TABLE 7–3
Specific
Techniques
for Active and
Interactive
Listening

Active Situation	Interactive Situation
Identify main and supporting points	Paraphrase
Organize the message	Ask open and closed questions
Summarize the message	Ask primary and secondary questions
Visualize the message	Ask neutral and directed questions
Personalize the message	
Take notes	

A manager must strategically determine the most appropriate questions for different situations. Three types of questions are appropriate to this discussion: open–closed, primary–secondary, and neutral–directed.

Open–Closed Questions

The phrasing of an open-ended question gives the respondent a wide choice of possible answers. At the other end of the spectrum is the closed question, which calls for a narrow range of possible answers. An example illustrates this point. Suppose a frustrated subordinate describes to you a major problem with a new project. In her agitation, the employee jumps from one point to another while describing the problem. Naturally, this disorderly description makes it difficult to listen, so you ask questions for both clarity and completeness of information. The following list includes open and closed questions that you might ask the employee for clarification.

- What do you think are the major causes of the problem? (open)
- What more can you tell me about it? (open)
- Did you check the steam gauge? (closed)
- Where do you think we should go from here? (open)
- Would it be a good idea to wait until tomorrow? (closed)

While open questions ask for additional information, they also allow possible digression. Closed questions are more direct and help one to focus on the problems or facts. Closed questions also call for commitment ("will you?"). Managers must use strategic analysis to determine the best type of question in each case.

Primary–Secondary Questions

Two other options open to managers are primary and secondary questions. A primary question is the first question about a topic. A manager may choose to follow up with a secondary question designed to obtain more specific information after the primary question has been answered. A secondary question is not merely an additional question; it also seeks to get at a deeper level of information than the primary question. Such probes call for clarification or elaboration. The following dialogue shows the strategic use of primary and secondary questioning.

Manager:	Do you think you'll be able to have the analysis done by Wednesday? (primary)
Employee:	That shouldn't be any problem, if everything goes right for a change.
Manager:	What might go wrong? (secondary)
Employee:	The accounting information is hard to get sometimes.
Manager:	What specific part is hard to get? (secondary)

Notice that each secondary question seeks further information on the preceding answer.

Neutral–Directed Questions

The third classification involves neutral versus directed questions. While a neutral question seeks information without attempting to lead the speaker to answer in a certain way, the directed question leads the speaker to a response the inquirer desires. A directed question, or leading question, opens with such phrases as "Doesn't it seem logical that . . . ," or "Wouldn't you agree that . . . ," or "Surely you won't . . . , will you?" Directed questions may be used to obtain confirmation or clarification on one specific point, whereas the neutral question can obtain an unintended response.

In summary, a manager who uses paraphrases and appropriate questions adds clarity to communication because of the interactive process that develops. Interactive listening is clearly not a passive activity; rather, it requires the involvement of the manager through the use of questions and paraphrases. To help us see these two techniques in action, let us examine an interview recently televised between a CNN anchorman and Jeffrey Toobin, author of several books on the U.S. Constitution. The topic was the possible ineligibility of Senator Hillary Clinton (D-NY) to serve as secretary of state in the Obama administration. The anchorman began the interview by reading Article 1, Section 6, of the Constitution and asking Mr. Toobin whether it was a legitimate argument. Mr. Toobin turned his chair toward the anchorman, leaned in toward him, and made eye contact. He began his response by paraphrasing the question, making it much simpler to understand and demonstrating that he understood it. "So, you are asking if Hillary Clinton is ineligible to be a member of the Obama Cabinet? Answer: No."

He further clarified that the gist of this section of the Constitution stated that "if a senator has voted to increase the pay of a Cabinet's post, he/she cannot be appointed to that post. Last year, Congress increased the salary of Cabinet members, thus raising this question."

The CNN anchorman, also maintaining eye contact, then summarized the answer and proceeded to probe Mr. Toobin by asking if there had ever been a time where the provision under discussion was applied. Mr. Toobin again paraphrased and provided details, explaining that the issue had come up a number of times in previous administrations, most recently during Gerald Ford's presidency. The CNN anchorman, maintaining eye contact as well, summarized and ended by saying, "So basically, they slashed the secretary of state's pay." Both participants in the interview demonstrated good listening skills, including paraphrases, open and closed questions and probes, and nonverbal cues.

LISTENING TO INFORMAL COMMUNICATION

So far, this discussion on listening has emphasized times in which a formal speaking–listening situation is established. But informal casual listening can also be extremely important—what begins as casual listening can quickly become factual or empathic listening. A manager should always be aware of the rumors that circulate on the grapevine. At times, these rumors can provide important information; at other times, it may be important to attempt to alter the content of the rumor; and at still others, it may be best to ignore the rumors. But managers must stay tuned in.

The term *grapevine* has an interesting history. It arose during the Civil War when intelligence telegraph lines were strung loosely from tree to tree in the manner of a grapevine. Because the messages from the line often were incorrect or confusing, any rumor was said to be from the grapevine.

What causes rumors in modern organizations? To answer this question, the following formula is helpful:

$$\text{Rumors} = \text{Ambiguity} \times \text{Interest}$$

Rumors are created when the available message is ambiguous. If all information were available and clear from the formal channels, no rumors would be created. When the message is ambiguous but interesting, rumors will result.

This relationship has an important implication for managerial communication. Management can determine what is interesting to employees by listening to the rumors. For instance, a vice president recently resigned from a computer company, but the rumors on the grapevine do not address the replacement. Rather, a new relationship between two employees is the major topic. This would imply that the employees are relatively secure about the management team and one replacement will probably not rock the boat. Compare this to a company where the president suddenly retired. All that was discussed whenever people gathered was the latest rumor about the replacement. Obviously, this matter was of great concern to the employees.

Research indicates that information transmitted via the grapevine in organizations is 70 to 90 percent accurate. However, some amount of distortion always exists.[14] This core of truth along with the degree of distortion is often what makes a message on the grapevine believable, interesting, and durable.

As information proceeds from person to person on the grapevine, it tends to undergo three kinds of change. The first is *leveling*, the dropping of details and the simplifying of context and qualifications. This process is especially prevalent when the rumor is extremely complex. It must be made rather simple to pass on to the next person. The second kind of change is *sharpening*, the preference for vivid and dramatic treatment of data. Employees work to make a story better and more entertaining as it is passed from one person to another. Third is *assimilating*, the tendency of people to adjust or modify rumors, to mold them to fit their personal needs. This makes the rumor more interesting to those on the grapevine.[15]

Effective managerial listening requires that managers critically assess informal communication to determine the extent to which leveling, sharpening, and assimilation have occurred. Inaccurate rumors can sometimes call for action. In one manufacturing plant, rumors maintained that a massive personnel layoff was about to occur because of the new machinery being installed. Management heard these incorrect rumors. Members of the management team met with employees to assure them no layoffs would occur. Listening to rumors helped prevent a loss of employee morale. As one manager once said, it is important to listen to "the talk on the street." Research shows that employees prefer to get their information

FIGURE 7–1
Three Dimensions of a Message

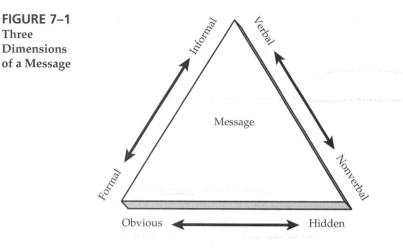

from the formal channels, and they turn to informal channels when the formal have dried up. Managers concerned about rampant rumors should remember the relationship between formal and informal channels.

LISTENING TO THE TOTAL ENVIRONMENT

This chapter primarily discusses listening to the spoken word. Chapter 8 discusses nonverbal communication. Managers must listen to spoken and nonverbal messages both separately and jointly in formal and informal settings. Strategic managerial communication requires listening to messages that aren't always obvious. Figure 7–1 graphically demonstrates the three possible aspects of a message: formal to informal, verbal to nonverbal, and obvious to hidden. The three possibilities are displayed in a triangle with equal sides because all three aspects should be considered equally.

It is necessary for managers to keep their eyes and ears open for all kinds of signals in their organization and its industry. When a person is aware of the signals of a forthcoming event, it is possible to take corrective action—but first the manager must listen to be aware. The magazine article discusses signals of potential restructuring, such as employees who voluntarily quit but are not replaced, increased debt, layoffs at other companies in the industry, rumors, and departures of top executives. It is possible that most employees could know about pending layoffs long before they were formally announced.

Of course, restructuring is a drastic action. It is important that managers listen to and analyze many other events in the company that can affect their careers. For example, which departments seem to be getting the best budgets? Employees in these groups will probably have the greatest opportunities for advancement. Although it is not always possible to determine budget allocations, it is possible to watch for the results of greater allocations. The hiring of additional support staff, the purchasing of newer and better computer equipment, the acquisition of new office furniture, and more frequent traveling to professional conferences can each signal a favored department.

The point is that managerial listening goes beyond listening to the obvious words. It requires listening to nonverbal behaviors and the continuous signals that come from the environment. Recall our discussion of the "onion" model in Chapter 2. The outer layer—culture and climate—is relevant here.

DEVELOPING A LISTENING CLIMATE

In addition to actually listening carefully, managers must also seem to be listening and establish a climate that demonstrates receptivity. Without this climate, the communication environment in an office can become like that in some homes:

Parent: Why don't you ever tell us what you are doing?
Child: I do, but you don't listen. You're always so busy.
Parent: We're never too busy to listen to you, but you just don't seem to want to tell us anything.

Are the parents too busy to listen, or do they just appear too busy? The same question may be asked of many managers. Is it possible that they appear too busy to listen? A manager may unintentionally establish a nonlistening climate by subtle behavior that says to the subordinate "Why talk if nobody is listening?"

While a manager is responsible for a tremendous amount of information and spends as much as 50 percent of the working day listening, one cannot listen if nobody is talking. Managers need to develop a listening climate to motivate people to open up. Consequently, managers should strive to eliminate listening habits that discourage communication. Table 7–4 lists 16 irritating listening habits.[16] A listener demonstrating these behaviors is not exhibiting a positive communication climate. Consequently, the speaker may not believe he is being listened to. This list can serve as a personal checklist for managers to see if they demonstrate any of the irritating behaviors.

Two levels of the listening climate require attention. The first is the micro level or the one-on-one situation. The second level is the macro or total climate. First we will review the micro level.

The Micro Listening Climate

A research study asked employees to indicate which of the poor listening habits in Table 7–4 they found the most common.[17] Two items seemed to stand out:

- When I'm talking, he finishes sentences for me.
- When I come in, he doesn't put down what he is doing and turn his attention completely to me.

This finding is especially revealing. Clearly, the listener needs to give undivided attention to the speaker, who does not want to be rushed to complete the message. This fact relates to the 25–75 rule discussed earlier. The listener's mind

TABLE 7–4
Irritating
Listening
Habits

- He doesn't give me a chance to talk.
- He never lets me complete more than a couple of sentences before interrupting.
- He never looks at me while I'm talking.
- He constantly fidgets with a pencil or a paper, studying it rather than listening to me.
- He never smiles.
- He always changes the subject with his questions and comments.
- Whenever I make a suggestion, he throws cold water on it.
- He's always jumping ahead of me to tell me what my next point is.
- He puts words into my mouth that I did not mean.
- Occasionally, he asks a question about what I've just told him.
- When I'm talking, he finishes sentences for me.
- When I have a good idea, he always says "Yes, I've been thinking about that, too."
- He overdoes nods of the head, yeahs, uh-huhs.
- He tries to insert humorous remarks when I'm trying to be serious.
- When I come in, he doesn't put down what he's doing and turn his attention completely to me.
- He asks questions that demand agreement with him. For example, he makes a statement and then says, "Don't you think so?" or "Don't you agree?"

moves so much more rapidly than the spoken word that the listener's impatience may show as she attempts to complete the speaker's sentence. Even though the listener is paying attention, this impatience to complete the speaker's communication may develop a negative listening climate. The same is true when the listener works on something else while attempting to listen. The speaker may soon get the feeling that the message being delivered is not very important.

Demonstrating a positive climate is most important when a manager is involved in empathic listening. As discussed earlier in this chapter, an empathic listener tries to understand the speaker's feelings. Most people have a very difficult time expressing their feelings, so an encouraging, supportive, receptive climate needs to be established. Managerial strategies include maintaining eye contact, leaning slightly toward the speaker, changing facial expression in relationship to the message, and taking notes. All of these behaviors demonstrate a positive listening climate.

For a valuable exercise, review the list of irritating listening habits and watch for them in your own behavior for a week. This form of personal feedback should provide insights for improving your micro listening climate.

The Macro Listening Climate

Managers must take responsibility for ensuring that those who work around them are free to exchange information in a timely and accurate manner.[18] They must develop a general atmosphere that promotes rather than hinders the opportunity to communicate. This macro level of listening is demonstrated by the manager's general demeanor and style. For instance, much has been said about managing by wandering around.[19] When managers are physically available and not locked away behind closed office doors, they create an atmosphere that says "I am here to listen to you."

In his popular book *Thriving on Chaos,* Tom Peters presents a number of suggestions that create strong listening environments.[20] First, he suggests that opportunities to listen be built into managers' daily routines. This can be done by frequently visiting the cafeteria or break room. Unfortunately, many managers do not work these activities into their schedules because of time pressures and do not realize this is an integral and critical part of their jobs.

Another technique is to have informal meetings—"huddles" or spontaneous gatherings of a few people to discuss a problem indicate the manager wants and needs to listen to employees' ideas. Another technique is to keep official titles and symbols of authority to a minimum. People are more willing to talk when they don't feel inferior to another. In some contemporary organizations, job titles not only have disappeared from office doors, but also have been deleted from business cards. The implication is that everyone works together—communicates together—to get the job done.

The "open-door policy" expressed in more traditional companies can be either a positive or a negative macro listening climate. Managers often pride themselves on announcing an open-door policy. They tell their employees to stop by anytime—their "office door is always open." But managers become frustrated when employees do not come through the open door.

Why is the open-door policy not used? A negative listening environment probably exists. First, it may be necessary to make an appointment with an administrative assistant before the door is opened. Second, the office may be located far from employee work areas. Wouldn't it be better to be easily and readily available? This would be a positive open-door climate. A supervisor in a large organization once remarked, "If they have to announce an open-door policy, it probably means there really isn't one!"[21]

The importance of the macro listening climate was aptly demonstrated by Celeste, a first-line supervisor in a foundry. Her company was on the far south side of the Chicago suburbs. Celeste was probably one of the most respected supervisors. She gained respect by always being available to the employees. For instance, one Saturday the company rented a bus and arranged for employees to attend a Chicago White Sox baseball game. Celeste was one of the first to sign up. During the bus trip and at the game, she was part of the group even though she was the only supervisor to attend. This is probably one of the reasons her employees truly believed that Celeste always had an open door when it was time to discuss a problem. She developed a positive listening climate.

A number of elements influence employees' perceptions that managers are willing to listen.[22] Employees' work and personal backgrounds, the organizational culture, the employees' roles within the organization, and the little symbolic behaviors of the manager all affect the macro listening climate. Managers would do well to take a periodic audit of their personal listening behavior and their environment to ensure they have established a climate that says "Yes, I am willing to listen."

Summary Managers need to work on their listening skills. The major benefit is improved understanding between people. Much of the data necessary for good decisions comes through listening. Listening makes a person more dependable. Good listeners are more respected and liked by co-workers. Better listening enables a manager to be better informed overall.

Managers must exert an active, concentrated effort to overcome listening barriers. One of the primary barriers is that people think about four times faster than they can speak. Consequently, the listener's mind tends to wander. Motivation and willingness are highly related barriers. Willingness develops before listening even begins, whereas poor motivation is largely caused by the 25–75 problem. Other barriers to listening include internal distractions, detouring, debate, and time.

Two main types of listening are *active* and *interactive*. Active listening occurs when a manager has little opportunity to respond directly to the speaker. Interactive listening occurs when the manager can verbally interact with the speaker by asking questions or summarizing.

Listening has three levels of intensity: *casual*, *factual*, and *empathic*. The level to use is determined by the importance and complexity of the message and occasion. Once the manager has determined the type and intensity level of listening called for, the manager must prepare physically and psychologically to listen.

Techniques for active listening include identifying the main and supporting points, organizing, summarizing, visualizing, personalizing the message, and taking notes. Techniques for interactive listening include paraphrasing and asking open/closed, primary/secondary, and neutral/directed questions. When listening to informal communication, a manager should remember that information transmitted informally undergoes some distortion. Leveling, sharpening, and assimilating occur. A manager who is a good listener will listen to the total environment—both spoken and nonverbal messages are important.

Finally, a manager should work to develop a climate that demonstrates receptivity so that people are motivated to communicate. On a micro level, a manager should avoid poor listening habits such as interrupting. On a macro level, a manager's general demeanor and style will indicate approachability.

Cases for Small Group Discussion

Case 7-1.

Holgate's Listening Problems

John Holgate, a section manager in a chemical plant, has several engineers reporting to him. As part of his job, Holgate attends meetings during any given day with some of his junior engineers, as well as with people outside his immediate group. Occasionally, people higher up in the company (the technical director or vice president, for example) attend these review meetings.

The engineers who work for Holgate believe he often misrepresents them, and also think Holgate doesn't listen to what is being said. He frequently interrupts the speakers and completes their sentences for them. Since the engineers do not want to disagree with their boss openly, they do not contradict him in front of higher management.

Naturally, this habit results in confusion, wasted time and effort, and poor morale. When members of higher management return for their next review, they usually find that the work they requested has not been done. In fact, they occasionally find that unrequested tasks have been carried out. As they listen to Holgate's project status review, management has lately been wondering what is going on. This doubt reflects not just on Holgate but on his subordinates as well. The subordinates' morale and productivity have been slipping.

Questions

1. Why does Holgate complete the speaker's sentences?
2. How can Holgate improve his listening skills?
3. Assuming you are Holgate's subordinate, how could you point out this problem to him?

Case 7-2.

Pardon Me!

Bob Pierce, a gentle man of about 50, is the president of ABC Construction Company. The company is considered the most progressive and innovative in highway, bridge, and dam construction in the area. Pierce has served in different functional areas of the company, is fairly well educated, and is oriented toward engineering.

Before becoming ABC's vice president of field operations, Walter Horton was the chief engineer of a rival firm. He has a reputation for being a very good project manager and for knowing intimately the details of ABC field operations.

Pierce has just returned from sick leave. His bad cold is still slowing him down. It is now noon, and Pierce, who has finally caught up with the backlog of work, is preparing to go to lunch. Just then, Horton walks into his office. Horton has been trying to get in touch with Pierce the past few days for his decision about the construction plan for the new dam. Horton spreads his blueprints on the president's desk and starts his presentation.

After the presentation, the following conversation occurs.

Horton:	Well, how do you feel about the plan?
Pierce:	(somewhat absently) Well, uh, pretty good . . .
Horton:	(a little too quickly) Is there anything I haven't made clear?
Pierce:	Mmm . . . no . . .

Horton:	Okay, good. Now I would like to present the plan to the board of directors and maybe . . .
Pierce:	Board of directors? Wait a minute. You're moving pretty fast.
Horton:	You agreed the plan's a good one, didn't you?
Pierce:	(not with it at all) Well, yes.

Questions

1. What are the physical and psychological listening barriers Pierce faced during the presentation?
2. What assumptions is Horton making about Pierce's ability to grasp the situation?
3. What could Pierce have done to prevent the situation?
4. What are Horton's shortcomings as a communicator that would complicate the situation for anyone listening to him?

Case 7-3.

Hearing but Not Listening

Cedar's Furniture and Appliance is a chain of five stores, two located in Youngstown, two in Akron, and one in Cleveland. Cedar's main office is in Akron.

Jane Pyle is the office manager at the main office. She supervises four word processing operators. Three of Pyle's employees are efficient and thorough. She tells them what she wants done once, and it is done. However, the fourth employee, Harriet Enders, seems to get little done right. She finishes her daily work, but she frequently has to redo it, thus putting an extra burden on the other three operators. They have to make up the work Enders has no time for because she is redoing her original work. The other three employees are beginning to complain to Pyle about the problem.

Pyle doesn't want to terminate Enders because Pyle knows her subordinate can be a hard worker. When she does follow directions, Enders is the first of the four word processing operators to finish. The office manager wonders why Enders doesn't understand directions while the other three people always seem to. She is almost sure that, although Enders is hearing, she is not listening. Enders' problem is preventing the office work from running smoothly.

Questions

1. Write the dialogue Pyle might use to open the discussion with Enders about this problem.
2. What environmental factors might be responsible for Enders' difficulty in listening?

Endnotes

1. C. G. Coakley and A. D. Wolvin, "Listening Pedagogy and Andragogy," *Journal of the International Listening Association* 4 (1990), pp. 33–61.

2. Judi Brownell, "Perceptions of Effective Listeners: A Management Study," *Journal of Business Communication* 27, no. 4 (Fall 1990), pp. 401–15.

3. B. D. Sypher and T. E. Zorn, "Communication Related Abilities and Upward Mobility: A Longitudinal Investigation," *Human Communication Research* 12 (1986), pp. 420–31.

4. Margot Denney, "CEO Drives Home Message," *Bryan-College Station Eagle*, April 10, 2003, p. 1A.

5. James R. Stengel, Andrea L. Dixon, and Chris T. Allen, "Best Practice: Listening Begins at Home," *Harvard Business Review*, November 2003, pp. 106–16.

6. Spherion Corp., "Talent Retention in Any Economy," *The Workplace Viewpoint* 13 (2004), www.spherion.com (January 23, 2006).

7. Philip V. Lewis, *Organizational Communication: The Essence of Effective Management*, 3rd ed. (New York: John Wiley & Sons, 1987), p. 146.

8. Franklin H. Knower, D. Philips, and F. Koeppel, "Studies in Listening to Informative Speaking," *Journal of Social Psychology* 40 (1945), p. 82.

9. Larry R. Smeltzer and Kittie W. Watson, "Listening: An Empirical Comparison of Discussion Length and Level of Incentive," *Central States Speech Journal* 35, no. 3 (1984), pp. 166–71.

10. R. N. Bostrom, *Input! The Process of Listening* (Northbrook, IL: Waveland Press, 1988).

11. L. R. Smeltzer and K. W. Watson, "A Test of Instructional Strategies for Listening Improvement in a Simulated Business Setting," *Journal of Business Communication* 22, no. 4 (Fall 1985), pp. 33–42.

12. Edward E. Lawler, *The Ultimate Advantage* (San Francisco: Jossey-Bass, 1992).

13. Bill Saporito, "A Week Aboard the Wal-Mart Express," *Fortune*, August 24, 1992, pp. 77–84.

14. Hugh B. Vickery, "Tapping into the Employee Grapevine," *Association Management*, January 1984, pp. 59–64.

15. Lewis, *Organizational Communication*, pp. 46–48.

16. Eugene Raudsepp, "Is Anybody Listening," *Machine Design*, February 24, 1977, p. 7.

17. Larry R. Smeltzer and Kittie Watson, "Barriers to Listening Comparison Between Business Students and Business Practitioners," *Communication Research Report* 1, no. 1 (December 1984), pp. 82–87.

18. E. H. Schein, *Organizational Culture and Leadership* (San Francisco: Jossey-Bass, 1985).

19. T. J. Peters and R. H. Waterman, Jr., *In Search of Excellence: Lessons from America's Best Run Companies* (New York: Warner Books, 1982).

20. T. Peters, *Thriving on Chaos* (New York: Alfred A. Knopf, 1988).

21. Charles E. Beck and Elizabeth A. Beck, "The Manager's Open Door and the Communication Climate," *Business Horizons*, January–February 1986, pp. 15–19.

22. Marilyn H. Lewis and N. L. Reinsch, Jr., "Listening in Organizational Environments," *Journal of Business Communication* 25, no. 3 (Summer 1988), pp. 49–67; and J. Brownell, "Listening Environment: Critical Aspects of Organizational Communication," working paper, Cornell University, 1992.

Chapter Eight

Nonverbal Communication

What you do speaks so loudly that I cannot hear what you say.

—*Ralph Waldo Emerson, American essayist and poet*

Understanding the importance of nonverbal communication is often difficult because it is such a natural part of any managerial interaction. To appreciate the contribution nonverbal communication makes to managerial communication, imagine yourself at a meeting with six others discussing an upcoming event—say the opening of a new facility for your company. It is a meeting like any number you have attended before, yet it is radically different because you cannot see the others. Something keeps you from this. It could be a fabric veil, fog, wooden panels—you decide. Your location is also a puzzle. Is it the boardroom for the corporation, or is it a meeting room just anywhere? How important is this meeting in the whole scheme of things? Your environment provides no clues. In addition, you cannot really hear the others very well. All voices have been altered by the device used during investigatory reports on television. You can hear the words, but the voices have little or no character. The words are slowed down and slurred to some extent.

You are all seated in the same room, but because of the room's setup, you cannot see who is seated where—who is at the head of the table (perhaps you are), and who is at the sides, not even who is seated next to whom. While you and several others flew in to attend the meeting, you did not have a chance to shake hands before the meeting began. In fact, today you have not seen the others or what they are wearing. Are they dressed as well as you are, or are they dressed informally? The only communication possible during the meeting is what you can get from you and the six others talking.

Unfortunately, even that part of the communication process is a challenge. You verbally trip over each other as the meeting proceeds since you have no efficient way to signal whose turn it is to speak. In addition, because speakers must identify themselves before speaking, the interactions take longer than usual. Furthermore, you must keep these verbal identities in mind as you listen because you have no visual or tactile cues to go on. As the meeting progresses, whenever you contribute, you are unsure of all but the verbal reactions because you cannot see the shrugs, posture shifts, or expressions on the other faces.

The interaction is also lengthened by the need to evaluate each remark for intent. Did he mean that ironically? Was she being sarcastic? Was that last remark meant as a joke? The audio scrambler makes quick judgments on these fine points nearly impossible. And while you can hear the voices, which voice belongs to whom? Someone suggests that all the employees in the store dress up as clowns. You are just about to say "ridiculous" when you check yourself—be careful, maybe the boss said that.

You know the meeting is scheduled to last two hours, but because you had to surrender your watch at the door, you have no idea about the time, although it seems an eternity. You know the agenda for the meeting, but are you going to be able to cover all the items in the time allotted? Are you giving enough time to each item? Are you going to get out of the meeting and find that only half the time has elapsed? Whatever the case, you wish you were out of the meeting now.

THE IMPORTANCE OF NONVERBAL COMMUNICATION

Nonverbal factors are clearly a crucial element of managerial communication. Without nonverbal communication as a source of information, most of the richness and much of the meaning in messages would be lost. In many cases, conversations would be complicated by the need to repeat messages for clarity, and the time required would multiply enormously.

Nonverbal communication accompanies oral and, by logical extension, written messages, while consisting of the signals delivered through means other than verbal. In short, it includes *everything but the words*. Managers send, receive, and interpret nonverbal messages in the same way they send, receive, and interpret verbal ones. The same communication dynamics come into play as the sender intends (although often unconsciously) to send a message and chooses some medium through which to do so (a gesture, for example) that receivers perceive and interpret just as they do with verbal messages. Nonverbal communication may bear a clear meaning in itself, but often it serves as an adjunct to the spoken words, adding nuance in one place and clarity in another. At other times, this complex source of messages may even contradict the words being spoken.

Nonverbal communication is an important part of our daily managerial interactions.[1] While the extent of the nonverbal aspect varies from interaction to interaction, one set of oft-cited statistics shows that 55 percent of a message comes from the speaker's appearance, facial expression, and posture, while vocal aspects deliver 38 percent, and the actual words deliver only 7 percent.[2] Nonverbal communication is a rich and complex source of communication data, and this chapter provides an overview of the areas relevant to the managerial function. But first, three generalizations about nonverbal signals should be stressed here. While the first two apply to most other signals, it helps to keep them in mind when interpreting nonverbal communication.

First, with the exception of so-called emblems, nonverbal signals rarely have one set meaning. Rather, they usually add to the message's meaning, as shown in the following section of this chapter.

Second, nonverbal signals vary from culture to culture, and region to region, in their meaning. Nonverbal signals derive from experiences within the communication environment (cultural, regional, or social) and are generally dispersed throughout it.[3] It is not enough merely to translate the verbal language; the nonverbal must be expressed as well.[4] The Japanese, for example, usually present a noncontroversial demeanor and are excessively polite by North American standards. In negotiation, the accompanying nonverbals can create confusion across cultures.[5] In cross-cultural situations, in fact, while the verbal takes on greater importance, knowing and using basic nonverbal signals—for example, bowing in South Korea—can communicate respect.[6]

Third, when nonverbal signals contradict verbal ones, the nonverbals are usually the ones to trust. When verbal and nonverbal disagree, credibility can suffer.[7] A speaker who says "I'm delighted to be here" while fidgeting nervously with his notes and glancing at the ceiling is perceived as lying. Nonverbal signals can provide valuable clues about the truth of a message.

The law enforcement community provides a contemporary example of nonverbal behavior's importance. When attempting to identify terrorists and criminals in public places such as airports and subways, officials are trained to "read" suspects' body language. The technique is called behavior detection and is rooted in the notion that people convey emotions such as fear in subconscious gestures, facial expressions, and speech patterns.[8] Since the September 11, 2001, attack on the U.S., behavior detection has been adopted by police, the Transportation Security Administration, and other authorities at over 40 airports, universities, and mass transit systems.

Telling people how to dress, talk, and even move is a far easier task than putting it all into play in one's life. While we can read about the importance of smiling behavior, for example, how much is too much? Women and men aspiring to be managers can view excellent models for nonverbal behavior on business-oriented TV programs. To get the maximum impact of the nonverbal elements in the conversations (with the exception of vocal style), watch these programs with the sound turned off. Not only do they show the kinds of gestures leaders make, but they also generally reflect current appropriate dress.

THE FUNCTIONS OF NONVERBAL CUES

Nonverbal communication is a broader concept than many realize. It is far more than just gestures and eye contact. A simple definition already offered is that in managerial interactions, nonverbal communication is everything but the words. A more precise definition is that offered by Harrison, a leading expert, who said it is "the exchange of information through nonlinguistic signs."[9] These nonlinguistic signs are like any kind of sign in communication in that they are something tangible capable of bearing meaning, just as linguistic signs are. They differ in that they are nonverbal.

Even color and how it's presented in the context of a message, can serve as a nonlinguistic sign. Some studies have looked at the impact colors have on cognitive performance. Researchers at the University of British Columbia conducted tests with 600 people to determine the effects of the colors blue and red. Red groups did better on tests of recall and attention to detail. Participants in the blue groups tested better with skills requiring imagination and creativity.[10] So if your team is tasked with brainstorming for a new product or service, you may want to have them meet in a room with blue walls.

Depending on the culture, color is a nonlinguistic sign of certain emotions. For instance, Western brides generally wear white, but Eastern brides wear red. In China, white is a sign of bereavement and loss, just as black is in the U.S.

A study of emotional responses to cell phone ads demonstrates how color creates different emotions in different cultures. Thirty-two people from six cultures (Finland, Sweden, Taiwan, India, China, and the U.S.) were asked to interpret a Nokia ad's external characteristics. The predominant blue and white colors, recognized by the Finnish respondents as their country's flag's colors, provoked a positive impression. Further, the Finns found the colors "reliable," "natural," "trustworthy," and "comfortable." By contrast, the Chinese and Taiwanese respondents said that white is a funereal color for them, creating a negative impression. The Swedes recognized that blue and white are "Finnish colors" and rejected them as "boring" and "cold." The respondents from India thought the colors warm and summery. The U.S. respondents were inconsistent about whether the blue and white colors were warm or cold, summery or wintery. Interestingly, several Americans connected the blue and white colors to "unlimited freedom" and "innovation," which no informants from other cultures mentioned.[11]

Unfortunately, nonverbal communication can result in frustratingly inexact interpretation. Scholars have carefully studied nonverbal communication but have only scratched the surface of the topic in many areas. If placed in the proper perspective, it can be a valuable source of cues in communication situations.

Burbinster sees six functions for nonverbal communication:[12]

- Complementing
- Accenting
- Contradicting
- Repeating
- Regulating
- Substituting

Nonverbal signals that *complement* the verbal message repeat it. Typically, these signals accompany what is being said. For example, a technician explaining the varying gap widths in faulty components in a heating system might hold up her thumb and index finger and vary the gap between them as she discusses the problem. Or a supervisor welcoming a subordinate back after a lengthy illness might give him a warm handshake to stress how pleased he is at the other's return.

Those nonverbal signals that *accent* call our attention to a matter under discussion. A common example is a person pounding on a desk as she makes an important point. People may also use vocalics, the nonverbal aspects of the voice itself, to highlight a point. Someone differentiating between one choice and another might say "I want *this* one and not *that*."

The nonverbal signals that contradict are less obvious. These are usually sent unintentionally by the subconscious to say nonverbally the opposite of what is being said verbally. Either subtly or obviously, nonverbal cues will often tell the careful observers the truth when the verbal cues don't. This complex area of nonverbal communication will be discussed later under the heading "Nonverbal Signs of Deception."

Repeating occurs when we have already sent a message using one form of communication and wish to emphasize the point being made. It differs from complementing in that it is not done simultaneously with the verbal comment. For example, a demonstration following a verbal description of a tool's use is a nonverbal repetition.

Regulating, the fifth purpose Burbinster suggests, is a subtle and important one. Regulating occurs during conversations to signal to our partner to "slow," "stop," and even "wait your turn" and let the other person know when we are ready to listen or to speak. Watch an ongoing conversation and you will quickly spot a variety of these cues. A speaker who is not finished with his point but is being interrupted might speak louder or faster to keep his turn (thus using vocalics). Another might hold up her hand to say "not yet, let me finish." On the other hand, a speaker will usually look directly at the listener to indicate that the listener's turn is imminent.

Substituting is a less common nonverbal signal than the others. When we can't send a message by verbal cues, we might choose to use nonverbal ones—especially emblems, which will be discussed in the next section on movement and gestures—to get the point across to our receiver. A supervisor visiting a loud factory might use the "OK" sign to signal an employee. This will likely be more effective than something shouted.

From a theoretical perspective, nonverbal communication also serves another important function: communication redundancy. This concept refers to the phenomena built into any language system that combat the effects of noise. It simply means that much of the meaning of a message can be deduced from other elements in the message that have already appeared. The TV game show *Wheel of Fortune* is an example of redundancy in that not every word or letter must be on the game board before one can guess the correct phrase.

While part of a message delivers new information, much of it exists to ensure the points being made are understood. Far from being a negative phenomenon, communication redundancy is vitally important because it helps ensure that our message gets past the various barriers that environmental, organizational, or interpersonal elements erect. When a message is made more redundant, that is, when the information in it has been made more predictable to the receiver, the message has a greater chance of transferring the meaning the sender intends it to convey.

Every communication system is redundant. Verbal languages build in redundancy through a variety of means including grammar and syntax. Most of the functions addressed by nonverbal communication serve in some way as redundancy. Thus, as we discuss an issue with someone, we will use nonverbal signals to complement, accent, repeat, and even substitute to get a point across. This may be done without even thinking about it. Even when a nonverbal signal contradicts the verbal, additional nonverbal signals are likely to follow to underscore the contradiction.[13] Thus, a shake of the head denying a request is followed by a smile to indicate goodwill.

Some nonverbal behaviors are *innate*, others are *learned* from the community around us, and some are *mixed*. For instance, eye blinking patterns and blushing appear to be innate—universal involuntary behaviors that occur in certain communication situations. Other cues such as the eyewink and the thumbs-up are learned, and they signal different meanings in different cultures. A third group of nonverbal behaviors (laugh, smile) is mixed in that they occur in every culture, but they can be controlled and their meanings can change. In some Asian cultures, for example, a small laugh may occur naturally but may convey discomfort and submission rather than affiliation and pleasure.

This chapter now explores several key areas of nonverbal communication and suggests how managers can use them to their advantage. It also looks at how nonverbal indications of deception can be detected through careful observation.

MOVEMENT

Say "nonverbal communication" to most people, and they probably think of movement, which is technically *kinesics*. Nonverbal communication consists of far more than just one general category, but movement is the most studied of the categories. It includes gestures as well as posture.

Gestures may include *emblems, illustrators, regulators, affect displays,* and *adapters*.[14] While people usually use gestures without thinking, a conscious awareness of them can help a manager communicate more efficiently. An understanding of, and training in, effective signals can open up the possibility of our strategic conscious use of them.

Earlier, we noted that nonverbal signals usually suggest meaning; they do not give direct meaning. *Emblems* are an exception in that they actually stand for something else. The OK sign is one example; another is the "time out"—one palm held at a right angle to the other.

Illustrators complement verbal communication by providing an example of, or reinforcing, what is being said. When a person is trying to explain an item that is not present, what is more natural than drawing it in the air?

Regulators are gestures that both subtly and obviously control what a speaker says. They arise from a variety of sources, including the hands—for example, when one holds up the hand palm outward to keep another from interrupting. Turning the palm toward you and wiggling the fingers is a beckoning gesture in the United States. We also regulate to draw some speakers out and rein others in with gestures.

The *affect display* is more complex than most gestures and involves several parts of the body. For example, suppose you are talking to someone who has a scowl on his face as he sits up straight but is turned slightly away from you. His arms cross his chest, and you have little doubt this person doesn't like the idea under discussion. The affect display signals to another person what we are feeling and can show pleasure as well as anger, boredom as well as interest. Reading such nonverbal signals from others is rarely a problem. The challenge lies in controlling these within ourselves in some situations. We may not always want to show what we are feeling, so we must control these nonverbals, particularly if it could affect our current communication strategy.

The adapter may be the least appreciated source of kinesic messages; however, it can be quite important. In many situations, when one behavior might be inappropriate, the body will adapt by sending signals that would provide a solution, if one could only implement it. For example, the person wishing to leave, but unable to do so, might start to move his crossed leg in imitation of walking. Another person under stress may begin to twist the paper clip she is holding as a socially acceptable substitute for what she would like to do with the person she is reprimanding. That employee being reprimanded may wrap his arms around himself as a sort of substitute hug to provide the comfort he needs at that moment. A nervous speaker may rock to calm herself. Adapters often appear as a pattern of seemingly irrelevant nonverbal signals, but to the careful observer their presence may suggest discomfort. Similarly, in stressful situations when projecting an image of self-control is crucial, be aware of the nonverbal signals you may be sending. Keeping a calm face while clenching your fists may reveal more than intended.

While gestures may be the most obvious example of meaningful movement, other kinesic behaviors contribute significantly to message meaning as well. Take posture, for example. Slumping, leaning, standing with weight on one leg, and rounding the shoulders all connote weakness and lack of confidence. By contrast, standing at military "attention" (head up, shoulders back, chest forward, and weight evenly distributed on both feet) connotes power, alertness, and confidence. Managers who have mastered the elements of good posture often are attended to even before they begin to speak.

Another example of kinesic communication is head movement. As mentioned in the previous chapter, a good listener often indicates that he is paying attention by nodding and/or tilting his head. On the other hand, a speaker who nods or tilts his head while talking may be interpreted as unsure of himself or even submissive.

Mimicry is a form of gesturing where two people mirror each others' movements. It is typically an unconscious and automatic behavior triggered by an abundance of mirroring neurons in the brain. Mimicry has been shown to positively influence the flow of conversation, as well as mutual liking. The back and forth exchange of smiles, head nods, arm crossing, and hand movements creates this social circuit that leaves two people feeling better and better about the other person. Studies have proven this to be true in salary negotiations and job interviews, where ample mimicking correlated to strong feelings of trust and likeability.[15]

We also communicate meaning by the way we walk. When a speaker strides quickly to the platform, she seems energetic, bold, and in command of the situation. Her credibility is enhanced by this nonverbal element. However, if she walks around while speaking, or perhaps sways, rocks, or shifts her weight from foot to foot repeatedly, her impression is diminished.

To summarize, movement is a very important category of nonverbal communication. We pay attention to various parts of a communicator's body—head, trunk, arms, legs—as we watch and listen, drawing inferences from their movements. A list of common interpretations of kinesic cues appears in Table 8–1. A cautionary note: As you will read in Chapter 9, our culture defines both verbal and nonverbal behavior, so keep in mind that the "meanings" of the kinesic cues in the table may change from culture to culture. For example, head nodding is a sign of affirmation in the United States, but it's a sign of disagreement in the South Slavic states, Iran, and Sri Lanka. Managers in any culture must attend to kinesics when they communicate so that their body language contributes to, rather than contradicts or detracts from, the intended meaning.

TABLE 8–1
Kinesic Cues

Body Segment	Movement	Interpretation
Head	Gazing	Attentive; honest
	Shifting, darting eyes	Uncertain; lying
	Eyebrows up	Challenging; open
	Smiling mouth	Enjoyment; pleasure
	Nodding	Listening; agreeing
	Tilting head	Interested
	Head down	Defensive
Trunk and shoulders	Leaning toward	Interested; rapport
	Leaning away	Lack of interest; skeptical
	Posture slouched	Low self-esteem
	Expanded chest	Confident
	Shrunken chest	Threatened
	Buttoning jacket	Formal; leaving
Hands and arms	Touching others	Powerful
	Touching self	Nervous; anxious
	Repetitive movements	Lying; unsure of self
	Hand over mouth while speaking	Want to escape
	Arms crossed	Bored; closed to ideas
	Fingers steepled	Confident
	Hands on hips	Challenging; arrogant
	Hands in pockets	Secretive
	Palms showing	Trusting
	Pointing	Authoritative; aggressive
	Clenched hands; wringing hands; picking cuticle	Need reassurance

SPATIAL MESSAGES

Proxemics refers to the space around us and how we and others relate to it. Space and distance can reveal much and merit careful attention. Most people hearing "proxemics" think only of personal space, the personal "bubble" surrounding a person. That is a good place to start, but the concept encompasses far more than just that.

Spatial Zones

Edward Hall studied use of personal distances and determined that Americans have four arbitrarily established proxemic zones, described in Figure 8–1, in which we interact.[16] Strategic managers are aware of these zones and appreciate how they and others react when their spaces are invaded.

Our language suggests we all are aware of personal space to some degree. We talk about someone "keeping his distance," or we complain when we perceive others "invading our space," or say "They are crowding me on this issue" when in fact what they are doing has little to do with territory. When someone is pressing another on an issue, the other person may respond, "Give me breathing room," or less politely, "Keep out of my face."

In the United States, businesspeople generally operate within four zones: intimate, personal, social, and public. In the discussion that follows, keep in mind that the figures are averages. They reflect the general culture, situational

FIGURE 8–1
Spatial Zones

Public zone: Beyond 12 feet

Social zone: 4 feet to 12 feet

Personal zone: 2 feet to 4 feet

Intimate zone:

18 inches to 2 feet

mandates, and the relationship between the parties. A number of factors enter into any interpersonal exchange. These can include personal appearance, culture, gender, and age. Thus, we may react differently to a tall person compared to a short person, and may draw nearer to an attractive person than to another who is less attractive.[17]

As discussed later in Chapter 9, "meanings" for nonverbal behaviors differ from culture to culture. In the United States, the *intimate zone* ranges from physical contact to roughly 1.5 to 2 feet. It is reserved for those who are psychologically close. When it is invaded by others, especially for more than a moment, a person usually feels uncomfortable and is likely to draw back or put up some sort of barrier, although often without consciously knowing why.

The *personal zone* extends from the edge of the intimate zone out to roughly 4 feet. Americans reserve it for close friends but permit others to enter it temporarily during introductions. Watch as two strangers come together for an introduction. As they shake hands, they will often stand with one leg forward and the other ready to back up. Then, when the greeting is over, both will usually retreat into the next zone. Cooperating on a task or simultaneously studying a document may bring people into their personal space, but they typically compensate by not making eye contact.

The next area is the *social zone*. It extends from about 4 feet to 12 feet and is the space in which we would like to conduct much of our daily business. Relationships between managers and their employees might begin in this area and continue for a time. They will often move into the personal zone once trust has developed, but this takes time.[18] In the U.S. culture, the *public zone* extends beyond 12 feet and reflects the distance at which most would like to keep strangers. Little communication of a business nature takes place in this zone. Perhaps the only spoken communication that occurs is the public speech. We see the formal institutionalized reflection of this distance in the arrangement of public auditoriums or even in the layout of many political rallies. Even if the latter is not too crowded, the audience will often keep its distance.

For managers, the value of understanding spatial zones is clear. An observant communicator can gauge the relative warmth that exists in a relationship by the distances individuals keep during interactions. As trust grows, distances generally diminish. Thus, allies sit next to each other in meetings. However, other factors determine spatial differences as well. Let's consider some of these.

Spatial Differences

As we have said, proxemic zones vary from culture to culture. For example, businesspeople in many South American and Arab countries typically interact with people at far closer ranges than do U.S. businesspeople. Often, when people from the United States interact with individuals from these cultures, the varying proxemic zones expected by the groups create awkwardness until someone adapts to the needs of the others and either gives up some ground or extends the distance.

Distance preferences also vary by gender. Men tend to maintain larger personal space bubbles than do women. Women are more likely to allow men or other women to come closer than men, and women will be more tolerant of temporary violations of their own space.[19] Men take up more space with their bodies and their artifacts, a tendency that is often perceived as indicating power.

A recent study of 850 workers at midsize companies resulted in interesting gender differences regarding workspace preferences. Women voiced preferences for privacy, natural light, and the option to personalize their space. Men, on the other hand, spoke out strongly for just one environmental attribute: the ability to control the room temperature.[20]

Naturally, circumstances may artificially affect our use of zones. The classic example of this is the crowded elevator, where people allow others to invade personal and intimate zones. Here, though, people will try to adapt by avoiding eye contact or blocking—that is, by folding the arms across the chest or putting up their briefcases as a sort of shield. If someone accidentally touches another, apologies quickly follow.

When traditional zones need to be ignored for an extended period, people will stake out their territory. One way is to create even spacing between participants, as when seated around a meeting table with movable seats. In other situations, people will erect some sort of barrier to signal the limits of their own space. Watch at meetings around a conference table as people unconsciously arrange notebooks, jackets, coffee cups, and other business artifacts around the perimeters of their territory. They are signaling where the boundaries of their personal space lie in that crowded environment. Similarly, students in a class typically occupy the same seat throughout the term, claiming it as "their" space and piling their belongings around them.

Permanent, or "fixed," spaces such as cubicles or large desks often are perceived as barriers. It is rude to come behind the boss's desk or peek over the top of the cubicle. But semifixed spaces such as conference tables can connote cooperation and shared responsibility (see Figure 8–2), as the next section explains.

Strategic Use of Space

Managers should be aware that intruding into another's territory without an invitation can be an annoyance or even a threat, no matter what a person's rank. Recognizing the boundaries of both fixed- and semifixed-feature spaces communicates respect to the individual. Artifacts belonging to another individual

FIGURE 8–2
Fixed and Semifixed Space in the Same Office

Semifixed space
Conference table

Fixed space
Executive's desk

should be regarded as personal. One should never rifle through a co-worker's desk drawers for writing implements or sit on the edge of that person's desk.

Managers can use space to create an air of power and authority or an air of collegiality and respect. Everyone reads the environment for nonverbal clues. The amount of space allotted to another, the amount of privacy that space entails, and where in the building that space is located can speak volumes about organizational power. Generally, more is better than less, bigger is better than smaller, new is better than old. In addition, the closer people are to the organization's leaders, the more power they are perceived by others to enjoy.

On the other hand, managers who value open communication will work in proximity to their subordinates and co-workers, will minimize status-filled artifacts such as heavy furniture, and will discourage territoriality. Indeed, contemporary organizations require that all employees share their "space" as a symbol of cooperation and teamwork. When Michael Bloomberg was elected mayor of New York City, he rearranged City Hall to resemble a giant open bullpen, eliminating private offices. This new look resembled the trading area at Salomon Brothers, the investment firm where he had been a partner. Again, his aim was to free the flow of information.

Office design can put the right people together. At WPP, a British marketing group, walls were removed and coffee areas created. Rather than assigning accountants and media people to separate floors, they work side by side in teams to ensure that they keep talking to each other.[21]

Some studies have noted differences in office space preferences among age groups. In one study, 40 percent of younger workers, commonly labeled Generation Y or Millenials (ages 18–29), preferred to work in open office plans; only 18 percent said they preferred cubicles with privacy panels. Older workers, on the other hand, said they worked best in private offices (45 percent); just 16 percent said they preferred collaborative spaces.[22]

PERSONAL APPEARANCE

What we wear says much about who we are, or at least who we want to be perceived as. Dress is an integral part of the first impression we form on meeting someone and is often the key to initial credibility.[23] Consequently, managers should pay close attention to what they wear in order to send the right message to others. This section will focus on general principles for effective dress since clothing styles are so changeable. One piece of advice is enduring though. Be neither the first nor the last to adopt a fashion. The key to dress is to fit in with the organization's culture, to show by your appearance that you have adopted the organization's values. Thus, financial institutions expect employees to look conservative, assuring customers and clients of their stability. Ad agency employees are often expected to dress more fashion-forward, indicating their flair, creativity, and contemporary style. High-tech organizations de-emphasize a "corporate" appearance, to the extent that executives are dressed as casually as the lowest-level employee.

The occasion will also dictate personal appearance. While observing people at events such as weddings and funerals may lead one to conclude that our culture is moving toward more informality, in many business settings casual dress is considered disrespectful. Job interviews, client visits, and sales presentations call for careful attention to appearance. Recruiters often draw conclusions about applicants based on the style and condition of their footwear and hair. Thus, when shopping for an "interview suit," applicants should also shop for dress shoes.

Managers must remember that everyday appearance also conveys important messages. Many contemporary organizations have developed a detailed dress code or employee uniform in recognition of the importance of personal appearance. According to a 2006 survey by the Society for Human Resource Management, 6 in 10 employers allow a dress-down day at least once a week. But the number of employers allowing casual dress every day has plunged from 53 percent in 2002 to a new low of 38 percent.[24] The reason for the return to more dressy attire is, in part, because of the confusion generated by business casual standards. But mostly, managers have the impression that when employees dress casually, the quality of the work suffers.

Legal issues can arise from dress policies, too. Employers must be careful to enforce dress codes on all employees, not just one group (such as women) to avoid accusations of discrimination. In 2007, a Phoenix jury awarded $287,000 to a Somali employee who had worked at Alamo Car Rental. The EEOC argued that the company engaged in religious discrimination for firing her when she wore a head scarf during Ramadan.[25]

Observers always assign meaning to details such as accessories, color, jewelry, and emblems worn on the jacket lapel or hat. A prominent example of the symbolic nature of clothing is IBM. In Lou Gerstner's book, *Who Says Elephants Can't Dance?* the former CEO describes how he revitalized the failing corporation. One of his major efforts was culture change, and one of his methods was prescribing changes in employee dress. The famous "old" IBM look had been crisp white shirts, dark suits, and conservative ties. Originally, it had been adopted to match customer expectations. But by 1993, when Gerstner took over, it seemed anachronistic, stuffy, and emblematic of the company's demise. The "new" IBM look was more casual and contemporary. Again, Gerstner advises, "dress according to the circumstances of your day and recognize who you will be with (customers, government leaders, or just your colleagues . . .)."[26]

In summary, no matter whether the organization's culture is formal or casual, no matter whether the occasion is special or ordinary, managers' appearance should reflect the expectations and values of their audience. By adhering to the principle of "fitting in," managers will enhance their credibility and improve their communication effectiveness.

VOICE

The final source of nonverbal signals this chapter will focus on is paralanguage, or vocal style. The spoken word contains more than linguistic cues. Nonverbal aspects of vocal delivery include the pitch, rate, volume, tone, onset, and duration of messages. These cues are among the least obvious to most listeners, with the likely exception of tone, yet they can be as important as, or even more important than, the actual words used.[27] The pitch of the speaker's voice, the onset of the message—that is, the time it takes between the person's taking the turn and the message's beginning—and the length of the message send subtle cues.

The following is an example. If we are asking someone about a serious issue and the person's responses come almost too quickly, we might suspect he is not serious or has rehearsed the responses. Similarly, when someone takes far longer to answer a question than expected, we begin to wonder if all that is being said is true. And, as the discussion in the next section on nonverbal signs of deception shows, we even monitor pitch and can read meaning into changes of it.

The importance of vocal cues to managers is obvious in sending as well as receiving. It is important to monitor the signals being sent, particularly for tone, to ensure that the intended communication strategy is not being undermined by subtle nonverbal cues.

Speakers have a typical vocal style that distinguishes their voice from that of other speakers. The elements consist of a basic pitch, rate, pause pattern, and volume. Certain characteristics of voice are also regional in origin, such as articulation and pacing. The southern U.S. drawl and the northeastern U.S. clipped dialect are examples. In addition to these basic vocal characteristics, speakers can vary their pitch, rate, and volume to emphasize their meaning and to communicate emotion. Failure to vary these vocal characteristics results in what is commonly known as a monotonal vocal style. In the U.S. business culture, a monotonal speaking style connotes lack of interest and even lack of authority. Managers may unintentionally undermine their message by the style in which it is delivered. Chapter 14 describes good vocal style in more detail, but these criteria apply to everyday speaking as well as to formal presentations.

Confidence

To summarize, in business, speaking in a clear, firm, low-pitched voice connotes confidence and results in more attentive listening. Nasal, shrill, quiet, breathy, or harsh voices are devalued. Excessive use of filled pauses ("uh," "well") gives an impression of uncertainty. Managers must learn to use their vocal characteristics to maximize the message, rather than detract from it, just as they must use the preceding nonverbal categories.

NONVERBAL SIGNS OF DECEPTION

In many situations, managers must evaluate other employees to determine if the data they work with are accurate. While the data set out in a report can usually be tested objectively, information derived from interpersonal interactions such as disciplinary and pre-employment screening interviews frequently offers little opportunity for immediate objective verification. Fortunately, some nonverbal signals can help managers assess the veracity of verbal statements. As we have seen, nonverbal signals usually complement verbal ones and serve as needed reinforcement to reduce the uncertainty in communication. However, they may also unintentionally contradict the verbal ones they accompany.

When contradictory nonverbal signals betray deception, they are called *leakage*. During deception, certain types of nonverbal signals often escape from the deceiver despite attempts at control. The subconscious apparently betrays the speaker through this nonverbal leakage. People also often unconsciously read and interpret these signals. Managers can learn to spot nonverbal signs of deception.

Several patterns of nonverbal behavior crop up during deception.[28] Since some sources of nonverbal signals can be controlled in deceptive situations better than others—for example, looking another in the eye while deceiving—we will focus on signals that are difficult to control consciously. These include movement, dress, personal space, and voice.

Remember that nonverbal behavior usually *suggests* meaning rather than having a one-to-one correlation with a specific word or concept. The meaning of nonverbal signs might vary, and a gesture might be motivated by something besides what is suggested here.

To detect possible nonverbal signs of deception, it is important to be in the right place. Often, interviewees are seated behind desks so significant cues go undetected. The face, always likely to be visible, can be a poor source of deception cues (although hand-to-face contacts are valuable cues). When possible, seat the other person in an open chair facing you. Nonverbal signs from the hands, trunk, legs, or feet then will be more evident.[29]

Baseline

Deception signs are behaviors that differ from normal nonverbal interactions, so you also need to know what behavior is normal for that individual. Researchers have found that when observers see an individual giving honest answers before the person is seen lying, the observers' ability to detect dishonesty increases significantly over situations with no behavioral baseline. You don't detect dishonesty by looking for the lie, according to psychologist Paul Ekman of the University of California–San Francisco, but by identifying the change in behavior that suggests a person is nervous when he/she shouldn't be.[30]

The individual's baseline is also invaluable because one person might behave differently from others in identical circumstances. A baseline allows one to gauge if nervous behavior reflects the overall situation or is a reaction to the question being asked.

In the job interview, a baseline is relatively easy. During the preliminary chat, ask nonthreatening questions. Begin with the résumé before moving into the unknown. Watch for nonverbal cues. An investigatory interrogation could use the same pattern. Small talk serves its traditional primary purpose of putting the other at ease, and a secondary one of providing a behavioral baseline.

Movement

Gestures and trunk movements, part of the broad category of kinesics, are probably the most valuable nonverbal signs of deception. Perhaps the most common deception-related gestures are the hand-to-face movements, and the most common of these is the mouth cover. More subtle is the single finger to the mouth, the moustache stroke, or the nose rub. Other gestures suggesting deception are nail biting and lip biting.

Conversational gestures vary as well. Generally, when one is comfortable with honest responses, gestures are open and outward. During deception, people both limit their gestures and keep them closer to the body. And, while smiling decreases and the frequency of gestures used to illustrate conversational points slows down in deception, the gestures suggesting deception increase. One of these is the hand shrug emblem. Researchers have found that deceptive speakers will shrug their hands—turning the palms up from palms down position—twice as frequently as in nondeceptive messages. This signal suggests a subconscious pleading for the listener to believe what is being said.

Some authorities also believe that an increase in leg and foot movements may indicate deception.[31] Foot tapping, leg rocking while the legs are crossed, and frequent shifts in leg posture are examples of this kind of activity. A rhythmic "walking" motion with one crossed leg has long been recognized as an intention gesture suggesting the person would like to walk away. But keep in mind the need to compare behavior with the baseline.

Signals of deception are not just confined to the body. They can involve dress, space, and voice.

Dress

With clothing, nonverbal leakage mainly shows up in the manipulation of dress, which may suggest a respondent feels threatened by a given question. An interviewee may suddenly close and button his or her coat or begin to tug nervously at a pants leg or skirt hem or pull sleeves down over his or her hands. This may betray a fear of having some deception uncovered. Other signals include straightening or tugging at the collar, smoothing the tie, picking at lint, or rubbing at a spot.

Personal Space

Proxemics, relating to the distance that one keeps from others as well as one's relation to the surrounding environment, may be a rich source of deception cues. An interviewee might shift the chair's position or might suddenly lean back on the chair's rear legs. Moving away from the interviewer may show a lack of cooperativeness or be a feeble attempt to put distance between the interviewee and interviewer by altering the environment. Often, when a person physically backs up, the other person comes closer. In formal conversations occurring while standing, the interviewee may lean back or step back during a deceptive response even while "blocking" by folding the arms across the chest.

An interviewee who has been relaxed may shift under pressure. For example, deception may leak out when the person suddenly crosses her arms and legs and leans back. The vulnerable forward posture is less comfortable when facing the fear of discovery. Conversely, an interviewee might "open up" during a response, suggesting openness and honesty. An interviewee may also try to erect "signal blunders" to hide behind. These may be such subtle activities as placing a purse or briefcase in the lap as a barrier.

Artifacts

One's personal possessions in the office and the physical environment of the office itself offer cues, and they can be manipulated to create the intended perception. Some people will meticulously decorate their offices in an attempt to manage the impressions of their visitors. For instance, a manager may mount every award and plaque he's ever received on a "brag wall" to enhance his status. Although many of these decorations can reflect honest identity claims, some can be strategic and even deceptive.[32] How many times have you been lured back to a car salesman's office to find an overabundance of religious symbols? How about cute kiddie photos? They seem to say, "You can trust me. I'm a man of faith and a family man, and I would never give you a raw deal." Personal effects in the office should be used as clues toward the bigger picture of who the real person is, but the impression they give off needs to be interpreted carefully.

Voice

Voice is another rich source of cues. Most relevant in detecting deception are the voice's pitch, tone, and volume, as well as the response's onset and duration. Authorities have long known that deceptive answers have a slower onset than honest ones.

In addition, deceptive answers are likely to be longer and less specific than honest ones. The deceiver may be attempting to fill in the gap with needless material. Some see length as an attempt to make a deceptive answer more elaborate and thus more convincing than the deceiver knows it is. The answer's length may also reflect the pauses and hesitations needed as the interviewee stumbles through the answer.

The final source of deception is pitch. Researchers have found that vocal pitch rises measurably in deceptive responses. While observers frequently could not say why they labeled such a response as deceptive, they knew it was, and research instruments could show the difference.[33]

In many interpersonal, managerial interactions, nonverbal elements are the source of most of the message. While not everything communicated nonverbally is done so consciously or intentionally, the unintentional signals may be as valid as the intentional ones and potentially more useful. Keep in mind, though, the suggestions about establishing a behavioral baseline for each person in specific situations. In addition, if deception is suspected, use that as an impetus for further investigation or at least caution, not as the final word.

Summary

Everything but the words themselves may be considered the domain of nonverbal communication. Every managerial interaction has nonverbal elements that add to or qualify the interaction. It is difficult to put precise meanings to nonverbal signals and they vary from culture to culture; however, when nonverbal signals contradict verbal ones, the nonverbal signals are usually the ones to trust.

Nonverbal cues have six functions: complementing, accenting, contradicting, repeating, regulating, and substituting. In addition, nonverbal cues add redundancy to the verbal message and increase the probability that the verbal message will be understood as intended by the sender.

The study of movement includes gestures, posture, head movement, and walk. Gestures may include emblems, illustrators, affect displays, regulators, and adapters. The space around us and how we and others relate to it are also important. Four zones are presented and discussed in this chapter, but care must be taken in interpreting them because zones may differ among cultures. Inappropriate use of space may make a manager appear rude, while an accurate analysis indicates much about the importance of power in an organization.

Personal appearance is another integral part of the impression we give, and often the key to credibility. Consequently, managers should pay close attention to their clothing, accessories, makeup, hairstyle, and grooming to be sure their appearance fits the expectations of the organization's culture and customers.

Voice is the final source of nonverbal signals discussed in the chapter. Vocal delivery includes the pitch, tone, onset, and duration of messages.

The first step to detecting deception is to establish a baseline. Once this has been accomplished, movement, dress, space, artifacts, and voice can each be used to evaluate the potential for deception in an interaction. But in all managerial communication situations, it is important to remember that no dictionary exists for the meaning of nonverbal cues.

Cases for Small Group Discussion

Case 8-1.

Facing a Series of Interviews

Hanna Jenson recently applied for a position that involves supervising the work activities of a large comprehensive insurance company. She has just received a letter notifying her to report for an interview for this position in four days. The letter indicates Jenson will be required to attend a series of interviews as follows:

9:00 A.M.	Rodney Custer, personnel manager
10:00 A.M.	Ahmad Syed, department chief
11:00 A.M.	Bobbie Kent, medical claims supervisor

If Jenson gets the job, she will receive a substantial raise in salary as well as her first opportunity to gain supervisory experience. Therefore, she wants the job very badly and is concerned about how to prepare for each of the interviews.

Although she has never worked in this particular department, Jenson has worked for the company for several years. She knows Custer and Syed on a casual basis, but she has never met Kent. Custer is 38 years old, meticulous in dress, and obviously very proud of the managerial accomplishments he has made since he became personnel manager two years ago. Jenson's friends in the department believe Custer is sexist and tends to hire men in supervisory positions if possible.

Syed is an elderly rotund gentleman who will be eligible for retirement in two years. He is somewhat unkempt in appearance, but his knowledge of policy and regulations has earned him the respect of managers throughout the company.

Jenson is especially concerned about the interview with Kent. If she gets the job, she will be working directly under Kent, yet she knows nothing about her.

Questions

1. What positive and negative suggestions would you give Jenson about her choice of dress for this interview?
2. What effective nonverbal signals would you suggest Jenson send during the interview, given the profiles of two of the individuals Jenson is to meet?
3. How could Jenson's strategy differ in each interview situation?

Case 8-2.

What Is Going On Here?

Art Margulis is the 45-year-old director of marketing research for a Fortune 500 consumer products company. He joined the firm 19 years ago after he received his MBA with a marketing emphasis. Because of his technical expertise, management skills, and outgoing personality, he was made director of this 50-person group four years ago. Six people report directly to him, but the management style is informal, so he frequently interacts with everyone in the department.

Two years ago, Margulis extensively recruited Maria Lopez, who had just completed her Ph.D. in applied statistics. Margulis had a difficult time persuading her to join the company because she had many attractive offers. Although she was only 34 years old, she had outstanding experience in marketing research and a unique educational background. Lopez came in and quickly made a number of significant contributions to the department. As manager of statistical analysis, she reports directly to Margulis but has nobody reporting to her. Soon after joining the company, Lopez and her husband divorced. Many employees in the department believe her personal problems are why she has not been more sociable with other employees.

Lopez and Margulis have always gotten along well and often have lunch together to discuss various projects. They seem to have much in common as they both understand the advanced statistics used in the research. Recently, the conversations have turned more personal as Margulis went through a divorce and seems to be seeking more social support. In particular, he seems to miss his two teenage daughters and needs someone to talk to about it.

But Lopez sees a problem developing, and she recently talked to a human resource manager about it. She explained that she has a lot of respect for Margulis and enjoys visiting with him. But she notices a definite change in his behavior around her. The eye contact is more prolonged and the personal physical space between them is reduced. Lopez feels uneasy about it and has tried to subtly change the trend. However, this only intensified what Lopez saw as "pressure" to spend more time with Margulis. Today, Margulis asked Lopez to have dinner with him so they could talk over a project. It seems they haven't had time to cover the project during working hours.

Questions

Discuss this case in terms of nonverbal behavior and other topics presented in this chapter. What are the implications of this situation?

Endnotes

1. Carol Lehman and Mark Lehman, "Effective Nonverbal Communication Techniques: Essential Element in the Promotional Strategies of Professional Service Firms," *Journal of Professional Services Marketing* 5, no. 1 (1989), p. 17.
2. Albert Mehrabian, "Communicating Without Words," *Psychology Today*, September 1968, pp. 53–55.
3. Scott T. Fleishmann, *Employment Relations Today*, Summer 1991, pp. 161–62.
4. Roswitha Rothlach, "Anglo-German Misunderstandings in Language and Behavior," *Industrial and Commercial Training* 23, no. 3 (March 1991), pp. 15–16.
5. Om P. Kharbanda and Ernest A. Stallworthy, "Verbal and Non-verbal Communication," *Journal of Managerial Psychology* 6, no. 2 (April 1991), p. 49.
6. Larry H. Hynson, Jr., "Doing Business with South Korea—Park II: Business Practices and Culture," *East Asian Executive Reports* 13 (September 15, 1991), p. 18.
7. Sandra G. Garside and Brian H. Kleiner, "Effective One-to-One Communication Skills," *Industrial and Commercial Training* 23, no. 7 (July 1991), p. 27.
8. Paul Ekman, *Emotions Revealed: Recognizing Faces and Feelings to Improve Communication and Emotional Life* (Henry Holt and Company, 2004).
9. R. P. Harrison, *Beyond Words: An Introduction to Nonverbal Communication* (Englewood Cliffs, NJ: Prentice Hall, 1974), p. 25.
10. Pam Belluck, "For a Creative Boost, Go Blue," *Houston Chronicle*, February 6, 2009.
11. Geraldine E. Hynes and Marius Janson, "Using Semiotic Analysis to Determine Effectiveness of Internet Marketing," *Proceedings of the 2007 Annual International Convention of the Association for Business Communication*. Available at www.business-communication.org.
12. S. Burbinster, "Body Politics," *Associate & Management*, April 1987, pp. 55–57.
13. John L. Waltman, "Communication Redundancy and Business Communication," *Journal of Business Communication* 21, no. 4 (Fall 1984).
14. P. Ekman and W. Friesen, "The Repertoire of Nonverbal Behavior," *Semiotica* 1 (1969), pp. 49–98.
15. Alex (Sandy) Pentland, *Honest Signals: How They Shape our World* (MIT Press, 2008), pp. 10–40, 105.
16. Edward T. Hall, *The Hidden Dimension* (New York: Doubleday, 1966).
17. Loretta A. Malandro and Larry Barker, *Nonverbal Communication* (Reading, MA: Addison-Wesley Publishing, 1983), pp. 226–30.
18. Phillip L. Hunsaker, "Communicating Better: There's No Proxy for Proxemics," in *Reading in Business Communication*, ed. Richard C. Huseman (Hinsdale, IL: Dryden Press, 1981), p. 52.
19. Lynn Cohen, "Nonverbal (Mis)communication Between Managerial Men and Women," *Business Horizons*, January–February 1983, p. 15.

20. Elizabeth Woyke, "Work Life: What Do Men Want? A Thermostat," *BusinessWeek*, May 29, 2006, p. 11.

21. "Press the Flesh, not the Keyboard," *The Economist* 364, issue 8287 (August 24, 2002), p. 50.

22. Woyke, "Work Life: What Do Men Want? A Thermostat."

23. Lynn Pearl, "Opening the Door to Rapport," *Agri Marketing* 30, no. 2 (April 1992), p. 97.

24. Stephanie Armour, "Business Casual Causes Confusion," *USA Today,* July 16, 2007. http://jobs.aol.com/article/a/business-casual-causes-confusion/200707161044 09990002 (retrieved July 17, 2007).

25. *Ibid.*

26. Louis V. Gerstner, Jr., *Who Says Elephants Can't Dance? Inside IBM's Historic Turnaround* (New York: HarperCollins, 2002), p. 185.

27. Patricia Buhler, "Managing in the 90s: Are You Really Saying What You Mean?" *Supervision* 52, no. 9 (September 1991), p. 19.

28. Paul Ekman and Wallace V. Friesen, "Detecting Deception from the Body and Face," *Journal of Personality and Social Psychology* 29, no. 2 (1974), p. 295.

29. John L. Waltman, "Nonverbal Interrogation: Some Applications," *Journal of Police Science and Administration* 11, no. 2 (June 1983), p. 167.

30. Jeff Gammage, "Good Liars May Be Wired Differently," *Houston Chronicle,* January 29, 2006, p. 2D.

31. Charles J. McClintock and Raymond G. Hunt, "Nonverbal Indicators of Affect and Deception in Interview Situations," *Journal of Applied Psychology* 5, no. 3 (1975), p. 420.

32. Sam Gosling, *Snoop: What Your Stuff Says about You* (Profile Books, 2008), p.13.

33. Paul Ekman, Wallace Friesen, and Klaus R. Scherer, "Body Movement and Voice Pitch in Deception Interaction," *Semiotica* 16, no. 11 (1976), p. 26.

Chapter Nine

Intercultural Managerial Communication

The real death of America will come when everyone is alike.

—*James T. Ellison, U.S. historian*

Do you see yourself as a candidate for an overseas assignment? Depending on the company you work for, the extent of its overseas operations, and the rules and regulations of the host country, people at various levels may be offered assignments abroad. Some companies with limited operations overseas prefer to send some of their newest people to staff those sites. This point will be addressed in greater detail later in this chapter. But whether or not you plan to work for a multinational corporation, cultural sensitivity is an important quality for managerial success.

RATIONALE

You should become familiar with intercultural business communication practices for at least three reasons. First, until the global recession began in 2008, the U.S. had witnessed tremendous growth in international trade for over three decades. Between 1990 and 2006, trade volumes grew by more than 6 percent a year. The total value of import/export trade in 2008 exceeded $4.38 trillion: over $2.52 trillion in imports and almost $1.86 trillion in exports.[1] But the world's economic machine went into reverse in 2008, and the World Trade Organization predicted that the volume of global merchandise trade would shrink by 9 percent in 2009. The immediate causes are a collapse in demand and a credit crunch. The speed with which international trade has fallen so uniformly around the world is likely due to vertical specialization, or global supply chains. This is in part because countries specialize not only in products but also in steps in the process of production. So, for instance, a tractor made in the U.S. may contain steel from India and be stamped and pressed in Mexico before being sold in China. Thus, changes in demand in one country affect the trade flows and economies of several countries. Going forward, this interdependence may be a key to revival. Once demand begins to increase again, vertical specialization and the open system of trade may bring more rapid world recovery.[2]

Despite the current global economic crisis, many countries depend on international trade as an important contributor to their gross domestic product (GDP). The U.S. has steadily become more "open" over the last eight years—that is, exports and imports have grown faster than GDP. In 2008, international trade accounted for over 30 percent of the United States' GDP.[3] But the U.S. is not the most globalized country, by far. For the past 40 years, KOF Swiss Economic Institute annually has ranked 158 countries according to their degree of globalization, as measured by 24 economic, social, and political factors. Who is number one? Belgium.[4] In addition to high levels of trade in goods and services, Belgium experiences the most foreign investment. Furthermore, the country is profoundly affected by ideas, information, and people from abroad. The globalization index for the U.S. has been continuously increasing since the 1970s. The U.S. ranked 38th in 2009, mostly due to economic activity rather than social and political globalization.

A second reason you should become familiar with best practices for intercultural business communication is that, even if you don't go overseas to conduct business, you may find yourself working for a firm owned by a company from another country. In the United States, for example, the direct investment of foreign-based companies grew from $9 billion in 1966 to more than $414 billion in 2008. Spending by foreign investors increased 67 percent in 2007 and 90 percent in 2008. The largest industry growth was in manufacturing, which accounted for almost half of the total investment outlays. Outlays were also sizable in transportation, utilities, mining, finance and insurance, real estate, and banking. Most outlays by foreign direct investors were to acquire existing U.S. businesses rather than to establish new businesses in the U.S. The top investors in U.S. businesses in 2007 were Canada, Britain, Australia, Spain, Germany, and the United Arab Emirates.[5]

The following are some examples of businesses owned by foreign-based companies: Motel 6 is owned by Accor SA, a French company; and Dannon Co., the yogurt maker, is owned by Danone Group, also a French company. Henkel, a German corporation, owns the Dial Corporation, makers of Dial soap, Renuzit air fresheners, and Armour Star canned meats. Great Britain's Diageo PLC owns Johnny Walker scotch, Bailey's Irish Cream liqueur, and Smirnoff vodka. British companies own French's mustard, Canada Dry (Cadbury Schweppes PLC), and Pillsbury (Pet). Wholly owned subsidiaries of the government of Dubai include Barneys and Loehmann's clothing stores. If you look around, you will find other examples. For instance, a major shopping mall in suburban St. Louis, Missouri, is owned by Paramount, a German real estate holding company.

Products that we think of as American may actually be manufactured by foreign companies. For instance, Dreyer's Grand Ice Cream, Purina Dog Chow, Nescafé instant coffee, and KitKat candy bars are among the 8,000 brands made by Nestlé, the world's biggest food company. Nestlé is based in Switzerland. On the other hand, products that we may think of as "foreign" may actually be domestic. Philip Morris makes Grey Poupon mustard in the United States. Michelin tires are manufactured in South Carolina. And Evian water is distributed by Coca-Cola. Truly, we live in a global economy.

A third reason to learn about intercultural business communication is the increasing likelihood that you will work with, or for, someone who is not a native-born U.S. citizen. According to the U.S. Census Bureau, Department of Labor, 13 percent of the work force was non-U.S. native in 2000. New streams in the labor pool include workers of Asian and Hispanic origin. Currently, 7 million workers in the U.S. are from Asian countries (China, Japan, the Philippines, India, Vietnam, Korea, Indonesia, and Thailand). But the most rapidly growing ethnic or racial group is the Hispanic work force. In 2008, over 20 million workers were of Hispanic origin. By 2016, the U.S. Bureau of Labor Statistics predicts that the number will be almost 27 million, a 30 percent increase. By comparison, the rate of increase of white non-Hispanics in the work force is predicted to be 1.4 percent.[6] As a result, managers will be leading a noticeably different work force in the years ahead.

Furthermore, employees often bring their culturally based behaviors to work. For instance, Muslims are required by their faith to pray five times a day. Most of the prayer times are flexible, but the sunset prayers must be said at dusk. Dell, Inc., and Electrolux Home Products accommodate their Muslim workers in U.S. plants with a "tag-out" policy that allows a few employees at a time to step away for prayers. As the work force becomes ever more diverse, such cultural differences in behavior will have a major impact on the likelihood of successful business/worker interaction.

In summary, whether or not you deliberately choose to conduct business internationally, you will need to be an interculturally sensitive communicator. Unfortunately, the quality of the training given to people headed for overseas assignments differs widely by company and by country. It's been estimated that 30 to 50 percent of American managers fail to perform adequately abroad because they have not been sufficiently prepared for adjusting to the foreign culture.[7] In a survey of emerging trends conducted by the Cendant Mobility relocation firm, 84 percent of companies said that they provide intercultural training to staff but less than 50 percent of employees take advantage of that training.[8] Companies in Japan and Australia, on the other hand, are noted for the high quality of training their workers are given before being sent abroad.

This chapter will not cover everything anyone ever needed to know about being an intercultural managerial communicator in all parts of the world. That ambitious goal is the subject of thousands of books and articles in any library and could not possibly be condensed into one chapter. Our goal instead will be an introduction to the types of issues, concerns, and mores that managers need to study to become successful in intercultural business communication. Additionally, we will make a number of suggestions about what managers can do now and in the coming years to better prepare themselves to conduct global business.

WHAT IS CULTURE?

Before we review the many aspects of intercultural communication, we might want to get an idea of the meaning of the word *culture*. Though definitions of this term abound and vary widely in terms of their complexity, Gould defines it in a clear and straightforward manner.

def'n of culture

Culture is what we grow up in. Beginning in childhood, we learn the behaviors, habits, and attitudes that are acceptable to those around us. These are transmitted to us orally, nonverbally, and in writing. As time goes on, we gradually acquire the knowledge, beliefs, values, customs, and moral attitudes of the society in which we mature. A body of common understanding develops with which we feel comfortable. We know what to expect, and we know what is expected of us.[9]

Defined in such a way, culture includes the religious systems to which we are exposed, the educational system, the economic system, the political system, the recreational outlets, the mores governing dress and grooming, the standards of etiquette, the food and how it is prepared and served, the gift-giving customs, the morals, the legal system, the quality and quantity of communication among the people, the greeting practices, the rituals performed, the modes of travel available, as well as the many other aspects of people's lives that they come to take for granted.

Malcolm Gladwell explores the importance of culture in individual behaviors in his recent best-seller, *Outliers: The Story of Success.* He concludes that "cultural legacies are powerful forces. They have deep roots and long lives. They persist, generation after generation, virtually intact, even as the economic and social and demographic conditions that spawned them have vanished, and they play such a role in directing attitudes and behavior that we cannot make sense of our world without them."[10] Whether you like it or not, culture is all encompassing and everlasting.

When we recognize how pervasive a person's culture is and how much it can differ from country to country, we can then begin to appreciate more fully the difficult job facing a manager in an intercultural environment. The people in, or from, another country are quite comfortable with a culture that may seem strange to a U.S. businessperson. Yet it is we who will have to make the adjustments and live with the uncertainty and the unusual occurrences and practices. If we want to succeed in this highly competitive global marketplace, we will have to learn to see and accept things as others see and accept them.

INTERCULTURAL MYTHS

Before we examine the various aspects of intercultural business communication, we need to dispel a few myths. The global village concept, end of history view, and universality myth are three theories worth examining.

The *global village concept* was introduced by Marshall McLuhan in his 1967 book, *The Medium Is the Message.* This concept proposed that advancements in communication and transportation technologies would ultimately shrink the world to a point where we would be one big happy global village. Some believe the global village concept has been realized because we now know instantly of happenings in even the most remote parts of the world.[11]

Others believe we are nowhere near fruition of the global village concept. They contend that the great advancements in communication and transportation technologies have only created a greater proximity among the various peoples of the world, and that proximity has only enhanced the perceived differences among those peoples.[12]

In conjunction with the latter view, it has been suggested that you, today's students, are responsible for whether or not we ever do see the fruition of the global village concept. To be successful in the global marketplace, you will need to adjust to other cultures, and you will need to gain and maintain the trust of your intercultural partners. In other words, you will need to bridge the cultural gap.[13] With each successful international business venture (successful for all parties involved), we move closer to the realization of the global village concept.

A second widely discussed theory is the *end of history view* advanced by Francis Fukuyama. His assertion was that the end of the Cold War meant the end of the war of ideas. After the Berlin wall crumbled in 1989, he predicted that one relatively harmonious world would unite in liberal democracy. Somewhat modeled after the global village concept, Fukuyama's theory included the idea that significant global conflicts would be a thing of the past as we blend into one.[14] Unfortunately, this illusionary vision of world peace was quickly destroyed when former Soviet bloc nations struggled to adapt to Western culture and ideas.

The third myth of which we should be wary is the *universality myth*. This myth is often promoted by people who have spent a short time in a foreign country. Initially, they notice all the differences between their own culture and that of the host country. Then, they start to note all the similarities. They come away from the experience concluding that, under the skin, we are all alike: brothers and sisters in the common family of humanity.

Milton Bennett, who describes six stages of intercultural sensitivity,[15] refers to this belief as *minimization*. He says that looking for similarities is a way to assuage our fears of difference and make us feel better about each other. A short visit does not provide people the deeper insight into a culture that would have revealed major differences in beliefs, values, and mores. To illustrate, we might look at some of the results of a survey conducted in a number of countries. One of the questions asked of the respondents was, "Do you agree or disagree with the statement: 'Most people can be trusted'?" The levels of agreement are listed next:

United States	55%
United Kingdom	49%
Mexico	30%
West Germany	19%
Italy	1%

One could argue that language differences might have been responsible for some of the variation. But even if we allow for some margin of error, we would still have a significant variation in a very basic belief.

Another example of differences in basic beliefs was the 2004 incident in Minnesota when a Hmong deer hunter was convicted of killing five other hunters and wounding three more. The group of hunters had found him in a deer blind on private land, accused him of trespassing, and ordered him to leave. Instead, he opened fire. About 60,000 Hmong people live in the Minneapolis region. Refugees from Laos, the Hmong social organization is founded on a clan system, and they do not understand the concept of private property. They hunt wherever they see fit. This tragic incident demonstrates that we truly are not all alike under the skin, brothers and sisters in the common family of humanity. We differ appreciably, and those differences must be recognized, understood, and accepted if we are to do business with one another.

SOME OF THE WAYS IN WHICH WE DIFFER

One of the most extensive studies of cultural differences was conducted by Geert Hofstede in a very large U.S.-based multinational corporation. He collected more than 116,000 questionnaires from this corporation's employees in 40 countries around the globe. A massive statistical analysis of his findings revealed six dimensions of national culture as shown in Table 9-1: power distance, uncertainty avoidance, individualism/collectivism, masculinity/femininity, high and low context, and monochronic/polychronic time.[16]

Power distance indicates the extent to which a society accepts the fact that power in institutions and organizations is distributed unequally. It is reflected in the values of both the more powerful and less powerful members of the society. The Philippines, Venezuela, Mexico, and the South Slavic states are countries with high power distances, while Denmark, New Zealand, Austria, the United States, and Israel are a few of the countries with low power distances.

A manager in a culture with high power distance is seen as having dramatically more power than a subordinate would have. This manager, who is usually addressed respectfully by title and surname, might favor a controlling strategy and behave like an autocrat. For instance, within the British Houses of Parliament, lawmakers can move to the head of the line at restaurants, restrooms, and elevators, while clerks, aides, and secretaries who work in Parliament must stand and wait. In a culture with a lower power distance, however, a manager is seen as having little more power than a subordinate, is often addressed by first name, takes her place in line, and manages by using an equalitarian communication strategy.

A dramatic example of how power distance affects business is provided by the airline industry. Between 1988 and 1998 Korean Air's plane crash ratio was at alarming heights—4.79 per million departures. That figure was 17 times worse than the crash ratio for major U.S. commercial airlines in that time period. Several investigations and studies were done to examine the cause of Korean

TABLE 9–1
Hofstede's Dimensions of Cultural Differences

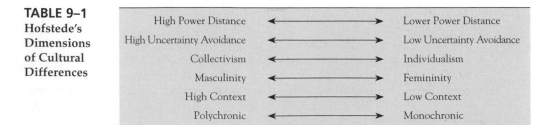

High Power Distance	←———→	Lower Power Distance
High Uncertainty Avoidance	←———→	Low Uncertainty Avoidance
Collectivism	←———→	Individualism
Masculinity	←———→	Femininity
High Context	←———→	Low Context
Polychronic	←———→	Monochronic

Air's crash ratio. Finally, it occurred to someone to apply Hofstede's power distance theory. What they discovered was fascinating. The first officers in the cockpit were paralyzed with fear to say anything that questioned the captain's ability. Afraid to speak up, they were trapped in subservient roles due to the high power distance ingrained in their culture. One Korean airline pilot revealed, "The captain is in charge and does what he wants, when he wants, when he likes, how he likes, and everyone else sits quietly and does nothing." Fortunately, by understanding the underlying importance of culture and how it relates to the airline industry, dramatic improvements were made. The Korean Air flight crews were retrained and have enjoyed a spotless safety record since 1999.[17]

Uncertainty avoidance relates to the degree to which a society feels threatened by uncertainty and by ambiguous situations. It tries to avoid these uncertainties and ambiguous situations by providing greater career stability, establishing and following formal rules, not allowing odd ideas and behaviors, and believing in absolute truths and the attainment of expertise. Greece, Germany, England, Portugal, Belgium, and Japan have strong uncertainty avoidance, while Singapore, Hong Kong, Denmark, the United States, and Sweden have weak uncertainty avoidance.

Belgium and Denmark are geographically close, and their people look similar. However, when it comes to uncertainty avoidance, the two nations are far apart because of different histories, politics, religions, literature, and other cultural factors. Recall that earlier in this chapter Belgium was identified as the most globalized of 158 countries. What do you think is the connection between that ranking and Belgians' avoidance of uncertainty, their respect for rules and plans, their insistence on following procedures regardless of circumstances? Uncertainty avoidance is probably a major dimension for most intercultural managers to contend with. Most likely, they will be expected to challenge the status quo and implement change, and uncertainty avoidance is a significant obstacle to change. Such managers ought to remember that using an equalitarian communication strategy to get people involved and highlighting the benefits of change can greatly help to reduce resistance.

On the *individualism/collectivism* dimension, *individualism* suggests a loosely knit social framework in which people are expected to take care of themselves and their immediate families only. *Collectivism*, on the other hand, is evidenced by a tight social framework in which people distinguish between in-groups and out-groups. They expect their in-group (relatives, clan, organization) to take care of them. Because of this, they believe they owe absolute loyalty to it. The United States, Australia, and Great Britain are the most highly individualistic countries on Hofstede's scale, while Guatemala, Pakistan, Colombia, Nigeria, Japan, and Venezuela are more collectivist countries.

The huge social-psychological gap between collectivist and individualist cultures can be illustrated linguistically. In Chinese, for instance, there is no word for "individualism." The closest one can come is the word for "selfishness." In Japanese, the word "I"—meaning the unconditional generalized self—is not often used in conversation. Instead, Japanese has many words for "I," depending on audience and context. This reflects the Eastern conviction that one is a different person when interacting with different groups.[18]

Managers from individualistic cultures and collectivist cultures conflict in many ways. In negotiations, for example, managers from collectivist cultures do not want to make decisions. They must first collaborate; consensus must be reached. But managers from individualistic cultures have difficulty collaborating, want to talk to a "decision maker," and cannot understand why the other group must spend so much time in conference.

Masculinity/femininity, as a dimension, expresses the extent to which the dominant values in the society are "masculine." This masculinity, according to Hofstede, would include assertiveness, the acquisition of money and things, and not caring about the quality of life. These values are labeled masculine because, within nearly all societies, men scored higher in these values. Japan, Austria, Venezuela, and Mexico were among the most masculine societies. Feminine cultures, by contrast, value family, children, and quality of life. Denmark, Sweden, and Norway are considered feminine cultures.

Consider the following comparison. In the United States, men are judged at least partly on their ability to make a good salary. Frequently, this judgment precludes traditional U.S. feminine values of caring for children. In Helsinki, Finland, however, a man may be called away from a meeting to tend to the baby in the child care center in the next building and no one considers this a wrong priority. Despite the passage of the Family Leave Act in 1993, far fewer working men than women take the full time they are eligible for when dealing with family and medical problems in the United States.

A fifth cultural difference an intercultural communicator needs to keep in mind is whether the culture is a high-context or low-context culture. These terms were first used by Edward T. Hall in 1977.[19] In a *high-context* culture, much information is either in the physical context or environment or is internalized in the person. In such a culture, people look for meaning in what is not said—in the nonverbal communication or body language; in the silences, the facial expressions, and the gestures. Japan and Saudi Arabia are high-context countries, as are Chinese- and Spanish-speaking countries.

In a *low-context* culture, most information is expected to be in explicit codes, such as words. In such a culture, communicators emphasize sending and receiving accurate messages directly, usually by being highly articulate. Canada and the United States are low-context cultures. As one might suspect, negotiations between low-context and high-context cultures can be fraught with peril when the parties are not warned of the differences in approaches.[20] The value of contracts also varies widely between high- and low-context cultures. U.S. business-to-business transactions rely on documents, not handshakes or personal relationships.

A recent study compared the "About Us" feature of Western and Eastern companies' websites. The results demonstrate how low-context and high-context cultural values can manifest in subtle but important ways. The researchers found that Western companies projected a strong image in the About Us page of their websites by directly stating their achievements, status, industry rank, and profits. By contrast, high-context Eastern companies used indirect methods to promote themselves, such as describing their heritage and history, relationships with high-status others, and links to the home country.[21]

The sixth dimension of cultural differences, according to Hofstede, is *monochronic versus polychronic* time. In a monochronic culture, such as Germany, the United States, and most westernized nations, we talk about saving time, wasting time, making time, and spending time. We measure time by the clock, often in nanoseconds. In hyper-punctual countries like Japan, pedestrians walk fast and bank clocks are accurate. In Western businesses, we read quarterly returns and define "long-term" projections as those going out three to five years into the future. Time is linear.

In polychronic cultures, such as Spain, Latin American nations, and most Asian countries, time just *is*. These cultures trace their roots back thousands of years. Time is measured by events, not the clock. Thus, promptness diminishes in value, and being "late" is a sign of status. In Ecuador, for instance, politicians, military officers, and businesspeople are less punctual than blue-collar workers. The story goes that when Ecuador's president, Lucio Gutierrez, realized that chronic lateness was costing his country $2.5 billion a year, he started a national campaign to promote the importance of clock time. But his spokesman arrived late at the television studio to make the announcement.[22] This example demonstrates how deep culture goes and how difficult it is to change.

In polychronic countries, "long-term" thinking is over generations and even centuries. The moment doesn't matter, by comparison. People in polychronic cultures are more patient, less interested in time management or measurement, and more willing to wait for their rewards than those in monochronic cultures. To them, time is flexible, unfolding naturally. And the fact that polychronic cultures typically are less economically successful than monochronic cultures is not a compelling reason for change.

Given the globalization of today's marketplace and the increasing pace at which firms are becoming multinational, it has been suggested that organizations around the world will begin to look very much alike. One theory states that as the companies become more similar, the organizational culture might dominate or diminish the effects of the larger culture. Research thus far does not support the likelihood of these developments. Laurent found that employees of different nationalities working for a multinational firm maintained and even strengthened their cultural differences. German workers became more German, American workers became more American, and Swedish workers became more Swedish.[23] The implication is that we must accept, even value, our cultural differences for business success.

One way that multinationals are demonstrating cultural sensitivity is in their hiring practices. PepsiCo, for instance, named Indra Nooyi as the company's CEO in 2006. Nooyi is a woman, born in India. Since 2001, half of all new hires at Pepsi are either women or ethnic minorities. And managers earn their bonuses in part by how well they recruit and retain them. Six of its top twelve executives are women or minorities. Pepsi argues that a diverse leadership helps the company better understand the disparate tastes of new consumers globally.[24]

Having explored some of the fundamental dimensions on which the people of the world differ and how profound the differences are, we now turn our attention to more practical matters. The next sections present approaches to success as intercultural communicators. More specifically, the rest of this chapter discusses dealing with language differences, being nonverbally sensitive, being a good intercultural communicator, and preparing for assignments or careers in international business.

SHOULD YOU LEARN THE LANGUAGE?

The first decision facing an international business traveler is whether to learn the language spoken in the country to be visited. People who have learned a second language will testify that it can be a long, involved, and tedious task. Furthermore, the difficulty level varies with the language to be learned. Some have many subtle nuances that non-natives have a hard time capturing. And the many dialects that exist within a country complicate the process even more. According to the U.S. State Department, despite our immigrant roots, just 10 percent of U.S. citizens can speak a second language. In contrast, more than half of the people in the European Union are bilingual, and 28 percent are trilingual.

Which languages are the most important to learn? According to the U.S. Department of Education, Chinese, Arabic, Farsi, Korean, Japanese, Russian, Hindi, and Urdu are the languages most vital to this country's future, although less than 1 percent of American high school students are studying any of these. By contrast, in China, English is mandatory for students from third grade onward.[25]

For short stays in a country, perhaps just to set up a partnership or sign a contract, most people would agree that one need not learn the language. Since English is the recognized language of business throughout the world, chances are good that the people one deals with will speak it. If they don't, one can always use an interpreter. Great care, however, should be exercised in selecting an interpreter, for they vary widely in ability and loyalty.

As the length of the stay increases, the need to learn the language, and the wisdom in learning it, also increases. Most authorities agree that an extended stay would justify the time and effort of learning the language of the land. Furthermore, familiarity with the local language enables familiarity with the culture, values, traditions, and business practices. The more that managers understand about the culture, the more likely they are to be successful in that environment.

One advantage of learning the language and learning it well is avoidance of interpretational disasters that have visited companies in their advertising and product labeling. For example, the Parker Pen Company unwittingly advertised in Latin America that its ink would prevent unwanted pregnancies. Similarly, Otis Engineering claimed on posters at a Russian trade show that its oil equipment would improve people's sex lives.

Sometimes slogans and product names backfire when translated into other languages. For example, Pepsi's slogan, "Come alive with Pepsi," in German reads, "Come alive from the grave with Pepsi." Ford had a similar experience with a product's name—one truck model was called the Fiera, which in Spanish means "ugly old woman."

One last caution is advisable about language usage. Some people choose a middle-of-the-road approach and learn only specific statements that are common or are pertinent to a particular setting. Such people should remember that in some languages, particularly the Eastern languages, the same word can be used to mean many different things. The tone of the voice varies to indicate a specific meaning. Sometimes a little knowledge can be more damaging than no knowledge.

NONVERBAL SENSITIVITY

Whether or not traveling managers choose to learn the verbal language of the land, they should try to learn as much as they can about the nonverbal language common in that culture. Chapter 8 provided an overview of the range of nonverbal behaviors used in business settings to communicate meaning. Interpretations of greetings, dress, space, touch, posture, gestures, and rituals vary widely among cultures. Business deals have been lost over a seemingly harmless American signal that was interpreted as a grave insult in another part of the world.

Greetings

From the start of any business contact, one should be aware that the form of greeting used may vary from culture to culture. Though the handshake is a fairly standard greeting in most parts of the world, the pressure used may differ. The high-pressure grip, which in America is supposed to suggest warmth and confidence, may be too aggressive where a lighter grasp is traditional.

In Japan, the bow is still practiced by older businesspeople. Sometimes the bow and handshake will both be used to signal respect for both cultures. Note, too, the different levels of bowing, each with significant meanings. In other parts of the world, a traditional greeting may be a hug, a nose rub, a kiss, or the placing of the hands in a praying position.[26]

On the subject of greetings, note too that business cards are treated differently in different parts of the world. In Japan, they are handed to the recipient with both hands with the information facing the receiver. Also, they are never put away hastily or scribbled on, but studied carefully and then arranged on the table during a business meeting. Finally, in any non-English-speaking country, printing the information on the reverse side of the business card in a second language is a courteous practice.[27]

Dress

While the business suit is considered acceptable attire for a business meeting in most parts of the world, it may or may not be acceptable for an evening of entertainment. For men in tropical climates, a *guayabera* or loose cotton shirt worn over a pair of slacks is considered acceptable at even formal occasions.

On the subject of dress, we should exercise caution even when we are not in business meetings or at official social functions. Standards of travel and entertainment dressing are much more conservative in some parts of the world than they are in the United States. Bare legs, arms, shoulders, or heads on the street or in holy buildings are considered offensive in many Arab and Eastern countries.

Space, Touch, and Posture

The space maintained, touching practiced, and postures assumed in business and social encounters vary appreciably across the globe. Americans are said to have a spatial bubble of up to 4 feet into which strangers should not encroach. In Arab countries and Latin America, people speak almost face-to-face and nose-to-nose. It has been said that an Arab wants to be close enough to smell your breath and body odor when he communicates with you. In the United States, we avoid smelling each other at all costs.

In some countries—Iran, Palestine, China, and Indonesia, for example—it is considered acceptable for two men to walk down the street holding hands as a sign of close friendship. However, in many of these same countries, it is not acceptable for a man and a woman to walk down the street hand in hand. This immodest public display of affection is frowned upon.

Also on the subject of touching, managers should exercise some care about what is touched. In Thailand, the head is considered sacred. It should never be touched, and objects should never be passed above it. In Tonga, touching someone's head could get you the death penalty. Finally, in Muslim countries, it is considered insulting to show the sole of your shoe to someone else. Businesspeople are cautioned never to cross their legs with one ankle on the other knee and never to lean back in an office chair with the feet on the desk.

Gestures

In Serbia, Iran, and Sri Lanka, nodding the head up and down means "no." In Italy, Greece, and some African countries, the gesture Americans use for "come here" means "good-bye." The "thumbs-up" gesture means "everything is good" in the United States, but to Australians it is an obscenity. The V-for-victory sign means something entirely different when reversed, with the palm facing the signer. In Britain, it then becomes an insult. In Ethiopia, pointing and the one-finger "come here" gesture are used only with children and dogs.

As demonstrated by the preceding illustrations, the gestures we use in international encounters can be fairly dangerous. A friendly or innocuous gesture can turn out to be a vivid and/or profane insult. Something that very clearly means one thing in one country may mean the opposite in another country. To increase our level of success in the increasingly competitive global marketplace, we are going to have to become interculturally sensitive.

Food

Perhaps we become most aware of cultural diversity when we discuss food—what foods are used to celebrate special occasions, how the food is eaten, even what is considered edible. Any traveler has tales of "exotic" meals, accompanied by value judgments.

Host nationals will want visitors to experience the culinary delights that bring so much pleasure to their taste buds, their national dining treasures. It is hard for them to imagine or understand that these same treats might bring forth horror and revulsion in someone not experienced with them.

Thus, as the special guest at a banquet one might be called on to try sheep's eyes in Saudi Arabia or Kazakhstan, shark's fin soup in China, a roasted gorilla hand in one part of Africa, or a live fish brought to the table and carved in Japan. While U.S. businesspeople may be reluctant to try such dishes, it would be supremely rude to refuse.

On the other hand, visitors to the United States are often critical of our daily consumption of processed foods and snacks such as popcorn and Jell-O. Corn is animal food in most parts of the world. Further, Americans' tendency to nibble throughout the day rather than sit through long meals is considered uncouth. Italians and Japanese, for instance, do not eat on the street or while standing.

The importance of sharing food when building intercultural relationships is exemplified by this Pakistani proverb: On the first cup of tea you're a stranger. On the second, a guest. By the third cup, you're family.

Gifts

The Foreign Corrupt Practices Act of 1977 specifies that bribing someone during the conduct of business is illegal. A violator's company may be fined up to $2 million, and the participants in the bribe individually may be fined up to $100,000 each and jailed for up to five years. Despite these stiff penalties, multinational corporations continue to take risks. U.S. federal prosecutors issued indictments in April 2003 against two executives representing ExxonMobil. They were accused of bribing officials in Kazakhstan in exchange for oil contracts in the mid-1990s. Payments allegedly included $20.5 million deposited in Swiss bank accounts of senior officers of the Republic of Kazakhstan, a new Gulfstream jet aircraft for the president, funds for tennis courts at his home, and four trucks with satellite dishes to be used by his daughter's television network. The indictments also cited speedboats, jewelry, fur coats, and snowmobiles. ExxonMobil denied knowledge that any improper payments were made.

Another dramatic example of international bribery involves KBR, an engineering and construction services company based in Houston, Texas. KBR was a subsidiary of the Halliburton Company until 2007. KBR was accused of steering more than $180 million worth of bribes to Nigerian government officials to win contracts valued at more than $6 billion between 1995 and 2004. In February 2009, KBR pleaded guilty in the case and agreed to pay $402 million in fines. In addition, a court-appointed monitor was assigned to oversee KBR's international transactions for three years, at a cost to the company of $3–5 million per year. Its former parent, Halliburton Company, agreed to pay most of the fine, along with an additional $177 million to settle civil complaints from the Securities and Exchange Commission. KBR admitted authorizing the bribes for contracts to build liquefied natural gas facilities on Bonny Island, Nigeria.[28]

Why would American corporations risk defying the FCPA? Antibribery laws are sometimes a source of competitive disadvantage when a company is trying to do business in a culture where gifts, fees, commissions, and "facilitation payments" to officials are normal practice and where other countries competing for lucrative contracts do not have antibribery restrictions.[29]

Gift-giving practices vary widely throughout the world. Common and expected in some countries, it is frowned upon in others. For example, while gift giving is important in Japan, it is generally considered inappropriate in Germany, Belgium, or the United Kingdom.[30] Tipping for good service, a common practice in the United States, is not expected in China, Denmark, Italy, and France.

Even where it is practiced, the nature and the value of the gifts may differ greatly. Though flowers are often safe if one is invited to dinner in someone's home, chrysanthemums should be avoided in many European countries because of their funereal association. In Japan, white flowers carry the same message, as do purple ones in Brazil and Mexico.[31]

Remember, too, that numbers and shapes might have some significance. The number four is associated with bad luck in Japan and China, as is seven in Kenya—though seven is seen as lucky in the Czech Republic. The triangle is considered a negative shape in Hong Kong, Korea, and Taiwan.[32]

Finally, investigate the interpretation of gifts bearing the company logo. While some people may interpret such gifts as a symbol of the business relationship being established or maintained, some might think the giver was simply too cheap to buy a gift on his or her own.

While not intended to be complete, the preceding discussion was designed to illustrate the very precarious world of the intercultural communicator. The dangers of nonverbal slippage are there whether or not a person chooses to learn the verbal language. In the end, the success of multinational firms will depend on how much effort their people expend toward being interculturally sensitive and thus sidestepping those dangers.

WHAT IS A GOOD INTERCULTURAL COMMUNICATOR?

While not a comprehensive profile, the following description portrays some of the most important qualities and characteristics of a good intercultural communicator. You are a good intercultural communicator if you avoid the pitfalls described earlier and if you maintain harmonious relations with your intercultural partners.

First and foremost, you are a good intercultural communicator if you avoid *ethnocentrism*. As mentioned previously, Bennett designed a six-stage developmental model of cultural sensitivity (see Table 9–2). His model identifies three stages of ethnocentrism: *denial, defense,* and *minimization*. An ethnocentric person may acknowledge the existence of cultural differences but sees his or her country as the best in the world and looks down on others as inferior because they are different. For whatever reasons, the ethnocentric person builds resentment rather than good relationships.

On the other hand, Bennett identified three stages of ethno-relativism: *acceptance, adaptation,* and *integration*. An ethno-relativistic manager recognizes and respects cultural differences and finds ways to make the workplace amenable to all.[33]

TABLE 9–2
Bennett's
Stages of
Intercultural
Sensitivity

Ethnocentrism	Ethno-relativism
1. **Denial**—no perception of differences	4. **Acceptance**—recognize and explore differences
2. **Defense**—hostility against other cultures	5. **Adaptation**—ability to empathize
3. **Minimization**—differences are superficial	6. **Integration**—recognize and embrace differences

Second, you are a good intercultural communicator if you are *nondefensive* about your homeland. For example, when someone from another country criticizes the United States for problems such as the high divorce rate, drug abuse, gang warfare, child abuse, teen pregnancies, AIDS, racial discrimination, and corrupt politicians, Americans should not defensively deny their validity. While you may not be able to explain fully how these problems came to be, a straightforward discussion of the problems and what things are being done about them would be appropriate.

Third, you are a good intercultural communicator if you are *curious* about other parts of the world and *brave.* You must have a genuine interest in the people and the places that exist outside your national boundaries. Intercultural managers realize that the comforts of home are not always available throughout the world and are willing to try new foods and lifestyle behaviors before condemning them out of hand.

Fourth, you are a good intercultural communicator if you are *empathic, understanding,* and *nonjudgmental.* You are able to see the world through the eyes of your intercultural partners with some degree of objectivity. You understand that the initially strange behaviors and mores of others have locally very justifiable, long-standing reasons. You do not try to push your culture's ways on people for whom these ways may not work.

Fifth, you are a good intercultural communicator if you are *patient.* You learn to live with ambiguity; you come to expect the unexpected. Meetings will not always go as planned. Businesses will not always be open during the hours posted. Conveniences will not always be readily available. Though much of your coping behaviors will involve riding out the unexpected, you will also sometimes use your industriousness to come up with alternatives to what was expected. If one mode of transportation proves too unpredictable, you simply look for another. If one means of communication fails, you just find another.

Finally, you are a good intercultural communicator if you are *genuinely personable* to the people of the other country with whom you are dealing. A good intercultural communicator truly likes and respects those people. It cannot be faked.

DEVELOPING INTERCULTURALLY SENSITIVE MANAGERS

Ambitious managers in multinational corporations should expect to work abroad sometime during their careers. A recent study by the Columbia University School of Business reported that successful executives must have multienvironment and multicountry experience to become a CEO in the 21st century.[34] In today's digital business world, why do managers and executives need to travel abroad in order to become fully informed citizens? Isn't everything available on the Internet? Probably not. The best way to get to know people who are different from ourselves, to understand and appreciate customs and beliefs that are unfamiliar, is to immerse ourselves in that new environment. Mark Twain observed over a century ago, "Travel is fatal to prejudice, bigotry, and narrow-mindedness."

In 2002, an estimated 3 to 5 million businesspeople were working as expatriates, and it is predicted that the size of the international work force will increase with increasing cooperation among nations.[35] IBM, a major corporation, has two-thirds of its workers abroad, both foreign nationals and American citizens. CEO Samuel Palmisano wrote in the 2007 annual report that IBM is a "globally integrated enterprise . . . which locates its operations and functions anywhere in the world based on the right cost, the right skills, and the right business environment." Corporations primarily send their best employees on international assignments to grow new markets, maintain existing operations, or develop high-potential employees who can both contribute to the company strategy and craft a global view of the corporation's business.[36] Further, a survey of human resource professionals at 300 Fortune 1000 companies revealed that half of the responding companies selected their best employees for international assignments.[37]

Lant Pritchett, an economist at the World Bank and the author of *Let Their People Come*, argues that the global pressure for employment movement across national borders will continue to rise. Cheap communication technologies make relocation easier psychologically, too, since it is less stressful to move when one can stay in touch with home base.[38]

You can do several things to prepare for a successful foreign assignment. As specified earlier, you may want to learn another language. You should explore training and educational opportunities in multicultural communication at your organization, in your community, and at nearby universities. On the social side, you might look into hosting an international student. This experience will not only help the student become acculturated in the United States; it will provide you with insight into the student's culture. Finally, stay abreast of business, political, and economic developments throughout the world. Read newspapers with an international focus, such as the *Christian Science Monitor* or the *Financial Times*. In our increasingly global marketplace, your cross-cultural expertise will bring competitive advantage.

In the meantime, what to do at home? Managers denied an overseas experience can still develop intercultural sensitivity. After all, managing diversity successfully brings high value to all contemporary organizations, not just multinational organizations. Michael Morris, a business professor at Columbia University, recognizes the common pitfalls managers face when trying to treat all employees fairly and respectfully. At one extreme, a manager may take the universalist approach, treating all employees the same. At the other extreme, a manager may take the particularist approach, adjusting the treatment according to the worker's culture. Both behaviors can have a negative effect on employees' perception of justice. "If justice issues are not well-managed in a diverse workplace, detrimental consequences ranging from poor morale and turnover to intergroup rivalry and balkanization may result."[39]

Morris offers 10 ways managers can create a more level playing field:

1. Rely on multiethnic strategies, not just on good intentions. For instance, a manager might implement a mentoring program to ensure that all employees develop important relationships.
2. Provide every employee constructive feedback so she/he may learn and grow.
3. Work to ensure that all cultural groups have access to opportunities.
4. Work to ensure that all cultural groups perceive that they are treated fairly.
5. Provide cultural competence training to supervisors who conduct performance reviews.
6. Monitor cultural boundaries to avoid engendering intergroup competition.
7. Manage misunderstandings by making staff aware that cultural differences may be the root cause of clashes rather than personality differences.
8. Be sensitive to obstacles facing members of certain cultural groups and be flexible about performance evaluations to even the playing field.
9. Call on those with cultural expertise just as managers would call on those with technical expertise for an IT problem.
10. Include all employees and all cultures in diversity discussions.

Women, non-native Americans, and people of color represented approximately 70 percent of new entrants to the U.S. work force in 2008. Therefore, cultural competence has taken on greater significance, both in recruitment and retention of multicultural workers and in reaching the multicultural consumer market. Managing diversity is every manager's challenge.

Summary

Given the changes occurring in the world marketplace and the increasingly competitive nature of markets both at home and abroad, firms must become more active internationally to survive and prosper. These trends and developments all suggest that today's students have a noteworthy chance of becoming tomorrow's international businesspeople. To be successful international businesspeople, they will have to be successful intercultural communicators.

A person's culture is pervasive, a body of common understanding with which he or she feels comfortable. But cultures differ appreciably, and those differences must be understood and accepted if cross-cultural business ventures are to succeed. The world has not yet become one big global village, and people are not all alike under the skin. In fact, the opposite is true—as we become globalized, we hold onto aspects of our cultural uniqueness. International businesspeople must still work to bridge the cultural gaps that exist among the peoples of the world.

For short business trips to another country, it is probably not necessary to learn the language of that country. For longer stays, it might be a good idea to do so. Learning the language frees the businessperson from having to rely on interpreters. It also lessens the chances of encountering the interpretational disasters some companies have experienced in their advertising and product labeling. Most importantly, it offers insights into the local culture.

Regardless of whether or not the language of the land is learned, international businesspeople need to be as nonverbally sensitive as they can. They need to be aware of greeting rituals and standards of dress. They should be aware that space, touch, gestures, and posture are dealt with differently in some cultures. They need to accept patiently others' interpretations of time, to be open to culinary adventures, and be familiar with gift-giving rituals.

A good intercultural communicator is ethnorelativistic, is nondefensive about his or her homeland in the face of questions about its problems, is curious about other people and brave with regard to the conditions he or she might have to confront, is empathic and understanding and nonjudgmental of intercultural partners, is patient in living with ambiguity and expecting the unexpected, and is genuinely personable to the people of the culture with whom he or she is dealing.

Finally, managers who accept the possibility of an international assignment or career should seize whatever opportunities are available to prepare themselves. They might consider learning the local language. They should investigate the social and academic programs available. Additionally, they need to stay abreast of business, economic, and political developments throughout the world and the opportunities that arise from them. Managers who are denied an international experience can still develop cultural sensitivity. By doing so, they ensure that their employees perceive the workplace to be just, respectful of differences, and fair.

Case for Small Group Discussion

Preparing for Sonora

You are a human resources training specialist working for a large automaker. Your company will soon complete construction of a plant in Sonora, Mexico. This plant will specialize in the production of your very popular subcompact, the Chaperone.

Initially, all the new plant's management will be transferred from various locations in the United States. Later, supervisors will be promoted from the ranks of the Mexican nationals hired to work on the production line. It is hoped that many of these supervisors will eventually rise to the ranks of at least middle management.

The company now faces a twofold problem, however. First, it needs to identify the criteria used to select the managers who are going to be transferred from the United States to the Sonora plant. Second, it needs to train them to function in a different culture.

Because you earned an international business certificate along with your degree in human resources management, your boss has decided that this job is right for you. She believes this to be true even though your familiarity with Mexico is limited to two coastal vacations there three and four years ago.

She wants a three-page proposal, in memo form, on her desk in two days. The first page should cover the criteria to be used in selecting the managers to be sent to Sonora. She notes that you needn't bother with their technical expertise. Others will screen the candidates on that basis. You should instead focus on the qualifications they should have to be good intercultural managers and communicators and how the company should assess those qualifications.

The remaining two pages of the memo should outline the training program through which the transferees would go. This program will have to cover, at a minimum, language training, the larger cultural variations, nonverbal sensitivity, managerial philosophies, and organizational cultures in the two countries.

Project

As a team, write a memo that will establish the foundation for success in this international venture. Your selection criteria should single out the candidates with the greatest potential for success. Your training program should then ensure the likelihood that they will achieve that success.

Endnotes

1. U.S. Department of Commerce, International Trade Administration, "Top U.S. Trade Partners," http://www.ita.doc.gov/td/industry/otea/ttp/Top_Trade_Partners.pdf (retrieved June 19, 2009).

2. "Globalisation and Trade: The Nuts and Bolts Come Apart," *The Economist*, March 28, 2009, pp. 79–81.

3. Source: U.S. Bureau of Economic Analysis, www.bea.gov (retrieved June 22, 2009).

4. KOF Swiss Economic Institute, "KOF Index of Globalisation 2009," http://globalization .KOF.ethz.ch/static/pdf/press_release_2009_en.pdf (retrieved June 19, 2009).

5. Peter S. Goodman and Louise Story, "U.S. for Sale: Foreigners Invest Big as Dollar Droops," *Houston Chronicle,* January 20, 2008, p. A16.

6. Charlotte Huff, "Powering Up a Hispanic Workforce," *Workforce Management,* May 18, 2009, pp. 25–26.

7. C. Glenn Pearce, Ross Figgins, and Steven Golen, *Business Communication Principles and Applications,* 2nd ed. (New York: John Wiley & Sons, 1988), p. 626.

8. Deedee Doke, "Perfect Strangers: Cultural and Linguistic Differences Between U.S. and UK Workers Necessitate Training for Expatriates," *HR Magazine* 49, 12 (December 2004). Retrieved from OCLC FirstSearch Database (October 10, 2005).

9. Norm Sigband and Arthur Bell, *Communication for Management and Business,* 4th ed. (Glenview, IL: Scott Foresman, 1986), pp. 69–70.

10. Malcolm Gladwell, *Outliers: The Story of Success* (New York: Little, Brown and Company, 2008), p. 175.

11. Dale Level and William Galle, *Managerial Communication* (Plano, TX: Business Publications, 1988), p. 379.

12. Sigband and Bell, *Communicating for Management and Business,* p. 67.

13. *Ibid.*

14. Samuel P. Huntington, *The Clash of Civilizations and the Remaking of World Order* (Simon & Schuster, 1996), p. 31.

15. Milton J. Bennett, "A Developmental Approach to Training for Intercultural Sensitivity," *International Journal of Intercultural Relations* 10 (1986), pp. 179–96.

16. Geert Hofstede, "Motivation, Leadership and Organization: Do American Theories Apply Abroad?" *Organizational Dynamics,* Summer 1980, pp. 42–63.

17. Gladwell, *Outliers: The Story of Success,* pp. 177–223.

18. Richard E. Nisbett, *The Geography of Thought: How Asians and Westerners Think Differently . . . and Why* (New York: The Free Press, 2003), pp. 51–56.

19. Edward T. Hall, *Beyond Culture* (Garden City, NY: Anchor Press/Doubleday, 1977).

20. Phillip Harris and Robert T. Moran, *Managing Cultural Differences*, 5th ed. (Houston: Gulf Publishing, 2000), p. 36.

21. Yong-Kang Wei, "Projecting Ethos through 'About Us': A Comparative Study of American and Chinese Corporations' Websites." Unpublished paper presented at First Annual General Business Conference, Sam Houston State University, Huntsville, Texas, USA, April 18, 2009.

22. James Surowiecki, "The Financial Page: Punctuality Pays," *The New Yorker*, April 5, 2004, p. 31.

23. A. Laurent, "The Cultural Diversity of Western Conceptions of Management," *International Studies of Management and Organization* 13, nos. 1–2 (Spring–Summer 1983), pp. 75–96.

24. Jia Lynn Yang, "On the Radar: Pepsi's Diversity Push Pays Off," *Fortune*, September 4, 2006, p. 32.

25. Simon Winchester, "How America Can Maintain Its Edge," *Parade*, December 21, 2008, p. 8.

26. M. Katherine Glover, "Do's and Taboos: Cultural Aspects of International Business," *Business America*, August 13, 1990, p. 4.

27. *Ibid.*

28. Tom Fowler, "KBR Pleads Guilty in Bribery Case," *Houston Chronicle*, February 12, 2009, p. D1, D4. See also, "Two Charged in KBR Case in Nigeria," *Houston Chronicle*, March 4, 2009, p. B1

29. "Bribery Has Long Been Used to Land International Contracts," *Alexander's Gas & Oil Connections* 8, 11 (June 3, 2003). http://www.gasandoil.com/goc/features/fex32399.htm (retrieved December 20, 2003).

30. Glover, "Do's and Taboos," p. 4.

31. *Ibid.*

32. *Ibid.*, p. 2.

33. Bennett, "A Developmental Approach to Training for Intercultural Sensitivity," pp. 184–86.

34. Rosalie L. Tung, "Attitudes and Experience of Expatriates on International Assignments." Paper presented at Pacific Region Forum on Business and Management Communication, January 22, 1998. Retrieved from http://www.cic.sfu.ca/forum/TungMarch181998.html.

35. "New Study: Facing Increased Uncertainty and Volatility on World Stage, Employees on International Assignment Often Feel Left on Their Own," *News Aktuell-DPA Firmengruppe*, May 15, 2002.

36. C. Brooklyn Derr and Gary R. Oddou, "Are U.S. Multinationals Adequately Preparing Future American Leaders for Global Competition?" *International Journal of Human Resource Management*, no. 2 (February 1991), pp. 227–45.

37. "KPMG Survey: Majority of Companies Select Top Employees for Overseas Assignments, However Fail to Successfully Repatriate," *PR Newswire Association, Inc.*, October 25, 2000.

38. Michael Mandel, "Globalization vs. Immigration Reform: Can We Have Free Flow of Goods and Capital without Free Flow of Labor?" *BusinessWeek*, June 4, 2007, p. 40.

39. Michael Morris and Kwok Leung, "Justice for All? Progress in Research on Cultural Variation in the Psychology of Distributive and Procedural Justice," *Applied Psychology: An International Review* 49, 1 (2000), pp. 100–32.

Interpersonal Communication Strategies

Chapter Ten

Conflict Management

Difficulties are meant to rouse, not discourage. The human spirit is to grow strong by conflict.

—*William Ellery Channing, U.S. abolitionist and Unitarian clergyman*

The world seems to be full of conflict. Continuing tensions in the Middle East, the Pacific Rim, and Africa make the likelihood of global peace remote. Conflict is also pervasive at the corporate level as demonstrated by the frequency of mergers, acquisitions, and unfriendly takeovers.

Within companies, tensions can also run high. Workplace violence is the number one cause of death for women, and the number two cause for men, on the job. And the incidence of workplace violence is increasing at an alarming rate.[1] Managers must protect workers from violence by developing intervention efforts, including training in conflict resolution.

According to a survey of American Management Association executives, managers are likely to spend about 20 percent of their time dealing with conflict.[2] Conflict may occur as a simple disagreement over the meaning of a work procedure, or it may be an argument over priorities and involve deciding which of two projects should draw from the limited funds available for project development. Or it might bring into focus a long-standing irritation that could result in a work stoppage.

Managers were asked to describe the type of conflicts in which they became involved. One manager described a situation in which four computer programmers wanted to go to a training seminar, but funds were available for only one. Another manager described how both she and a colleague wanted to take their vacations at the same time. Their manager said they could not do that and told them to work out the schedule between them. In both these situations, conflicts had to be resolved.

Organizational conflict is a natural part of the traditional organizational structure because a built-in opposition between units often exists. Increases in conflict correlate positively with such factors as increases in an organization's levels of hierarchy, standardization of jobs, and increases in the number of workers.[3] In fact, organizational conflict is so pervasive that over 75 university-affiliated centers, institutes, associations, and consortiums are dedicated to research on this subject. One such organization, the Association for Conflict Resolution, has over

6,000 members: mediators, arbitrators, facilitators, educators, and others involved in the field of conflict resolution and collaborative decision making. The ACR has chapters in 20 states of the U.S.

An increasing number of companies are also creating programs that help employees resolve their problems quickly and without external intervention. The policies are integrated into the corporate culture and use a variety of approaches, including hotlines, peer review panels, mediation, and arbitration to resolve conflicts. Current research indicates that about 10 percent of American employers have implemented such internal systems.[4]

BENEFITS OF CONFLICT

Conflict generally has a negative connotation; however, conflict is a positive occurrence if managed properly. Conflict requires managers to analyze their goals, it creates dialogue among employees, and it fosters creative solutions. Without conflict, employees and organizations would stagnate.

Generational conflict in the workplace is one example of how conflict can have positive effects. For the first time in U.S. history, four generations are working together. Possibilities for conflict run high due to differences in work style and philosophy. Older workers view "work" as a place—a location you go to at a specified time, such as 9 a.m. to 5 p.m. Younger workers tend to view "work" as something you do—anywhere, anytime. They grew up in a digital world where information is always available. So it's easy for Boomers to conclude that Millenials who arrive at 9:30 are working less hard than they, who arrived at 8:30, not realizing that the younger generation may have already put in time at their home computers or BlackBerrys while still in pajamas. To Millenials, the extent of scheduling that goes on in most workplaces is stultifying. Learning that much of today's work can be done asynchronously, Boomers benefit from their younger colleagues' preferences for maximum efficiency.[5]

Conflict also may foster creativity. Conflict helps to overcome individual psychological distortions and biases by forcing people out of their traditional modes of thinking. In this way, conflict promotes the unstructured thinking that some see as required for developing good novel alternatives to difficult problems.[6]

In addition, studies show a higher decision quality when there is open opposition and resistance by subordinates than when the resistance of subordinates is weak or even passive. In one study, high-quality decisions occurred in 45.8 percent of the situations with strong subordinate resistance, but in only 18.8 percent of the situations where the resistance was weak or nonexistent.[7]

Thus, managers who pride themselves in running a smooth ship may not be as effective as they think. The smooth ship may reflect suppressed conflict that could have potential benefit if allowed free play. In fact, the conflict might not be as harmful as its suppression.

What causes conflict? When is it functional and when is it not? What methods can be used to resolve conflict? Is any one method best? The following discussion answers these questions, but first we review the relationship between communication and conflict.

THE RELATIONSHIP BETWEEN COMMUNICATION AND CONFLICT

As is true with many other terms, conflict has both a colloquial meaning and a long list of specific definitions. However, a quick review of these definitions will help describe the nature of conflict. Katz and Kahn state that two systems—which could include persons, groups, organizations, or nations—are in conflict when they interact directly in such a way that the actions of one tend to prevent or compel some outcome against the resistance of the other.[8] Another author states that conflict characterizes a situation in which the conditions, practices, or goals of individuals are inherently incompatible.[9] A third definition presents conflict as a struggle over values or claims to scarce resources, power, or status. In this struggle, opponents aim to neutralize, injure, or eliminate their rivals.[10]

These three definitions help define the nature of conflict and indicate the role of communication in conflict. The first definition uses the word *interact*, implying a communication interaction of some kind. The second definition uses the phrase *inherently incompatible*, and the third definition includes *a struggle over values*. Communication is the method by which managers determine if something is inherently incompatible, and the struggle over values is carried out through communication behaviors. Thus, the ability to communicate effectively may eliminate conflict immediately; however, ineffective communication may cause a situation to appear inherently incompatible, and thus a struggle over values may ensue. The conclusion is that communicative behavior may cause, as well as resolve, conflict.

Let's examine the specific characteristics of conflict and the corresponding implications for communication. The following are four axioms that are particularly relevant to communication.[11] These axioms are reviewed to demonstrate how effective communication can make conflict a constructive positive process.

1. **Conflict involves at least two parties.** Because conflict involves at least two parties, communication is an integral component. Conflict can be generated or resolved only through communication. Consequently, managers must understand the types of communication interactions that can cause conflict, and the communication patterns that are most functional after conflict has developed. In fact, a good communicator can bring conflict to the surface and make it a productive process.

2. **Conflict develops from perceived mutually exclusive goals.** Mutually exclusive goals may exist as a result of objective facts or an individual's values and perceptions. However, the key factor is that the parties involved perceive the objectives as mutually exclusive; frequently, through communication, the involved parties see that the goal actually isn't mutually exclusive. But only through communication can the parties in conflict determine the existence of a superordinate goal that may meet both parties' goals. Again, the positive nature of conflict is evident because without conflict the parties may not know about the superordinate goal.

3. **Conflict involves parties who may have different values or perceptions.** To illustrate how conflictive parties may have different value systems, consider

how a first-level supervisor, who was once a member of a trade union, would have values much different from that of a young engineer who has been out of college only two years. This value difference may result in a potential conflict when the two employees consider implementing a computerized production control system. The supervisor could perceive the computerized system as too difficult to learn and as a threat to employees' job security. However, the young engineer might perceive it solely as an engineering challenge. In this case, values affect perception.

The selective attention principle says that we tend to perceive what is important and pleasing to us and avoid what is not. The following example shows how differences in perception led to a major conflict.[12] A textile mill allowed a conflict to develop that resulted in a big labor turnover. The mill had informed employees when they were hired that it gave automatic raises each year and merit raises for deserving employees after 9 and 18 months. The employees, however, understood this to mean they would receive an automatic raise at *all three* of these periods—9, 12, and 18 months. When they did not obtain their raises, many of them quit because they thought the employer had not maintained the original promise to grant wage increases. In this case, the differences between employee and employer perception led to conflicting views.

When conflicting parties have different values or perceptions, communication is important in two ways. First, exposure and communication between two individuals will likely result in the individuals eventually sharing values and becoming more friendly toward each other.[13] Second, as more accurate communication develops between two managers, the perceptual differences will subside, and hence, the probability of conflict will be reduced.

Chapter 1 mentioned that cultural diversity is increasing in organizations. This diversity will create conflict, but it will be exciting and productive because diverse viewpoints, when managed appropriately, will result in more creative outcomes.

4. **Conflict terminates only when each side is satisfied that it has won or lost.** Win–lose situations seem to dominate our culture—for instance, law courts use the adversary system and political parties strive to win elections. Competition to win in sports is so keen that fights among spectators are not uncommon. The pervasive win–lose attitude in our culture has made it difficult to imagine that both parties may "win" in any situation labeled a conflict. This problem recalls the first axiom, which states that conflict develops from mutually exclusive goals. However, accurate communication may reveal that a "win" or a "loss" is not the only alternative.

SOURCES OF CONFLICT

When managers perceive conflict in the workplace, they may assume it's due to incompatible personalities. "Why can't everyone just get along with each other?" they plead. But managers need to understand that the sources of conflict are often deeper than individual personality. Then they will be better able to select the appropriate communication strategy. The underlying causes or sources of conflict situations often are built into the organization's hierarchy and ways of doing business.

The lines of authority in an organization can encourage conflict. For example, the lending and the savings departments are interdependent in all banks. The lending department cannot lend funds until the savings department has collected funds. By the same token, the savings department would be hard pressed if the lending department had no customers. These two areas have common goals within the bank (profit and continued operation of the bank), but their interdependence can lead to conflict over their respective authority. While the savings department would like to give high interest rates to please its customers, the lending department wants to provide low interest rates to please its clientele. When the interdependence of these departments becomes a central issue, conflict will arise over whose authority takes precedence or whose responsibility for the bank's profit goal is more relevant.

The distribution of the limited resources available in an organization is another source of conflict. If resources were unlimited, few conflicts would arise, but this condition seldom exists. When resources are limited, and more than one person or group wants a share, conflict develops. The most obvious conflict occurs during the annual budget review. With funds traditionally limited, it is necessary to decide which department will get what amount. Since each department manager's goal appears most important from her own perspective, the funds allocated to one department may appear to be funds taken from another. The interdependency of the various departments vying for budget allocations thus can become a major source of conflict.

Diverse goals are a third source of organizational conflict. For instance, clashes may occur between quality assurance managers and production managers in a manufacturing environment. The goal of the quality people is zero defects, while the goal of production is filling the customer's order on time. Conflicting goals and roles can also explain why a company's salespeople routinely ignore the accounting staff's requests for expense forms and receipts. Or why a shift foreman refuses to let his workers attend an employee development session offered by Human Resources. To alleviate such traditional conflicts between functional units, senior executives should remind their managers of the overarching goals, mission, and vision.

Conflict and Perception

The relationship between conflict and perception has already been briefly discussed. Perceived conflict is present when the parties recognize the conditions or when the parties misunderstand one another's true position.

Clearly, failure to identify potentially conflictive situations may prevent conflicts from developing immediately. More often though, the inaccurate or illogical perception of a situation causes unnecessary conflict. An example of inaccurate perception is the case of manager praise. A recent poll by Maritz Incentives found wide-ranging opinions on appreciation in the workplace: 55 percent of employees said their bosses never or rarely thank them for their efforts. On the other hand, only 6 percent of supervisors said they never praise their subordinates;

34 percent said they daily praise their direct reports, and 45 percent said they do so weekly or monthly.[14] It is easy to see how this discrepancy of perceptions can lead to conflict.

The grid in Figure 10–1 shows why inaccurate perceptions create conflict in the managerial process. Assume two managers are discussing an issue. Two possibilities exist for each manager: each correctly perceives the existence of a potential conflict or incorrectly perceives it. This results in the four possibilities diagrammed. The grid shows that an accurate mutual perception could possibly exist in only one of four occurrences. Of course, this is not always the case, but numerous conflicts not warranted by the actual situation may develop.

Further, two managers may be aware of serious disagreement over a policy, but it may not create any anxiety or affect their feelings toward one another. Competition for budget allocations, for example, don't need to be personalized.

Personally felt conflict may find expression in fear, threat, mistrust, and hostility. Consider the bank teller who called in a bomb threat on the day he was fired so he could meet his former co-workers for drinks. No one knows the financial costs of such workplace revenge behaviors, but everyone agrees that a lack of communication causes most employee sabotage. "Getting back is the way of communicating when you can't, or when you're afraid to speak up for yourself," explains William Lundin, a workplace relations specialist.[15] According to one Phoenix management consultant, about 30 percent of workers try to "get back at the boss" on a regular basis. Incidents of workplace violence continue to increase. Based on Labor Department statistics, across the U.S. each week, more than 10 employees are slain at work.[16] And just as we prepare for natural disasters, we need to prepare for workplace violence.

What can managers do to prevent violence and acts of hostility? It's important to maintain a communication program that allows employees (1) to understand how their performance level is being evaluated, (2) to know the consequences of changing (and not changing) their behavior, (3) to discuss their problems, (4) to explore options for solutions, and (5) to defuse anger. The venting of hostility can be therapeutic rather than detrimental, if managed properly. Group discussions can act as a safety valve for this hostility, as can periodic meetings between supervisors and subordinates. Effective managers do not become defensive even when

[handwritten margin note: maintain communication]

FIGURE 10–1
Accuracy of Perceptions and Conflict

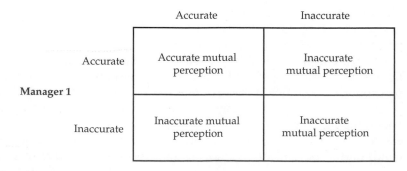

		Manager 2	
		Accurate	Inaccurate
Manager 1	Accurate	Accurate mutual perception	Inaccurate mutual perception
	Inaccurate	Inaccurate mutual perception	Inaccurate mutual perception

FIGURE 10–2
Ways to Manifest Conflict

they are the focus of the hostile communication. Nondefensive communication is the key to managing personally felt conflict.

The observable behavior of the manager, based on conditions, perceptions, and feelings, may be seen as either conflict or an attempt to establish mutual goals. The most obvious manifestations of conflict are open aggression or violence at one end of a continuum and integrative problem solving at the other end, as depicted in Figure 10–2. A continuum is used because generally neither totally open aggression nor completely satisfactory problem solving is manifest. However, the goal is to move as close as possible to integrative problem solving. As the remainder of this discussion shows, managers have numerous ways to manage conflict along this continuum as they attempt to resolve it.

STRATEGIES IN CONFLICT RESOLUTION

Now that we have looked at the relationship of conflict to managerial communication, discussed constructive conflict, and reviewed the sources of conflict, we can identify strategies for conflict resolution. Managerial communication strategies for managing conflict could be put into many categories. For our discussion, we use the system presented in Figure 10–3. This figure demonstrates that during

FIGURE 10–3
Strategies for Managing Conflict

High 9

Accommodating (1,9)
Disagreements are smoothed over. A state of peaceful coexistence is the ultimate goal.

Problem solving (9,9)
Problem solving takes place with varying points of view objectively evaluated; emotions and doubts are examined and worked through.

Compromising (5,5)
Compromise, bargaining, and middle-ground positions are accepted so that no one wins and no one loses.

Forcing (9,1)
Conflict is suppressed through authority-obedience approach. Win–lose power struggles are fought out, but often forced by the boss.

Avoiding (1,1)
Neutrality is maintained at all costs. Withdrawal relieves the necessity of dealing with situations that would arouse conflict.

Concern for People

Low 1

1   2   3   4   5   6   7   8   9

Low   High

Concern for Production

a conflict, managers may emphasize interpersonal relations, task production, or a combination thereof. Five possible strategies are presented: avoiding, accommodating, forcing, compromising, and problem solving.[17]

While reviewing these strategies, the contingency approach to managerial communication should be kept in mind. Various conflict situations require different strategies, so effective communication requires that managers match the strategy to the situation.

Avoiding

The avoidance or withdrawal strategy combines a low concern for production with a low concern for people. The person using this style sees conflict as a hopeless, useless experience. Rather than undergo the tension and frustration of conflict, managers using the avoidance or withdrawal style simply remove themselves from conflict situations. This avoidance may be physical or psychological. The person using this strategy will avoid disagreement and tension, will not openly take sides in a disagreement among others, and will feel little commitment to any decisions reached. This conflict management style is the second most popular among U.S. managers.[18]

Avoidance need not be dramatic. Many managers avoid by ignoring a comment or quickly changing the subject when conversation begins to threaten. Another way to avoid is to place the responsibility for an issue on a higher manager. A third way to withdraw is to use a simple response of "I'm looking into the matter," with the hopes that the other party will forget the issue.

This strategy is frequently used in large bureaucracies that have an overabundance of policies. Rather than attempt to resolve the conflict, managers simply blame it on "policy." Managers who lack self-confidence in their communication abilities may hope the problem just disappears. However, this usually does not work. In fact, withdrawal from conflict has been negatively correlated with constructive conflict resolution. Withdrawal has been further negatively correlated with knowledge of the supervisor's feelings and attitudes; open upward communication; helpfulness of the supervisor; and adequacy of the planning relationship. Thus, managers who avoid conflict do not operate effectively in these critical managerial areas.[19]

Accommodating

In accommodating, the second type of conflict resolution, managers try to deal with conflict by making everyone happy. When using this approach, the manager emphasizes maintaining relationships with fellow employees and de-emphasizes achieving productive goals. Since the manager wants others' acceptance, he will give in to others' desires in areas that conflict with his own. Managers using this style believe confrontation is destructive.

Typical attempts to accommodate may include such things as calling for a coffee break at a tense moment, breaking tension with humor, changing the topic, or engaging in some ritual show of togetherness such as an office birthday party. Since these efforts are likely to reduce felt conflict, they are more beneficial than simple avoidance. This reduction of felt conflict will probably have short-range effects and may even have some long-range benefit. However, just because someone does not experience a hostile or negative feeling does not mean the real cause of the conflict is resolved. In fact, accommodating is a camouflage approach that can break down at any time and create barriers to progress. Thus, research has found that it is used more in low- or medium-performance organizations than in high-performance organizations. In addition, accommodating correlates negatively with open upward communication and with participation in goal setting.

Forcing

Forcing, the third conflict management strategy, is used by the manager who attempts to meet production goals at all costs, without concern for the needs or acceptance of others. For such a manager, losing is destructive because it is viewed as reduced status, weakness, and the loss of self-image. Winning must be achieved at any cost and gives this manager a sense of excitement and achievement. Not surprisingly, it is the number one conflict resolution strategy used by managers.[20]

A situation characterized by the forcing strategy will probably cause later conflicts. The language managers use to describe conflict situations in their organizations often reflects the negative effect this style may have: opposition, battle, fight, conquest, head-to-head, coercion, and smash. Such language and imagery can result in long-lasting emotional wounds.[21]

While force can resolve immediate disputes, the long-term effects will probably include a loss of productivity. Forcing in conflict situations negatively correlates with such factors as adequacy of planning, helpfulness of the supervision, and participation in goal setting. The major difficulty of a forcing strategy is that employees are reluctant to plan or carry out plans when they perceive that the ultimate resolution of the conflict will put them on the losing side of a win–lose position.

Interestingly, while little doubt exists that forcing has limited use, managers consider forcing to be their favorite backup strategy for dealing with conflict.[22] Immediate compliance is misperceived as a long-term solution in these cases.

Compromising

Compromise, the fourth strategy for conflict resolution, assumes that half a loaf is better than none. This approach falls somewhere between forcing and accommodating. Since compromise provides some gain for both sides rather than a unilateral victory, many participants judge this approach as better than the other strategies just discussed.

Compromise is used when one of two conditions exists: (1) neither party involved believes he or she has the power to "force" the issue on the other party, or (2) one or both of the parties believes winning may not be worth the cost in money, time, or energy. Compromise is often highly related to negotiating, which is the topic of the next chapter; however, several important points are pertinent here. First, compromise may lead to both parties' perceiving themselves as winners, but they may also both feel like losers. A negative overtone may develop in the working relationship between the employees involved, and any sense of trust may break down. While both parties involved probably entered the negotiations with a cooperative attitude, a sense of competition may be the result of compromise.

A second concern with compromise is that the party with the most information has the better position. This power of information may restrict open communication among employees. This situation in turn often results in a lopsided compromise. A third factor is the principle of the least-interested party: The party that has the least interest in the outcome is in the more powerful position in the negotiations. As a result, an employee who has little concern about the welfare of the company may have an inordinate amount of influence in a compromise.

PROBLEM SOLVING: THE WIN–WIN STRATEGY

Thus far, it may seem that no totally acceptable, productive strategy exists to manage conflict. Everything has been discussed in terms of loss. Fortunately, this is not the case. Problem solving, the fifth strategy to be discussed, is a win–win strategy for conflict. This complex and highly effective style requires skillful strategic managerial communication, but it reaps a big dividend; thus, the remainder of our discussion centers on this strategy. Let's first describe the win–win strategy and then examine specific techniques for implementation.

Description of the Strategy

The key to this strategy is that it follows a mutual problem-solving approach rather than a combative one. In contrast to managers who use a forcing or compromising strategy, managers engaged in this type of problem solving assume a high-quality mutually acceptable solution is possible. The parties direct their energies toward defeating the problem and not each other.

The following example presents a clear description of the problem-solving approach to conflict resolution. It details a meeting in Wisconsin that set out to explore possible prison reforms.

Nine of the state's top prison officials met to design an ideal correctional institution. In the course of the discussion, one group member proposed that uniforms traditionally worn by prison guards be eliminated. The group then began a lengthy argument about whether or not uniforms should be worn. One group member suggested that the issue be resolved democratically by vote. As a result, six people voted against uniforms and three voted in favor of them. The winning members looked pleased while the losing members either got angry or withdrew from further discussion.

A group consultant present at the time suggested that the members take another look at the situation. Then he asked those in favor of uniforms what they hoped to accomplish (establishing goals). Those officials stated that part of the rehabilitative process in correctional institutions is that of teaching people to deal constructively with authority, and they saw uniforms as a means for achieving the goal. When asked why they opposed uniforms (analyzing the problem) the other group members said that uniforms created such a stigma that guards had an additional difficulty laying to rest the stereotypes held by inmates before they could deal with them on a one-to-one basis. The group consultant then asked the group what ways might be appropriate to meet the combined goals, namely, teaching people to deal with authority and avoiding the difficulty of stereotypes held about traditional uniforms (generating solutions). While working on the problem, the group identified 10 possible solutions, including prison personnel using nametags, color-coded casual dress, or uniforms for guard supervisors but not for guards in constant contact with prisoners. After discussing the various alternatives, the group decided upon the third solution (selecting the best solution).

In their first discussion, the group engaged in clear conflict that was only partially resolved by vote. In the discussion led by the consultant, the group turned to problem solving, eventually reaching consensus and a win–win solution.[23]

Beliefs Necessary to Implement the Strategy

We are suggesting that the problem-solving strategy is the most desirable; however, a manager wanting to effectively use this approach must hold a series of beliefs.

Belief 1: Cooperation Is Better than Competition

The manager must first believe cooperation is better than competition. American management seems to be based on competition, so it is difficult to envision cooperation as a viable possibility at times.[24] This competition may develop out of Darwin's concept of survival of the fittest: A manager who has a self-image of weakness may fear extinction. Lacking confidence, this person feels a sense of competitiveness with others in the company.

Competition also has an important role in stimulating employees to achieve more. However, as technology becomes more complex and employees more specialized, interdependence is required. Few tasks can be completed without the cooperation of many employees. The group as a whole becomes greater than the sum of all the individuals, so cooperation is required. This is not to say that differences of opinion should be prevented.

Different opinions can lead to new insights and creativity as long as the opinions do not disrupt the group process. A manager must enter the conflict situation believing others' opinions are beneficial. He must be willing to listen. The emphasis on teamwork in today's work environment makes cooperation mandatory.

Belief 2: Parties Can Be Trusted

The second belief is that the other parties involved in the conflict can be trusted. Managers who are trusting will not conceal or distort relevant information, nor will they fear stating facts, ideas, conclusions, and feelings that would make them vulnerable.

A researcher compared problem-solving groups. Half the groups were directed to trust other people, to express their views openly, to share information freely, and to aim at a high level of mutual confidence. The other groups were directed to behave in opposite ways. The research found that problem-solving groups with high trust will:

- Exchange relevant ideas and feelings more openly
- Develop greater clarification of goals and problems
- Search more extensively for alternative courses of action
- Have greater influence on solutions
- Be more satisfied with their problem-solving efforts
- Have greater motivation to implement conclusions
- See themselves as closer and more of a team
- Have less desire to leave their group to join another[25]

Trusting behavior causes reciprocity. Trusting cues will likely evoke trusting behavior from others. Conversely, when a manager does not trust others, the cues to mistrust will evoke mistrustful behavior on the other's part. So it is best to assume a person can be trusted and to change that view only with evidence to the contrary.

Belief 3: Status Differences Can Be Minimized

The third belief that managers must possess is that status differences between parties can be minimized in a conflict situation. Differences in power or status that separate two individuals into a we–they orientation inhibit conflict resolution. A manager who is in a higher power position may yield to the temptation to use the power inherent in the position as the rationale for forcing the solution. If that happens, the participants, rather than confronting the problem and treating each other as equals, will regress into a win–lose style, and the result is much less productive. Managers who do not rely on status will spend time listening to everyone involved. The section in Chapter 7 on developing a listening climate provides ideas for managers who want to minimize their perceived power and encourage communication both upward and laterally.

Belief 4: Mutually Acceptable Solutions Can Be Found

The final belief managers must hold is that a mutually acceptable and desirable solution exists and can be found. Unless both parties believe this is possible, a win–lose strategy will result. Conflict resolution can be extremely frustrating and time-consuming unless both parties remain optimistic about finding a mutually acceptable answer. This is not to say that both parties are meeting the same goal. Rather, both parties can reach their different goals in an acceptable manner.

Each of these four beliefs—cooperation, trust, equal status, and mutually acceptable goals—is important. A manager must believe in these concepts to implement an effective win–win conflict resolution strategy. But belief in these concepts is not enough. Managers must also use the appropriate communication skills in a strategic manner. The next part of this discussion describes these skills and the appropriate method for implementing them.

Implementing the Strategy

Specific steps should be followed to achieve the problem-solving strategy. However, before these steps are reviewed, key communication principles must be identified.

- Use neutral rather than emotional terms. "I still tend to prefer my approach" is better than "Your idea is not functional."
- Avoid absolute statements that leave no room for modification. "I think this is the way . . ." is better than "This is the *only* way."
- Ask open-ended questions.
- Avoid leading questions. This rule is especially important where status differences are present.
- Repeat key phrases to make sure all parties are communicating on the same wavelength.
- Use terms that all parties clearly understand.
- Allow the other person to complete statements. Do not interrupt.
- Use effective listening skills, especially paraphrasing, to ensure the other person's ideas are fully understood.
- Be aware of the importance of physical arrangements. For instance, sitting in front of a big desk may cause a person to feel defensive.

When managers use the communication principles just presented as they follow the sequence given next, they should be able to resolve conflicts successfully.

The first step in implementing the problem-solving strategy is to maximize environmental conditions, as follows:

- **Review and adjust conflict conditions.** Earlier we identified sources of conflict inherent in the organization, including goals and resources. When a manager can identify these conditions, it is sometimes possible to adjust them to promote cooperation.
- **Review and adjust perceptions.** Managers should adjust and correct their perceptions through reality testing. "Am I viewing the situation or the behavior as it actually exists?" Perceptions become more accurate as an individual learns more facts about the condition and has resulting impressions confirmed by others' perceptions.
- **Review and adjust attitudes.** Since an optimal outcome depends on trust, mutuality, and cooperation, little success will result if the parties are distrustful, hostile, and competitive. Accordingly, one should identify the attitudes and feelings of the parties engaged in the conflict as far as possible. Often, the best strategy is to start with the easily solved problems. Once the easier problems are solved, a more positive attitude develops for the more complex conflict situation. The trust that results may make cooperative communication easier.

Once environmental conditions and perceptions have been identified and perhaps adjusted, you are ready to begin the actual problem-solving strategy.

John Dewey, an American educator who lived and wrote in the early part of the 20th century, first articulated this process in one of his books, *How We Think*. Over 100 years later, this rational problem-solving process is still frequently and successfully used in contemporary businesses. The reason for its popularity is that it *is* "how we think." In Chapter 13, you will learn more about Dewey's problem-solving process and how to apply it in meetings and team projects. For now, let's examine five steps in the problem-solving process.

1. **Define the problem.** A statement of the problem in a conflict situation is usually much more difficult than it seems. People tend to discuss solutions before they clearly define the problem. Because of this, our inclination is to state the problem as a solution rather than as a goal. This results in ambiguous communication, and it is common for the parties to focus on the solutions without having a clear definition of the problem. The outcome may be increased conflict. Second, managers must state the goals in the form of group goals rather than individual priorities. Third, the problem definition must be specific. One helpful strategy is to clearly write out the problem statement so everyone can see it and agree on it. Alternatively, the group can agree on a problem stated in a question format.

2. **Analyze the problem.** Again, managers tend to want to skip this step. After all, they may argue, they live with the problem. What is the point of spending more time wallowing in it? Dewey's answer is that by exploring the depths of the problem, by looking at its history, causes, effects, and extent, one can later come up with a solution that addresses more than symptoms, and that is more than a bandage. It will address the root cause of the problem, thus improving its chances of being successful.

3. **Brainstorm alternatives.** All parties should offer potential solutions. One idea may stimulate other ideas. The more employees communicate in an open trusting environment, the greater the potential for generating effective solutions. Trust, of course, evaporates when an idea is criticized during a brainstorming session. As soon as someone says, "That's a terrible idea. It'll never work," who would be willing to take the risk of offering another idea? Managers must ensure that premature judging of solutions is avoided during this step.

4. **Develop criteria for a good solution.** These criteria, or standards, may already be in place and available. Other times, the organization's executives will specify to the problem-solving managers what a good solution must look like. Occasionally, the managers are expected to develop their own criteria. Common criteria for an optimal solution include the following: it must be cost-effective, it must be easily or quickly implemented, it must use only resources that are currently available, it must be legal, and it must be consistent with the organization's mission or values.

5. **Evaluate the brainstormed alternatives using the independently developed criteria for a good solution.** This is really the easiest step. By this time, attention to the problem is unified, and an open communication environment has been achieved with active participation by all the parties involved. The best solution appears automatically as the brainstormed alternative that matches your list of criteria.

CONFLICT AND MANAGEMENT SUCCESS

The basic nature of organizational dynamics creates conflict.[26] Consequently, managers must understand and learn to manage conflict. And as this chapter has explained, communication is at the foundation of conflict management. Since conflict is a pervasive, vital, but often troublesome aspect of organizational life, effective conflict management has become a major task for business and industry training programs.[27] Whether one is a college student anticipating a career in management or a practicing manager with years of experience, it is necessary to continually seek constructive communication strategies for conflict management.

Summary

Managers are likely to spend at least 20 percent of their time dealing with some kind of conflict, so it is important to understand the causes of conflict and productive methods for resolution. Because miscommunication is an integral element behind conflict, effective managerial communication is one key to resolution.

Conflict can be constructive as well as destructive. The nature of the word *conflict* implies opposing positions with negative results; however, when properly managed, conflict may be a positive force. An important managerial role is to be able to identify the difference between destructive and constructive conflict.

Managers can use one of five strategies to resolve conflict: avoiding, accommodating, forcing, compromising, or problem solving. The first four strategies are termed win–lose or lose–lose because one or both parties in the conflict will lose. However, the fifth strategy is termed a win–win approach because both parties in the conflict are potential winners; consequently, the effective manager should strive for the win–win style.

The problem-solving strategy can be achieved when the manager believes in cooperation, trusts the other party, minimizes status differences, and believes a mutually acceptable and desirable solution is available. These beliefs are a prerequisite to success, but satisfactory results cannot be obtained unless sound communication principles are used to put the beliefs into action. A sequence of steps should be followed when implementing the win–win strategy: review and adjust conflict conditions, perceptions, and attitudes; develop a problem definition; analyze the problem; brainstorm alternatives; evaluate alternatives according to criteria; and develop the best solution.

When a manager uses strategic communication skills, believes in the win–win approach to conflict resolution, and follows the correct sequence of activities, a constructive approach to conflict resolution can result.

Cases for Small Group Discussion

Case 10-1.

Conflict over Job Duties

Linda Sims is the manager of the accounting department and Jose Martinez is the manager of the sales department for a production company. This is a fast-growing firm, and the staff of the accounting department (11 employees) is often overwhelmed with work.

Since the accounting department is located immediately next to the credit department, Ruth Rankin, the administrative assistant in credit, sometimes works on journal entries assigned to her by Sims.

The company has experienced especially rapid growth over the past six months, which has caused everyone to be busier than usual. With the increase in sales volume, the credit office is under pressure to process applications more quickly, and Rankin is available to help Sims out with accounting overflow less often.

Sims complains to Martinez that she needs Rankin to work in accounting more than he needs her in credit. Martinez's response is "If I can't move the credit applications through the pipeline in a timely manner, soon there'll be no need for an accounting department, because this company will be out of business."

Questions

1. What is the cause of this conflict?
2. Write a problem statement for this situation.
3. If you were Sims, how would you approach Martinez in this situation?
4. What style did Sims initially use?
5. What could Sims do to gain Martinez's cooperation rather than make him defensive?

Case 10-2.

Conflict Between the Team Members

Rod Edwards, the advertising manager for Waterlite Advertising and Associates, has two assistants. One is Gina Reese, an account executive who gets clients for the company. Edwards's second assistant is Mina Patel, a copywriter. She does the actual writing and designing of the ads for the clients.

Reese and Patel usually have a close working relationship because they work as a team on all clients' accounts. Reese gets the clients and discusses their needs with them. Afterward, she tells Patel about the conversation and the clients' needs so Patel can design the right ad. Once Patel finishes the ad, Reese presents it to the client. If the ad is a success, it is usually Reese who gets the praise and recognition because she is the one who interfaces with the client.

In the past, Patel was not bothered by the recognition Reese got because she always knew she was the one who designed the ad. But the last ad Patel designed brought in a $1 million contract to the firm. Edwards immediately gave Reese a raise for bringing in the client but did not give Patel any recognition.

Naturally, this caused friction between Reese and Patel, and their relationship began to deteriorate. Four days after Reese got the raise, their conflict reached a climax. Reese borrowed Patel's stapler (a trivial occurrence) and forgot to return it. Patel caused a scene and refused to talk to Reese for the next few days.

The problem was brought to Edwards's attention because his department's productivity was declining. For the ads to be developed, the assistants had to work as a team.

Edwards called both employees into his office and immediately started lecturing them. He insisted they get along and begin working on the next ad. He told them he expected an ad finished by noon the following day. Reese and Patel walked out of Edwards's office without resolving the problem. They did get some work done the next day, but their close relationship was never resumed.

Questions

1. What kind of conflict resolution strategy did Edwards use? What kind should he have used?
2. This is an example of destructive conflict. Could it develop as a constructive situation?
3. What steps should Edwards have followed to develop a win–win strategy?

Endnotes

1. National Institute for Occupational Safety and Health, Centers for Disease Control and Prevention, U.S. Department of Health and Human Services, "Homicide Alert," no. 94–101. Retrieved from http://www.cdc.gov/niosh/94–101.html (December 22, 2003).
2. Warren H. Schmidt, "Conflict: A Powerful Process for (Good or Bad) Change," *Management Review* 63, no. 12 (December 1974), p. 5.
3. Ronald Corwin, "Patterns of Organizational Conflict," *Administrative Science Quarterly* 14, no. 3 (December 1969), pp. 507–20.
4. Association for Conflict Resolution, Frequently Asked Questions. Retrieved June 2, 2009, from http://www.acrnet.org/about/CR-FAQ.htm.
5. Tammy Erickson, "The Four Biggest Reasons for Generational Conflict in Teams," Harvard Business Publishing—for Managers, February 16, 2009. Retrieved March 24, 2009, from http://blogs.harvardbusiness.org/erickson/2009/.
6. L. Putnam and S. Wilson, "Argumentation and Bargaining Strategies as Discriminators of Integrative and Distributive Outcomes," in *Managing Conflict: An Interdisciplinary Approach*, ed. A. Rahim (New York: Praeger Publishers, 1988).
7. L. R. Hoffman, E. Harburg, and N. R. F. Meier, "Differences and Disagreements as Factors in Creative Problem-Solving," *Journal of Abnormal and Social Psychology* 64, no. 2 (1962), pp. 206–24.
8. Daniel Katz and Robert L. Kahn, *The Social Psychology of Organizations*, 2nd ed. (New York: John Wiley & Sons, 1978), p. 613.
9. Clagett G. Smith, "A Comparative Analysis of Some Conditions and Consequences of Intra-Organizational Conflict," *Administrative Science Quarterly* 10, no. 3 (1965–1966), pp. 504–29.
10. K. W. Thomas, "Conflict," in *Organizational Behavior*, ed. S. Kerr (Columbus, OH: Grid Publishing, 1979), pp. 151–81.

11. Charles E. Watkins, "An Analytical Model of Conflict: How Differences in Perception Cause Differences of Opinion," *Supervisory Management* 41, no. 3 (March 1974), pp. 1–5; and J. L. Hocker and W. W. Wilmot, *Interpersonal Conflict,* 2nd ed. (Dubuque, IA: Wm. C. Brown, 1985).

12. Lewis Benton, "The Many Faces of Conflict: How Differences in Perception Cause Differences of Opinion," *Supervisory Management* 15, no. 3 (March 1970), pp. 7–12.

13. Robert Zajonc, "Attitudinal Effects of Mere Exposure," *Journal of Personality and Social Psychology Monograph Supplement* 9, no. 2 (June 1968), pp. 1–27.

14. "Does the Boss Say Thanks?" *St. Louis Post-Dispatch,* September 19, 2003, p. C9.

15. Carol Vinzant, "On the Job: Messing with the Boss's Head," *Fortune,* May 1, 2000, p. 329.

16. L. M. Sixel, "Preparing for Violence," *Houston Chronicle,* April 19, 2007, p. D1.

17. This diagram is based on the works of R. R. Blake and J. S. Mouton, "The Fifth Achievement," *Journal of Applied Behavioral Science* 6, no. 4 (1970), pp. 413–26; J. Hall, *How to Interpret Your Scores from the Conflict Management Survey* (Conroe, TX: Teleometrics, 1986); R. W. Thomas, "Conflict and Negotiation Processes in Organizations," in *The Handbook of Industrial and Organizational Psychology* 2, ed. M. D. Dunnette and L. Hough (Palo Alto: Consulting Psychologists Press, 1992), pp. 651–718; and K. W. Thomas and R. H. Kilman, *The Thomas-Kilman Conflict Mode Instrument* (Tuxedo, NY: Xicom, Inc., 1974).

18. E. Phillips and R. Cheston, "Conflict Resolution: What Works?" *California Management Review* 21, no. 4 (Summer 1979), p. 76.

19. W. A. Donohue, M. E. Diez, and R. B. Stahl, "New Directions in Negotiations Research," in *Communication Yearbook* 7, ed. R. N. Bostrom (Beverly Hills, CA: Sage Publications, 1983), pp. 249–79.

20. Phillips and Cheston, "Conflict Resolution: What Works?" p. 76.

21. Gareth Morgan, *Images of Organization* (Newbury Park, CA: Sage Publications, 1986).

22. Jay W. Lorsch and Paul R. Lawrence, eds., *Studies in Organizational Design* (Homewood, IL: Irwin-Dorsey, 1970), p. 1.

23. Alan C. Filley, *Interpersonal Conflict Resolution* (Glenview, IL: Scott Foresman, 1975), p. 33.

24. N. J. Adler, *International Dimensions of Organizational Behavior* (Boston: Kent Publishing Co., 1986).

25. D. E. Zand, "Trust and Managerial Problem Solving," *Administrative Science Quarterly* 17, no. 1 (1972), pp. 229–39.

26. Daniel Robey, *Designing Organizations* (Homewood, IL: Richard D. Irwin, 1986), pp. 176–201.

27. Linda L. Putnam, "Communication and Interpersonal Conflict," *Management Communication Quarterly* 1, no. 3 (February 1988), pp. 293–301.

Chapter Eleven

Managerial Negotiation

We cannot negotiate with those who say, "What's mine is mine and what's yours is negotiable."

—*John F. Kennedy, 35th U.S. president*

Negotiation is an integral aspect of management. Successful managers negotiate for increased budget allocations, better purchasing prices, higher salaries for themselves and their subordinates, increased time to finish important assignments, more favorable annual objectives, or even better salary offers when starting with a new company. Many managers, however, shy away from negotiation. They do not feel comfortable doing it because either they have not succeeded in previous negotiations or they have not learned the process of dynamic negotiation. Most knowledge about negotiation, unfortunately, comes from limited personal experience.

Managers should take advantage of situations in their personal life that give them the opportunity to negotiate. They can learn from those experiences and improve their negotiating ability, which can then transfer to their management position. Personal experiences can range from buying a car or selling items in a garage sale to negotiating chores and compensation with children. By thus building one's skills, managers will avoid ineffective negotiations in the workplace, which can reduce organizational productivity, demoralize those involved, and generate hostile feelings among other parties.[1]

Furthermore, recent research shows gender differences in the use of negotiation. In general, men initiate negotiation four times more often than women do. This tendency has important consequences in business, particularly concerning pay, promotion, and recognition. Linda Babcock and Sara Laschever report in their book, *Women Don't Ask,* that only 7 percent of female MBAs graduating from Carnegie Mellon University negotiated for a higher salary than the one initially offered by a potential employer, while 57 percent of male MBAs did. On average, those who negotiated raised the initial offer by $4,053. The starting salaries for males were more than 7 percent higher than those for females, overall.[2] Babcock and Laschever believe that a different negotiating style explains most of the gap in women's starting pay, and this gap explains a large part of the persistent pay differential between men and women throughout their careers.

NEGOTIATION AND NETWORKING

Networking skills are relevant to managerial negotiation skills. Since negotiating is a process, not an event or a one-shot deal in most business situations, it's important to maintain relationships while negotiating. Negotiating strategically means thinking long-term, building our networks. It means balancing relationships and results, cooperation and competition. It also means using our networks to help us negotiate successfully.

Again, research has identified gender differences in the ways managers use their networks during negotiations. When asking for a pay raise or promotion, women are more likely to rely on their job performance alone. Conversely, men are predisposed to ask for a raise when they feel it is warranted by comparison to others' performance. Men use their networking abilities and relationships as leverage for their personal goals. Women tend to be less outcome-oriented and more concerned with preserving goodwill. Often, women are also inclined to wait for someone else to sing their praises. All of these tendencies can be a detriment at the negotiation table.[3]

Networking is a skill. And like all skills, practice and preparation make perfect. When combined with merit, networking can be a valuable tool in influencing job searches, negotiations, and interviews. Building and using business relationships effectively can have a significant impact on your success. People enjoy mentoring people they like, and then claiming credit for their mentee's career success.

When negotiating, a manager has to strike a balance between what's good for a business relationship and what's good for the manager and her organization. It is also important in a management position to network with other managers so you can ensure you are on par with industry and company standards when negotiating.

NEGOTIATION AND CONFLICT

Before discussing the dynamic process of negotiation, we should first specify exactly what the term means. Chapter 10 dealt with conflict resolution in terms of win–lose, lose–lose, and win–win strategies. That discussion urged that a win–win solution to conflict is best, and it reviewed the beliefs necessary to implement this approach successfully. However, such an outcome is not always appropriate. When one or both parties see a situation as that in which one party will lose or gain something in exchange for the other party's loss or gain, a negotiation strategy is best. In this situation, one party cannot easily determine the needs or desired outcome of the other party, and one of the parties may not fully trust the other.

Win–lose situations occur every day in a manager's life. When managers consider the term *negotiation,* they may often think of special formal situations such as collective bargaining between labor and management or a sports agent negotiating for an athlete. These examples are generally termed third-party negotiations. Research indicates managers are more frequently becoming involved in third-party negotiations.[4] However, this discussion emphasizes the type of every-day negotiation situations any manager may face, such as obtaining additional office space for an employee, winning a budget increase, or securing additional support from another department. Effective managers win more than they lose.

Every negotiator has two universal concerns. The parties must balance their concern for the outcome of the negotiation with the relationship needs between the parties.[5] However, the degree of these concerns varies from one situation to another. In some situations, winning is all that matters, but in other situations, the value of the relationship may outweigh the need to win. In between these opposite extremes is the risk of obtaining a winning outcome while damaging the relationship, which affects the losing party's willingness to fulfill the agreement. A manager may need to work with this party in the future, and if the relationship is damaged, future transactions could be controversial. For example, when a subordinate requests a salary increase, the manager must weigh the need to manage the budget at the lowest cost with the need to maintain a positive relationship with the subordinate. If the subordinate's work performance is highly valued, the manager may want to make concessions to ensure continued good work.

A manager's approach to the negotiation process may be served by referring to the negotiation styles that balance these universal concerns, as demonstrated in Chapter 10 (Figure 10-3), where a manager's concern for production is balanced against the concern for people. Knowing the appropriate negotiation strategy can help a manager reach success.

A STRATEGIC MODEL FOR NEGOTIATIONS

The best way to approach the negotiation process is through the strategic analysis of managerial communication illustrated in Chapter 2.

The basic model of strategic managerial communication presented in Chapter 2 is shown here in Figure 11–1. To use the analogy from Chapter 2, we must peel

FIGURE 11–1
Strategic
Managerial
Communication
Model

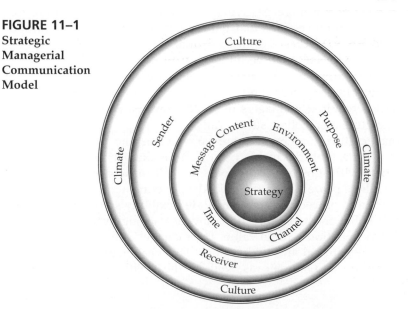

away the layers of the onion to develop a strategy. Discussion first focuses on the culture and climate (layer 1).

Next, the sender (manager), the purpose or goal of the negotiations, and the receiver's (the adversary's) style are explored (layer 2). To develop a negotiation strategy systematically, one must also analyze style. One must analyze the time, environment, channel, and content of the message. These are the third layer of the onion. Although the following discussion treats these items independently, managers must consider all the layers simultaneously when developing a negotiation strategy (the core of the model) because they all affect each other. This chapter concludes with a description of six negotiation strategies at the core (or fourth layer) of our onion model.

LAYER 1: CULTURE AND CLIMATE

As mentioned in many places in this book, culture is a primary concern in any communication situation. "First seek to understand, then to be understood" is Stephen Covey's fifth habit of the *Seven Habits of Highly Effective People*.[6] Managers must review and analyze the situation that initiates the need to negotiate and the culture/climate that surrounds each negotiation scenario. Then the manager can begin to identify alternative ways to resolve the need for the negotiation process. True understanding requires both talking and listening. The manager does not have to agree with the other party, but does need to understand the other party's position. In addition, the manager can show empathy without feeling sympathy and evaluate the difference between fact and emotion that may derive from the nature of the culture or climate.

Both national and organizational culture must be considered when negotiating. Some cultures support an assertive, almost demanding, negotiation style, whereas in other cultures a more passive approach is expected. A culture may encourage long negotiation sessions that require patience, while others support quick resolution. Some cultures encourage initial offers close to an expected settlement, while in other cultures the initial offer is nowhere near an expected outcome. In some cultures, it is important to develop a personal relationship before negotiating, but in others, only a superficial knowledge of the other persons involved is required. Managers must be thoroughly aware of the other party's national culture to negotiate successfully.

Organizational culture largely determines who has the power within an organization and the extent to which a person can make decisions. There is no reason to negotiate with someone if that person can't make decisions, and this is often the case where power is centralized. Also, in bureaucratic organizations, numerous policies and procedures may preclude flexibility so there is little that can be negotiated. But most organizations are not so highly centralized and bureaucratic that negotiation is of no value. The manager's challenge is to determine what can be negotiated and with whom. This challenge is a result of the organizational culture and climate as well as the political structure within the organization.

LAYER 2: SENDER, RECEIVER, AND PURPOSE

We next examine elements in the second layer of our onion model (Figure 11–1)—the negotiator's personal style and purpose. Just as some people are outgoing and talkative, and others are withdrawn and quiet, some managers enter a negotiation with confidence and a positive attitude, while others see defeat from the outset, believing they do not have a chance. Before negotiators can succeed, they must believe in themselves. E. H. Harriman, one of the U.S.'s leading railroad pioneers and a man bubbling with self-confidence, once remarked to a young financier, "Let me be one of 15 men around a table, and I will have my way."[7] A manager can gain confidence by becoming aware of the negotiation process and properly preparing for the interaction. In addition, practice in negotiation, if done properly, leads to greater confidence because of the positive results.

A manager creates power in negotiations when confident. Being confident, however, is not enough; during negotiations, you must also act and look confident. To begin, do not look as if you are expecting a long fight. One of the poorest practices is to remove your jacket, roll up your shirtsleeves, pour a cup of coffee, or otherwise appear to be settling in for an extended session. In addition, take care not to project a tired listless image. An adversary's hope and confidence increase dramatically when an opponent looks tired.

In negotiation, appearance is an important source of communication; during much of the discussion, negotiators watch one another closely. You can promote success with a neat appearance that suggests you are well organized and a person that cannot easily be exploited. We dealt with nonverbal messages in Chapter 8 and will do so again later in this chapter, but remember that nervous habits such as tapping a finger on the desk or playing with a pencil can project a nervous vulnerable image.

While the negotiation process may be conducted by phone, this medium has some disadvantages. Negotiating by phone restricts the manager's ability to read body language. Phone communication can result in the message being misunderstood or appearing last minute in nature. Negotiation by phone may take the receiver by surprise as he has not prepared for the conversation, and the resulting negotiation may become more competitive.

Some tension is always part of the negotiation process. This tension generally results from two separate unknowns inherent in any negotiation. The first is whether or not a deal can be struck. A second unknown is how long the negotiations will take. Simply knowing that it is natural to feel these tensions and being aware of their source helps to lessen them considerably.

Purpose

The purpose of the negotiation process is simple: to maximize your advantage. Initially, that purpose is one of the most critical elements to consider when developing a negotiation strategy. The purpose of the negotiation may translate to "know what you want" or, more appropriately, "know what is reasonable to expect." Obviously, wants and expectations are vastly different, but unless you have clearly differentiated between the two, confusion and failure can result.

Negotiation is useless in certain situations. Consider, for example, a production manager who has successfully negotiated personal salary increases in the past. Unfortunately, poor market conditions have affected the company, and nobody is receiving a salary increase. If the manager tries to negotiate now, he or she not only will fail to get an increase but also might create resentment because demands are made during hard times.

If the time is ripe and the other party is committed to the negotiation, then the manager can establish the negotiation goal. The following discussion presents three strategies: determining the maximum supportable outcome (MSO), the least acceptable outcome (LAO), and the best alternative to negotiated agreement (BATNA).

Defining the Maximum Supportable and Least Acceptable Outcomes

The maximum supportable outcome is the absolute most one can ask for in the opening position within reason. A negotiation can be quickly terminated if the MSO is beyond reason.

The LAO is the least acceptable result you will accept from the negotiation. If the outcome of the negotiation is anything less than your least acceptable outcome, it would be better to terminate the negotiation. Planning is important so the LAO is established before the negotiation.

Of course, both the LAO and MSO also reflect primary, secondary, short-term, and long-term considerations. An outcome frequently is complex and includes more than one aspect.

Since the least acceptable outcome (LAO) and the maximum supportable outcome (MSO) are the guideposts for negotiation, their terms must be clear before you enter any negotiation. It is a critical error (and possibly the most common) for a person to modify either of these two points after the negotiation has begun. Doing so suggests your adversary is influencing you unduly.

Keep in mind throughout our discussion of LAO and MSO that the terms are reversed for your adversary in the negotiation. Consider the example of a sales manager for a clothing distributor who is negotiating the price of 100 new suits with the purchasing manager of a clothing store. Table 11–1 demonstrates how the two see the terms differently.

It is important to keep this "reversal of terms" in mind when studying the following material. One outcome may be desirable to one person, but undesirable to another. In negotiation, as with other aspects of communication, individual perception and frame of reference are important to remember.

TABLE 11–1
Reversed Terms

Sales Manager		Purchasing Manager
Maximum supportable outcome (MSO)	$15,000	Least acceptable outcome (LAO)
Least acceptable outcome (LAO)	$11,500	Maximum supportable outcome (MSO)

Finding the LAO and MSO

Because the guidelines provided by the least acceptable outcome and the maximum supportable outcome are so critical, give careful thought to finding these outcomes. The LAO is probably easiest to establish. This is the point below which nothing could be accepted because of the potential loss. In effect, when a negotiator commits to this point, loss is unlikely.

The LAO is both objective and subjective, a combination of the facts surrounding the situation and the value placed on them. Because it is subjective, no magical formula determines the LAO. Thus, make every effort to separate what is acceptable from what is wanted.

In determining exactly what your LAO is, it is worthwhile to develop some kind of decision worksheet to ensure a systematic and objective process. Table 11–2 presents an example for determining the LAO of a job offer.

Any format that helps you think through the process is of value. Of course, we would all prefer to be at the other extreme of the range, the MSO. The MSO is the furthest point from the LAO that the negotiator can reasonably justify.

That area between the MSO and the LAO is the settlement range.[8] Both parties in the negotiation will have a conscious (or unconscious) settlement range. To help achieve success, the negotiator must be able to justify the MSO convincingly. Otherwise, the MSO may be set at a point that is beyond the opponent's LAO. Even though the negotiator might be willing to settle for much less, this possibility may be obviated because the opponent will see no reason to continue the discussion. But the reciprocal of this is also true; the maximum should not be too low, because once the MSO is out, one cannot readjust it. Negotiation will surely cease at that point.

The establishment of the MSO reflects the "one-trip-to-the-well" principle. You get to state your opening position only once, and it is vital to make the most of it. It is almost impossible to reverse directions and ask for more when, after looking more closely at the situation, you belatedly realize your MSO was set too low.

But what is maximum? It is whatever one can support, and this justification may require some creativity. In developing the maximum supportable outcome, look for unique attributes to include. Do not become so fixed on one or two items that you never consider other possible combinations. Consider a marketing manager who is negotiating with the vice president for an additional employee

TABLE 11–2
Establishing the Least Acceptable Outcome

Item	Relative Importance	LAO
Salary	4	$68,000
Location	3	Within 500 miles of hometown near a lake
Company size	1	Member of the Fortune 500
Job duties	5	At least 20% of the job should involve use of computers so I can use these skills
Social climate	2	Several young unmarried people (like me) in the department

position in the marketing department. The additional position may not be as big an obstacle to overcome as the salary requested for the position. How can the manager justify a salary of $80,000 for the position? It may be possible to divert attention to something positive like increased sales to distract the vice president from the salary. Do not hesitate to make a reference list that outlines the benefits to upper management of agreeing to the salary request as well as an undisclosed list of possible responses that could negatively affect your negotiating position. By establishing such lists, you can prepare possible responses to overcome criticism regarding the salary request.

Defining BATNA

So far, we have seen that to achieve your negotiation's purpose, you must determine your LAO and MSO. But sometimes negotiating with a bottom line is less effective and beneficial than developing a solid BATNA (best alternative to a negotiated agreement). BATNA was the brainchild of Roger Fisher and Bill Ury of Harvard, first described in their series of books on Principled Negotiation that started with *Getting to Yes*.[9] The basic idea is that each party in a negotiation needs to identify what, if any, options are available if there is a stalemate. If there is no alternative, you will walk away from the table empty-handed. You should decide on your BATNA prior to the start of negotiations.

An example is that you have an offer from a dealer to buy your old car for $1,000. You decide to advertise your car in the newspaper classifieds for $1,200 (the MSO). Your BATNA is now $1,000, since you know you can fall back on that dealer's offer if no individual sale is successful. But wait. Other offers that you might consider include selling your car to your little sister for $750. This might or might not be a better alternative than the dealer's offer, because of your relationship value. Thus, finding BATNA requires weighing a broad range of factors.

BATNAs prevent you from accepting terms that are too unfavorable and from rejecting terms that you should accept. If the proposed solution is better than your BATNA, then it's your MSO, and you should take it. If the agreement is not better than your BATNA, you should reopen negotiations. However, your BATNA is not the same as your LAO, the minimum acceptable offer. Instead, it's where you will go if you don't get even the least acceptable offer. When the parties have similar BATNAs, then the negotiation is ripe for agreement. Much time and money can be saved by "settling" for a BATNA rather than continuing a dispute. In the U.S., about 90 percent of lawsuits settle out of court because the lawyers understand the strength of each side's case and how likely each is to prevail in court. Thus, when negotiations threaten to break down, parties should reveal their BATNAs to see if they are similar.

LAYER 3: TIME, ENVIRONMENT, CONTENT, AND CHANNEL

After peeling away the first two layers of our onion model (Figure 11–1), we come to four new and more specific strategic considerations. The first one we shall describe is time.

Time

Time is a vital component of strategy.[10] Two issues should be addressed when considering time factors: (1) when to negotiate and (2) how to best use the time within the negotiation. The answer to the second question also provides insights for the best time to make an offer or counteroffer. First, let's look at when to negotiate.

To optimize energy and prevent major setbacks, try to conduct a negotiating session when you feel healthy and rested. Many individual idiosyncrasies exist, but the consensus seems to be that most people are at peak efficiency about 11 a.m.[11]

Although the ideal is to select the best time to negotiate, it is not always practical. Thus, the savvy negotiator is always fully prepared and never loses an opportunity to negotiate. A quick meeting in the cafeteria, a chance encounter in the elevator, or an apparently spontaneous telephone call can represent opportunities for negotiation. To quote John Ilich, author of several best sellers on power negotiation, including *The Complete Idiot's Guide to Winning through Negotiation*, "Never lose an opportunity to negotiate, but never negotiate until you are certain it's an opportunity."[12]

In any negotiation, the main question to ask is, "When do I have the most power and when is my adversary the weakest?" Naturally, the answer changes. Assume a manager wanted to adopt a flextime policy for her staff. The best time to negotiate this with upper management is probably just after some major accomplishment or even when another department has changed its work schedule. Strategic timing can add significantly to a person's power in negotiation.

A second question is how to best use time within the negotiation. Generally, one expects most significant concession behavior and settlement action to occur close to the deadline.[13] An approaching deadline puts pressure on the parties to state their true positions and thus does much to squeeze any elements of bluff out of the latter steps of negotiation. A number of major studies verify the power of time limits on the negotiation.[14]

Because of the significance of deadlines, note the following guidelines.

1. **Do not reveal the true deadline.** When an adversary knows the other person's deadlines, negotiations stall until the deadline acts as a pressure for concession. When a person has an extremely tight deadline, she may be wise to extend the deadline rather than to enter the negotiations at a disadvantage.

2. **Be patient.** This may also be referred to as forbearance.[15] Negotiators should take time to answer questions, provide information, and make decisions. This includes keeping defensive reactions under control as well as avoiding the tendency to take an offensive posture when being verbally attacked. The time provided through patience allows the opportunity to organize, understand issues, test the opponent's strengths and weaknesses, and weigh risks. Also, it creates a sense of pressure in the opponent, especially when the deadline approaches.

3. **Use the clock.** Because most Americans are so conscious of time, you should seek concessions or even provide minor concessions toward the end of a time period. Thus, you might elicit action on the part of the opponent immediately before lunch or dinner because people like to have a sense of accomplishment when taking a break. And a flurry of action can be used to the negotiator's advantage if taken at the right time.

Environment

In addition to time and timing, the physical environment is strategically important. This section explores two aspects of the physical environment: site and physical arrangement.

Site selection is often important because it bears directly on the amount of control each party may exercise over the physical arrangements at that site as well as the psychological climate in which the exchange occurs. In negotiations conducted in one's home territory, the host has a legitimate right to assume responsibility for arranging the physical space. This is similar to the home-field advantage in sports; the home team is more likely to come out the winner in both situations.

What is the best way to arrange a conference room or office for negotiations? First, prevent distractions such as phone calls. These can be costly if they occur at an awkward time in the negotiation. Second, avoid sitting in a position that suggests subordination or even equality. If in a conference room, sit at the head of the table. If in your office, sit behind the desk. Also, have appropriate equipment such as flip charts, computers, or writing tables ready. Having these items ready underscores the sincerity of your position. On the other hand, if the importance of the relationship of the negotiating parties is primary, this power arrangement may be less important. Sitting at a roundtable and showing mutual respect may provide the manager with more power because the manager has chosen an environment that indicates compassion for the other. This strategy may actually elicit more concessions based on the trust established between the two parties.

Observing the physical arrangements of a room and physical position that an opponent takes in a negotiation provides valuable information. Figure 11–2

FIGURE 11–2
Seating
Arrangements

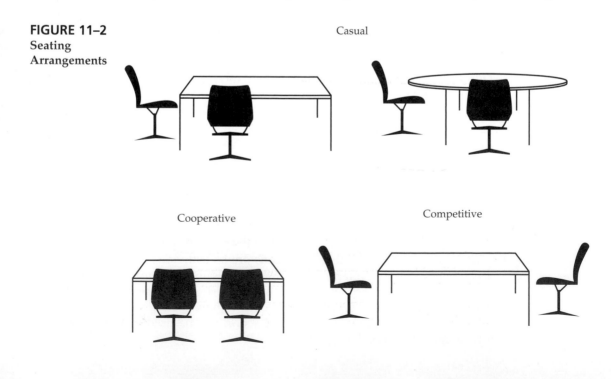

Casual

Cooperative

Competitive

summarizes several possibilities. For example, a researcher conducted observation and questionnaire studies of seating preferences in several social contexts and found that Americans engaging in casual conversation normally prefer to sit at right angles to each other (if seated at square or rectangular tables), or beside one another when seated at circular tables. He also found that side-by-side seating occurred in cooperative relationships. However, face-to-face seating was the most preferred configuration in competitive relationships, with a moderately wide space separating the parties. He also noted less conversation when people were seated far apart than when they were side by side or opposite one another.[16]

Other nonverbal elements come into play in negotiations. For example, one can use distance to gain power. Famous anthropologist and author Ray Birdwhistell found that when two parties are in competitive situations, they find proximity threatening.[17] Consequently, if a manager wants to create stress in an opponent, he might move closer physically. Eye contact can also be a strong tool in negotiation. Research indicates people avoid direct visual contact in competitive encounters because it is stressful.[18] They find it intimidating, dominating, or overly revealing of motives they wish to keep hidden when engaged in competitive relationships.[19] In this same regard, other researchers have found that people have greater difficulty telling a convincing lie when they are being watched closely than when not.[20]

If you cannot use home ground for negotiation, try for neutral territory. Thus, in a negotiation with a high-level manager, it might be inappropriate to ask her to come to a lower-level manager's office. However, one could suggest that both parties meet in a conference room to avoid interruptions by saying, "I know you're busy and get a lot of interruptions. How about meeting in the conference room so we can get away for a few minutes?" Or a meeting at lunch might be an easy way to neutralize a situation. The adversary may be comfortable at lunch, and it may be possible to offset any status advantage.

When you have no alternative to meeting in the adversary's office, you do not need to assume a subordinate role immediately. Typically, the adversary is at a desk and you are in a side chair, or worse, in a low-slung occasional chair; you can quickly offset the disadvantage merely by standing up and moving around while speaking. With this little nonverbal technique, it is now possible to look down on the adversary.

Message Content

Sender, receiver, purpose, time, and environment all help to set the stage for what is really the essence of the negotiation: the message itself. Negotiation revolves around the amount of information that each party decides to relate (or not to relate) about true motives and preferences. Negotiators base such a decision not only on their own standards but also equally on their opponents' behavior, openness, and honesty before and during the exchange.

Although nonverbal messages are important, the spoken word is the predominant form of communication in negotiation. The major types of verbal messages appropriate for discussion here are making concessions and responding to and presenting questions. But first, we will consider the opening messages.

Opening Messages

Should the negotiations begin with an immediate discussion of key issues, or is it best to begin with a friendly neutral conversation? The answer depends on the total time allowed for the negotiations, the type of previous relationship with the parties involved, and whether the general atmosphere is friendly or hostile.

In the United States, the accepted practice is to begin with a general conversation on neutral topics. But the conversation moves rather quickly toward the issues. The same pattern is true with many western Europeans; however, in Mexico, the Arab world, and most Asian countries, the initial neutral conversations are generally much longer.

Concessions

We have mentioned that it is important to establish the LAO and MSO before negotiating. But it is not advisable to state these early in the negotiation. Rather, it is best to determine the other person's LAO. You then begin to move away from your MSO toward your LAO and toward the other person's MSO. This is generally accomplished through a series of concessions.

When and how to make concessions is determined by information obtained from questions—our next topic. However, principles of the equality rule can serve as a guideline for making concessions. The first equality principle suggests negotiators generally expect one another to make an equal *number* of concessions from their initial starting point. The second principle is that of an equal sacrifice. By this rule, "equality" is judged by *how much* an individual concedes relative to his aspirations—in other words, who makes the bigger sacrifice.

Imagine a situation in which two managers are negotiating a reorganization among several departments. A third manager has left and has not been replaced; consequently, the duties of her department will be assigned to the two remaining departments. During this negotiation, the two managers must perceive that each has made an equal *number* of concessions as well as an equal *amount*. But numbers and amounts are difficult to quantify when negotiating such items as job duties, reporting relationships, and budgets. Consequently, the manner in which these concessions are made is important. An effective negotiator uses positive language to ensure concessions appear frequent and large.

Questions

Making concessions is closely related to asking and responding to questions. Dorothy Leads discusses the power of questions in her book *Smart Questions*.[21] Leads indicates that individuals pay more attention to a question than to a statement since the other party knows they will be expected to do more than listen: they will need to respond. While closed questions can be appropriate at times, open-ended questions often gather more valuable information that can be useful in the negotiation process. It is through these questions that an effective negotiator determines when and how much of a concession to offer.

A negotiator may unintentionally strike an emotional chord with a question and arouse antagonism; consequently, it may be necessary to prepare the ground before asking questions. One way to accomplish this is by explaining the reason or reasons for asking a question if the potential exists for embarrassment.

Questions serve five purposes:

1. To arouse attention: "When did that change?" or "Did you know about . . .?"
2. To obtain information: "What is the difference between the two items?" or "What's the value of that point?"
3. To clarify: "I still am confused about your motive here. What else is key to you?" or "What are the terms we've settled on so far?"
4. To stimulate thinking: "Could you give me your reaction to the second item?" or "Is there another alternative?"
5. To bring to a conclusion or summary: "How would you summarize your proposal?" or "Are we ready to act?" or "Have we got a deal?"

While it is usually a good idea to prepare several questions, some people get so involved in asking questions that they stop listening. Also, few people can think of all the right questions during the actual negotiation. Preparation will help to overcome both possibilities.

If you want a particular answer, ask a *leading question*. A leading question directs the person who is answering from statement to statement until the logic of the questioner's argument is made. Here is a series of leading questions:

> Is research included in your cost? Where? How is it prorated between jobs? Exactly why do you include it in our charges when you just said that this job requires no research?

In this example, the questioner may or may not know the answers, but she led her opponents to a planned conclusion.

When no need exists to lead the opponent in a particular direction, use *open-ended questions*—questions that usually begin with how, why, or what. For example, "How would you recommend we close the gap?" "Why is plan A preferable to plan B?" "What is the proposal?" Open questions invite people to express their thinking freely. These are the types of questions that Dorothy Leads refers to as smart questions.

A third type of question, the *rhetorical question*, is one that is asked not to get an answer, but for effect. Rather than seeking an answer, this type of question attempts to draw attention to a particular item. Examples of rhetorical questions include "What do you think the vice president would say to something like that?" or "Do you really want us to believe that?"

In general, avoid *bipolar, either-or,* or *shotgun* questions. Such a question as "Would you prefer a corner office with a computer, or would you rather have a larger desk and no extra chair?" needs to be divided into two questions. As the question is presently stated, confusion will result, or the opponent may even ask for both. Similarly, forced-choice questions will make your opponent feel cornered and may end the negotiations. Also, a wise negotiator avoids a rapid-fire questioning approach. An opponent needs time to respond, and the questioner needs to listen to the responses.

A final effective use of questions is to get negotiations back on track when an opponent has been diverted. A simple question like "How can we relate what you're saying to . . . ?" should get the most recent comments turned in a different, more relevant direction.

To summarize, do not ask questions just for the sake of asking a question. Keep the purpose of the question in mind, listen for the right time, and then phrase the question to meet the prevailing needs.

Answering Questions

Negotiation is a game of asking and answering questions. The preparation and mental alertness required to ask purposeful questions are just as essential for answering them. Perhaps the most important preparation is to brainstorm and write down in advance questions most likely to arise. Ask an associate to act as devil's advocate and raise a host of hard questions before negotiation. The more a person prepares possible answers, the better those answers will be.

Keep two universal guidelines in mind when answering questions: (1) never answer until the question is fully understood, and (2) take time to think through your answer. Besides applying these two guidelines, you can exercise two options in answering. First, you may answer the question accurately and completely. However, since such directness is not always advisable in many negotiations, the second option is to not be totally open when answering.[22] For instance, when negotiating for the salary to go with a new job, it is not wise to directly answer the question "What is the salary you are looking for?" It is probably best to respond with a comment like "What do you generally pay for this type of job?" If your MSO and BATNA are below the other party's lower limits, you will not have revealed your limits too soon.

When you do not wish to give an answer, several alternatives are available. First, you may choose to answer only part of the question. For instance, a question may be, "What is required to have this project completed by May 1?" You respond by listing all that is required to have the job done without relating to the date. By receiving complete and detailed information, the interrogator thinks the question has been answered. Meanwhile, you can stay away from potentially damaging information.

Another possibility is to ask for clarification even when the question is fairly clear. Often when people are clarifying a question, they intentionally or unintentionally change the question substantially or provide additional insight into the type of answer sought. Also, the time it takes to restate the question provides additional maneuvering time for you to consider possible answers. A variation is to ask for clarification for part of the question, thus diverting attention away from the remainder of the question—as a result, you may end up having to answer only part of the question.

A third possibility is to answer a different question. In such a ploy, the question being answered is so similar to the one asked that the interrogator actually considers the answer satisfactory. For instance, when asked which budget item would be the best to drop from next year's request, you might answer that inflation is affecting all areas of the budget, and then provide a specific example of inflation's effects. This, in turn, could be followed by the next alternative: answering the question with a question—for example, "Where do you think inflation has had the greatest impact on the entire company?" This tactic may or may not divert attention away from the initial question but is often better than giving a direct answer.

A fourth alternative is to answer a negative question with a positive response. When negotiating salaries, a typical scenario has the opponent asking, "What do you consider to be the biggest weakness you'll bring to this job?" Naturally, a thorough and accurate answer would put you at a disadvantage. A positive strategic answer might be, "Well, sometimes I get too caught up in my work and I'll stay until late at night. This really isn't fair to my family, so I have to learn to balance my time between family and work." This answer takes the advantage away from the opponent because it is difficult to fault a hard worker who is also a family person.

The real key to answering questions, then, is the ability to think on your feet. This task becomes easier with experience, but no substitute exists for rehearsing the possible questions and being prepared.

Channel

Face-to-face negotiation used to be considered the only viable channel, but this is no longer the case. Negotiators today must consider several communication channels when developing their negotiation strategy.

Whether the negotiation is conducted face-to-face, via the telephone, or electronically, written media often play a key role.[23] The most common use is the *letter of intent*, which follows many negotiations. A person's memory is always much better five minutes after a conversation than five days later. The letter or memo of intent ensures that all the critical items are mutually agreed on.

The person who writes the memo or letter has the advantage, for this person interprets meanings and shapes words to reflect his understanding of the discussion. The question is not one of exploiting the party or catching the opponent in some trap. It is simply getting the area of agreement laid out in your own way, rather than leaving it to the opponent.

Of course, you do not write the letter in such a tone that it sounds as if the opponent cannot be trusted. You can achieve such tact easily. In one situation, a manager hosted several employees from an out-of-town office. She submitted an expense voucher for $400, but the next paycheck did not cover the expenses. A discussion with her supervisor followed, and after a long negotiation, he agreed to pay $300 of the $400. After the negotiation, the manager sent the following short e-mail:

DATE: March 11, 2010

TO: Chris Averson

FROM: Pat Harolds

SUBJECT: Expense Voucher

Thanks for taking the time to sit down with me and discuss the expenses incurred while hosting the engineers from St. Paul. I'll be looking forward to receiving the $300 with the next paycheck.

This quick e-mail not only confirms the result of the negotiation, but it establishes goodwill.

Managers can also use written correspondence to de-emphasize an issue or soothe a highly emotional situation. Correspondence brings an issue back into perspective merely by tactfully showing that a matter is not of great importance. Often, the printed word can lend credibility that face-to-face communication lacks since some people are more apt to take seriously what they see than what they hear. Also, a carefully written memo tends to be less emotional than a face-to-face interaction.

Finally, managers can use written correspondence to present a position when a complex explanation is required. It is difficult to present a complex argument that includes cost figures and diagrams with only an oral presentation. A written statement or even a chart can be helpful when presenting such an argument. In addition, if the opponent has no such aids, counterarguments might be harder to formulate. Managers who believe that the only communication channel is face-to-face severely limit their options.

LAYER 4: CORE STRATEGIES

We have arrived at the core of our strategic managerial communication model (Figure 11–1). How a manager acts and looks, how she communicates the maximum supportable outcome, reacts to the adversary's style, uses time, establishes the environmental conditions, and asks and answers questions all contribute to the negotiation strategy. Managers combine these communication variables either by design or by accident to develop a core strategy for negotiating. Six general strategies reviewed in the following paragraphs can assist you in combining the different aspects of communication systematically. No particular approach is recommended over another; rather, these six approaches represent possibilities that may best fit a particular situation.[24]

Surprise

The surprise strategy involves unexpectedly introducing a goal or concession into a negotiation. For instance, a manager negotiating budget items with a vice president might suddenly request a new title. The total surprise may catch the other off guard so the additional request is approved, especially since it does not add additional expense.

A quick concession on a nonessential item is another form of surprise. Once again, this concession may be on an item unrelated to the main focus of the negotiation in hopes that the concession will foster a reciprocal concession by the opponent. Surprise may be particularly valuable with an opponent who is under time pressure, because it may stimulate some quick concessions.

Bluff

When playing poker, you may bluff by placing a large bet even though you do not have a strong hand to back it up. By bluffing, you hope to scare your opponent. This tactic is also occasionally appropriate in managerial negotiation. Bluffing, the act of creating illusions without the use of lies or outright misrepresentations, is fair play in negotiations because each side is attempting to maximize its own benefit. A difference exists between withholding information and presenting wrong data. For instance, when a person is negotiating to buy an office desk, it is not the same thing to say "I would like to pay no more than $900" as it is to say "I have only $900 to spend." A person may want to spend no more than $900 but has additional funds if they are needed.

Stacking

The stacking strategy is used when one idea is attached to another. For instance, a public relations manager might use this approach when negotiating a new strategy with her administrative vice president: "I was just reading in *Fortune* that ABC International has changed its approach for its stockholders' meeting. ABC used an approach similar to what I'm suggesting." This manager is stacking her approach on top of ABC's to build credibility.

Legislators also use a form of stacking when presenting bills. They will attach a controversial item as a "rider" onto something that has wide support. Managers use this tactic in negotiations when they stack an undesirable characteristic onto a desirable one. For instance, a person may be asked to take a transfer (undesirable) in combination with a promotion (desirable).

Fait Accompli

The *fait accompli* is a type of bluff that says, in effect, "Here it is, it is accomplished." You state the terms of an offer and act as if the terms are acceptable to the opposing party. The expectation is that when an issue is phrased as if it were a negotiated final settlement, the opponent will accept it with little or no protest. Assume an item has been discussed for some time, but no solid agreement has been reached. You may write a letter of intent regarding the negotiation and state the issue as settled. Using this approach, real estate agents will occasionally push stubborn buyers into action by jotting down the buyer's tentative terms onto a contract. Once the details are down, the buyer is asked to sign and often does.

Take It or Leave It

The take-it-or-leave-it position lets an opponent know this offer is your best one; it represents the maximum goal adjustments a person is willing to make. In making a take-it-or-leave-it offer (which is, in fact, an ultimatum), you take the risk that the offer will be rejected, so there may be no chance to improve it or even revive the negotiations. You could follow with a different offer if the initial take-it-or-leave-it proposal was rejected; however, credibility would be lost. You can only use this strategy once.

Screen

In negotiation, a screen is a third party used by the negotiator as part of the process. You act like a screen between the opponent and the final decision maker. For instance, assume you are negotiating with an outside contractor. You can say that certain conditions proposed by the contractor need to be approved by others in the company. When these conditions are not approved, the adversary may find it necessary to grant concessions to keep the deal going. The third party may actually be a phantom person in the background, but this procedure generates thinking time and may take away some of the opponent's offensive advantage. Instead of negotiating one on one, the opponent has two adversaries, and it is difficult to negotiate through a "barrier" or screen.

Negotiators often use the screen, but it has a serious drawback: It gives the impression that you have limited power. Use this procedure sparingly when negotiating salaries and budgets with your subordinates, because it will soon appear that you have little decision-making authority, and thus both respect and influence are weakened.

If possible, do not let an adversary use the third-party technique. Instead, try to get directly to the decision maker. The screen filters out the communications, so much of the strategy used on the adversary is weakened.

These six strategies are only suggestions. Combinations of these or even other strategies are possible. Every strategy has potential drawbacks, strengths, and risks depending on the variables discussed in this chapter and summarized in our onion model (Figure 11–1). Formulating the appropriate strategy is not an easy task. Good negotiation strategy requires analytical ability, an understanding of communication, a refined set of skills, and creativity. However, after you have studied this chapter, you should be able to enter a negotiation confidently.

Summary

Negotiation is an appropriate tool for compromise in conflict resolution situations. Before negotiating, the manager should establish the maximum supportable outcome (MSO) and least acceptable outcome (LAO) to know the negotiation range. Both limits must be carefully thought out so managers can protect their best interests while negotiating in a credible manner. The MSO must be one the manager can support convincingly, and the LAO must be one the manager can live with. It is also wise to define BATNA (the best alternative to a negotiated agreement) to prevent a stalemate.

Negotiators need to consider when to negotiate, how long to continue, and when to make a counteroffer. Since negotiation is liable to be most fruitful when close to an opponent's deadlines, several suggestions about deadlines are appropriate: (1) do not reveal the true deadlines, if possible; (2) be patient; (3) use the clock. Strategic negotiators should also seek an optimum physical environment that benefits them without giving advantage to the opposition.

Another consideration is language used during the negotiation. Negotiators should use common basic language, should strive for clarity, should be specific, and should not be apologetic. Questions asked during negotiations have five purposes: to create attention, to obtain information, to clarify, to stimulate thinking, and to conclude or summarize. In phrasing questions, strategy dictates whether to use open-ended, leading, or closed questions. In answering questions, the negotiator must protect his or her interests by taking time to think through the answer and respond only when the question is fully understood. The chapter suggests strategies for adapting answers to suit one's interests.

The channel chosen for negotiation is important. Which channel is chosen depends on the circumstances. The letter or memo of intent that follows many negotiations requires care in preparation and can work to the advantage of the person preparing it.

Six core strategies can be applied in negotiations—*surprise,* unexpectedly introducing a goal or a concession; *bluff,* creating an illusion without lying; *stacking,* linking one idea with another for argument's sake; *fait accompli,* acting as if terms are acceptable to the opposition before any agreement has occurred; *take it or leave it,* letting the opponent know that this offer is the last; and the *screen,* using a third party as part of the negotiation.

Role Play Scenario

Employment Agreement

Background: Managers seeking new positions may find there is far more to agree to than just pay, benefits, and job responsibilities. Today, companies want to protect their trade secrets, inventions, and clients. To do so, they ask new executives and managers to sign employment agreements that safeguard their interests.

Instructions: In pairs, students should negotiate the conditions for employment in the following scenario. One student is the candidate; the other is the hiring agent. The negotiators should determine the MSO, LAO, and BATNA for each topic to be negotiated.

Company: Bio-Analytics, Inc., a scientific software development company. The organization's chief clients are pharmaceutical companies, research and development laboratories, and universities. Products are software programs that support scientific research.

Position: Director of Marketing.

Responsibilities: Manage the Marketing Department, which is responsible for finding clients, selling Bio-Analytics products, and servicing the accounts.

Topics for Negotiation:

1. Noncompete clause—When the Director leaves, s/he can't work for similar types of companies for a specified period of time, and also in a defined geographical area. S/he also can't work for a competitor while employed in the current job.
2. Invention clause—The company, not the employee, owns whatever the employee developed or invented while working for the firm.
3. Nonsolicitation of clients—When the Director leaves, s/he can't seek business from former clients for a specified time.
4. Nonsolicitation of employees—When the Director leaves, s/he can't try to attract former colleagues to the new firm for a specified time.
5. Confidentiality agreement—When the Director leaves, s/he may not disclose to outsiders the company's private business and technical data, such as products in development, formulas, test results, and sales strategies.

Negotiation Tips for the Candidate:

- With noncompete clauses, try to limit the time in which you can't work for a competing company. As a bargaining chip, point out that your useful knowledge about a company lasts only a limited time, such as a few months after you leave the company.
- With clients, ask to be allowed to identify which clients you can and can't contact after you leave the company.
- Focus the negotiation on conditions worth fighting for. For instance, the duration of noncompete and nonsolicitation provisions can limit your future ability to earn a living.

Cases for Small Group Discussion

Case 11-1.

Purchasing and Accounts Payable

Saul and Latisha are both administrative managers in a machine tool company. Latisha is the director of purchasing and has four purchasing agents and a secretary reporting to her. Saul is the director of accounts payable and has two people reporting to him. The secretary for the accounts payable group also works for the accounts receivable group, so in effect the accounts payable group has only a part-time secretary.

Saul and Latisha both have business degrees and graduated from college three and five years ago, respectively. They are both ambitious, and there is a high level of competition between them. The following discussion occurs in Latisha's office, which is down the hall from Saul's. Latisha is busy and has many papers spread across her desk. It is about 45 minutes before the normal quitting time, but it looks as if Latisha may not get away by then.

Everything has been rather hectic lately because it is nearing the end of the month. Both Latisha and Saul have numerous activities that need to be completed within the next few days.

Questions

1. Analyze the following conversation and indicate what could be done to improve the effectiveness of this interaction.

> **Saul:** Latisha, could I use your secretary for a few hours tomorrow? We are really behind, and I've noticed that your secretary doesn't seem to be too busy.
>
> **Latisha:** What do you mean "too busy"? We all have work backing up on us.
>
> **Saul:** Well, you have one secretary, but we have to share time with accounts receivable.

Latisha:	Well I'm sorry, we're just too busy.
Saul:	How about asking her to work some overtime but charge it to our department? Does she like to work overtime?
Latisha:	She might want to do that. You can ask.
Saul:	Would you please ask? That might be better because you're her supervisor.
Latisha:	No, you go ahead and talk to her. Also, remember you will have to pay the time and a half for overtime.
Saul:	I really think you should talk to her.

As Saul says this, the telephone rings, and he walks out of the office.

2. Return to Figure 11–1. What are the major variables presented in the figure that influence the communication presented in this case?

Case 11-2.

Negotiating a Purchase

Reggie Blanchard's delivery van was recently totaled when someone ran a stop sign and struck the van. The other person's insurance company is going to pay Blanchard for the damages to his van, and for a week now Blanchard has been looking at new vans while he temporarily leases one. The following scenario transpired when Blanchard talked to Kelly, a salesperson who tried to sell him a new van.

Kelly:	Yes, sir, may I be of service to you?
Blanchard:	I recently lost my delivery van in an accident. I am temporarily leasing a van, so I would like to get one as soon as possible.
Kelly:	What kind of van did you have?
Blanchard:	A 2005 one like this (pointing to a low-priced van). It had low mileage and was in great shape.
Kelly:	I know how you must feel. It is discomforting to lose a service van like that. And then you really don't get enough money from the insurance company to buy a van just like the one you had, do you?
Blanchard:	Yes, sir, that's exactly right.
Kelly:	How did the accident happen?

Blanchard then proceeds to explain how the other person ran the stop sign and demolished the passenger side of his van, and as he does this, Kelly nods his head in agreement with Blanchard's every word.

Kelly:	That sorry old soul must have had mud in his eyes not to have seen you in that intersection.
Blanchard:	Ha, ha. I guess you're right.

Kelly: Well, now don't worry, because you've come to the right place at the right time. We're making good deals on all this year's models to be ready for the shipment of next year's vans due any week now.

Blanchard: That sounds good. Let me ask you, how much for this one?

Kelly: Well, these models are going like hotcakes. They're excellent vehicles and the prices are outstanding for the quality in the van. I can let you have this one for $37,000.

Blanchard: I hate to say it, but that seems a little high for this model.

Kelly: Oh, but this van has some great features, including our consumer protection package for $1,970 (smiling). This includes paint treatment, a sound shield underneath the van, and a three-year rust prevention guarantee. It also includes a membership in our motor club plan, which has some excellent benefits for business-people.

This last sentence was spoken while Kelly put his hand on Blanchard's shoulder.

Blanchard: Is that so?

Kelly: How much are you looking to spend?

Blanchard: I'm not exactly sure, but judging from what the book value of my old van is, and the amount of the notes I was paying on it, I'd like to spend not much more than $30,000.

Kelly: Well, like I say, I can give you this van for $37,000. We've already lowered the sticker price by $2,500. It normally sells for $39,500 (pause). If you can spend $30,000, then $7,000 more won't add that much to your payment. Besides, we're the only dealer in town that offers the consumer protection plan, and we feel that the benefits far outweigh the cost. It's a steal, I tell you.

Blanchard: Oh well, in that case I guess $37,000 is fairly reasonable. Let me think about it, but it sounds good.

Questions

1. What negotiation style did Kelly use to move Blanchard toward this sale?
2. List some things Blanchard could do to improve his own position at the beginning of the negotiation.
3. Discuss some negotiation strategies that Blanchard should have used as the negotiation proceeded.

Endnotes

1. D. G. Pruitt, *Negotiation Behavior* (New York: Academic Press, 1981).

2. Linda Babcock and Sara Laschever, *Women Don't Ask: Negotiation and the Gender Divide* (Princeton, NJ: Princeton University Press, 2003).

3. Barbara Safani, "Nuances of Negotiation," *Insider's Guide to Job Search,* http://www.teglaloroupepeacefoundation.org.

4. Deborah M. Kolb and Blair H. Sheppard, "Do Managers Mediate, or Even Arbitrate?" *Negotiation Journal,* October 1985, pp. 379–88.

5. Roger Fisher, William Ury, and Bruce Patton, *Getting to Yes: Negotiating Agreement Without Giving In,* 2nd ed. (Boston: Houghton Mifflin Co., 1992).

6. Stephen R. Covey, *The 7 Habits of Highly Effective People* (Simon & Schuster, 1989).

7. John Ilich, *The Art and Skill of Successful Negotiation* (Englewood Cliffs, NJ: Prentice Hall, 1983), p. 33.

8. Michael Schalzki, *Negotiation: The Art of Getting What You Want* (New York: Signet, 1981), p. 33.

9. Fisher *et al., Getting to Yes.*

10. Peter J. D. Carnevale and Edward J. Lawler, "Time Pressure and the Development of Integrative Agreements in Bilateral Negotiations," *Journal of Conflict Resolution* 30, no. 4 (December 1986), pp. 636–59.

11. David D. Seltz and Alfred J. Modica, *Negotiate Your Way to Success* (New York: New American Library, 1980), p. 52.

12. Ilich, *The Art and Skill of Successful Negotiation,* p. 22.

13. Herb Cohen, *You Can Negotiate Anything* (New York: Bantam Books, 1980), p. 92.

14. Jeffrey Z. Rubin and Bert R. Brown, *The Social Psychology of Bargaining and Negotiation* (New York: Academic Press, 1975), p. 122.

15. Gerald I. Nierenberg, *Fundamentals of Negotiating* (New York: Hawthorn, 1973), p. 150.

16. R. Sommer, "Further Studies of Small Group Ecology," *Sociometry* 28, no. 2 (1965), pp. 337–38.

17. R. L. Birdwhistell, *Introduction to Kinesics* (Louisville, KY: University of Louisville Press, 1952).

18. P. A. Andersen and J. F. Andersen, "The Exchange of Nonverbal Intimacy: A Critical Review of Dyadic Models," *Journal of Nonverbal Behavior* 8, no. 12 (1984), pp. 327–49.

19. M. Cook, "Experiments on Orientations and Proxemics," *Human Relations* 23, no. 1 (1970), pp. 62–76.

20. R. V. Exline, J. Thibaut, C. Brannon, and P. Gumpert, "Visual Interaction in Relation to Machiavellianism and Unethical Acts," *American Psychologist* 16, no. 3 (1961), p. 396.

21. Dorothy Leads, *Smart Questions, A New Strategy for Successful Managers* (McGraw-Hill, 1987).

22. Linda L. Putnam and M. Scott Poole, "Conflict and Negotiation," in *Handbook of Organizational Communication,* by F. Jablin, L. Putnam, K. Roberts, and L. Porter (Newbury Park, CA: Sage Publications, 1987), pp. 549–99.

23. Joseph F. Byrnes, "Ten Guidelines for Effective Negotiation," *Business Horizons,* May–June 1987, pp. 7–12.

24. These strategies are partially drawn from Roy J. Lewicki and Joseph A. Littere, *Negotiation* (Homewood, IL: Richard D. Irwin, 1985).

Chapter **Twelve**

Conducting Interviews

Patience is the most necessary quality for business; many a man would rather you heard his story than grant his request.

—*Lord Chesterfield (1694–1773), British statesman and author*

A manager conducts many different kinds of interviews: performance appraisal, employment, persuasive, grievance, exit, problem solving, and informational. No matter what the situation, the process is an intensive communication transaction designed to obtain or share certain predetermined kinds of information. But successful managers must learn to avoid the special communication barriers that accompany the process. Accordingly, this chapter examines interviews from the perspective of the interviewer, suggests ways to overcome the special barriers, and offers guidelines for conducting the most common kinds of interviews.

BARRIERS TO EFFECTIVE INTERVIEWS

All the communication dynamics discussed in Chapter 2 are present in the interview, but six barriers are particularly relevant: (1) differing intentions of the people involved, (2) bias, (3) the fact-inference fallacy, (4) nonverbal communication, (5) effects of first impressions, and (6) organizational status.

Barrier 1: Differing Intentions

Managers cannot always assume all participants agree on the information that should be exchanged in an interview. In fact, rarely do both the interviewer and interviewee agree. One obvious instance is the employment interview. While the interviewer wants to know all the strengths and weaknesses of the applicant, the applicant (interviewee) wants to reveal only strengths to the interviewer.

Differences in intention operate at one of three levels. First, both parties consciously may intend to have a clear and accurate exchange of information. This type may be particularly relevant in a performance appraisal interview. This type is equally important during informational interviews at networking events. At the second level, one of the parties does not intend to disclose certain relevant information. This often occurs in exit interviews when the employee does not reveal the real reason for leaving. At the third level, both parties do not intend to disclose certain relevant information. This may happen when an employee interviewed for a promotion discusses the potential salary. The employee will probably not reveal the lowest acceptable salary, and the interviewer does not indicate the highest possible salary. Figure 12–1 depicts these three levels of intentions.

Skillful questioning, which is reviewed in the next section of this chapter, helps overcome this barrier. Listening to the other person and understanding her point of view also helps reduce this barrier. However, the key is to remember that the other person's goal may not always be the same as the manager's in the interview process.

Barrier 2: Bias

Bias is a barrier because it slants people's perceptions so they tend to see and hear only what they want to see and hear.[1] The most prevalent type of bias is the *halo effect*, which managers fall prey to when they allow the evaluation of one characteristic to be influenced by another characteristic or by a general impression.[2] One aspect of the job may affect the manager's impression of the employee in other areas. If an employee has a tendency to be late, for instance, the manager could let this shortcoming influence her impression of the employee on other unrelated characteristics such as technical skills. The bias creates problems in performance evaluation interviews.[3]

Another type of bias is the *recency effect*. This occurs when the latest information disproportionately affects all the earlier information. Still other types of bias are *leniency* or *harshness*. In these instances, interviewers see everything as either positive or negative—they do not differentiate.[4]

Questions can also subtly bias an interview. For instance, one manager asked this loaded question: "Should the consumer group continue its generous support of the marketing research department when the research has proven to be of little value?" The question is obviously biased and would be difficult to answer in the affirmative. Appropriate ways to phrase questions will be discussed in the following section of this chapter.

Managers frequently become biased by co-workers' opinions. For instance, the following is the type of statement frequently heard: "You'll get nothing but trouble from Patrick, but you'll find Semkins easy to work with." Smart managers wait to form their own impressions of these subordinates.

Research has found that people who try hard can control their bias.[5] Thus, before entering the interview, the manager should try to review any bias that may interfere with her main goal and then make a special effort to remain objective.

FIGURE 12–1
Differing
Intentions

Barrier
increases

| Both parties do not want full exchange of information. |
| One party does not want full exchange of information. |
| Both parties intend to have full exchange of information. |

Accuracy
increases

Barrier 3: Confusing Facts with Inferences

Managers actually deal with very few facts in an interview. Rather, they must make inferences based on the words and actions of the interviewee. Sometimes, managers can be "almost certain" about their conclusions from an interview, but other times they are not too sure.[6] When they are not sure, however, problems can arise. Table 12–1 reveals some problems caused by discrepancies among words, facts, and inferences.

Managers need to be on the alert to determine when they are making plausible inferences and when they are jumping to unfounded conclusions. Many of the techniques discussed later in the chapter help overcome this barrier. The simplest method for avoiding this confusion is to remember that a fact can be measured and proven, while an inference is an opinion or judgment and by definition subjective.

Barrier 4: Nonverbal Communication

A quizzical look, a frown, a shrug, a look of indifference—all are important nonverbal messages, but those reading them must exercise caution before interpreting them. Nonverbal information can be a problem in an interview because interviews are generally short and intensive.[7] If a person slouches in a chair for a few minutes during a 20-minute interview, this behavior is more noticeable than if he slouches for a few minutes during a four-hour meeting. Because of the compact time span, nonverbal signals have a greater impact.

Accurately reading nonverbal signals in a compact time is complicated by the *primary effect*—one piece of information overpowering all others. In a short period, one nonverbal cue can more easily overpower the others.[8] This is especially the case when one has no baseline of nonverbal signs for judging

TABLE 12–1
Facts and
Inferences

Words	Facts	Possible Inference
"I like selling office equipment."	The record shows that the person has been selling for two years but before that was unemployed for six months.	This is the only work the person is able to get.
(When asked to fully describe college activities) "I did well in college and was involved in some extracurricular activities."	The person tends to avoid discussion on these activities and changes the subject when asked specifically about grades.	The person did not do well in academic work in college and had little involvement in extracurricular activities.
"I did not care for the atmosphere in that department" (by applicant for a job transfer).	The person received a poor performance review.	The applicant is a troublemaker.

the candidate. The careful interviewer is also aware that she can use nonverbal signs from the interviewee to judge the honesty of responses. Research has indicated that through training and practice, we can improve our ability to detect nonverbal deception.[9] This is further elaborated in the discussion of nonverbal leakage in Chapter 8.

Barrier 5: Effects of First Impressions

A manager may form a quick first impression that colors what he sees during the rest of the interview. If the interview is short, this strong first view may affect his overall impression since he does not have the time to find data to the contrary. Further, research indicates interviewers are influenced more by unfavorable than by favorable information, and the earlier in the interview the unfavorable information, the greater its negative effect.[10] In addition, it is more likely that the interviewer's impression will change from favorable to unfavorable than the opposite.[11]

This barrier may also be referred to as "hypothesis testing," meaning the interviewer establishes a hypothesis early and then seeks information that supports it. The fear is that any information that doesn't support the hypothesis will be ignored.[12]

Since this barrier is so pervasive, managers must act to limit its impact. Part of the solution is simple: be cautious about making value judgments until evidence other than that available from first impressions has been considered. Then, too, be aware that short interviews encourage the manager to make a decision prematurely.

Barrier 6: Organizational Status

Perhaps the most pervasive communication barrier results from hierarchical rank.[13] In any interview situation, the parties involved know who holds the balance of power.[14] While a higher-ranking person may encourage candor, the lower-level person may fear the consequences of such openness. It is only human to worry about the reactions of people in powerful positions, so candor frequently suffers.

Several suggestions can prevent it. For one thing, managers should recognize that employees almost always want to make the best impression when communicating with the boss. An effective manager should try to create an open supportive communication climate that minimizes power differences. And when a manager hears something unpleasant, harsh, or unwarranted from a subordinate, the manager should check her defensive reaction and try to remain open-minded and fair.

QUESTIONS THAT LEAD TO EFFECTIVE INTERVIEWS

Thorough analysis and planning are required for effective interviews. We believe the numerous contingencies can best be managed by addressing the following seven questions.

Question 1: What Is the Interview Objective?

First, consider the interview objective. Are you trying to obtain general information, gather specific data, or persuade someone to accept an idea? The interview objective indicates the format. However, the objective is not always clear, or the interview may have more than one objective. Consider the employment interview in which a person is simultaneously trying to gather general information about the applicant and specific information about her skills in order to determine whether the applicant will fit in to the workplace. All the while, the manager is trying to sell the applicant on the benefits of joining the company. Because several goals may apply at one time, it is important to clarify the purpose of the interview and set priorities.

Question 2: Where Is the Best Place to Conduct the Interview?

Time and place have an impact on the success of an interview. Managers should select a time that is mutually convenient. Managers should also allow adequate time so neither party in the interview feels rushed. Finally, managers should be aware of the primacy-recency effect when scheduling a series of interviews. That is, people tend to recall most favorably the first and the last of a series of events. This psychological phenomenon can affect hiring decisions, in particular.

Privacy is also a primary concern. It ensures confidentiality and minimizes interferences. Many managers find they can best eliminate distractions by conducting the interview in a place other than their work area or office. Remember that a neutral setting also reduces the status barrier present in many interviews.

Question 3: What Is the Best Way to Begin the Interview?

This question and the next are closely related. The opening statements lay the foundation for the questioning to follow. The opening of an interview generally serves two purposes: (1) it establishes the communication climate and (2) it explains the purpose of the interview.

The interview climate is established as soon as the manager meets the interviewee. At that point, nonverbal communication plays a crucial role. A friendly greeting, handshake, or smile will break the ice and help put the interviewee at ease. Friendly conversation about a neutral topic also puts everyone at ease. No matter what the purpose of the interview, managers should always begin by establishing rapport. This makes the interviewee feel safe and ensures two-way communication.

Next, the manager should affirm the interview's purpose. Typical starters are:

- Summarizing the problem or task at hand.
- Requesting advice or assistance.
- Mentioning an incentive or reward for taking part in the interview.
- Requesting a specific time commitment for the interview.

In addition to stating the purpose of the interview, the manager should check to be sure the interviewee agrees. This encourages a participatory attitude and may stimulate the other person's involvement in the interview. Thus, the opening, which may take the least time of all the segments in the interview process, is a crucial part and sets the stage.

Question 4: What Is the Best Questioning Strategy?

Exact questions and their precise sequence cannot always be planned for an interview. However, developing a questioning strategy before the interview helps a manager reach the interview's goal. One strategy is the *structured interview*, in which the interviewer writes out preliminary questions in sequence. This may be effective for inexperienced interviewers or for situations where each question must be repeated exactly the same way and in the same sequence with each interviewee.[15]

Because a structured interview restricts the interviewer's flexibility and makes it difficult to adapt to unique situations, certain cases require an *unstructured interview*. Here, the interviewer has a clear objective but has prepared no specific questions in advance. With an unstructured format, the interviewer initiates the discussion, letting the initial responses lead into the next question. This type of interview is particularly valuable when it is important that the interviewee helps set the direction—as in some appraisal interviews or certain counseling sessions. Also, this type of interview facilitates the communication flow in informational interviews at networking activities.

A compromise between the structured and unstructured interview is the *semistructured interview*. In this format, the interviewer prepares a list of critical questions to make sure she covers all important points by the close of the interview. Meanwhile, she maintains flexibility because the sequence of the questioning is not completely planned. Many consider this the most appropriate format for most situations faced by experienced managers.

Question 5: What Is the Best Sequence for the Questions?

For a semistructured interview, a funnel or inverted funnel question sequence is recommended. The funnel sequence opens with broad open-ended questions and proceeds with increasingly restricted questions. The inverted funnel sequence begins with closed questions and gradually proceeds toward open-ended ones. Figure 12–2 shows these two sequences.

The appropriate strategy depends on the situation.[16] The funnel sequence works best when the interviewee is able and willing to talk freely, such as in a job selection interview. The inverted funnel works best when the interviewee is reluctant to participate or is hostile toward the manager. Thus, for example, during an exit interview, the manager might begin with specific, factual questions and move gradually toward general questions about changes the interviewee feels are needed in the workplace.

Question 6: What Are the Best Types of Questions?

The various types of questions have already been discussed in Chapter 7 and are reviewed next.

Interview questions fall into three wording categories: open–closed, primary–secondary, and neutral–directed. *Open* and *closed* questions are best explained

FIGURE 12–2
Question
Sequence

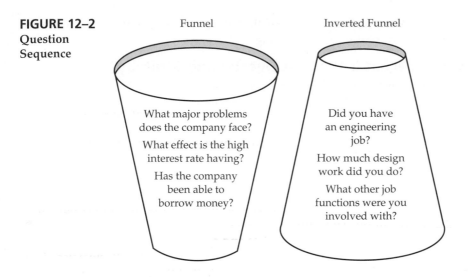

Funnel

What major problems
does the company face?

What effect is the high
interest rate having?

Has the company
been able to
borrow money?

Inverted Funnel

Did you have
an engineering
job?

How much design
work did you do?

What other job
functions were you
involved with?

using a continuum. An open-ended question has virtually no restriction on the type of response that is received. At the other extreme is the closed-ended question, which calls for specific short responses. Look at the following examples of the two types of questions.

Open-Ended	Closed-Ended
1. How was your last job?	1. What part of your last job did you dislike?
2. Tell me more about the Niles project.	2. What percentage of the Niles project is completed?
3. How is everything in the Denver Division?	3. Did you complete the quarterly report for the Denver Division?
4. Tell me about yourself.	4. Have you ever been to Los Angeles?

Managers often use closed questions when they should be asking open-ended questions. Managers need to ask themselves if they are looking for a general response or a specific answer. Are they trying to solicit information (open), trying to make the interviewee comfortable (open), or trying to get to a specific point or commitment as quickly as possible (closed)? The answers to these strategic questions help one decide when to use open or closed questions.

The second category of questions is *primary* and *secondary*. A primary question introduces a topic in an interview, while a secondary question follows up, probing further into the response to the primary question. A secondary question is most valuable when the primary question did not elicit all the desired information.

The following dialogue gives an example of the use of primary and secondary questions.

Interviewer:	What was your most recent job? (primary)
Interviewee:	I supervised the AR Department.
Interviewer:	What is the AR Department? (secondary)
Interviewee:	That's the accounts receivable group that does all . . .

In this example, the secondary question elicited additional information for the interviewer.

A subtle form of secondary questions is a probe. Table 12–2 presents seven types of probes. Again, notice that in a relaxed interview, although these probes obtain additional information, they may not appear to be questions but rather part of the conversation. They are subtle but effective.

Secondary questions help gain complete and accurate information, but they also establish a positive communication climate in the interview. The effective use of secondary questions and probes can help demonstrate that the manager is interested in listening. Initially, the interviewee may not know how much information is wanted, or whether the manager is really interested in her comments; however, the use of secondary questions and probes helps establish a willing and open atmosphere.

Neutral and directed questions, the third category, may also be considered in terms of a continuum with neutral questions at one end and directed questions at the other. Since the correct answer is not implied in the question, a neutral question does not lead the interviewee to answer in one particular way. The directed question, at the other end of the continuum, leads the interviewee to give a particular answer. The classic example of a directed question is the courtroom ploy, "Isn't it true that . . . ?" In reality, this type of extreme directed question may be considered a plea for agreement rather than a true question even when an interrogative tone is used.[17]

Examples of neutral and directed questions (listed in the following table) show the difference.

Neutral Questions	Directed Questions
1. What kind of car do you prefer?	1. Don't you think that foreign cars are superior to American cars?
2. What is your reaction to decentralization?	2. You are opposed to decentralization, aren't you?
3. What do you think of unionization?	3. Naturally, you are opposed to any kind of unions?
4. Do you feel we should hire more employees?	4. I don't think we should hire any more employees. Do you?

The skillful use of directed questions can be valuable since such questions can help keep the interview on track and be used effectively for persuasion. In

TABLE 12–2 Seven Probes

Probe	Definition of Probe	Illustration of Probe
1. Brief assertion of understanding	Person A indicates interest and understanding, thus encouraging B to continue.	"So, first I said to him, how'd you like a cup of coffee . . . sort of thought it would break the ice."
2. Neutral phrase	Person A elicits more information from B without affecting (biasing) the information.	"I don't know . . . kids today seem to be getting away with murder." "Uh-huh."
3. Silence	Person A does not speak and looks attentively at B. The period of time involved is under 10 seconds.	"Wow . . . what a day I've had." Silence—2 seconds. "I mean, I didn't have a minute to myself the way they kept me working."
4. Echo	Person A converts the last portion of what B says into a question . . . generally with almost all the same words.	"I'm not sure that I can take any more . . . I'm at the end of my rope." "At the end of your rope?"
5. Clarification	Person A tries to get a definition or further explanation from B that is not understood.	"I'll tell you that lowering the voting age ain't right." "Oh . . . how so?" "Well, for one thing, it's increased the likelihood of political conspiracies."
6. Elaboration	Person A requests new information that is directly related to something B already said.	"Chief, I'm really worried about the parade tomorrow." "How do you mean worried?" "Well, I think we might be in for some trouble." "Oh . . . what indication do you have that we might have some trouble?"
7. Summary	Person A tries to pull together the main points made by B during the past few minutes.	"And finally, Hank, there's the question of pay . . . we just don't get paid enough for the work we do." "Let me see if I have it straight, Ralph. First, you say the work is dirty, not carefully scheduled, and finally, you're underpaid for the work you do, correct?"

persuasion, they point the interviewee in a particular direction and help him think about the benefit of some concept.

Question 7: What Is the Best Way to Close the Interview?

When it is time to close the interview, as with many other communications, it is important to summarize the main information and ensure understanding. The close also provides the opportunity to arrange for any follow-up activity and to express appreciation. Goodwill is always appropriate, whether the interviewee is a job applicant, a disgruntled customer, a networking associate, or a long-term loyal subordinate. End with agreement, a statement of appreciation, and a handshake.

So far, we have given an overview of the barriers to interviews as well as the most frequent questions managers ask about the interview process. Next, we will focus on three specific interview situations that managers experience as well as the appropriate strategies for each: employment interviews, performance appraisal interviews, and networking.

EMPLOYMENT INTERVIEWS

Selecting the most qualified people available for a position is a major managerial responsibility. Many screening tools are used in employee selection, including application forms and aptitude and personality tests, but the most common is the interview.

While a member of the human resources department often screens applicants, the applicant's future manager generally makes the final decision. The ability to match competent applicants with the correct job leads to the success of an organization. Making good hiring decisions also reduces the cost of turnover, which can be significant. The U.S. Department of Labor estimates that it costs a company one-third of a new hire's annual salary to replace an employee. More than 75 percent of turnover can be traced back to poor interviewing and hiring practices, according to a Harvard Business School study.[18] Managers have a responsibility to both the organization and the applicant to see that an applicant–job match exists.

As a manager, one way to create an edge for yourself is to rely on networking with peers and acquaintances for potential candidates. If a referred applicant is trusted and well qualified, this can save your company crucial overhead dollars and time by eliminating the search process. According to *BusinessWeek* contributor Stephen Baker, the increasing popularity of social and professional networking sites, such as LinkedIn and Facebook, is making networking easier than ever before. An online network of friends has turned into a turbocharged rolodex for job seekers inside and outside companies. In addition, every hand we shake or business card we exchange can lead to an online friendship invitation that can extend our professional network beyond limits.[19]

Yet, employment interviews are typically not used to their best advantage. While research shows that the interview is low in both reliability and validity,[20] no adequate replacement exists. It is the only technique that gives managers the chance to personally evaluate the candidate and to pursue questioning in a way that tests cannot.

Planning

The employment interview, like all communication situations, requires planning, but in a more specific way.

Position Requirements

A manager's first step is to ensure a clear understanding of the job's requirements. This effort helps avoid putting too much weight on irrelevant information. An interviewer familiar with extensive details about the job to be filled (such as that provided by detailed job descriptions and job titles) enhances the reliability of employment selection decisions.[21] When no comprehensive job description is available, it may be necessary for the interviewer to complete a job analysis.

When reviewing the nature of the job, be careful not to compare the last *person* holding the job with present candidates. Doing so can inaccurately affect your impressions of a candidate. Also, many job incumbents change the nature of a position slightly to match their personal capabilities and interests. A good time to analyze the present and future qualifications required for performance on a job is when personnel changes are made.

Time

Time and timing are also important parts of the planning process. The amount of time allocated for an interview varies. In general, it is better to allocate too much rather than too little time.

Timing is important in the employment interview due to the contrast effect, namely, the influence that earlier interviews may have on later interviews. The job candidate who is only average but follows a number of poor candidates will likely make a better impression than if she had followed other average candidates. One way to reduce this effect is to avoid interviewing a long series of candidates without a break.

In addition, allow enough time between interviews and arrange your schedule so fatigue does not become a factor. Applicants interviewed when the interviewer is tired may receive lower ratings than other applicants. These suggested strategies are valuable considerations when planning the interview.

Applicant Preview

Interviewers should review the application or the résumé before the interview to plan specific questions. Remember that the interview's objective is to get information that written material cannot easily reveal, including motivation and personality characteristics. Clearly, time is wasted if the interview covers the same material that appears in the documents. But you can also use the interview to clarify inconsistencies or fill in gaps. In short, use the documents as a springboard for the interview topics.

Legal Concerns

By now, almost all managers are familiar with the Americans with Disabilities Act of 1990 and the Civil Rights Act of 1964, which was amended by the Equal Employment Opportunity (EEO) Act of 1972. Unfortunately, knowledge of the legal restrictions of employment interviewing is too often misapplied. Either managers may become too cautious in their questioning out of fear of the law and miss valuable information, or they may ignore the legal restrictions. Although the following paragraphs do not constitute a comprehensive discussion of the legal components of employment, several suggestions may help you in your employment interviews.

Probably the first thing that comes to managers' minds when discussing EEO is what is a legal or illegal question. To answer this, one needs to be aware of the concept of bona fide occupational qualification (BFOQ), which is *any characteristic that is a valid criterion of job performance.* Race, age, national origin, general health, religion, gender, ethnic background, number of children, and marital status are generally not bases on which people should be judged.

Firms with affirmative action programs are committed to ensuring that members of what are called protected groups (people over 40, people with disabilities, minorities, and females usually fall into this classification) will be actively sought for employment.[22] Equal employment opportunity and affirmative action are often confused because their goals have some similarities. However, EEO seeks a level playing field where all have an equal chance at gaining employment based on qualifications. A commitment to affirmative action is a commitment to make extra effort to identify and recruit individuals from protected classes.[23]

Generally, education, experience, abilities, and skills are the basic elements of BFOQs. Each job must be analyzed. In most situations, managers can follow guidelines that ensure no condition of the Equal Employment Opportunity Act is being ignored. The best advice is to only ask questions related to BFOQs or directly related to making an objective employment decision.

Keep in mind, too, that casual conversations with job applicants should respect the guidelines set out here. For example, suppose a job applicant is being treated to lunch. Don't confuse this with a truly social situation and make small talk about family or religion. These could be misconstrued by the candidates as irrelevant non-BFOQ questions and represent grounds for later disputes should a job offer not materialize.

Table 12–3 presents useful guidelines regarding lawful and unlawful questions during the employment interview. These same considerations also apply to application forms. Discrimination occurs when an individual who has an equal probability of being successful on a job does not have an equal probability of getting the job.[24] A manager is responsible for seeing that discrimination does not occur.

The Employment Interview Process

During the employment interview, the manager tries to find out as much as possible about a candidate that relates to potential job success. The best way to do this is to be aware of the various barriers and suggested strategies discussed previously. Also, to be fully effective, managers should be familiar with certain conditions specific to the selection interview. The following guidelines assist managers in their efforts to increase the reliability and validity of the employment interview.

Use Appropriate Questioning Strategy

Research indicates the form and sequence of questions profoundly influence the outcome of the interview.[25] Most interviews open positively with the manager attempting to put the interviewee at ease. The résumé can be a useful guide for selecting some strong point from the candidate's background to help make the interviewee comfortable in the beginning.[26] It is generally best to use a semi-structured interview that ensures a definite direction is taken but also allows the

TABLE 12–3 Question Guidelines for Employment Interview

Focus on Question	Nondiscriminatory	Possibly Discriminatory
Name	Have you ever used a different name in other jobs?	What was your name before you changed it?
Birthplace and residence	Which state do you presently live in? How long have you lived in Cedar Falls (or a given state)?	Where were you born? In which country were your parents born?
Physical characteristics including race	Do you have any distinguishing marks or scars?	Are you Asian?
National origin or ancestry		You're from Mexico aren't you? Are you related to the Manuels from Hermosa?
Sex, living arrangements		How many children do you have? Are you married?
Religion		Are you Jewish? What religious holidays will you be taking off if we hire you?
Citizenship	Does your visa allow you to work in the United States?	Are you a German?
Organizations	Do you belong to any charitable organizations?	Are you in the D.A.R.? Were you a member of the Catholic Students Club?
Arrest record and convictions		How often have you been arrested, and for what (unless related to job performance)?
Physical abilities or limitations	This job requires lifting and carrying; do you see any problems with that?	Are you handicapped (similarly, avoid questions about the type and severity of the handicap)?
Education	Have you received your CPM certification yet?	Do you have an MBA degree (or similar questions when educational achievement has no relation to the skills needed for a given job)?
Financial status		Have you ever had your wages garnished? What is your approximate net worth? How much is your house mortgage?

opportunity to prepare additional questions as the interview proceeds. Table 12–4 shows possible questions that you might use as an interviewer.

When designing the questions for the interview, remember the difference between open and closed, primary and secondary, and neutral and directed

TABLE 12–4
Question
Options

Openers

Why would you like to join our company?
Why do you feel qualified for this job?
Tell me about your experience.

Determining Motivation

Why do you want to change jobs?
What led you to enter this profession?
Where would you like to be in your career five years from now? Ten years?
What do you see as the perfect job for you?

Determining Experience

What did you do while you were in the military?
How would you go about improving our operations?
Who or what has influenced you the most? Why?
What aspects of your last job did you like best/least? Why?
What are your greatest strengths/weaknesses for this position?
What kinds of people do you like most/least as work associates?
What are your greatest achievements to date?
What equipment are you familiar with?
Why have you changed jobs so often?
What has been the biggest crisis in your career?
Why did you quit your previous employment?
May I see examples of your work?

Evaluating Educational Background

Describe your education for me.
Why did you choose your major field?
What extracurricular activities did you participate in?
What honors did you earn?
Do your grades reflect your full ability? Why not?
What courses did you like best/least and why?
What special training have you had for this job?

questions. Know the benefits and shortcomings of each of these types of questions so you can implement an effective questioning strategy. An employment interview generally uses open-ended questions, but it can also use closed and directed questions as probes.

A special-type of question that is successfully used in employment interviews is the *behavioral question.* Based on the premise that past behavior predicts future behavior, these questions ask about specific instances of a particular action. Managers can use behavioral questions to probe for more information behind useless generalizations such as "I'm a people person" and "I'm a team player." Typically, behavioral questions begin with "Tell me about a time when you . . ." and follow with situations or qualities relevant to the position, thus requiring evidence to "prove" the applicant's claims. Behaviors demonstrating leadership, conflict management, handling difficult customers, goal setting, teamwork, and the like can be effectively explored using behavioral questions.

Another special type of question that is becoming popular in certain employment interviews is the *problem-solving question*. Its purpose is to seek out creative talent, a necessity for companies where competitive advantage is gained through its people. Microsoft, Boeing, IBM, Southwest Airlines, and Weyerhauser are among the 20 to 30 percent of companies using situational or problem-solving questions, according to Professor Vandra Huber of the University of Washington.[27] The following are some sample problem-solving questions used during Microsoft interviews:

- Estimate the number of gas stations in the United States.
- If you could remove any of the 50 states, which would it be and why?
- Design a bathroom for me.
- If you have a fishbowl with 200 fish and 99 percent are guppies, how many guppies do you need to remove to get to the point where 98 percent of the remaining fish are guppies?[28]

Clearly, the answers to such questions are not as important as the process the candidate uses to (a) determine the problem and (b) develop solutions. A description of the steps in the rational problem-solving process can be found in Chapters 10 and 13.

Don't Do Most of the Talking

In employment interviews, the manager is generally more talkative when reacting favorably to an applicant than when reacting unfavorably.[29] In other words, when an interviewer is impressed by the applicant, the interviewer is inclined to do less listening.

For whatever reason, extensive talking is efficient only when attempting to sell a candidate on a position; information relevant to hiring decisions is obtained through listening, not talking. Thus, be careful not to talk too much. A good rule of thumb is that the manager should talk only 30 percent of the time during an employment interview.

Keep Records

Given all the information revealed during an interview, it is unrealistic to expect that it can be remembered accurately for any length of time. One study showed that half the interviewers could not accurately recall the most critical information produced in a 20-minute interview.[30] Thus, record notes or a summary of the interview immediately after its completion. One option is to use a rating system. This minimizes the possibility of erroneously making an early decision or letting one or two negative characteristics predominate. Another option is to have a routine form that reports on the same areas for each candidate interviewed or records answers to the same questions.

PERFORMANCE REVIEW INTERVIEWS

Periodically, managers are called on to conduct performance appraisal interviews. Over 45 years ago, Maier cited several purposes for the performance review interview,[31] and current objectives remain much the same.[32]

- Let employees know where they stand.
- Recognize good work.
- Communicate to subordinates directions in which they should improve.
- Develop employees in their present jobs.
- Develop and train employees for higher jobs.
- Assess the department or unit as a whole and where each person fits into the larger picture.

While the potential benefits of the performance review interview seem evident, its infrequent and ineffective use in organizations is widely recognized. This contradiction exists for several reasons, including that managers do not like to be put into the role of evaluator. Some managers may fear their working relationship with subordinates will be destroyed because of the discomfort created in the appraisal process.[33] Another reason may be that managers often are not adequately trained in conducting these interviews.[34] Knowledge of the following information should encourage managers to conduct performance appraisal interviews.

Purpose

The performance interview can meet two purposes: (1) it can focus on the worker's past performance in an effort to determine growth, or (2) it can focus on future activities and involve setting goals that will lead to increased employee performance. A critical question is relevant here: Does a manager discuss goals, performance improvement, and personal development in the same interview as salary increases? Extensive review of the available research on this question makes it clear that one should not combine specific developmental topics and salary discussions in one interview. The importance of the salary review typically dominates the interview so neither the manager nor the employee is in the proper frame of mind to discuss plans for improvement in a positive manner.[35] Instead, two separate interviews would be more appropriate. This requires more time but generally yields a more positive response from the employee.

Types

Three types of performance reviews are possible and vary according to the nature of the job and the employees.[36] *Developmental* appraisal interviews are used for high-performing, high-potential employees who have discretionary jobs giving them the opportunity to implement performance improvement.

The second type, the *maintenance* interview, is used for those who have performed at a steady satisfactory level for some time and are not likely to improve due to constraints of ability, motivation, or the nature of their jobs. In this situation, the interviewee focuses on maintaining performance at the currently acceptable levels.

The third type of interview, the *remedial* appraisal, is used for low-performing or marginal subordinates in an attempt to raise performance to acceptable levels. This category involves two processes: evaluation and development. First, evaluate the present and past performances, and then determine how they can be developed.

Each type of interview calls for a different degree of evaluation and development. More development is emphasized in the developmental and remedial interviews and more evaluation in the maintenance interview. A performance review interview does not always meet the same purpose; consequently, different communication strategies must be implemented to meet the established goals of either evaluation or development. In implementing the appropriate strategy, planning is required just as it is in other interview formats.

Planning

In terms of the onion model presented in Chapter 2, the three main areas to be analyzed in the planning process are the timing, the environment, and the message content—that is, when, where, and what—as shown in the third layer of the model.

Timing

Formal appraisals are most often conducted on an annual basis. Once a year seems to be a practical time frame; however, this should not preclude the feedback that should be provided to employees whenever needed.

Why perform a formal review once a year when more frequent feedback is provided? For one thing, an annual review helps overcome the various communication errors discussed in Chapter 2. A formal review also provides the opportunity to systematically review the possibility that different assumptions have developed between subordinates and managers. Periodic "course correction" makes sense for even very satisfactory subordinates. Also, certain situations, such as the completion of a major project or unusually poor performance, require formal feedback. Consider the entire situation when determining the best time for a performance interview.

Once the time is selected, inform the employee of the interview well in advance. The lead time required may vary from several hours to several weeks, depending on the employee and the type of job involved. In any event, avoid the "stop by my office as soon as you get a chance" type of preparation, which deprives the employee of the opportunity to prepare psychologically for the interview.

Environment

Once the necessary time and timing are determined, consider the best place for the interview. Managers tend to schedule the performance review interview in their own offices without realizing how potentially threatening this environment may be, especially when the subordinate is not accustomed to spending much time in the manager's office. Often, the best place for the interview is in a neutral, safe, private location to maximize two-way interaction.

Message Content

Once the time and place of the interview are established, focus on the content of the session. Regardless of the specific interview purpose, review expectations and goals. To appreciate these fully, review the dimensions of the subordinate's job. In addition, review notes from the previous performance review and recent job performance items. You may even want to solicit information from customers or other managers who have observed the employee's performance. All these procedures allow a manager the opportunity to list specific items that must be discussed in the interview.

To give subordinates the opportunity to prepare for the interview, have them complete a self-evaluation form before the interview. Managers can use the standard performance evaluation form or a separate form similar to that shown in Table 12–5.

The more opportunity an employee has to participate in the process, the greater the possibility that open and valuable communication will result. Studies show that performance appraisal discussions based on a self-review of performance are more satisfying than those based strictly on manager-prepared appraisals.[37] For the performance review to provide feedback to an employee and to establish goals, a trusting environment must be established.

The next section describes the process that will lead to a trusting environment.

Process

Although the parties involved already know each other and the purpose of the meeting is well established, it is still necessary to begin in a friendly, warm manner. It is a good practice to state the purpose of the session to ensure mutual agreement, as well.

Once the climate is established, choose one of three approaches: tell and sell, tell and listen, and problem solving.[38] The *tell-and-sell* approach is used to tell an employee what is expected without any discussion and then to sell the employee on the idea. Those using this style assume employees desire to correct weaknesses if they know them. Unfortunately, employees' defenses may be raised as a result, and any independent judgment on the subordinate's part may be suppressed.

TABLE 12–5
Employee Self-Appraisal Checklist

The purpose of this form is to help you prepare for your performance review.

Be ready to discuss any of your specific accomplishments or problems that have occurred since the last performance review.

Set aside some time and review your job since the last review so you can answer the following questions:

1. What are some unusually difficult problems you have solved?

2. What do you regard as your major strong points in knowledge, skills, or experience?

3. What do you regard as your weaker areas in knowledge, skills, or experience?

4. What are some working relationships you are pleased about?

5. What are some working relationships you feel need strengthening?

6. Did you carry out any special assignments with distinction or handle emergencies skillfully?

7. Determine one or two areas where you think you could improve something if you had the right assistance from your manager.

TABLE 12–6
Supportive and Defensive Climates

Defensive Climate	Supportive Climate
Evaluative	Descriptive
Control	Problem orientation
Neutrality	Empathy
Superiority	Equality
Certainty	Provisionalism

This style is often appropriate for the subordinate who has little knowledge about the job (such as a relatively new employee). However, the possibilities for this style are limited because most employees generally have something to say.

The second style, *tell and listen*, includes the element of listening. As Chapter 7 emphasizes, listening is the key skill to learning. Tell employees that they are doing a good job, but listen to the reasons they give for such performance. The response probably indicates the cause behind the behavior.

The third strategy, *problem solving*, expands on the second approach. The problem-solving approach is based on the premise that two-way communication leads to a mutually acceptable plan for performance improvement. This approach allows subordinates more freedom and responsibility than the other two; however, the climate must be right for subordinates to express themselves.

Supportive Environment

Table 12–6 draws on Gibb's classic work to differentiate the communication process that leads to a supportive rather than a defensive environment.[39]

Examples of communications from each of these categories assist in developing an effective communication strategy for the appraisal interview.

Evaluative vs. Descriptive

Communication that blames a subordinate naturally leads to a defensive climate. Avoid statements that make moral assessments of another or that question an individual's values and motives. Descriptive communication provides specific feedback and does not judge the receiver. The examples that follow show the difference that might occur during a performance review interview.

Notice that the evaluative examples typically are less specific and make inferences about the receiver's personality. These types of comments lead to defensiveness.

Evaluative	Descriptive
You simply have to stop making so many silly mistakes.	We're still getting more than three errors per run with the new system.
Betty, you're tactless and rude.	Betty, some people say they are offended by your humor.
The delay was definitely your fault because you didn't follow instructions.	There seems to be some confusion about the instructions.

Control vs. Problem Orientation

Problem-oriented communication defines a mutual problem and seeks a solution. Controlling communication tries to do "something" to another person such as forcing a change in a behavior or an attitude. The problem orientation conveys respect for the employee's ability to work on a problem and to formulate meaningful answers to the problem. The following are some examples of control and problem-oriented communication.

Control	Problem Orientation
Here is what you can do to reduce errors.	What do you think could be done to reduce errors?
You definitely have a problem with that project.	We've got a problem with this project.
Stop being so negative around here.	How do you think we could develop a more positive approach?

The problem-oriented comments develop more opportunities for two-way communication by using open-ended questions and indicating a concern for solving the problem in a cooperative manner. Listening is also a productive by-product of the problem-solving approach.

Neutrality vs. Empathy

Neutrality expresses a lack of concern for the well-being of the employee, whereas empathy shows that the manager identifies with the subordinate's problem, shares her feelings, and accepts the emotional values involved. Compare the following examples.

Neutrality	Empathy
That really isn't much of a problem.	Sounds like you're really concerned about it. Tell me more about the situation.
Everybody has to face that at one time or another.	That can be a tough situation. I'll tell you how I've seen it handled before, and then you can give me your reaction.
Well, everyone is entitled to an opinion.	I think we disagree. Let's discuss this further and compare viewpoints.

Managers show empathy in the appraisal interview when they are willing to listen, when they inquire how employees feel about something, and when they attempt to understand and accept the employee's feelings. Empathy cannot be developed when a person is hastily cut off from communicating any further or the listener demonstrates lack of interest in the message.

Superiority vs. Equality

The less the psychological distance between the manager and the subordinate, the greater the probability of a productive assessment interview. Managers often inhibit subordinates by subtly indicating both verbally and nonverbally their superiority in position, wealth, power, intellectual ability, or even physical characteristics. The following are examples of verbal communication demonstrating superiority and equality.

Superiority	Equality
After working on this kind of problem for 10 years, I know how to handle it.	This solution has worked before, so it should work here, too.
I'm getting paid more than you so it is my responsibility to make this kind of decision.	It's my ultimate responsibility to make the decision, but I sure want your recommendations.
The type of problems I face shouldn't be of interest to people at your level.	I want to share with you the type of situations I'm involved with.

Managers demonstrate superiority or equality by nonverbal as well as verbal communication patterns. Sitting behind a big desk, putting your feet on the desk, looking uninterested, and acting busy, are all signs of superiority. Showing superiority can only add to defensiveness and reduce two-way communication.

Certainty vs. Provisionalism

Managers who emphasize certainty often phrase what they say as if the decision cannot be changed. This dogmatic approach makes the employee feel that offering new ideas or a different solution is futile. Provisionalism demonstrates that a manager is willing to be challenged to arrive at the best possible solution. Provisionalism promotes enthusiasm and provides a challenge to employees, as these examples demonstrate.

Certainty	Provisionalism
I know what the problem is, so there isn't much reason to talk about it.	I have some ideas, but it would be good to talk about it.
This is the way it's going to be done.	Let's try it this way for a while and see what happens.
I want it to be completed by June 1.	What needs to be done to ensure that it's completed by June 1?

These five elements of an effective communication strategy—description, problem orientation, empathy, equality, and provisionalism—are major factors in reducing defensiveness and developing trust. Once trust has been developed, managers must provide feedback to subordinates.

Providing Feedback

Performance evaluation gives feedback on the employee's past performances. The performance appraisal interview allows managers to motivate their employees to higher levels of performance through positive feedback. Subordinates will see feedback as constructive criticism rather than as negative criticism if managers keep in mind the following principles.

1. **Identify concrete behavior.** Statements that identify specific, concrete behaviors are easier to accept than ambiguous abstract statements. For instance, "You seem to have lost your self-confidence" is rather abstract. It is better to say, "You have not asked for any new projects since the hydraulic overhaul. I'd like to know why."
2. **Avoid inferences about motives, intents, and feelings unless you can cite specific behaviors to support these inferences.** A statement such as "You have lost interest in your job" is strictly an inference that does not lead to a constructive performance review.
3. **Focus feedback on a limited number of observable behaviors.** Employees can act on only a few feedback statements at a time. If one must deal with a large number of items, it is probably better to schedule several sessions.
4. **Time feedback to follow closely the behavior being discussed.** Immediate feedback almost always has more impact on the receiver than does delayed feedback. Accordingly, certain employees may require more than an annual review.
5. **Give feedback to help the employees rather than to make you feel better.** Avoid giving feedback when feelings are not under control.

Managers who experience difficult situations may ask, "What about the employee who receives extensive negative feedback? How can I continue to administer it in a positive environment?" Once again, the manner in which the feedback message is structured is important. Another factor to consider is that no matter how much negative feedback the situation calls for, positive comments can usually also be used; however, the old "sandwich" approach is not recommended.

In the sandwich approach, a manager places a negative statement between two positive comments. However, most employees quickly recognize the manager's attempt to manipulate the situation; consequently, the strategy usually falls short of its intended purpose. The current recommended procedure is to dispense supportive feedback almost exclusively at the beginning of the interview. This tactic helps establish an initial positive climate, and once aware that the manager duly appreciates past success, the subordinate becomes more receptive to a thorough analysis of those areas where need for improvement exists.[40]

Goal setting is a valuable process when structuring feedback in a positive manner. The following discussion points out several implications that need to be considered when establishing goals that help build a positive climate.

Establishing Goals

The performance review interview ought to be constructive. Instead of dwelling on past failures, focus on the actions an employee can take to improve and develop. Performance goals help keep the focus on the future. When these goals are clear, the performance appraisal is positively related to subordinate satisfaction with the interview process.[41]

Managers clearly state objectives when they include the elements of *time, quality, quantity,* and *priority.* Consider the following example:

> During the next 60 days, you will set aside 20 minutes each day to meet with your crew and state what is expected in terms of their production and work schedules. Subordinates whose work schedules are not up to standard you will counsel on a daily basis. If your turnover rate continues to be the same, and you fail to counsel your employees, we will change your supervisory responsibilities.[42]

Notice that this activity is clearly stated: Quality is stated in terms of production and work schedules; quantity is established in terms of turnover and the frequency of the meetings. These are important priorities for the supervisor because, if the conditions are not met, the supervisor could be demoted.

To ensure that the objectives or action plans are clear, write down the agreed-on activity. This allows both parties to review the statements and ensure that all the meanings are mutually clear. Action plans guide employees' future activities to achieve established goals. Clearly stated expectations can reduce risk exposure from litigation if personnel or responsibilities change due to unmet objectives. The following section describes how to avoid potential legal issues that frequently arise from the performance review process.

Legal Concerns

According to the Bureau of Justice Statistics, the number of employment lawsuits filed in federal court from 1990 to 1998 more than tripled. When Congress declared that Title VII of the Civil Rights Act of 1991 granted employment law cases the right to request a jury trial, the number of cases filed in federal and state courts continued to increase as well as the average award amount. Regardless of the outcome, businesses must allocate a significant amount of financial and human resources on the legal process.[43]

The number of lawsuits filed as a result of performance appraisals increased dramatically during the last two decades.[44] In response, firms have attempted to reduce risk by improving their performance review processes. Approaches involve two main components: (1) a legal performance appraisal system, and (2) procedural consistency. Risk is further reduced when the forms, tools, and processes implemented for performance reviews are evaluated annually to validate expected outcomes. Legal, regulatory, and operational changes may require more frequent updates.

A legal performance appraisal system must pass a number of tests. First, employers must be able to show that their "selection" procedures do not disproportionately eliminate protected groups unless required for a "safe and efficient" performance. Second, the tool used for appraisals must be able to measure performance as it relates to the important aspects of the employee's responsibilities. (Recall the concept of BFOQ explained earlier in this chapter.) Third, to avoid bias by the manager, performance appraisals should be based on precise and objective criteria. Fourth, the appraisal should be performed by the employee's direct manager who observes the employee's performance daily. Finally, the manager should be adequately trained to perform appraisals appropriately.[45] Employers will find it difficult to prove nondiscriminatory practices during litigation if they fail any of these tests.

A biased and inaccurate appraisal is not illegal, but becomes so if it results in adverse outcomes for protected groups. It has been estimated through studies that approximately 50 percent of merit raises and promotions result from discriminatory performance appraisals. Employers who provide due process and employee grievance channels can often resolve conflict before it results in litigation.[46] The key component in due process is to ensure consistency in the way employees' grievances are addressed.

Managers are responsible for overseeing the performance appraisal process. They are challenged with balancing the needs of the organization and the needs of their subordinates. Managers that approach performance reviews fairly and free of bias can achieve their objectives and limit their organizations' risk exposure. Managers can acquire valuable information to improve their techniques for delivery of performance reviews and other duties through networking channels.

NETWORKING

Our discussion of managerial interviewing strategies warrants attention to a third application: networking. Social and professional networking provides excellent resources for intellectual and career management. Managers are very aware that knowledge is power and shared knowledge fosters beneficial relationships. Networking involves time and energy commitment to maximize managers' potential rewards. A clear understanding of purpose, mode, and potential outcomes enhances networking efforts.

Purpose

The main purpose of networking is to build relationships through informational interviews. As we saw in the previous chapter, networking skills can be useful during negotiations. But managers will fail at networking activities if their goals are merely to obtain something for themselves. Their motives may be transparent to others and hinder successful communication. Networking is a two-way street that succeeds when participants' intent is to share information in a mutually beneficial relationship.

Networking skills improve over time as participants are exposed to a variety of settings. Participants learn how to assist others and create long-lasting relationships. Participants provide assistance through their own expertise or by referring expert contacts. Activities as simple as sharing information on relevant events and articles with other participants are forms of assistance. By helping others, participants demonstrate that they are a contact worth keeping and provide a reason to follow up with them again. These actions reinforce professional ties that may lead to reciprocity when the newcomer is in need of assistance.

Effective networking involves meaningful connections, relationships, and rapport developed through trust. According to a recent study by Pepperdine University's Graziadio School of Business Management, successful professionals with annual incomes in excess of $200,000 cite networking as a critical factor in career advancement.[47] Networking activities allow participants to share experiences and develop best practices that continue to improve as they move through different networks. The number of contacts increases and participants build a large pool of long-lasting relationships that are mutually beneficial.

How to Network

The number of networking associations and activities is endless. The most frequently used channels to exchange information for networking activities include electronic media such as Facebook and LinkedIn as well as face-to-face interactions. Networking occurs in formal and informal settings, and applying appropriate networking etiquette improves communication.

Managers can acquire valuable knowledge specific to their occupation, firm, and industry through a diverse group of professional contacts. Influential contacts within the company include mentors, colleagues, and other professionals. External network groups include professional associations as well as specialized groups for minorities, women, and executives. Internet searches reveal numerous sites to acquire specific activities for individual groups. Social networking through university alumni, former supervisors, previous colleagues, and casual gatherings increase one's pool of resources. Successful networking requires planning, setting goals, and tracking results.

Basic steps for successful networking include:

- Identify networking groups that foster mutually beneficial interaction.
- Join professional associations and attend local and national meetings.
- Volunteer as a speaker, committee member, and/or officer.
- Know and promote your strengths, not your title.
- Display an attitude of enthusiasm, confidence, and sincerity.
- Listen carefully to identify opportunities to contribute to others.
- Mingle and meet several new contacts at every event.
- Ensure business cards are readily available.
- Follow-up with former and new contacts.

Frequently, important relationships are created and maintained outside the work environment. It is important to recognize that every conversation and activity creates networking opportunities and career advancement.[48] First impressions are permanently embedded, so appearance is important. The rules of body language are as critical here as in other interview settings. Networking groups have a set of acceptable standards and expectations of group members.

Networking etiquette is founded on the golden rule that members are expected to reciprocate. It is equally important to recognize that the group's purpose is to share information. Other networking etiquette guidelines are:

- Never ask for a job.
- Return calls and e-mails promptly.
- Always respond as promised.
- Recognize participants' time constraints.
- Treat all participants as equals.
- Be knowledgeable on current events.
- Be helpful and grateful.
- Maintain participants' confidentiality.

These and other factors create an environment to develop mutually beneficial relationships that can lead to career advancement. Networking also requires the participants to be open-minded, prepared, persistent, and patient. These characteristics combined with clear goals lead to successful outcomes.[49]

Outcomes

Many advantages for managers' career advancement occur as a natural turn of events with acquired knowledge. As time progresses, your credibility strengthens and you gain a reputation as an expert in your field. You earn respect from your colleagues and upper management as you gain knowledge about your company or industry. You increase your pool of internal and external contacts through leveraged introductions. Opportunities arise to increase your potential customer base and you may obtain consulting opportunities. You may connect with people who can assist, support, and accelerate your career advancement.

Promotion decisions are based on a number of factors: performance, image, style, and networks. Studies suggest that 60 percent of promotion decisions are based on networking activities within the organization.[50] This reinforces that visibility and communication within the company can accelerate career advancement. A manager's ability to generate new ideas and problem-solve gains attention by upper management. According to Melanie Howard, a social trends forecaster and business advisor, "Professional networking has become central to the success of senior executives, and those who excel at it tend to rise to the top of their fields due to the added influence and problem-solving ability effective networking can confer."[51] Self-improvement is a continuous process that networking can make substantial contributions to. Managers who build strong relationships with key people are on the road to success. A critical element for building strong relationships is effective communication.

Summary

This chapter presents general principles for conducting interviews and then applies them to two special situations. The term *interview* includes many daily interactions that have a time limit and an identifiable purpose. It is an opportunity to gain and share information, but it is important to be aware of special communication barriers that make this difficult. First, the interviewer and interviewee might have different intentions. Second, personal bias results when people hear and see what they want to hear and see. The third barrier is the fact-inference problem. Nonverbal communication, the fourth barrier, presents problems because the interview is generally a short intensive communication interaction where one nonverbal behavior may result in faulty conclusions. The last two barriers are the powerful effects of first impressions and organizational status.

To help overcome these barriers, seven questions should be asked by managers. A semistructured format is recommended for most interviews. This means some of the questions should be established before the interview, but others will depend on how the interview develops. Either the funnel or inverted funnel sequence of questions may be used. Three categories of questions are reviewed when discussing the phrasing of questions—open and closed, primary and secondary, neutral and directed. Each may be appropriate at the correct time. Seven types of probes also are presented. Strategic analysis is required to use the appropriate questions in different situations.

Finally, consideration is given to ending the interview. Both the manager and the interviewee must be clear on the main points, future action, and goodwill close.

All managers conduct employment and performance appraisal interviews during their careers. Consequently, they need to be aware of several aspects of each of these interviews. The employment interview requires planning to ensure the manager clearly understands the job opening. Legal concerns are unique during the employment interview, so it is necessary to be aware of the general guidelines for lawful questions.

An appropriate questioning strategy is important, and the manager can draw on a large number of potential questions to evaluate the applicants' motivation, education, experience, and fit. Each type of question has a specific purpose. The most common errors to avoid in the employment interview are talking too much rather than listening, and keeping inadequate records.

Performance appraisal interviews are critical for a number of reasons. Unfortunately, they are often not conducted or are ineffective. The effectiveness can be increased by scheduling the interview at the appropriate time, conducting it in the correct place, and discussing relevant topics. Legal issues can be avoided when performance appraisal interviews are fair, consistent, objective, and unbiased.

Strategic communication is essential when appraising performance; otherwise, defensive behavior may be aroused in the subordinate. Strategic communication allows the manager to develop a supportive nondefensive environment that encourages a problem-solving approach. This communication should contain messages that are descriptive, problem-oriented, empathetic, equal, and provisional. These characteristics should also be present when giving feedback and setting goals.

Networking is founded on informational interviews. The main purpose of networking is to share information through mutually beneficial relationships developed through social and professional network channels. Following basic steps and etiquette for networking improves successful outcomes that can accelerate career advancement.

Cases for Small Group Discussion

Case 12-1.

Kern and the Quiet Nurse

Kay Kern is the director of the Corporate Safety Department for a large multiplant manufacturing company in the Midwest. The company has six major manufacturing plants, and each has its own industrial nurses.

Twice a year, Kern has individual formal interviews with the nurses to find out if they have any major concerns or if Kern can help in any way. Since these nurses report to the personnel manager of each plant and not to Kern, this is not a performance review. Kern gets a lot of valuable information from the nurses through the interviews and seems to have developed a positive relationship with them. There is only one nurse, Joe James, who does not really open up to Kern and say much. On several occasions, Kern has tried to get information from James, but generally when Kern asks a question, all she gets is a one-word or superficial response. For instance, several months ago all the plants instituted a new program for monitoring the number and types of visits to the nurses' offices. Kern asked James if everything was all right with the new program. James merely shrugged and said, "Yes."

This worries Kern because James is a young nurse with only two years of experience and he probably has questions and could use some help. Kern has even asked some of the other employees in the plant if James was naturally quiet, but everyone said he was rather outgoing and easy to get to know. Kern is getting frustrated, because in her 25 years of experience she has never had this much trouble getting someone to open up.

Questions

1. What are some possible incorrect interview strategies that Kern may be using?
2. What would you recommend to Kern?

Case 12-2.

Is It Harassment?

Jack Simpson, newly appointed human resources director for Geridan Contracting Corporation (GCC), had had an unusual morning. First on his agenda was an exit interview with Maria Johnson, the company president's executive secretary. Johnson had simply informed Simpson she was quitting, giving no reason. Judging from her performance reviews over the last few years, Simpson believed her to be a competent, enthusiastic, and dedicated employee. Even though Simpson had little knowledge of her workload, he could see no obvious reason for the resignation. He had set up this exit interview hoping to find out why she had quit.

Next on Simpson's agenda was an interview with Ryan Ross, the president of GCC, who wanted to talk to Simpson before Simpson began interviewing later in the day for the secretary's replacement. Simpson had never conducted an interview for a president's secretary before, but he had planned on getting a good idea of what to look for during his talk with Johnson. He believed Ross would also advise him on what he expected from the secretary's replacement.

However, when Simpson and the resigning executive secretary, Johnson, sat down in a quiet conference room at 8:30 a.m., the HR director's ears began to burn. Johnson explained that for the last six months she was being sexually harassed by Ross and that she was considering suing GCC (and Ross in particular).

Simpson needs to know more about this accusation in case it does develop into a more serious situation. Also, the more facts he has, the better prepared he will be to discuss the situation with the president. What interview strategy should Simpson use with the secretary?

Questions

1. What type of questions would you recommend? What sequence?
2. What do you think will be the major barriers in this interview? Why?
3. What can Simpson do to be sure he is getting the facts?

Case 12-3.

Motivation and the Performance Appraisal

Samuel Jones has worked diligently for his supervisor, Eric Donnell, during the past three years in the accounting department of a local bank. During that period, he has never been reprimanded for any of the work he has done. In fact, only recently, he received his first, supposedly annual, performance review. Although he received a raise in each of the two prior years, this was the first time he was formally evaluated. The first year he received a memo from Donnell stating the amount of his raise. The next year, Donnell did not even inform him of a raise. Rather, Jones had to figure it out for himself from his paycheck stub.

After sitting through his first formal evaluation, Jones is stunned. Donnell informed him his work effort is just average and he does not always show enough motivation in the tasks he undertakes. This is the most Donnell has said to Jones concerning his work since Jones began working there over three years ago.

Donnell works on important matters alone in his office and shuts himself off from his employees' activities. Some of Jones's fellow workers see this as a sign the boss has faith in them to get the job done and to accept responsibilities on their own. But Jones believes Donnell is just avoiding responsibility and is not interested in involving himself with his employees. Jones believes his boss thinks "I've got my own problems, so don't come to me with yours."

Jones has healthy working relationships with several other supervisors in the bank, and they all have told him more than once that his performance is above average. Because of this, Jones feels hurt that Donnell called him "average." As far as motivation goes, Jones does not see what there is to be motivated about. He never receives rewards, verbal or otherwise, at those times when he does good work. Consequently, he is confused about what levels of effort and performance will lead to the recognition he feels he deserves.

Questions

1. List some needs that Jones's boss could fulfill for him to increase his work effort.
2. List some elements of job performance that Donnell must make sure are present to get better performance from his employee.
3. What can Donnell do to get the most out of his performance evaluations?
4. What, if anything, can Jones do to increase the flow of feedback from his supervisor?

Endnotes

1. Susan T. Fiske and Steven L. Newberg, "A Continuum of Impression Formation, from Category-Based to Individuating Process: Influences of Information and Motivation on Attention and Interpretation," in *Advances in Experimental Social Psychology*, vol. 23, ed. Mark P. Zanna (New York: Academic Press, 1990), pp. 1–74.

2. Kevin R. Murphy and Douglas H. Reynolds, "Does True Halo Affect Observed Halo?" *Journal of Applied Psychology*, May 1988, pp. 235–38.

3. Elaine Pulakos, Neal Schmitt, and C. Ostroff, "A Warning about the Use of a Standard Deviation across Dimensions within Rates to Measure Halo," *Journal of Applied Psychology*, February 1986, pp. 29–32.

4. Terry L. Leap and Michael D. Crino, *Personnel/Human Resource Management* (New York: Macmillan, 1989), p. 332.

5. Fran F. Kanfer and P. Karoly, "Self-Control: A Behaviorist Excursion into the Lion's Den," *Behavior Therapy* 3, no. 2 (1972), pp. 298–300.

6. James P. Walsh, "Selectivity and Selective Perception: An Investigation of Managers' Belief Structures and Information Processing," *Academy of Management Journal*, December 1988, pp. 873–96.

7. S. L. Ragan, "A Conversational Analysis of Alignment Talk in Job Interviews," in *Communication Yearbook*, vol. 7, ed. R. M. Bostrom (Beverly Hills, CA: Sage Publications, 1983), pp. 502–16.

8. R. L. Birdwhistell, *Kinesics and Context* (Philadelphia: University of Pennsylvania Press, 1970), p. 97.

9. J. K. Burgoon, D. B. Buller, and G. W. Woodall, *Nonverbal Communication: The Unspoken Dialogue* (New York: Harper & Row, 1989), p. 76.

10. Loren Falkenberg, "Improving the Accuracy of Stereotypes within the Workplace," *Journal of Management* 16, no. 1 (March 1990), pp. 107–18.

11. K. J. Williams, A. S. DeNisi, B. M. Meglino, and T. P. Cafferty, "Initial Decisions and Subsequent Performance Ratings," *Journal of Applied Psychology* 71, no. 2 (1986), pp. 189–95.

12. M. Snyder and B. H. Campbell, "Testing Hypothesis about Other People: The Role of the Hypothesis," *Personality and Social Psychology Bulletin*, 1980, pp. 421–26.

13. H. J. Bernardin and Richard W. Beatty, "Can Subordinate Appraisals Enhance Managerial Productivity?" *Sloan Management Review*, Summer 1987, p. 69.

14. R. I. Lazar and W. S. Wilkstrom, *Appraising Managerial Performance: Current Practices and Future Directions* (New York: The Conference Board, 1977), p. 46.

15. G. Johns, "Effects of Informational Order and Frequency of Applicant Evaluation upon Linear Information-Processing Competence of Interviewers," *Journal of Applied Psychology* 60, no. 3 (1975), pp. 427–33.

16. C. D. Tengler and F. M. Jablin, "Effects of Question Type, Orientation, and Sequencing in the Employment Screening Interview," *Communication Monographs* 50, no. 2 (1983), pp. 243–63.

17. Charles Stewart and W. B. Cash, *Interviewing: Principles and Practices*, 5th ed. (Dubuque, IA: Wm. C. Brown, 1988), p. 21.

18. Elizabeth Bradley, "Hiring the Best," *WIB, Magazine of the American Business Women's Association*, July–August 2003, pp. 12–15.

19. Stephen Baker, "What's a Friend Worth?" *BusinessWeek*, June 1, 2009, pp. 32–36.

20. Terry L. Leap and Michael D. Crino, *Personnel/Human Resource Management* (New York: Macmillan, 1989), p. 245.

21. Michael M. Harris, "Reconsidering the Employment Interview: A Review of Recent Literature and Suggestions for Future Research," *Personnel Psychology* 42, no. 4 (1989), pp. 691–726.

22. Jeanne C. Poole and E. Theodore Katz, "An EEO–AA Program That Exceeds Quotas—It Targets Biases," *Personnel Journal*, January 1987, p. 103.

23. James R. Redeker, "The Supreme Court on Affirmative Action: Conflicting Opinions," *Personnel*, October 1986, p. 8.

24. "Employment Discrimination: A Recent Perspective from the 'Burger Court,'" *Industrial Management*, September–October 1986, p. 3.

25. Stewart and Cash, Jr., *Interviewing: Principles and Practices*, p. 133.

26. Fredrick M. Jablin and Vernon D. Miller, "Interviewer and Applicant Questioning Behavior in Employment Interviews," *Management Communication Quarterly* 4, no. 1 (1990), pp. 51–86.

27. Wendy Kaufman, "Job Interviews Get Creative," *All Things Considered*, National Public Radio, August 22, 2003, www.npr.org/display_pages/features/feature_1405340.html.

28. William Poundstone, *How Would You Move Mount Fuji: Microsoft's Cult of the Puzzle* (New York: Little, Brown & Company, 2003).

29. C. W. Anderson, "The Relation Between Speaking Times and Decision in the Employment Interview," *Journal of Applied Psychology* 44, (1960), pp. 267–68.

30. R. E. Carlson, D. P. Schwab, and H. G. Henneman III, "Agreement among Selection Interview Styles," *Journal of Industrial Psychology* 5, no. 1 (1970), pp. 8–17.

31. R. F. Maier, *The Appraisal Interview: Objectives and Skills* (New York: John Wiley & Sons, 1958), p. 3.

32. Robert D. Bretz, Jr., George T. Milkovich, and Walter Read, "The Current State of Performance Appraisal Research and Practice: Concerns, Directions, and Implications," *Journal of Management* 18, no. 2 (June 1992), pp. 321–52.

33. R. M. Glen, "Performance Appraisal: An Unnerving yet Useful Process," *Public Personnel Management* 19, no. 1 (1990), pp. 1–10.

34. B. Dugan, "Effects of Assessor Training on Information Use," *Journal of Applied Psychology* 73 (1988), pp. 743–48; and Timothy M. Downs, "Predictions of Communication Satisfaction During Performance Appraisal Interviews," *Management Communication Quarterly* 3, no. 13 (1990), pp. 334–54.

35. Michael E. Stano and N. L. Reinsch, Jr., *Communication in Interviews* (Englewood Cliffs, NJ: Prentice Hall, 1982), p. 101.

36. L. L. Cummings and C. P. Schwab, "Designing Appraisal Systems for Information Yield," *California Management Review* 20, no. 1 (1978), pp. 18–25.

37. B. E. Becker and R. J. Klimoski, "A Field Study of the Relationship Between the Organizational Feedback Environment and Performance," *Personnel Psychology* 42, no. 3 (1989), pp. 343–58.

38. Maier, *The Appraisal Interview*, p. 22.

39. Jack R. Gibb, "Defensive Communication," *Journal of Communication*, September 1961, pp. 141–48.

40. Douglas Cederblom, "The Performance Appraisal Interview: A Review, Implications, and Suggestions," in *Readings in Organizational Communication*, ed. Kevin L. Hutchinson (Dubuque, IA: Wm. C. Brown, 1992), pp. 310–21.

41. M. M. Greller, "Evaluation of Feedback Sources as a Function of Role and Organizational Level," *Journal of Applied Psychology* 65, no. 1 (1980), pp. 24–27.

42. Judith Hale, "Communication Skills in Performance Appraisal," *Industrial Management*, no. 22 (March–April 1980), p. 19.

43. Robert J. Grossman, "Law in the Slow Lane," *HR Magazine* 45, no. 7 (July 2000), pp. 62–70.

44. Peter A. Veglahn, "Key Issues in Performance Appraisal Challenges: Evidence for Court and Arbitration Decisions," *Labor Law Journal* 44, no. 10 (October 1993), pp. 595–606.

45. Giovanni B. Giglioni, Joyce B. Giglioni, and James Bryant, "Performance Appraisal: Here Comes the Judge," *California Management Review* 24, no. 2 (Winter 1981), pp. 14–23.

46. N. B. Winstanley, "Legal and Ethical Issues in Performance Appraisals," *Harvard Business Review* 58, no. 6 (November–December 1980), pp. 186–192.

47. Paula Ketter, "Social Net-What?" *T + D* 63, no. 2 (March 2009), p. 22.

48. Judy Estrin, "Networking: It's the Way to Grow," *T + D* 62, no. 10 (October 2008), pp. 100–101.

49. "Networking & Professional Etiquette," n.d., www.career.caltech.edu/resources/handouts/Networking%20Handouts.pdf (June 1, 2009).

50. "Need to Know Networking," *Personnel Today*, March 24, 2009, p. 19.

51. Melanie Howard, "Social Networking: An Old Process in a New Form," *Market Leader*, no. 44 (Quarter 2, 2009), pp. 66–68.

Part Five

Group Communication Strategies

Chapter **Thirteen**

Managing Meetings and Teams

> Groupthink leads "to weak and faltering decisions, or rather, indecisions. When you take the most gallant soldier, the most intrepid airman or the most audacious soldier, put them at a table together, what do you get? The sum total of their fears."
>
> —*Winston Churchill, in describing meetings during World War II*

Meetings are an important organizational communication process that continues to be useful for coordination of work functions. In fact, 90 percent of all U.S. businesses and 100 percent of the Fortune 500 companies use some form of group structure. Their need lies in the complexity and interdependence of tasks, which make it difficult for one person to have the knowledge to make decisions and solve problems in today's organizations. The contemporary regulatory environment illustrates this interdependence and the high cost of decisions. Governmental regulations on how and what an industry can do often require that lawyers, industrial relations managers, tax specialists, accountants, and governmental experts discuss ideas before a decision is made.

From a broader perspective, it is easy to see why teams have been adopted as a key personnel configuration in the postmodern business environment. As discussed in Chapter 1, today's workplace is fast paced. The traditional management hierarchy has been replaced by flexible, cooperative, mission-driven managers who expect their subordinates and associates to participate fully in the task or project at hand.

Managing teams—and the meetings that teamwork requires—calls for special skills. Just because a work group is labeled a team doesn't mean it automatically functions as a team. As a team leader, you must use a variety of communication strategies to maximize your team's effectiveness. This chapter describes those key strategic considerations. But first, we briefly review the range of functions that meetings and teams perform.

Managers use meetings for several functions: informational, fact finding, problem solving, decision making, and coordinating. While a meeting may be labeled team, staff, marketing, committee, ad hoc, or whatever, any meeting should allow members to share information, obtain ideas, solve problems, coordinate efforts, make decisions, and build working relationships. A gathering of workers who simply sit and hear the manager make announcements is not a true meeting.

Managers use informational meetings to explain important new decisions or company activities to employees, answer questions, or help them understand how to perform a desired task. The essential aim is to communicate a company point of view and have it accepted by employees. Such meetings succeed when they get the employees to examine, articulate, and align their own interests with the company's.

Managers conduct fact-finding meetings to tap the expertise of several employees and at the same time obtain facts for planning and decision making. For example, a sales manager may call in all the sales representatives to find out about such matters as business conditions, competition, customer desires, and complaints. A production manager having trouble with a specific operation might meet with all the key people who have knowledge of a situation.

In a problem-solving and decision-making meeting, team members pool their specialized expertise with the objective of developing a solution. This meeting goes beyond simply finding facts; it seeks to identify the issues and discuss the probable gains and losses resulting from alternate actions.

In coordination meetings, project teams keep each other informed of their progress and plan each stage of their joint efforts. Whatever their purpose, meetings are a way of managerial life; however, managers must use meetings prudently to maximize their benefits and minimize their costs.

An outstanding example of meetings that accomplish the goals described here was the Katrina Working Group sessions led by the mayor of Houston, Texas, Bill White, following the devastation of Hurricane Katrina in September 2005. Every morning he presided over a session of community leaders, corporate executives, church leaders, emergency services staff, and elected officials to determine how to serve the thousands of evacuees from New Orleans and other Gulf Coast areas who were seeking shelter in Houston. Forty people sat at long tables arranged in a square in a large room, with dozens of others sitting in rows behind the tables. Mayor White refused to allow speeches or grandstanding. Instead he asked participants to raise issues and helped them formulate response plans. As a result of the efficient methods that the mayor's team used to handle the crisis, ensuring humanitarian aid to evacuees while maintaining the city's normal functions, Houston re-elected Bill White in November 2005 with 91 percent of the vote.[1]

ADVANTAGES AND DISADVANTAGES OF WORKING IN TEAMS

Whether participating in a team or leading one, managers should be aware of advantages and disadvantages of group work.

Advantages of the Team

One advantage is that a group decision may be of a higher quality than that made by an individual. But, before using a team, you must analyze the nature of the problem. Teams are better at solving problems for which there is no single correct solution or for which solutions are difficult to verify objectively.[2] Such problems require decisions that cannot be programmed. Nonprogrammed decisions are the result of infrequent situations that require creativity, insight, and the sharing of ideas and perspectives regarding a problem.[3] Groups, especially heterogeneous groups, bring a greater variety of information and a wider choice of solutions.

A second advantage to a team is that when members have had an opportunity for discussion, they are more likely to be committed to the information presented or the decision made. In other words, they become "owners" of the decision. A classic study conducted by Coch and French over 55 years ago investigated workers' resistance to technological changes in their jobs. When workers participated in discussions regarding implementation of the changes, significantly less resistance resulted than that which occurred among workers excluded from participation.[4] Each employee who participated in the meeting had increased ownership of the outcome, and the responsibility felt for making the solution or program work was enhanced.

A more recent study of employee retention factors found similar results. When asked which improvement would make the biggest difference in their organization's ability to retain employees, 42 percent of the executives surveyed chose empowering workers to participate in decision making. By contrast, only 6 percent cited more attractive compensation packages as an effective tool for lowering turnover.[5]

Another advantage of a meeting is that it may reduce the chance of communication problems. When a group of people hears the same message at the same time, the possibility of misinterpretation declines. Participants' questions can clarify the message, and each participant has the opportunity to hear the answer and ask additional questions. Feedback is increased and timing is reduced as a barrier to communication.

An old tale illustrates yet another benefit of working in teams. A man was lost while driving through the country. As he tried to read a map, he accidentally drove off the road into a ditch. Though he wasn't injured, his car was stuck deep in the mud. So the man walked to a nearby farm and asked for help.

"Warwick can get you out of that ditch," said the farmer, pointing to an old mule standing in a field. The man looked at the haggard mule doubtfully, but figured he had nothing to lose. The two men and Warwick made their way back to the ditch.

The farmer hitched the mule to the car. With a snap of the reins he shouted, "Pull, Fred! Pull, Jack! Pull, Ted! Pull, Warwick!" And the mule pulled the car from the ditch with very little effort. The man was amazed. He thanked the farmer, patted the mule, and asked, "Why did you call out all of those other names before you called Warwick?"

The farmer grinned and said, "Old Warwick is just about blind. As long as he believes he's part of a team, he doesn't mind pulling."[6]

Disadvantages of the Team

We have seen that working in teams can improve quality, productivity, creativity, loyalty and commitment, even retention. But there is a downside. Richard Hall put it well when he noted the "time spent on meetings is time not spent on other activities."[7] While the hourly cost of a meeting in terms of the base pay of the participants is already high, to determine the real cost, one must add payroll taxes, fringe benefits, and general overhead. The meeting participants' base pay would probably need to be doubled to determine the actual cost. Meeting costs often go unnoticed because they are not budget line items. Meetings are a hidden cost that can either impede or improve the effectiveness of a work group.

In addition to the high cost, the team may develop low-quality decisions. Pressures to conform, premature decisions, hidden agendas, extensive conflict, disruptive and dominant individuals, lack of planning, and poor leadership can easily reduce effectiveness.[8] Later in the chapter, we detail these factors and techniques for managing them.

A common disadvantage of meetings is their frequent overuse. Organizations often develop a "meeting" style of management. Management must meet for every little thing. Meetings generally are not necessary for routine or repetitive programmed decisions that can be handled by an established procedure. Unfortunately, too frequently meetings are held just because "we always have a meeting at this time." Overuse of meetings may cause employees to find them a nuisance, so they avoid them. Consequently, employees may miss truly important meetings or be unable to distinguish between a critical and a useless meeting.

Another problem is that the weekly team meeting might be a waste of time if members are not required to gather facts before the meeting, make decisions at the meeting, or present information. The manager must analyze each meeting to determine need. Still another often useless meeting pattern finds the manager telling a group about a new event or presenting a progress report without providing an opportunity for questions or interactions. Clearly, it may be more efficient to share information through a memo or e-mail rather than a meeting.

Groupthink

After extensive analysis, Irving Janis wrote a book titled *Victims of Groupthink*.[9] Groupthink is the tendency of a group to conform to ideas simply because the general sense of the group has moved in a particular direction and the members of the group feel committed to continue in the same line of thought. Although the group may be pursuing an incorrect conclusion, the group does not alter direction for fear of offending a group member. It is the extreme form of cohesiveness and is especially likely when a group has a high sense of teamwork and desire for consensus or harmony.

Groupthink is especially important because of its potential for disastrous effects. Some say the disaster of the space shuttle Challenger was a result of groupthink,[10] and many other disasters are partially attributed to groupthink.[11]

Based on Janis's concept, Von Bergen and Kirk describe symptoms of groupthink that managers should watch for.[12]

1. The illusion that everyone in the group holds the same viewpoint with an emphasis on team play.
2. The belief that the group can make no mistakes.

3. The belief that disagreements are to be avoided, faulty assumptions are not questioned, and personal doubts must be suppressed in favor of group harmony.

4. The tendency to comfort one another and to ignore or at least discount warnings that an agreed-on plan is either unworkable or highly unlikely to succeed.

5. The tendency to direct pressure on any dissenting group member who expresses strong challenges to the consensus opinion of the group.

6. The presence of inordinate optimism that predisposes members to take excessive risks.

When in a decision-making meeting, the effective manager is alert to groupthink symptoms and takes appropriate action. Or more appropriately, she takes actions to ensure that groupthink does not develop. Three actions help avoid the tendency toward groupthink:

1. *Do not make an early decision.* Do not commit early or become locked into a position early in the problem analysis. When a manager begins a discussion by saying "This is what I would like to see" or "This is the best solution . . . but I would like your comments," he is probably preventing an open discussion and is setting the stage for an early unanimous decision.

2. *Be open to criticism.* This is easy to say but difficult to do. It is natural to defend one's idea, but a wise manager will encourage employees to "push back." Criticism of an idea should not be taken as criticism of another's self-worth. When criticism cannot arise within the group, it may be solicited from an outsider who will generally be less susceptible to status and conformity pressures.

3. *Use a "devil's advocate."* If one member of the group is asked to provide opposition to any ideas expressed, this will ensure alternatives. This procedure works best when other members know that the dissenter is playing the devil's advocate role; otherwise, they may consider the person to be an agitator who should be ignored. In addition, the same person should not play the devil's advocate in every meeting. Constantly stating opposing viewpoints not only puts pressure on the person, but also may result in a negative image of the individual.

STRATEGIC CONSIDERATIONS FOR MEETINGS

As we have seen, meetings have advantages as well as disadvantages, and groupthink adds to their complexity. The following discussion of seven strategic considerations, which are listed in Table 13–1, is provided to assist managers when considering the various contingencies.

Strategic Consideration 1: Should We Meet?

There are good reasons to have a meeting, and poor reasons to do so. As we have seen, the best reason is to get everyone's input on a complex problem or task. A poor reason to meet is to show others that one has the power to call people together or to be the center of attention. Another wrong reason is social or

TABLE 13–1
Strategic
Considerations
for Meetings

1.	Should we meet?
2.	Who should attend?
3.	Premeeting arrangements
4.	Leadership style
5.	Decision-making format
6.	Managing disruptions
7.	Follow-up

recreational—a meeting is an opportunity to get away from the desk, to visit with Bill from Accounting about the football game, or to be seen with some influential decision makers. Often, a brief informal group conversation may be better than a formal meeting. A good way to handle the former is to hold the meeting with everybody standing up.[13] This strategy ensures involvement, attention to the meeting's purpose, and brevity.

Strategic Consideration 2: Who Should Attend?

Once you have decided to hold a meeting, you need to select the meeting participants. Among the criteria to consider are (1) how many people to invite, (2) who the members will represent, (3) the members' functions in the meeting, and (4) their team-ability.

First, choose a manageable group size. Remember the guideline that increasing the size limits the extent to which individuals want to communicate. Research shows that as a group grows, communication becomes distorted and stress between members increases. However, a decrease in group size may also be dysfunctional. Thus, small groups may engage in superficial discussion and avoid controversial subjects.

But what is the ideal size? Filley, who has conducted extensive research on work groups, believes the optimum size is generally about five.[14] But when the problem is more complex, relatively larger groups—as large as 12 to 13 members—have proved more effective. Smaller groups are often faster and more productive, on the other hand. Generally, the larger the group, the less inclined an individual group member is to participate.

Sometimes it may not be possible to limit the size of the group to five or seven employees. In such cases, a manager could break the large group into smaller subgroups. The improved decisions or more accurate sharing of information may justify the time and effort required to coordinate several groups.

Second, when selecting members, an important thing to remember is that the team should reflect the organizational members the problem affects. For instance, if the concern is a departmental one, then members of the department should be represented. If two departments share the problem, team membership obviously should be drawn from both areas. When possible, membership should also include people with authority to follow through on the chosen action with time, personnel, and financial resources. But salience of the meeting's topic should be considered more important than organizational status when selecting participants.

Third, consider participants' potential functions within the team. When scheduling a problem-solving meeting, include people who are familiar with the different aspects of the problem. Also, include people who will actually carry out the solution to ensure implementation of the decision. In short, subject-matter expertise should be a prime criterion for membership in a team or work group.

Finally, consider participants' team-ability. Task knowledge is an insufficient qualification for meeting participation. Ability to work with others may become even more of a concern for cross-functional teams and virtual teams because of the special communication challenges they involve. Members of teams may be too passive, tactful, or constrained to work together in a satisfying manner. They fear alienating one another.[15] On the other hand, members may be too passionate, stubborn, and aggressive. They might be unable to cooperate and compromise in a team setting. Clearly, your group must have the needed team skills to function in a meeting and resolve the problem.[16]

If a manager has difficulty finding employees with team-ability, training may be called for. Teamwork is a skill that can be acquired, not a gift one is born with. Understanding group dynamics comes with study and practice. Parts 3 (Strategies for Understanding Messages) and 4 (Interpersonal Communication Strategies) of this book offer guidelines for developing some of the process skills required for meeting participation, including collaborating, listening, giving constructive feedback, negotiating, compromising, and other conflict resolution strategies.

Strategic Consideration 3: Premeeting Arrangements

Premeeting arrangements fit into three categories: preparing the agenda and other appropriate materials, maximizing the physical environment, and determining the seating arrangements.

Materials

The agenda may be the first thing that comes to mind when considering materials for a meeting. More than a list of the meeting topics, the agenda is the script or working paper from which the meeting operates. As the cliché says, "What gets scheduled gets done." Consequently, the agenda deserves the manager's special consideration. Careful planning is half the battle. However, be sure to follow the agenda during the meeting. When others try to introduce new elements during the meeting, refer to the written agenda.[17]

Regardless of the type of meeting, the agenda needs to communicate the *what, why, when,* and *who* (the Ws) of a meeting. Frequently, one or several of the elements of an agenda are often omitted, yet each is important. For instance, if time frames for each agenda topic are included, the meeting is less likely to run long and more likely to address all the topics. And if expected outcomes for each topic are specified, the meeting participants are more likely to reach the stated goals. An agenda template is shown in Figure 13–1.

FIGURE 13–1
Meeting
Announcement
and Agenda
Template

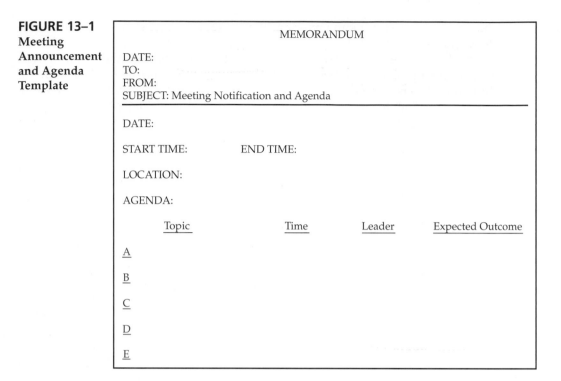

MEMORANDUM

DATE:
TO:
FROM:
SUBJECT: Meeting Notification and Agenda

DATE:

START TIME: END TIME:

LOCATION:

AGENDA:

	Topic	Time	Leader	Expected Outcome
A				
B				
C				
D				
E				

What People first need to know the *what,* the topic under discussion, so they may understand exactly what is to be discussed. Let the agenda make this clear. A topic listed as "Maintenance" will not communicate as fully as one that reads "Maintenance Status of the Emergency Generator." A more complete description enables participants to gather any special information or prepare questions relevant to the discussion.

Everyone knows that agendas are important, but half of business meetings are held with no agenda. Maybe the extra effort of an agenda seems unjustified, or the lack of an agenda may merely reflect a lack of planning. It may also be that agendas are not the common practice in many companies. Agendas are often not needed in small informal meetings where two or three employees get together or when one obvious topic is the only point for discussion. However, some managers assume agendas are never needed for small meetings. Agendas require planning time—an asset that ineffective managers rarely possess. Many managers would rather spend additional time in a poorly conducted meeting than take the time to plan. In many cases, a manager may wish to solicit input on the agenda from members. In these cases, it should be done in a systematic way to ensure orderly input. Few leaders like surprises at meetings.

Why People attending a meeting need to know the goal for each agenda item. Describe this clearly so participants can work toward it. Failure to clarify a group discussion's goal leads to circular talk and anxiety among participants. When people do not know why they are attending a meeting, apprehension arises.

When Setting the time involves several strategic factors. First, what time of day is best for all the participants? A quick review of the organization may indicate that the first thing in the morning is bad if many other activities are competing for attention, whereas immediately after lunch may be a difficult time for people to stay alert.

Second, how long should the meeting last? If a meeting schedule does not allow sufficient time, critical issues may receive superficial coverage. But remember that people value time highly and resent its waste or misuse. Be sure to list both the start time and the end time on your meeting announcement to allow participants to plan their day.

A standard time limit that applies to all meetings is impossible to set. However, some ground rules on length are possible. The most effective meetings last no longer than one and a half hours. After this long, people need to break for coffee or fresh air. Short, single goals can be met in less than an hour, and this should be the time span a manager aims for. Individual agenda items should also be assigned a time limit. Too often, meetings go on and on because no one has established definite time parameters.

"When" applies to the appropriate time to send out the agenda as well. The purpose of the agenda and any supporting material is lost if none of it arrives until the last minute. Neither should one send the materials with so much lead-time that the participants forget about it. A rule of thumb is that the longer a meeting is (and, consequently, the more scheduling and preparation required by the participants), the greater the lead-time required for the agenda and supporting materials. However, try to avoid too long a lead-time since this could bring about forgetfulness. Generally, participants need two or three days' notice to prepare for a meeting.

Who It is not a mere courtesy to inform the participants about the others who will be at the meeting. This knowledge allows the participants to complete their own audience analysis. Knowing who else will be present lets the participants prepare any material or information that others in the meeting may request.

A list of participants also forces the meeting manager to think about possible group dynamics. For instance, will a verbally dominant person attempt to control the group? Will the correct mix of expertise be present? Answers to these questions can influence meeting outcomes.

Physical Facilities

Once the participants have been selected and the agenda, along with any supporting material, has been prepared, questions arise such as "Where is the best place to hold the meeting?" or "What physical arrangements must be considered?"

Physical surroundings are important. A few simple guidelines will help to make a meeting productive:

- Use a room where the chairs and tables can be arranged to meet group needs.
- Match the size of the room with the size of the group. Meetings held in close cramped rooms with the members jammed together around narrow tables make for an unpleasant conversational climate and hamper decision making. Tension, a prime breeder of conflict, builds in a close and uncomfortable meeting room. At the same time, however, a room seating 45 can be cold and overwhelming to a group of five.
- Check for comfortable chairs, ventilation, and lighting. Remember, though, that soft overly comfortable chairs can affect concentration and even prolong the meeting.
- Make sure space exists for visual aids if they are to be used. If you know you will be needing equipment, writing materials, and so on, be sure they are available. Keep the audience in mind. Thus, providing place cards may be useful if the participants are strangers.
- Above all, arrange to have the meeting in a meeting room rather than the meeting leader's office. It will create an environment that emphasizes the participants are coming together for specific purposes at a specific time on neutral turf. The atmosphere created is one of urgency and seriousness, which helps keep the meeting on the topic.

Seating Arrangements

After designating the appropriate facility for the meeting, managers should consider which of several possible seating arrangements to use. Depending on the situation, more than one arrangement may be possible; however, a few arrangements should be avoided. The first arrangement to avoid is the long narrow table that makes it nearly impossible for all participants to see one another. A manager can use eye contact to gain attention or to control a participant. Consequently, such a seating arrangement works against the manager's attempts to use all the nonverbal techniques available.

A second arrangement to avoid is one that divides up sides. For instance, if two groups are in natural opposition, they should not sit across from each other. Similarly, one should keep two hostile participants apart or in such a position that they cannot easily see each other.

Several seating arrangements lend themselves to effective meetings: the table with the leader at one end, the round table or circle, and the U shape.[18] When the leader sits at one end of the table, control of the meeting is easier because all communication will tend to flow toward the head. However, this arrangement loses effectiveness with a group larger than six or seven participants. As groups get larger, sidebar comments tend to increase and eye contact is difficult to maintain.

When the size of the meeting becomes larger than 10 to 12 members, a U-shaped arrangement is preferred. The manager sitting in the middle of the U can maintain eye contact with all the participants. At the same time, communication among subunits of the group is less likely. A variation is the oval-shaped table.

FIGURE 13–2
Seating
Arrangements

When the President of the U.S. meets with his Cabinet (most senior appointed officers), for instance, everyone sits at an oval table, with the President at the middle, directly across from the Vice President. Other members are seated according to the *order of precedence,* with higher-ranking officers sitting closer to the center of the table.

The manager using the round table or circle arrangement has less direct control of the group than with other arrangements. Because the manager has a less dominant position, participants tend to address each other rather than the leader. A table is, in a sense, a kind of communication line, as the contour of the table establishes the flow of communication. Thus, the round table is best when seeking a true participative form of decision making and trying to minimize status differences. Figure 13–2 illustrates the different arrangements.

In review, three major types of premeeting arrangements require analysis: what materials to prepare, what physical setting to use, and how to arrange seating. These factors do not guarantee an effective meeting, but strategic analysis in these areas will increase effectiveness.

Strategic Consideration 4: Leadership Style

The problems facing organizations are so varied and complex that no one style of leadership suits all situations. Consequently, a manager must be flexible and diagnose the situation to determine the appropriate leadership behavior from one situation to another.

When diagnosing the situation to determine the most effective style, managers need to consider three factors: the group, the objective of the meeting, and the type of leadership behavior with which the manager personally feels most comfortable.[19] Figure 13–3 shows how these three factors operate together.

Each group differs but needs a leader with some degree of interpersonal orientation; therefore, tight control is generally inappropriate. Less control is required when the group is mature and knows the topic, whereas a new or immature group needs a leader who provides more control and direction.

A routine or structured meeting may call for more leader control and task orientation, but a democratic or more laissez-faire approach may be required for a solution to an abstract problem or one requiring a creative solution. A highly emotional task requires less control, while more control may be best for a nonsensitive objective.

FIGURE 13–3
Determining
Leadership
Style

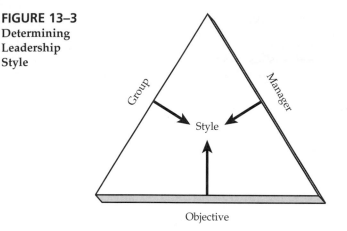

Finally, a manager must be aware of the type of leadership behavior with which she is personally most comfortable. This awareness helps a manager monitor her own behavior and remain flexible rather than use the same behavior repeatedly. Increasing one's repertoire of management tools is a requirement for today's fast-paced, constantly shifting workplace.

Leading Project Teams

Managing project teams calls for special leadership skills. Among them is the ability to select team members who communicate information freely and honestly. One nontraditional tool for objectively evaluating project team members is Social Network Analysis (SNA). SNA begins with a survey about who respondents go to for advice or information, who they communicate with most frequently, and who is their most valued contact in the organization.

Survey results are analyzed and "sociograms" are designed that reveal employees' social networks and connections. From these sociograms, a project leader can identify people with *centrality*. Centrality is a measure of a person's relative importance based on the person's location in the social network. Thus, when putting together a project team, or when analyzing a dysfunctional team, a manager should consider whether individuals have high degrees of centrality. These people control the flow of information and collaboration, bridging potential communication gaps in the team and in the organization.

One manager who uses SNA to evaluate project teams is Steve Randle, vice president of IT Operations for XO Communications. Headquartered in Virginia, XO Communications is one of the U.S.'s largest communications service providers to businesses and government. Randle reports, "Teams with members who show high centrality will be able to more effectively access needed resources across the organization and will more readily share information with other groups who need to be involved with a project in a timely manner. With better planning I can expect better results."[20]

The following are some other strategies that will help you maximize your project team's effectiveness.

- *Be a facilitator.* Managing teams is less about supervising than it is about motivating members to do their best. Avoid the tendency to micromanage once the team's objectives and responsibilities have been defined.
- *Support the team.* Provide resources, run interference, and resolve internal conflicts. Give them all the information they need, and more, to encourage trust. Remember that people cannot work in a vacuum.
- *Delegate.* Managers occasionally have trouble admitting that they cannot do it all. Instead of trying to manage every aspect of a meeting or project, trust members to perform their tasks. This also engenders respect for you as a leader and maintains morale.
- *Seek diversity.* As discussed in Chapter 10, heterogeneous groups experience more conflict but often produce higher-quality results than homogeneous groups. Stress the importance of collaboration, flexibility, and openness toward unfamiliar viewpoints and work styles.[21]

Strategic Consideration 5: Decision-Making Format

A diagnosis of the task, group, and personal preference will help to determine the appropriate decision-making format for the meeting. A formal plan is essential. Do not fall into the trap of believing that once the participants are together and know the goal, everything will automatically fall into place. Both experience and research suggest group members are haphazard and unorganized in their discussion and decision attempts when managers fail to use organizing formats.[22]

Three approaches to a meeting follow. The appropriateness of each of these is determined by the objective of the meeting, the participants in the meeting, and the leader.

The Rational Problem-Solving Process

In 1910, John Dewey described the steps that rational individuals use to solve a problem.[23] Most know these as the six stages to problem solving: (1) defining the problem, (2) analyzing the problem, (3) brainstorming the possible solutions, (4) determining the criteria that must be met to eliminate the problem, (5) selecting the best solution, and (6) implementing the solution. This process was introduced in Chapter 10 as an excellent conflict-resolution strategy.

When using this process in a meeting, it is critical to follow the sequence. People tend to begin to discuss solutions or even the implementation of a solution before the problem has been precisely defined. However, it is critical to get everyone to agree on the problem being discussed before addressing solutions. One way of doing this is to write the problem on a flip chart so everyone can see it. This same procedure can be followed for each step to ensure progress and focus.

After agreeing on the definition and scope of the problem, the group must spend time analyzing it fully. Again, you may meet resistance, especially if the members are intimately familiar with the problem. However, exploring the causes, effects, extent, and history of the problem may help the group avoid solutions that address mere symptoms rather than root causes of the problem.

The third step, brainstorming possible solutions, has received much attention in business literature. Alexander Osborn, an advertising executive, first described brainstorming as a special technique for facilitating the idea-generating portion of the decision process.[24]

The objective of brainstorming is to generate ideas rather than evaluate or analyze those ideas. A group can brainstorm successfully and produce a maximum number of ideas by adhering to three rules:

- Ideas are expressed freely without regard to quality. All ideas, no matter how unusual, are recorded.
- Criticism of the ideas produced is not allowed until all ideas have been expressed.
- Elaborations and combinations of previously expressed ideas are encouraged. The major strength of brainstorming is that one idea will create another. The ratio of high-quality ideas to the total number is not high, but often only one creative idea is needed for the solution.

Groups allowed to produce for longer work periods typically produce more ideas under brainstorming instructions than do individuals. Most groups continue to produce indefinitely, while individuals taper off.[25]

The fourth step is also important. The group must understand and honor required criteria for a "good" solution. Upper management sometimes imposes these criteria, or standards, on the group. Other times, the decision-making team may develop its own. Typical criteria are that a solution must be cost-effective, legal, timely, practical, and consistent with the organization's mission and/or values.

Step 5 in the rational decision-making process, selecting the best solution, is automatic in that it is a matter of comparing the list of criteria or standards with the list of brainstormed solutions. The idea from step 3 that best fits the criteria developed in step 4 now becomes the best solution. Following this process prevents groups from choosing a solution that is favored by someone with authority or someone who dominates the discussion. Rather, the best solution is chosen rationally.

As a final step, the group considers implementation of their solution. In today's business environment, where continuous quality improvement is stressed, it is important to put systems in place that will monitor how well the new solution is working. The monitoring systems can detect weaknesses and shortcomings before they create major damage and wipe out the good work of the problem-solving team.

Two other decision-making formats widely used in business are based on Dewey's classic process. They are the nominal group technique and the Delphi technique.

The Nominal Group Technique

When using the nominal group technique (NGT), the meeting leader directs each participant to create separate lists of the advantages and disadvantages associated with the problem and solutions under discussion. After a predetermined time, the participants present their advantages and disadvantages, which are posted so everyone can see them. Then members are directed to work alone again to rank all advantages and disadvantages from highest to lowest priority. After this, a master list is compiled. The participants can then discuss the issue based on the information presented in the master list. When groups follow this procedure, they generate a basis for group discussion that reflects all the participants' views that were individually developed by working alone.

The NGT has several advantages that a manager should consider when planning a meeting. One is that all participants can express their views without intimidation from more powerful or vocal group members. The procedure also ensures that each step in the rational problem solving is followed. Finally, it can save time because the meeting participants can generate their initial lists before the meeting. The NGT thus integrates the advantages of both group and individual creativity.[26]

The Delphi Technique

The Delphi technique is a unique group problem-solving process that differs greatly from the typical meeting. Unlike the typical discussion meeting or NGT, which requires physical proximity of group members, the Delphi technique does not require participants to meet face-to-face. This technique has been beneficial when team members are geographically dispersed or their schedules preclude a common meeting time. It is generally used with an ad hoc meeting of experts, and with virtual teams who meet only electronically.

Delphi uses an initial questionnaire that elicits the participants' expert opinions on a topic. Once these opinions have been collected, all group members receive a second questionnaire listing others' contributions, and all are asked to evaluate each idea using several specified criteria. This step is then followed by a third questionnaire that reports the second-round ratings, a mean rating, and any consensus. The participants then revise their earlier ratings considering the average or consensus. A final questionnaire includes all ratings, the consensus, and remaining problems.

The advantages of the Delphi technique are that it does not require physical proximity and that it controls some of the possible disadvantages of group decision making. The most vocal or highest-status person does not have an opportunity to control the group because everyone's comments are pooled. Also, the coordinator can guarantee the decision-making process does not omit any critical steps or ignore important comments.

A study conducted by Van De Ven and Delbecq[27] verified the value of the nominal group technique and the Delphi technique. They compared the effectiveness of group decisions when made with ordinary group discussion, with the nominal group technique, and with the Delphi method. They also compared participant satisfaction with the three techniques. They concluded that the quality of decisions was higher with the nominal group technique and Delphi than with ordinary group discussion; however, participants preferred the ordinary discussion technique. This preference has important implications for managers. Managers should consider decision-making formats to maximize group effectiveness.

Strategic Consideration 6: Managing Disruptions

One of the most aggravating behaviors is when a team member continually disrupts the communication flow. This person may be unskilled in group dynamics or may be coming to the meetings with a hidden agenda (that is, private objectives) that conflicts with the stated agenda. Disruptive behavior may include continuous clowning, dominating the conversation, attempting to change directions, or making accusations. These disruptions need resolution; otherwise, teams can quickly deteriorate.

Before the Meeting

A manager can minimize disruptions by taking a preventive point of view. John Jones suggests seven tactics that managers may use ahead of time when they believe a person will disrupt a meeting.[28]

1. Before the meeting, ask for the disrupter's cooperation.
2. Give the person a special task or role in the meeting, such as posting the viewpoints of others.
3. Work out your differences before the meeting (possibly with a third-party facilitator) to present a united front to all other members.
4. Structure the meeting to include frequent discussion of the meeting process itself.
5. Take all the dominator's items off the agenda.
6. Alert the person to the consequences of disruption. For example, say, "I have learned that a number of people are angry with you, and plan to confront you in the meeting."
7. Arrange allies to support you in dealing with the disruptive behavior of the individual.

During the Meeting

While prevention is preferred, a manager also needs to have options for controlling disruptive behavior during a meeting. The following are some strategies.

1. When dealing with an emotional conversation, make sure only one person speaks at a time, paraphrase each statement to ensure accuracy before allowing anyone else to speak, and be sure that everyone takes turns. One surprisingly effective technique is to move on to the next agenda item. One can return when tempers cool.[29] You might also stand and move to the flip chart or screen, or casually stand near the parties involved. This will help keep control in a nonverbal manner.
2. A less obvious disruptive influence occurs when participants do not get involved in the discussion. One way to ensure that participants become involved is to use the Delphi technique discussed earlier. When the participants need to have answers prepared for specific questions before the meeting, ask for these answers during the meeting.

3. Ask participants to jot down answers on a notepad when sensitive issues are discussed. Ask the participants to submit their written reactions anonymously to you, and then read them to the group. Participants thus have an opportunity to present viewpoints in a "safe" manner.

4. Ask questions throughout the meeting to help keep the participants involved. When worded correctly and addressed to the right audience, questions develop a participative climate. Questions have the greatest chance of soliciting participation when they are open ended, brief, unbiased, easily understood, and immediately pertinent to the topic.

A manager needs to consider four possible alternatives when asking a question.[30] When an *overhead question* is asked, anyone in the group may answer. A good idea is to begin with an overhead question and continue until forced to change. Either domination or nonparticipation by certain individuals may require a *direct question,* simply one that is directed to an individual. With direct questions, keep a balance instead of continually asking a verbal person or an assumed expert.

A *reverse question* is one originally asked by a group member. The leader then directs it back to the person who asked it. Do this when it is apparent that the participant really wants to make a statement but is not quite sure it would be appropriate. A final alternative is the *relay question,* which is asked by a group member and is relayed by the leader to the group: "Mary's question is interesting. What is a good answer?" The relay question gives you an opportunity to keep the communication moving among all the members of the group.

Strategic Consideration 7: Follow-Up

At meeting's end, reanalyze the original goals to ensure you have met them, make appropriate follow-up assignments, and evaluate the meeting process to determine if and how future meetings could be improved. One way to determine if the goal has been met is to review the rational problem-solving process to ensure each step was followed. If the group has defined the problem and has reviewed alternative solutions to this problem, it can be assumed the original objective has been met.

Another easy way to determine if the objective is met is to write out the decision or summarize the discussion in a few sentences. This clear statement allows the participants to review it and make sure they understand it. A summary of the decision reached will bring to the surface any individual misunderstandings or disagreements.

A good idea is to point out differences that exist at the end of the meeting. This recognizes that disagreement is not always bad; also, the disagreements will probably be vital to future discussions. A clear understanding of differences at the end of that meeting should make future meetings go more smoothly and help prevent unnecessary meetings.

Appropriate postmeeting follow-up is also an important component of team management. Before closing the meeting, clearly set out the next steps each member is to take. Also announce the next meeting, if necessary. Written confirmation of the decisions reached and any future actions to be taken by the participants is

FIGURE 13–4
Meeting Follow-Up Memo

Subject of meeting _____

Name of sender _____

Where and when held _____

Present _____

Major conclusions _____

Future actions _____

Next meeting _____

a good practice. Such a memo or e-mail serves as a reminder of the results and informs other personnel who are interested but did not attend the meeting.

Stress the positive when writing the follow-up memo so the participants can see the fruits of their labor. A follow-up memo or e-mail becomes a record of the meeting, ensures follow-up, and establishes accountability for future action. Some companies have a standard form for the follow-up memo (shown in Figure 13–4) that helps keep it short, simple, and accurate.

In a meeting, much happens that is lost forever. A manager may need to provide more detailed minutes. Minutes are particularly valuable as a starter for future meetings on the same topic. Traditional minutes should capture a summary of the meeting that includes action items, decisions, and open issues.

- *Action items.* Action items are to-dos assigned to meeting participants. Record the task, the person responsible, and the date agreed upon to complete the task.
- *Decisions.* All decisions that may affect future choices of the group should be recorded.
- *Open issues.* New issues raised at the meeting but not resolved there should be recorded so they can be carried over to a future meeting.[31]

The minutes should record these three results for each topic on the agenda. In addition, any significant comments about that topic should be recorded. Participants appreciate having their comments displayed in a way that is visible to everyone. Conventional minutes are often distributed to all meeting members. For political or corporate culture reasons, a manager may want to summarize the information for larger distribution and post it to an intranet site.

The final step in the management of a meeting is the evaluation of the meeting itself, an important self-development activity. One extreme form of evaluation is audio recording of the meeting and evaluating it step-by-step. This may be especially worthwhile for project teams that meet regularly over extended time periods. In fact, your organization may require this of all project managers when they begin a project with a new team of specialists.

FIGURE 13–5
Evaluation
Sheet

Listed below is a series of statements about a meeting. Circle the number of the scale that best describes the meeting in which you just participated.

1. The objective of the meeting was clearly defined.

Strongly agree   5   4   3   2   1   Strongly disagree

2. A systematic approach was used to solve problems.

Strongly agree   5   4   3   2   1   Strongly disagree

3. All the participants were involved in the meeting.

Strongly agree   5   4   3   2   1   Strongly disagree

4. Disruptions were effectively managed.

Strongly agree   5   4   3   2   1   Strongly disagree

5. An appropriate format was established for the meeting.

Strongly agree   5   4   3   2   1   Strongly disagree

6. Appropriate premeeting details (agenda, room, etc.) were arranged.

Strongly agree   5   4   3   2   1   Strongly disagree

7. Time was well managed.

Strongly agree   5   4   3   2   1   Strongly disagree

8. The stated objectives could have been met without a meeting.

Strongly disagree   5   4   3   2   1   Strongly agree

9. The objective of the meeting has been met.

Strongly agree   5   4   3   2   1   Strongly disagree

The evaluation sheet in Figure 13–5 represents one tool that can be used to evaluate a meeting.

Summary

The team is a common personnel configuration today. Team meetings have advantages and disadvantages, including groupthink, with which managers should be familiar. To make effective use of meetings, a number of contingencies need to be reviewed. The first and most obvious consideration facing a manager is the stated objective. If the objective is a programmed decision, or if a commitment does not present a special problem, a meeting may not be required.

Once it is clear that a meeting should be conducted, it is important to consider who should attend. Criteria for selecting meeting members include how many to invite, whose interests they represent, their knowledge and authority, and their team-abilities.

Next, a manager must make the premeeting arrangements. These involve deciding what should be on the agenda, which additional materials should be attached to the agenda, and what should be the physical arrangements (including seating)

for the meeting. Overlooking any one of these questions may cause an omission that reduces meeting effectiveness.

After the arrangements have been prepared, managers need to select the appropriate leadership style for the situation, group, and objective. The selection of the appropriate leadership style will assist in the format choice. Project team leadership calls for special skills.

This chapter presents three decision-making formats for a meeting: The rational problem-solving approach, the nominal group technique, and the Delphi technique (which can be used for virtual meetings or geographically dispersed group members). Each of these approaches has inherent strengths and challenges.

Regardless of the format selected, disruptions can occur during a meeting, but they can be prevented if a manager takes precautions, including talking to potential disrupters ahead of time or planning special activities for them during the meeting. Once a disruption occurs, strategic communication can control it.

Finally, a manager's responsibility as the leader of a meeting includes the postmeeting follow-up. This follow-up may take the form of traditional meeting minutes, a short memo, or an e-mail and an effort to ensure that various commitments have been met. Also, formal evaluation of the meeting helps determine ways a future meeting could be improved.

Cases for Small Group Discussion

Case 13-1.

The Regional Relationships

Jerry Blaire is the regional manager of a national electronics franchise retail store. This franchise has over 200 locally owned stores throughout the eastern United States. As the regional manager, Blaire is responsible for an urban area in which there are eight stores, plus the remainder of the state, which has another six stores.

The regional manager is the liaison between the manager-owner of the stores and the corporate offices in Boston. Responsibilities include monitoring the individual stores to ensure the provisions of the franchise agreement are maintained, dealing with any complaints from managers, taking product orders, introducing new products, and managing the regional advertising program.

Blaire has been with this company for seven years, and before that he worked with a home entertainment retail store for three years after he earned his degree in marketing.

Blaire is responsible for coordinating the advertising campaign for all 14 stores in the region. A major part of the campaign involves store hours, which had traditionally been from 10 a.m. to 8 p.m., Monday through Saturday. The minimum number of hours required by the national office is 40 per week. However, several of the managers have been pressuring lately to change the store hours, especially those from downtown areas. They maintain that their business is minimal after 6 p.m., so they would like to close earlier. Meanwhile, the suburban stores want to stay open later because they do more business in the evening. According to the provisions of the franchise agreement, all the stores in a region must maintain the same store hours.

The problem is getting more attention from the store managers and is a frequent topic of discussion as Blaire makes his visits. Blaire has decided to have a meeting for all the managers so he can systematically analyze the problem of store hours.

Questions

1. What type of leadership style should Blaire use in this meeting? Why?
2. What meeting format would you recommend?
3. What special problems would you anticipate for this meeting?
4. What preliminary arrangements are particularly important for this meeting?
5. Do you think it is a good idea for Blaire to have a meeting, or should he make this decision about hours himself?

Case 13-2.

Keeping the Meeting on the Topic

Waith Manufacturing Company's data processing department was preparing to implement a new computerized production information system at its new Madison plant. The project was divided into two parts. One consisted of the installation of a new computer network at the plant and the development of new database programs. The second involved hooking the plant's network into the company intranet so all departments had access to the production reports.

Alonzo Mendoza was the systems analyst responsible for the development and implementation of the project. Janet DeLaura was a lead programmer under Mendoza working on the plant side of the project. Bill Synge was the other lead programmer responsible for the intranet. Mendoza scheduled a series of weekly status meetings with DeLaura and Synge to ensure the project was moving along as scheduled and to allow for discussion of critical problems. One month before the scheduled implementation of the project, Mendoza called a special meeting to develop the actual series of tasks needed for the final system conversion. During this meeting, Mendoza outlined the major tasks concerning the whole project that had to be done on that last day.

He then solicited input from DeLaura and Synge. DeLaura spoke up immediately and began talking about several new problems that had surfaced on her side of the project. Mendoza interrupted her, saying those problems would be discussed at the regular status meeting since this meeting had been called to develop final conversion tasks only. DeLaura became irritated and was silent for a few minutes. Synge said he had a few items to add to the conversion list and covered the first two tasks. Then he said the last task covered reminded him of a current problem he had in the interface program. Mendoza replied brusquely that only conversion tasks would be discussed at this meeting. Neither DeLaura nor Synge had much to say during the rest of the meeting.

Questions

1. What would you have done to keep the meeting on the right topic?
2. What technique might Mendoza have used to avoid interfering with the flow of ideas?
3. What might DeLaura and Synge have done to improve communications?

Endnotes

1. Rick Casey, "The Katrina Coffee Klatch," *Houston Chronicle*, September 14, 2005, p. 1B
2. H. Simon, *The New Science of Management Decision* (New York: Harper and Row, 1960).
3. P. S. Goodman, E. Ravlin, and M. Schminke, "Understanding Groups in Organizations," in *Research in Organizational Behavior*, vol. 9, eds. I. B. M. Staw and L. L. Cummings (Greenwich, CT: JAI Press, 1987), pp. 121–73.
4. Lester Coch and John R. P. French, Jr., "Overcoming Resistance to Change," *Human Relations* 1, no. 4 (1948), pp. 512–32.
5. "Korn/Ferry International Executive Quiz," n.d., www.ekorn-ferry.com (April 9, 2006).
6. Adapted from James W. Moore, *Some Folks Feel the Rain: Others Just Get Wet* (Nashville, TN: Dimensions for Living, 1999).
7. Richard H. Hall, *Organizations*, 5th ed. (Englewood Cliffs, NJ: Prentice Hall, 1991), p. 180.
8. M. E. Gist, E. A. Locks, and M. S. Taylor, "Organizational Behavior: Group Structure, Process, and Effectiveness," *Journal of Management* 13, no. 2 (1987), pp. 237–57.
9. I. L. Janis, *Victims of Groupthink* (Boston: Houghton Mifflin, 1972).
10. G. Moorhead, R. Ference, and C. P. Neck, "Group Decision Fiascoes Continue: Space Shuttle Challenger and a Revised Groupthink Framework," *Human Relations* 44, no. 4 (1991), pp. 539–50.
11. T. Hensley and G. Griffin, "Victims of Groupthink: The Kent State University Board of Trustees and the 1977 Gymnasium Controversy," *Journal of Conflict Resolution* 30, no. 4 (1986), pp. 497–531.
12. C. Von Bergen and R. J. Kirk, "Groupthink: When Too Many Heads Spoil the Decision," *Management Review*, March 1978, p. 46.
13. Robert Towensen, *Up the Organization* (Greenwich, CT: Fawcett, 1970), p. 171.
14. A. C. Filley, R. F. House, and S. Kerr, Managerial Process and Organizational Behavioral, 2d ed. (Glenview, IL: Scott Foresman & Company, 1976).
15. P. Slater, "Contrasting Correlates of Group Size," *Sociometry* 21, no. 1 (1958), pp. 129–39.
16. J. M. Levine and R. Moreland, "Progress in Small Group Research," *Annual Review of Psychology* 41 (1990), pp. 585–634.
17. K. G. Stoneman and A. M. Dickinson, "Individual Performance as a Function of Group Contingencies and Group Size," *Journal of Organizational Behavior Management* 10, no. 1 (1989), pp. 131–50.

18. J. R. Hackman and C. G. Morris, "Group Tasks, Group Interaction Process and Group Performance Effectiveness: A Review and Proposed Integration," in *Advances in Experimental Social Psychology*, vol. 8, ed. I. L. Berkowitz (New York: Academic Press, 1975), pp. 1–50.

19. N. Shawchuck, *Taking a Look at Your Leadership Style* (Downers Grove, IL: Organizational Research Press, 1978).

20. Brad Johnson, "Secrets of Successful IT Teams: Socially Connected Employees," *CIO*, May 9, 2008, www.cio.com/article/print/354814 (retrieved June 5, 2008).

21. Liz Hughes, "Do's and Don'ts of Effective Team Leadership," *WIB, Magazine of the American Business Women's Association*, January–February 2004, p. 10.

22. David R. Weibold, "Making Meetings More Successful: Plans, Formats, and Procedures for Group Problem-Solving," *Journal of Business Communication* 16, no. 3 (Summer 1979), p. 8.

23. John Dewey, *How We Think* (Boston: D. C. Heath, 1910).

24. Alexander F. Osborn, *Applied Imagination* (New York: Scribners, 1957).

25. Marvin E. Shaw, *Group Dynamics*, 3rd ed. (New York: McGraw-Hill, 1981), p. 57.

26. Andrè L. Delbecq, Andrew H. Van De Ven, and David H. Gustafson, *Group Techniques for Program Planning* (Glenview, IL: Scott, Foresman, 1975).

27. A. H. Van De Ven and A. L. Delbecq, "The Effectiveness of Nominal, Delphi, and Interacting Group Decision-Making Processes," *Academy of Management Journal* 17, no. 4 (December 1974), pp. 605–21.

28. John E. Jones, "Dealing with Disruptive Individuals in Meetings," *1980 Annual Handbook for Group Facilitators*, ed. J. William Pfeiffer and John E. Jones (San Diego: University Associates, 1980), p. 161.

29. D. J. Isenberg, "Group Polarization: A Critical Review and Meta-analysis," *Journal of Personality and Social Psychology* 50, no. 4 (1986), pp. 1141–51.

30. Lawrence N. Loban, "Question: The Answer to Meeting Participation," *Supervision*, January 1972, pp. 11–13.

31. "3M Meeting Network: Articles and Advice," n.d., www.3m.com/meetingnetwork/readingroom/meetingguide_minutes.html (June 12, 2006).

Chapter **Fourteen**

Making Formal Presentations

It usually takes me more than three weeks to prepare a good impromptu speech.

—*Mark Twain, American humorist and author*

Managers today find that presentation skills are important for a multitude of situations. At any time, they might be called on to present a product report, a marketing status report, a persuasive report to convince upper management to accept a new product design, a financial report, or an after-dinner speech to honor the winner of a cost-saving campaign.

For several reasons, the value of competency in presentational speaking is likely to grow.[1] First, as organizations become more complex, managers are often called on to present proposals and make explanations to large numbers of people. Second, products and services also are becoming more complex. The public may require detailed explanations of their function and/or design.

No matter what the topic, a presentation is a critical form of communication. It is generally given to a group of decision makers on an important topic. It is essential that these decision makers have timely and understandable information.[2] To be effective in making such presentations, managers need to understand essential strategies. To assist you in meeting these challenges, this chapter describes steps in planning, organizing, and delivering formal presentations.

PLANNING YOUR PRESENTATION

When beginning to think about your presentation, consider your purpose, length of time to speak, and audience.

Purpose

The first step in planning an effective presentation is to determine the purpose. The purpose of business presentations is generally to inform, convince, or cause action. Some presentations have multiple purposes. When, for example, an engineering

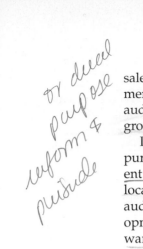

sales representative presents a product design to a client's engineering management group, she might have two purposes in mind. She will want to inform the audience of the product's technical features, and she will want to persuade the group to order the product.

In some situations, the exact purpose is easy to determine, but in others the purpose may be complex because the speaker and the audience have two different goals. For instance, the audience may want to know the most cost-effective location for a new manufacturing plant. The speaker, however, may want the audience to accept a certain location that has a special need for economic development. In other words, the audience wants to be informed, whereas the speaker wants to persuade.

The purpose may also vary within the group. Consider an audience that consists of five people: a vice president, a production superintendent, a director of finance, a marketing manager, and a personnel director. Suppose they were all attending a presentation comparing the relative success of two products introduced in a test market three months ago. What is "relative success" to each audience member? Each will look at the products from a different perspective because of differing functional responsibilities. The marketing manager may think in terms of market share, whereas the finance manager may look at only the cost factor. What type of information should the speaker emphasize?

The power and status of the different audience members can also influence the overall purpose. One member's viewpoint may initially differ from that of another member, but the more powerful person can quickly influence the less powerful member. In the previous example, the vice president may simply say that the most important consideration is the expansion of production facilities required by the two new products. Suddenly, the definition of "relative success" has changed again. Though the goal of informing the audience has remained the same, the information required to meet this goal has been shaped by the audience.

The best way to ensure clarity of purpose is to write out a purpose statement. Not only does this act force you to think about the purpose, but also the written statement can then be presented to an associate or to likely audience members for their reaction. The feedback will help you define the purpose clearly and accurately. Figure 14–1 will help you write out your purpose statement. Just fill in the blanks.

Once you have clearly established your purpose, you are ready to consider cost and time to determine what expense can be justified. One five-minute presentation might involve hundreds of work hours and cost thousands of dollars; another could require a minimum of effort. As with any managerial communication, a manager must make strategic decisions.

FIGURE 14–1
Your
Presentation
Purpose

I want to tell you _____
                                    (content)

So you will _____
                              (purpose)

Length of the Presentation

Sometimes managers have no choice here, as when they are given a set amount of time to speak during a meeting or conference. In such cases, it is crucial to stay within the assigned time limit. The audience is probably listening to a number of such presentations. When many speakers exceed their time limits, the audience becomes less and less receptive to the proposals of the transgressors.

Even when speakers are given some choice on the length of the presentations, most make them too long rather than too short. Remember that it is difficult to hold people's attention beyond 20 minutes. When a presentation goes beyond 15 minutes, divide it into major segments by using reviews, questions, or graphics. One of history's most inspirational public speakers, President Franklin Delano Roosevelt, advised that, when presenting, one should "be sincere, be brief, be seated."

Audience understanding does not necessarily last as long as the speaker's. Just because a speaker is eloquent for an hour does not mean others are listening and understanding. To improve effectiveness, watch the audience for nonverbal and verbal feedback to evaluate comprehension.[3] This feedback will probably indicate it is best to keep the presentation short.

Audience Analysis

At the same time that effective managers analyze the purpose, they begin to analyze the audience. In any communication process, people naturally tend to become self-centered. Thus, a speaker may concentrate on his or her interests and forget about the audience. One group of consultants on oral presentations noted that managers often prepare messages that fail to tell the listeners what they want and need to hear, but instead focus on the speaker's interests.[4]

The most successful presentations are prepared with a particular audience in mind and are organized to suit their knowledge, attitudes, likes, and dislikes. Many presentations are technically well delivered, but they fail because the speakers do not anticipate audience reaction.

Though audience analysis is part of the "pretalk" preparation, a speaker should also be ready to analyze on the spot. During delivery, the presentation may be modified to reflect audience factors not available in advance. For instance, you would need to alter your presentation if you found that a critical decision maker needing special information decided at the last minute to attend the presentation. Nevertheless, when a thorough audience analysis precedes a presentation, few last-minute adjustments should be required.

The Audience Analysis Guide Sheet provided at the end of this chapter is designed to assist you in analyzing audiences. Once all the questions have been answered, it might be beneficial to ask another person to answer them as well, to compare answers. This feedback is especially important when the presentation is critical but little is known about the audience.

If you already know the audience well, say, for an internal presentation, a thorough analysis is not necessary. For instance, an internal auditor who gives a quarterly report to a bank's board of directors may not need a separate analysis each quarter. However, a periodic review of the audience may remind the speaker about some of its special characteristics. It may be easy to forget that the interests, technical knowledge, or attitudes differ from one board member to another; thus, a quick audience analysis will help reorient the speaker.

ORGANIZING YOUR PRESENTATION

The second step is organizing the presentation. Every presentation has a beginning, a middle, and an ending. These three main parts are described next. However, to a great extent, your purpose and audience will determine how you structure your presentation.

Introduction

The most crucial part of a presentation is the introduction. A presentation should begin with a statement that captures the audience's attention.

Quite often, a speaker will begin with humor or trite remarks. Depending on the gravity of your message, these timeworn openings may not be appropriate.

Though common, a speaker should rarely begin with an apology. Beginning with "I know that you do not want to be here," or "I realize that it is late in the day," or "I am not much of a speaker" does little to enhance speaker credibility and may detract from the audience's perception of the meeting. Instead, begin the presentation with a positive statement that has impact. Strategies for getting the attention of business audiences are listed next:

- **A startling statement:** "If our costs continue to increase over the next five years at the rate they have in the past five, we will have to charge over $150 for our lowest-priced shirt. Today, I will present four strategies for reducing costs in . . ."

- **A hypothetical statement:** "What would happen if we could no longer obtain the silver we need to produce XY 115? I am going to show you a viable substitute for that metal."

- **Some historical event or story:** "It was just eight years ago this week that we purchased the Bordin division, our first major acquisition. This presentation will review the progress of our purchases."

- **A rhetorical question:** "What will the inflation rate be in 2010? Will the energy problem continue? This presentation will outline the reasons why we need a market projection plan."

- **Reference to some current event:** "On Tuesday, February 19, Millville had a chemical fire that killed 5 people and injured 15. To avoid that kind of disaster in our operations, we need to increase our budget for safety training."

- **A quotation:** "The national director of the health department has stated, 'The number one health problem today is alcoholism. One in ten Americans has a drinking problem.' This serious problem is one of the many reasons we need an employee assistance program."

- **A personal anecdote:** "The other day I was talking to one of our long-time customers when she said the reason she keeps banking here is that nothing ever changes. That got me thinking about our reputation for stability in a chaotic economy. But I also began to wonder whether we've become stagnant."

Whatever strategy is selected, a speaker's first goal is to develop a dynamic attention-getting opening.[5] Its success will set the tone for the rest of the presentation. Next, the speaker should clearly state the purpose (inform, convince, cause action, inspire, introduce, congratulate, and so on) and the topic. Even if your purpose and topic were disclosed on the agenda or by your meeting moderator, it's a good idea to restate them in your introduction to avoid any confusion.

The discussion of listening in Chapter 7 indicates the difficulty of maintaining attention for a long period. By telling your listeners what is to come and why, you encourage them to make an effort. Thus, the third part of your introduction should establish the audience's motivation to listen. The speaker explains the significance of what the audience is about to hear and how it pertains to their interests and needs. A common error is to focus instead on the significance of the content to the *speaker*. While statements such as "I care deeply about this" might increase speaker credibility, they do not always lead to the listeners' agreeing to care, too. The best word to use at this point is "you," as in "After hearing my presentation, *you* will be able to . . ." Focusing on audience benefits will also help build the speaker's credibility, which is especially critical in persuasive speaking.

In some situations, it may also be appropriate to give the audience some directions regarding interruptions. For instance, you may ask them to jot down their questions and raise them after your remarks are finished. Unfortunately, in small meetings, the listeners will often feel free to interrupt with questions. It is important not to let the audience take control of your presentation. On the other hand, you can ask meeting members for their reaction and maintain a dialogue throughout the presentation. Effective speakers usually stay away from the "I talk, you listen" syndrome, which often loses the interest of the group.

One optional subsection of the introduction is the establishment of the speaker's credentials. Obviously, if the audience knows the speaker well, this can be omitted. For external or new audiences, however, it is important that they perceive the speaker as an expert on the topic. It is risky to rely on the meeting moderator's introduction to achieve this goal. Instead, during your opening remarks you might describe the research you conducted, the extent of your involvement in the topic, your position title, or even an anecdote that will enhance your credibility.

The final subsection should be a preview of the main points you will cover. Forecasting your main points will clarify the structure of the presentation and help your audience stay on track. You might even enumerate the points so your audience can "count down" as they listen. This preview acts as a transition between the introduction and the body of your presentation.

TABLE 14–1
Parts of the
Introduction

Parts of the Introduction
Attention step
Purpose statement
Motivation to listen
Directions about interruptions (optional)
Speaker credibility (optional)
Preview of main points

Table 14–1 summarizes the parts of a presentation introduction: an attention-getting opening, a purpose statement, motivation to listen, any ground rules regarding questions/participation, establishment of speaker credibility (optional), and a preview of the main points. Next, we will describe strategies for organizing the body of your presentation.

Persuasive Presentations

As mentioned earlier, the purpose of a business presentation is generally informative or persuasive. The body of your presentation should be organized according to your purpose. This section shows you some basic organizational structures for the body of a persuasive presentation. The following section covers organizational structures for the body of an informative presentation.

Howell and Bormann discuss three patterns that provide meaningful strategies for persuasive situations: the problem-solving pattern, the state-the-case-and-prove-it approach, and the psychological-progressive pattern.[6]

The first pattern, *problem solving*, is most often effective in the discussion of a relatively complicated problem, especially if the audience is largely ignorant of the facts or is likely to be hostile to the message. With this approach, the speaker leads the audience through a series of steps, beginning with a definition of the problem, then moving to an exploration of the problem (which includes an examination of causes and effects), then enumerating and evaluating representative solutions, and, when appropriate, recommending the best solution.

The manager using this plan must be especially well prepared on all aspects of the situation. The audience may not be familiar with the problem, its causes, and potential remedies, or an objective and logical solution. It is the most common pattern of argument in business presentations.

The second pattern of organization for persuasion, *state the case and prove it*, is relatively simple. It entails the straightforward development of a central thesis with supporting arguments. Normally, each supporting element begins with a contention or topic sentence followed immediately by substantiation. Typically, the pattern consists of an introduction followed by a thesis statement; then each supporting contention has appropriate elaboration and support. The presentation closes with a summary repeating the proposition.

Whereas the problem-solving pattern is an inductive organizational approach, the state-the-case-and-prove-it approach is deductive. It begins with a general conclusion and then justifies it. This second approach is appropriate for organizing discussions of familiar much-argued topics. The audience familiar with a topic has no need to explore it gradually and comprehensively. It is also used in advocacy, such as courtroom settings.

The third organizational strategy for persuasive presentations, the *psychological-progressive pattern*, involves five steps: (1) arouse, (2) dissatisfy, (3) gratify, (4) visualize, and (5) act. Applying this pattern, a manager first uses an appropriate attention-getter. The next task is to demonstrate the nature and urgency of the problem in a way that sets out the difficulties, tensions, or pathos of a specific situation of immediate concern. Then, the speaker links his or her recommendation with the problem so the decision-making audience can understand the proposal as a viable solution.

The accepting audience usually needs to be moved both rationally and emotionally. Thus, the manager should focus on helping the audience to visualize how the recommendation will remedy the situation. Demonstrating the solution's implementation or providing a "free sample" often will clinch the audience's decision to comply. Finally, the speaker should state specifically and concretely what the audience must "do" or "believe" after listening to the presentation. Basically, the psychological-progressive pattern is a problem-solving approach that is ideally suited to presentations designed to innovate or effect change. It is the typical structure of television commercials.

A city manager asking the city council for an additional $300,000 in the budget for snow-removal equipment gives a clear example of the psychological-progressive approach. The request was made during June because the new budget began July 1.

> Remember last February when we had to cancel our city council meeting because of the snow and ice on the streets? Not only did we cancel the meeting, but some of us couldn't get to work, children couldn't get to school, and in some cases it was even difficult to buy groceries (**arouse**).
>
> This was not only an inconvenience, it was a potentially dangerous situation. Emergency health care could have been a problem. Fortunately, no emergencies developed. Furthermore, it cost employees lost work time, and it made our city look inefficient. Our city works manager, who has been with us more than 15 years, was extremely demoralized at the inability to do anything about the situation due to the shortage of equipment (**dissatisfy**).
>
> This problem can be solved with the purchase of four additional plows. These plows have been offered at a special price from Kast Manufacturing in Minneapolis, which has more than 20 years of experience with snowplows. They also provide free delivery of the plows and a three-year warranty on all the hydraulic systems, and an eight-year warranty on the main blade and all structural components. In other words, this purchase will take care of our needs for a long time.
>
> With this addition and the resolution of the snow-removal problem, this council will be identified as a group with vision and the ability for long-range planning rather than short-term reactions (**gratify and visualize**).
>
> I am asking you to approve an additional $300,000 for next year's budget so that we can purchase four more snowplows. This could then become part of the city works equipment budget (**action**). This action will resolve our snow-removal problem next year and for many years in the future.

Persuasion Variables

As the preceding discussion indicated, different persuasive approaches are suited to different occasions or circumstances. To be a truly strategic attempt at persuasion, however, your efforts and ultimately your success should be moderated by a number of variables. These variables are categorized under the labels of sender, message, receiver, and context (see Figure 14–2).[7] The onion model discussed in Chapter 2 provides background information about each of these variables. Context is described as a factor in the model's first, outermost, layer. Sender and receiver variables are described in the second layer of the model. And message variables appear in the third layer.

Among variables associated with the *sender* of a persuasive message, probably the most significant variable is the speaker's credibility. Dimensions of speaker credibility include competence and trustworthiness; education, occupation, and experience; the citation of evidence; and the position advocated (in other words, how much of a change in attitude the speaker is asking for). Whether or not the speaker is liked will probably affect success in persuading. Also, the degree of similarity between the speaker and the audience frequently affects success. Even physical attractiveness has been linked to persuasiveness in some studies.

A number of *message* variables can contribute to the success of a persuasive effort. The order of the information is one variable. Should a persuader be direct or indirect? Research indicates that the indirect approach is generally best for hostile audiences. Another factor involves whether a person should be explicit or implicit in stating what is desired. Though most studies indicate that being explicit is generally best, some evidence supports being implicit for audiences that are highly intelligent and educated and/or familiar with the subject.

Another issue relevant to message content is whether a persuader should ignore or refute opposing arguments. Usually it is best to refute them. The persuader should usually address relevant obstacles. Finally, most studies conclude

FIGURE 14–2
Persuasion
Variables

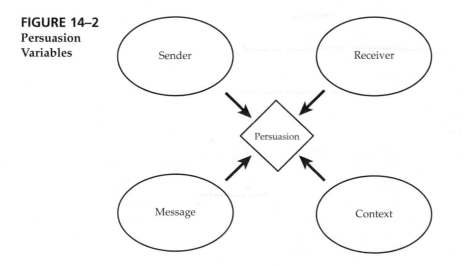

that concrete examples are more persuasive than statistical summaries, because they are more vivid and bring the evidence to life. Business presenters often believe that "the numbers" are automatically persuasive. However, specific cases, stories of dissatisfied customers, and the like can be far more convincing due to their emotional impact.

Among *receiver* variables, one might consider the general persuasibility of the person. Some people are simply more susceptible to persuasion than are others. Are there personality traits related to ease or difficulty with which a receiver is persuaded? Research provides inconsistent answers to that question. For example, some studies show self-esteem positively related to persuasibility, while others show a negative relationship. One possible explanation is that some personality traits provide effects that both enhance and prohibit persuasion. For example, intelligent receivers would be better able to understand persuasive messages, but they would also be better able to see weaknesses in a message and think of counterarguments.

Receiver readiness to accept appeals is a complex factor. Successful persuasive speakers conduct extensive audience analyses and plan to present appeals that are most likely to move their listeners. Audience demographics, knowledge levels, and attitudes all must be considered when choosing material for presentation. For example, a manager persuading an audience of factory workers to adopt a new process should explain the benefits of the process to the workers, such as improved safety, rather than benefits to the company, such as increased profitability or productivity. Hourly employees may interpret management buzzwords such as "efficiency" as "layoffs," or "quality" as "more work."

Context variables include primacy/recency effects, media, and persistence effects. In general, the order of points in a persuasive message (first or second) is not related to success. There is, however, some evidence that primacy effects are more likely to be found with interesting, controversial, and familiar topics, so begin with your strongest reason when persuading a hostile audience. Recency effects are more common with topics that are relatively uninteresting, noncontroversial, and unfamiliar, so build toward your strongest reason when persuading an apathetic audience.

With regard to the many media available today, research shows that audiences are more easily persuaded in face-to-face situations than when the message is filtered through media such as telephone or video. One exception is the written word—audiences tend to believe what they read, either in books, onscreen, or online. But electronic, visual, and auditory media appear to act as a buffer. A disembodied voice or a televised image can be dramatic, but the most powerful speakers prefer to look directly at their listeners as they present their case. This phenomenon helps to explain the amount of time, money, and effort that political candidates expend traveling and speaking to voters instead of relying solely on media coverage.

The last context variable is the persistence of the persuasive message. Generally, persuasive effects will decline over time. Thus, for maximum effectiveness, persuasive messages should be delivered as temporally close as possible to the point of decision or action. Thus, politicians usually spend the bulk of their advertising budget in the week before the election.

Though no one can prescribe a guaranteed plan for persuading people, managers should consider the variables earlier described as they develop their persuasive strategies. To the extent that you do, you should find that your rate of persuasive success increases appreciably.

Informative Presentations

We have seen that managers generally use three organizational patterns to develop the body of their persuasive presentations: the problem-solving pattern, the state-the-case-and-prove-it pattern, and the psychological-progressive pattern. But what if the purpose of the presentation is to describe or inform? In these situations, it is best to organize the information in a definite sequence. Clarity may demand that a subject be presented one way as opposed to another, or the subject itself may suggest the best pattern or arrangement. Some arrangement possibilities and examples of appropriate topics for each sequence are listed next.

- **Spatial or geographic:** Description of our new facility's layout
- **Political and economic categories:** Sales of our product line for various social groups
- **Importance:** Changes to employees' benefits package
- **Chronological:** History and future of our company
- **Advantages and disadvantages:** Various models of fax machines on the market
- **Comparison and contrast:** Where we stand among competitors in our industry
- **Structure and function:** New management layer being added to our company

A typical informative speaking situation is when a manager must explain new work procedures or processes. Giving instructions can be a challenge. The wrong strategy is simply telling employees once what to do, ending with "Do you have any questions?" Listeners may hesitate to ask questions for fear of seeming uncooperative or unintelligent. So instead they return to their tasks, try out the new procedure, and make mistakes. Rather than risk the boss's criticism, they may ask a co-worker for help, thus often compounding the problems and errors.

A better strategy for giving instructions is to use "tell—show—do." First the manager explains the steps in the new procedure, contrasting it with the current one. If the task is complex, the manager should cluster the steps into groups or stages. For example, instead of describing a 12-step procedure, the speaker could describe three stages, with four steps per stage. Dividing a body of information into smaller gulps makes it less daunting to listeners. After "telling" the audience about the new procedure, the manager "shows" the audience how to do it, either demonstrating it personally or using a model. More audiences are visual learners than auditory learners, so a demonstration is often very effective. Finally, the manager lets the employees try the new procedure themselves. The manager should offer liberal feedback and encouragement as she observes their efforts, since positive reinforcement is a powerful motivator for learning.

Whatever the division of the topic or the order in which it is to be presented, it is important to have a definite, logical, and strategic plan for the body of an informative presentation. And smooth transition is the key to the clarity of the plan's

TABLE 14–2
Types of
Transitions

Function	Example
Show the relationship between ideas	and, in addition, also, or, however, on the other hand, by comparison, furthermore
Enumerate ideas	first, to begin, my second point is, finally, in conclusion
Summarize ideas	Now that we have discussed its features, let's turn our attention to its benefits.
Emphasize ideas	If you remember nothing else, please remember this:

organization. A bridge or link must exist between units so the audience can follow the organizational plan. As the speaker moves to a new unit, this link may take the form of a simple announcement that a new unit will now be discussed. More helpful to the audience, however, is a transition that explains how the next point will compare with the previous one. Another device is the repetition of key words or phrases for emphasis. Examples of transitions at four levels of complexity appear in Table 14–2. A wise informative speaker will use them liberally to keep the audience on track.

Evidence

Whether the speaker's purpose is to inform or persuade, the speaker relies on evidence in the body of the presentation. The type of information and corresponding research required largely depend on which of the two types of evidence is required: fact or opinion. Evidence of *fact* is an objective description of something using empirical evidence without interpretation or judgment. A fact can be proven—that is, it is either true or untrue. Evidence of *opinion* is the application of interpretation and judgment rather than truth.

Business speakers often are expected to present facts, especially statistics, as evidence for their main points. Audiences respect speakers who "deliver the numbers." However, research consistently shows that facts, such as the features of a product, are not persuasive in themselves. Audiences may value rational thought but instead make decisions on the basis of their emotions.

A body of recent research in neuroscience and psychology highlights the important role that emotions play in decision making.[8] In particular, empirical studies of investor decision making support the belief that individuals do not act rationally and consider all available information when trading stocks. Both professional and amateur investors let emotions drive their investment decisions instead. Whitney Tilson, a highly successful U.S. money manager and founder of Tilson Capital Partners, suggests that overconfidence is the emotion that most often trumps rationality. Moreover, the more difficult the task (such as predicting the price of a stock), the greater the degree of overconfidence. Overtrading is one example. Tilson reports a study of 78,000 investors at a large U.S. discount brokerage whose average annual turnover was around 80 percent. The least active quintile, with an average annual turnover of 1 percent, scored a 17.5 percent annual return. The S&P return was 16.9 percent over the same period. The most active 20 percent of investors, with annual turnover of greater than 100 percent, scored just a 10 percent annual return. Tilson concludes that investors habitually chase performance irrationally, although it doesn't work.[9] The take-home point here is that business speakers who rely on factual evidence should be aware of its limitations in convincing people to behave in certain ways.

Turning to opinions as a form of evidence, three types of opinions may be used in a presentation: personal, lay, and expert. While all managers probably support their presentations with personal views from time to time, success in using personal opinions for support largely depends on the manager's credibility with the audience. A manager uses lay opinion when citing the opinions of ordinary people (nonexperts) such as customers, workers, or the public. This source is prevalent in presentations on marketing or personnel problems.

A manager uses expert opinion when citing an authority to provide evidence. This form of evidence works well when objective facts are difficult to find or when the speaker is unknown to the audience. However, the expert chosen must be respected, objective, and possess actual expertise. For instance, a baseball player may be an expert in baseball but not on the quality of paint, advertising notwithstanding.

Different presentation strategies require different evidence. In persuasive presentations, the psychological-progressive pattern generally requires less factual information and more emotional appeals. Consequently, it places more emphasis on opinion than on empirical information. The state-the-case-and-prove-it and problem-solving patterns call for extensive facts in most situations. Opinion is advisable in the latter cases when the manager has a high degree of credibility, and expert opinion is valuable when there is no doubt about the authority of the expert.

Audiences judge evidence, whether fact or opinion, according to its timeliness and its source. Personal opinion is the weakest type of evidence, unless the speaker has high credibility—authority, power, dynamism, trustworthiness, and expertise. Thus, a manager is wise to cite details about the research conducted, including when and from where the evidence was retrieved. In situations where the audience does not know the speaker, the credibility of the evidence becomes crucial to speaker credibility.

To summarize, the body of any presentation is the longest and most complex part. It must be carefully organized, and the organizational pattern must be made apparent to the audience. Speakers' options for organizing the main points in the body of their presentation are determined by their purpose (informative or persuasive). After the main points have been selected and arranged in a logical sequence, they each must be supported and developed by evidence (opinions or facts). The most common organizational patterns for the body of persuasive and informative presentations appear in Table 14–3.

Closing

The end of the presentation is relatively easy to prepare, yet crucial to the presentation's final impact. It should contain a brief summary of the purpose and the main points covered in their appropriate order. Once the presentation is finished, make sure it is finished. Do not present any new information or leave a question

TABLE 14–3
Sequencing
Options for
Main Points

Persuasive Purpose	Informative Purpose
Problem-Solving	Spatial/geographic
State-the-Case-and-Prove-It	Political/economic categories
Psychological-Progressive	Importance, chronological, advantages/disadvantages, comparison/contrast, structure/function

unanswered. Repeat the significance of the message to the audience, as stated in the introduction, to ensure retention. If some action is to be solicited from the audience, make the expectations clear. And leave the audience with a powerful "final thought" or challenge. Whatever the specific nature of the ending, it should strongly and clearly communicate that the speaker is ending. Too often, speakers just trickle off with a "Well, that's it; thanks for listening" ending. Your audience is listening closely at this point. They will be affected by your final impression as well as your first impression.

Table 14–4 summarizes the parts of a presentation's conclusion.

Questions

Speakers solicit questions after the presentation to allow for appropriate additions and clarifications. In a situation where the group may be inhibited, but questions are important to open the dialogue, the speaker may want to ask one member of the audience to be ready with a question to stimulate further questions.

Several suggestions are helpful when answering questions:

- If the original question was not audible to everyone, repeat it.
- Do not allow one person to ask all the questions.
- Select questions from all areas of the room, not just from one section.
- Do not evaluate a question by saying, "That's a good question." Such a response could be inadvertently telling others that their questions are not good.
- Do not answer with responses such as "as I said earlier," or "well, obviously," or "anyone would know the answer to that." Such responses can be quite demeaning.
- Look at the whole group when answering a question, not just the person who asked it.
- When you have finished, do not ask "Does that answer your question?" because that makes you seem tentative. If you didn't answer their question satisfactorily, they will likely let you know.

TABLE 14–4
Parts of the
Closing

Purpose statement
Main points
Significance of the message
Call to action (optional)
Final thought/challenge

- Do not point a finger to call on a questioner. It is a scolding pose and may appear authoritarian.
- If you have no answer to a question, it is best to admit it.
- Allow sufficient time to answer all questions.

PREPARING YOUR VISUAL AIDS

Visual aids are a must for all but the most informal business presentations. They represent another way of maintaining audience attention and involvement. Since the spoken word is, at best, limited in communication, and since its sound is transitory, the listener may miss the message, and the opportunity to hear it again may never arise. However, visual support can help overcome these limitations. Additionally, visual aids can clarify complex information. You can successfully use visual aids in the introduction, body, and closing of a presentation.

Criteria

Good visual aids make a positive impression on the audience and justify the time spent in their preparation. An effective aid is one designed to fit the speaker, the audience, and the room. Four criteria for an effective visual aid are:

1. *Visibility.* The visual aid must be easy to read. Some speakers attempt to make visual aids from printed material, but these are generally poor because lettering on visual aids must be larger and bolder than normal printer lettering. Also, technical drawings cannot easily be used; lines on many of the drawings are lost because they are so faint. Little is more irritating to an audience than to be told there is something important on the visual aid that they cannot see. Have the artwork drawn to eliminate unnecessary lines and to make essential lines heavier on the drawing. Use a readable and consistent font, especially when using PowerPoint. Generally, a sans serif font is appropriate, such as Calibri, Arial, or Helvetica. Be careful not to overuse uppercase, bold, and italics, all of which are harder to read than regular font in sentence case.[10]

2. *Clarity.* Clarity refers to what an audience understands from a visual. Make the main points easy to identify. Color is a good way to focus the audience's attention on the important parts of the visual. Though statistics show that audiences remember only 20 percent of what they hear but 80 percent of what they see, they must be able to understand what they see to remember it.[11] When designing a slide for PowerPoint, use basic solid background colors. Choose light colors for text. Avoid busy backgrounds, distracting color combinations, and low-contrast color combinations, such as black on red or medium blue on dark blue.[12]

3. *Simplicity.* After determining the content of a visual aid, look for ways to simplify it. Nothing should appear on the visual aid except the content relevant to the specific ideas to be communicated. Decorating a PowerPoint slide with clip art, borders, even the company logo, can be distracting. Most templates for computer slide shows include extra design elements that may be colorful

but are irrelevant to the speaker's message. Additionally, overused templates can communicate a lack of originality.

4. *Relevance.* Do not use a graphic or sound effect just because it is handy or pretty when it was originally prepared for some other purpose. Impressive special effects can backfire if used merely to impress. For example, in *Guide to PowerPoint*, authors Mary Munter and Dave Paradi suggest not using any of the 3-D chart or graph effects in a PowerPoint presentation because they are unnecessary and confusing for the audience.[13]

Keep several rules in mind when designing your visual aids. These are not magic formulas, but they are helpful guidelines. First, no text visual aid should contain more than six lines. Second, no line should contain more than six words. To meet these first two rules, a speaker may need to use more than one visual aid or design overlays to build a more complex visual. In a PowerPoint presentation, overloading a slide with too many lines of text will divert the audience's attention from listening to reading. Avoid full sentences, unless you decide to quote an entire passage. Think of the slide as a billboard; just because you have the space doesn't mean you have to fill it. With PowerPoint, less is more.

Third, rows or columns of data should be shown a single line at a time by using an accentuation technique to keep the audience's attention on the point of discussion. Simple accentuation techniques include pointing with a pencil or laser pointer, cutting a sheet of paper on the flip chart to reveal only the items under discussion, or using the "build" feature of PowerPoint. During a PowerPoint presentation you can change the cursor from an arrow to a pen by pressing Ctrl-P on the keyboard. Then, you can use the cursor to circle or underline data or words for accentuation. Ctrl-E changes the cursor to an eraser. Ctrl-A brings back the arrow.

Along with visibility, clarity, simplicity, and relevance, the timing of the visual aid contributes to its effectiveness. Since the visual aid is a graphical message intended to complement the verbal message, both messages should be presented at the same time. An aid should not be visible until it is used, and it should be removed from sight after it has been discussed so it does not distract the audience. A common mistake of many managers is to leave a flip chart open or keep a slide on screen after the need for the visual has passed.[14] An easy way to hide a slide while you are presenting is to press B on the keyboard (the screen goes to black). Pressing B again brings back the slide. Similarly, the W key makes the screen go white.

Types

The criteria for effective visual aids are universal, but a speaker must still choose a particular type of visual aid. Though the choice will be influenced by the size and type of audience, most business conference rooms still are equipped with *overhead projectors,* and many business speakers still use the overhead transparency or foil. Because the room lights are left on and the speaker faces the audience, the overhead projector allows the maximum relationship with the audience. Additionally, overheads ensure flexible presentation of the material: covering the visual and gradually revealing certain parts during the presentation, using overlays for added detail, and writing on the overhead with a marker. This simple method works well for internal, informal, or brief meetings.

The *whiteboard* and *flip chart* are impromptu speaking tools to be used only when there is insufficient time to prepare anything else. A right-handed speaker writing on the board or flip chart should stand to the right of the chart, facing the audience. If the speaker's back is turned and eye contact is lost, the audience's attention may dwindle. Handwritten visuals are rarely professional looking. However, spontaneous diagrams and flow charts can sometimes be a dramatic way to clarify complex processes under discussion or can be effective during brainstorming sessions.

The most common type of visual aid used for business presentations, of course, is <u>computer-generated graphics</u> such as those created in Microsoft PowerPoint. In the 15 years or so since it was introduced, PowerPoint has become the standard. One writer compared delivering a presentation without PowerPoint slides to serving French fries without ketchup. In busy corporate settings, absent audience members have been known to request copies of the slides, assuming that the visual aids contain all relevant information from the presentation. Another reason for its popularity is that the software is very user-friendly and, perhaps most importantly, almost universally available. One survey found over 90 percent of responding firms making presentations use PowerPoint graphics in-house.[15] In fact, companies are now incorporating presentation graphics software into their day-to-day internal communications and into their decision-making process.[16]

Recently, however, there has been a backlash against PowerPoint use, or more accurately, its abuse, in business presentations. Edward Tufte, one of the world's leading authorities on the presentation of visual information, condemns the software because it reduces the analytical quality of a presentation. Because only about 35–40 words fit on each slide, and because a typical slide is viewed for only about eight seconds, he argues that audiences cannot adequately link information together in a cohesive argument. Tufte criticizes the style-over-substance approach of the PowerPoint design guidelines and points out that the bureaucracy of bullets and multilevel lists not only oversimplifies ideas for the audience, but also damages the credibility of the presenter. There is growing concern that presenters have come to rely on PowerPoint as a crutch and use it in place of detailed technical reports.[17]

A tragic example of PowerPoint's misuse is the 2003 crash of the space shuttle Columbia. The Columbia Accident Investigation Board reported that NASA engineers, tasked with assessing possible wing damage during the mission, presented their findings in a confusing PowerPoint slide so crammed with bulleted items that it was almost impossible to analyze. The CAIB report noted, "It is easy to understand how a senior manager might read this PowerPoint slide and not realize that it addresses a life-threatening situation."[18]

One alternative to the traditional list of bullet points on PowerPoint slides is gaining popularity. The design strategy calls for placing an "assertion" as a complete sentence in the headline space at the top of a slide. Then images, equations, or charts that support the assertion appear in the body of the slide. Call-outs with arrows are sometimes added to explain the images (see Figure 14–3). This design at least partially assuages Tufte's challenges because it graphically displays relationships between ideas on the slide.[19]

Another point of controversy Tufte has called attention to is the lack of plagiarism controls included in the PowerPoint software. He believes the presentation software should be held to the same standards as any other scholarly paper or research report.[20] For better or worse, PowerPoint is the standard in American business presentation graphics. As such, managers need to learn to use computer-generated slide shows properly, following the principles outlined here.

Handouts are another form of visual aid. These written materials are different from the other visual aids because each member of the audience receives a copy, which may be used for reference during and after the presentation. Handouts are particularly valuable when the subject calls for such items as complicated charts and graphs, detailed regulations, points of law, or company policy. Often, the material can be distributed to the participants before the meeting, so less time is spent during the meeting for review. It is then possible to go directly to the discussion phase of the presentation.

When planning to distribute materials during the meeting, limit the information to what is required and do not distribute it until it is needed. Too many materials in front of the audience may distract them from the verbal message. The audience will be tempted to review the handout for one topic while you are discussing a different one. Naturally, this reduces the impact of the message.

FIGURE 14–3
Sample
PowerPoint
Slide Design

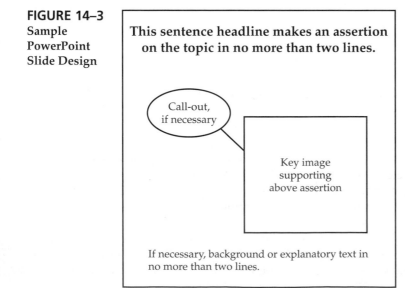

DELIVERING YOUR PRESENTATION

Now is the time for the real test: delivering the message. Thorough preparation will allow concentration on a number of elements that require attention during the delivery. A well-prepared speaker will have analyzed the audience and will have an idea of what to expect from the various members. The purpose and audience have been analyzed, the opening statement is ready, the message is organized, the closing is prepared, and visual aids are created.

Speaking Anxiety

What about stage fright? It might be consoling to know that about 60 percent of all speakers experience anxiety to some degree before speaking. A survey of 3,000 Americans revealed that the prospect of giving a speech brings forth people's greatest fear; they fear it even more than dying.[21] On this very subject, George Jessel, the late entertainer, once said, "The human brain is a wonderful organ. It starts to work as soon as you are born and doesn't stop until you get up to deliver a speech."

The best solution to anxiety is preparation. As you become better prepared to perform a task, your confidence generally increases, which, in turn, reduces anxiety. Rehearsal of the entire presentation is advisable when anxiety is particularly high. You should become more comfortable with each rehearsal.[22]

But no matter how well prepared you might be, some anxiety may remain. A small amount of tension or anxiety is good because it keeps a speaker alert; however, several techniques may be used when anxiety is so great that it may interfere with the presentation's effectiveness.

First, consider the value of the presentation and remember that the material is important. Believe that the audience is there to listen and that you have an opportunity to provide a valuable service. Carly Fiorina, former CEO of Hewlett-Packard, explains her poise and persuasiveness when before an audience thusly: "It doesn't matter whether I'm talking to 2 people, 10 people, or thousands of people. I think about it as though I'm talking to just one person. Every communication is a conversation."[23]

Second, it helps to sit with your eyes closed and take a few deep breaths. With hands relaxed and dangling to the side, rotate your head slowly while you concentrate on an especially pleasing thought (a mountain valley with beautiful flowers; soothing fluffy clouds floating across the sky; waves breaking on a beach).[24] Deep breathing oxygenates your brain, thus increasing alertness. It also relaxes tense muscles in your throat and neck. As a bonus, increasing the amount of air in your lungs ensures your voice will project farther. One minute of relaxation can be worth an hour of frantic preparation.

A third way to reduce anxiety is to memorize the first few remarks in the presentation. By the time these memorized comments have been presented, some of the initial anxiety should have subsided. Even though this part of the presentation has been memorized, it may be a good idea to have notes available just to increase confidence.

Fourth, planned bodily activity can help reduce anxiety. Strategic movements during the delivery can be used to control the higher level of energy produced by the anxiety. This movement may take the form of appropriate gestures or of walking to a laptop, flip chart, or screen.

Speaker Notes

How can notes be best arranged and used to support a managerial presentation? Traditionally, some people have advocated a precise outline following all the "proper" rules; others have maintained that 5-by-8-inch cards are essential. The "notes pages" feature in PowerPoint is handy. It gives you a printed sheet for each slide, with a representation of the slide at the top of the sheet and your notes about that slide appearing below it. Many speakers just use their PowerPoint slides as cues. Each person must find what works best for him or her.

Good speaker notes will help you channel your efforts toward effective delivery. Notes written clearly and concisely make it easy to maintain eye contact with the audience. The need to maintain eye contact with the audience supports the recommendation that speaker notes rather than graphics be used. Standing with your back to the audience while you read the speech off the screen is an all-too-common unprofessional speaking style.

Although notes can be a valuable source, they can easily become a psychological crutch. To make sure they don't become so, keep the following don'ts in mind.

- Don't twist, bend, smooth, or fold the notes in an aimless way because of nervousness. This behavior does nothing to relieve a speaker's anxiety, and it may increase the anxiety of the audience.
- Don't gaze at the notes out of a feeling of insecurity. Looking down to keep from looking at the audience can get to be a bad habit that physically and psychologically separates you from the audience.
- Don't write out your notes (or slides) in full sentences. You will be tempted to read the presentation aloud rather than speak extemporaneously from key points.
- Don't try to hide from the audience the fact that you are using notes. Why play games with the audience? The best procedure is to use notes openly, but only when necessary.

Nonverbal Aspects

Several nonverbal aspects of communication need to be considered during the delivery of a presentation, including eye contact, facial expressions, posture, gestures, and movement. Speakers are integral parts of the messages they convey, so how they present themselves affects the message directly.

The nonverbal components of communication discussed in Chapter 7 can apply to the speaking as well as to the listening role. For instance, just as eye contact is important when listening for the total message, eye contact can be used to complement the delivery of a message. By looking at different members of the audience, effective speakers use eye contact to involve the audience in the presentation. Speakers can also use the rest of their faces to show concern or excitement about the message. A smile, a puzzled frown, a grimace—all complement the verbal message.

Review Chapter 8 to recall how a speaker's posture, gestures, and body movement may also add to the spoken word. A forward-leaning posture may emphasize or show involvement, and walking toward a member of the audience may psychologically draw that person and others into the message. The most important thing to remember is that body movements have meaning, and they should be used to enhance the message, not distract from it.

Another aspect of nonverbal communication is proximity. Few would question the speaker's need to stand when the audience includes more than seven or eight people; however, many managerial presentations involve audiences of fewer than seven people in a conference room. This latter situation calls for managers to analyze the group, the purpose, and themselves to determine whether to stand or sit.

Voice Quality

Other nonverbal aspects important to the delivery of a presentation reside in the quality of your voice. Among the major vocal considerations of nonverbal communication discussed in Chapter 8 are rate, pitch, and volume.

The best speaking rate depends on your material. Generally, present ideas that are potentially difficult to comprehend at a slower rate than ideas that are easy to understand. Slow down to emphasize an important and/or primary point and speak faster when presenting secondary information. If you are feeling nervous, make a special effort to slow down, since nervousness usually speeds up a speaker's speech rate, and you don't want to seem out of control. Also, out of consideration, you might slow down for an audience that may have difficulty understanding your dialect or terminology. On the other hand, if your regional dialect is a drawl, make an effort to increase your rate for more liveliness and energy. Vary your rate to keep the attention of the audience; a voice that never changes speed becomes boring.

Speakers who talk at a constant pitch will also find it difficult to hold the audience's attention. Use wide variations in pitch for emphasis and interest. Usually, failure to vary pitch is a habit, commonly known as monotonal speaking. Read the following sentence aloud three times, raising the pitch on the italicized word each time. It is easy to see that understanding can be drastically affected by pitch.

I never said he promoted *her*. (Give him some credit. He has better insight than that.)

I never said *he* promoted her. (I just said she got promoted, not by whom.)

I never *said* he promoted her. (But I might have implied it in a number of ways.)

The third voice quality, volume, can add to a presentation by making it lively and easy to follow. The correct volume depends on group size and the physical surroundings; however, regardless of the situation, changes in volume improve emphasis and add variety. A speaker who is difficult to hear may be perceived as incompetent and shy. Keep in mind one special warning about volume: a speaker does not gain attention or make stronger emphasis merely by being loud. In fact, an effective speaker may lower his voice during distractions so his audience is forced to quiet down to hear him.

You can use several exercises to prepare your speaking voice. One simple but effective technique is to read aloud a few paragraphs from the editorial or sports section of the newspaper as though you were giving a presentation. This tactic draws attention to your voice quality. You should pay attention to the way professional speakers, such as TV news readers and announcers, use their voices to convey information and emotion.

In summary, research shows that 55 percent of your impression is the result of how you look, 38 percent is the result of how you sound, and just 7 percent is the result of what you say. So when you announce, "I'm delighted to be here tonight," while your voice shakes and your eyes dart to the door and you fumble with your notes, the audience is more likely to believe that you are *not* delighted to be here.

Practice

The cliché "Practice makes perfect" definitely applies to presentations. Practice is essential for managerial presentations because in U.S. business you should speak extemporaneously, not give memorized recitations or verbatim readings, as is the custom in other cultures. Unfortunately, many managers skip practice because they believe either that they are too busy or that practice is not important.

Even in the case of busy executives, however, practice is essential. It allows you to increase self-confidence and poise and to improve wording so the speech flows smoothly. Additionally, practice permits you to identify any flaws or gaps in the presentation, to deal with distractions, and to make sure the visual aids are smoothly integrated.

Lee Iacocca once said that perfect practice makes perfect.[25] Practice does not mean simply reviewing the basic outline or slide show while sitting at a desk. Rather, it means rehearsing it aloud in a situation that simulates the actual situation as nearly as possible. Also, it means applying all the guidelines available for good presentation development and delivery.

Look for a speech ally among your co-workers who can play the role of the audience and ask questions. Generally, whatever effort is expended in practice could make the difference between a mediocre presentation and an outstanding one.

Whenever possible, use the actual room and all the planned visual aids during the practice session. Doing so allows you to arrange the room properly. For example, though a semicircular arrangement would permit easy eye contact with all the participants, the room may dictate a theater-style arrangement. Knowing such things ahead of time allows you to make adjustments and avoid last-minute anxieties.

A practice session with the visual aids also helps you evaluate timing and get used to the remote. You can also determine such simple things as where to plug in the computer projector and where a light dimmer is located. Many veteran speakers always pack an extension cord, just in case. Such precautions can help prevent disaster after hours and hours have gone into preparing a presentation.

Finally, practice will help you arrange notes for maximum benefit. Managers who are completely familiar with their subject and feel they do not need notes may wind up embarrassing themselves, their audience, and their organization. A rehearsal helps settle the number of notes required and how detailed they should be. Also, additional notations can be made for clear transitions or ideas that need to be spoken more slowly, loudly, or clearly. And you won't be tempted to read from your PowerPoint slides during the presentation.

USING ELECTRONIC MEDIA EFFECTIVELY

The camera and microphone appear everywhere. A manager needs to learn to use these devices to maximize their potential. Unfortunately, many managers still take a defensive posture toward these audio and video presentation possibilities. Most people do not want to get involved in games for which they do not know the rules; thus, they shy away from the camera or microphone.

But the media offer many possibilities, from public service announcements to internal informative or motivational messages to employees. Managers sometimes receive requests from local radio or television stations for informative or persuasive presentations. While television and radio are different forms of communication, they can be rewarding and valuable media for your message.

To take advantage of these media, managers need to know the special rules that apply to the microphone and the camera. The first rule is to speak as though the audience is right there. Think of the microphone or camera as a friendly trusting person. This approach reduces the likelihood of insincere, overly dramatic, inappropriate communication styles.

A second rule is to use the face, hands, and body as in ordinary conversation to keep the presentation as natural as it would be in person. Normal gesturing helps to communicate honesty, and it can complement the ideas being expressed. Some caution, however, should be exercised. Grins, frowns, grimaces, and sweeping gestures are magnified by the camera and are seldom appropriate. Keep gestures close to your upper body so they can be seen in close-up shots.

A third rule is to use a script. What may seem to be an ad-lib presentation by a professional performer is probably the result of an extensive script. A script is a means of coordinating the audio, visual, time, content, and human variables. In addition to the words, it also contains instructions about production matters for crew members, enabling them to visualize how to integrate their responsibilities with the overall show. It helps establish the occasion's structure, organization, and timing. In other words, the script helps all parties know the sequence—how it will begin, move, and conclude.[26]

A fourth rule is closely related to the third: prepare and practice. We have already seen the importance of practice in relation to the face-to-face presentation; however, practice is even more important for a television or videoconference presentation. All the new stimuli make it difficult to concentrate on the task, so be prepared for distractions.

Another reason for the extra practice is the strict time limitations. Media presentations must be implemented in terms of seconds. In reaction to the tight scheduling, the novice media speaker should resist the tendency to speak rapidly and thus appear nervous.

Extensive practice is called for because of the higher level of refinement required for a media presentation. The audience expects polished professional speakers on the air. Remember, too, that every detail becomes a permanent record when captured on tape.

A fifth and final rule relates to the clothing appropriate for a video appearance. The obvious recommendation is to wear what you want others to see you in, but you'll also want your outfit to be unobtrusive. The following are some tips:

- Do not wear large patterns. They have a stroboscopic effect and appear to be moving.
- Do not wear clashing or loud colors (especially red). They can be easily distorted on the monitor.
- Avoid wearing black and white. Black absorbs too much light and white reflects it.
- Avoid large, glittery, or moving jewelry.

Professor Tom Hajduk, director of the Center for Business Communication at Carnegie Mellon University, developed a communication audit form for evaluating TV/videoconference presentations.[27] The audit provides a useful checklist of the unique delivery requirements for media presentations, as summarized in Table 14–5.

These rules should help managers take full advantage of the opportunities presented by the camera and microphone. Such appearances can be challenging but enjoyable experiences that provide a valuable service to your company while offering a tremendous opportunity for professional self-development.

TABLE 14–5
Delivery of Media Presentations

Vocal Impact	Nonverbal Impact	Visual Image Impact
Maintain normal volume (don't shout into the microphone)	Avoid white, black, stripes, patterns that vibrate on TV	Design clean uncluttered visuals that can be read in 30 seconds
Use a conversational rate (approximately 110 wpm)	Maintain eye contact with the camera	Keep all text at 40 points or larger
Project extra vocal enthusiasm and energy	Stand tall and straight	Avoid textual lists of bullet points
Articulate clearly	Use natural but slower chest-high gestures	Label chart columns, rows, and parts to help speed understanding (avoid legends)
Maintain fluency; avoid filled pauses (uh, ok, so)	Move slowly and stay within microphone and camera range	Keep right side of visuals empty so presenter picture in picture (PIP) won't mask visual image
Pause before important points for drama	Use natural facial expressions and head movements	Point to visuals on document camera or draw on computer slides

Summary   To ensure an effective presentation, a manager should thoroughly analyze the purpose, time restrictions, and audience, complete all necessary preparations, and use appropriate delivery techniques. A thorough analysis of the purpose means the speaker should determine if everyone involved has the same goal for the presentation.

Once the goal has been clearly established, the necessary preparations must be completed. Preparation includes the development of an introduction, a sequence of main points that is appropriate for an informative or persuasive purpose, and a strong closing. The sequence of main points should be determined by the speaker's purpose. Support for each main point takes the form of evidence, which can be facts or opinions. Transitions must be added to bring unity and coherence to the completed presentation plan.

In addition, visual aids must be prepared. Visual aids help maintain interest and accurately communicate the key ideas. Visibility, clarity, simplicity, relevance, and timing are important to ensure that the visual aids complement the verbal communication.

Both nonverbal and verbal characteristics of the speaker are important for an effective professional delivery. Eye contact, facial expressions, posture, gestures, and movement all need to be considered. Voice rate, pitch, and volume affect the impact of the presentation.

A speaker should schedule sufficient time for questions and answers at the end of the presentation. When this part of the presentation is well managed, feedback and two-way communication develop.

A special presentational situation that more and more managers face today is speaking before a camera and microphone. Most of the rules that apply to a traditional face-to-face speaking situation apply also to this form of a presentation. However, several additional rules dealing with nonverbal cues and the use of a script will help a manager present an effective message via the electronic media.

AUDIENCE ANALYSIS GUIDE SHEET

1. How many do I expect in the audience?
2. Who are the most powerful or influential members?
3. What is their knowledge of the content area?
   _____ High, may be higher than mine
   _____ About the same as mine
   _____ Less than my knowledge of the subject
   _____ Probably do not have even basic knowledge
   _____ Varies
4. What types of evidence will most impress this group?
   _____ Technical data
   _____ Statistical comparisons
   _____ Cost figures

_____ Historical information

_____ Generalizations

_____ Demonstrations

_____ Stories and examples

_____ Opinions of the speaker

5. What is the group's attitude toward the subject?

_____ Exceptionally positive

_____ Somewhat positive

_____ Neutral

_____ Somewhat negative, reluctant

_____ Definitely negative

_____ Group varies, some positive and some negative

6. What is the group's attitude toward me as the presenter?

_____ See me as credible and knowledgeable

_____ Neutral, probably do not have an opinion

_____ See me as having little knowledge and credibility

7. What is the group's attitude toward the organization I represent?

_____ See the organization as reliable and trustworthy

_____ Neutral

_____ Might question its capabilities and reliability

8. What will be the group's disposition at the time of my presentation?

_____ Will have listened to many other presentations similar to this one; could be tired.

_____ Will have been sitting for a long time; may need a minute to stretch.

_____ This presentation will be unique, so it should be easy to grab their attention.

_____ This is an early item on the agenda; they should be fresh.

9. What are the *most important* audience characteristics to consider in the presentation?

Exercises for Small Groups

Exercise 14-1.

Prepare a 10-minute informative presentation for your class on the latest developments in office ergonomics. Begin by analyzing your audience and selecting your topics and their order of presentation. Your discussion should address the following elements:

- How will you introduce your subject so you grab the audience's attention?
- What type of supporting information will most impress your audience?
- What kind of closing should you use?

- How will you encourage questions at the end of your presentation?
- What would be the best type of visual aids to maintain the audience's attention?

Exercise 14-2.

Pick a computer presentation graphics package or multimedia package with which you are familiar. Assume you are a new sales representative for the company that developed this software. For instance, PowerPoint is a Microsoft product. In three days, you will be making a sales presentation on the latest version of this software to a group of executives at a large company. Obviously, you will want to inform them of all the features offered by your software and its advantages over the competition and previous versions. You will also want to persuade them to purchase the software. How would you accomplish your goals?

Exercise 14-3.

Pick one of the following topics to use in the development of a persuasive presentation.

- Lie detectors should (or should not) be used in the hiring process.
- Lie detectors should (or should not) be used by businesses in attempting to deter employee theft.
- Businesses should (or should not) be permitted to subject employees to random drug testing.
- Top executives should (or should not) be held criminally liable for their companies' illegal (or unethical) actions.
- Social responsibility should (or should not) be a major concern of today's CEOs.
- A manager should (or should not) be concerned about the personal problems of his or her employees.
- An international code of ethics should (or should not) be developed.
- Unionization is (or is not) appropriate for today's white-collar workers.

After picking a topic, visualize an audience to whom you would speak on the subject. Of the three persuasive presentation patterns described in this chapter, which would be most appropriate for your presentation? Given the topic you have chosen and the audience you have visualized, what type of evidence would you use to persuade them to accept your point of view?

Exercise 14-4.

Pick one of the following scenarios and develop a 10-minute informative presentation:

- For an audience of graduating seniors in business administration, discuss the topic of appropriate dress for employment interviews.

- For an audience of business executives, discuss the topic of appropriate dress for television interviews.

Endnotes

1. S. Clay Willmington, "Oral Communication for a Career in Business," *Bulletin of the Association for Business Communication* 52, no. 2 (June 1989), pp. 8–12.

2. Robert J. Olney and Anita S. Bednar, "Identifying Essential Oral Presentation Skills for Today's Business Curriculum," *Journal of Education for Business* 64, no. 4 (January 1989), p. 161.

3. Carol A. McFarland, "Teaching Students the Elements of Oral Business Presentations," *Bulletin of the Association for Business Communication* 43, no. 1 (March 1980), pp. 15–17.

4. Ernest G. Bormann, William S. Howell, Ralph G. Nichols, and George L. Shapiro, *Interpersonal Communication in the Modern Organization* (Englewood Cliffs, NJ: Prentice Hall, 1982), p. 197.

5. Lawrence L. Tracy, "Taming the Hostile Audience," *Training and Development Journal* 44, no. 2 (February 1990), p. 35.

6. William S. Howell and Ernest G. Bormann, *Presentational Speaking for Business and the Professions* (New York: Harper & Row, 1971), pp. 122–30.

7. Daniel J. O'Keefe, *Persuasion Theory and Research* (Newbury Park, CA: Sage Publications, 1990), pp. 130–88.

8. Baba Shiv, George Loewenstein, Antoine Bechara, Hanna Damasio, and Antonio R. Damasio, "Investment Behavior and the Negative Side of Emotion," *Psychological Science* 16, no. 6 (2005), pp. 435–39.

9. "Human Behavior: The Greatest Barrier to Trading Success," *Australasian Investment Review,* n.d., www.aireview.com (January 20, 2006).

10. Mary Munter and Dave Paradi, *Guide to PowerPoint* (Upper Saddle River, NJ: Pearson Prentice Hall, 2007), pp. 65, 94.

11. Donna Barron, "Graphics Presentations at Your Fingertips," *The Office,* July 1990, p. 32.

12. Robert P. Sedlack, Jr., Barbara L. Shwom, and Karl P. Keller, *Graphics and Visual Communication for Managers* (Mason, OH: Thomson South-Western, 2008), p. 71.

13. Munter and Paradi, *Guide to PowerPoint.*

14. James Wyllie, "Oral Communication: Survey and Suggestions," *Bulletin of the Association for Business Communication* 43, no. 2 (June 1980), pp. 14–17.

15. "The Pros and Cons of High-Tech Presenting," *Presentations* 13, no. 4 (April 1999), p. 34.

16. Patricia L. Panchak, "Capitalizing on the Graphics Edge," *Modern Office Technology,* June 1990, p. 63.

17. Edward R. Tufte, *The Cognitive Style of PowerPoint: Pitching Out Corrupts Within* (Cheshire, CT: Graphics Press, 2006).

18. "Over-Reliance on PowerPoint Leads to Simplistic Thinking," *The New York Times,* December 14, 2003, http://partners.nytimes.com/2003/12/14/magazine/14POWER.html (retrieved January 12, 2006).

19. Michael Alley, "Teaching the Assertion-Evidence Design of Presentation Slides," from *Rethinking the Design of Presentation Slides: Assertion-Evidence Structure,* www.writing.engr.psu.edu/slides.html (retrieved January 31, 2009).

20. Tufte, *The Cognitive Style of PowerPoint: Pitching Out Corrupts Within*.

21. David Wallechinsky and Irving Wallace, *The Book of Lists* (New York: William Morrow, 1977).

22. Kenneth R. Meyer, "Developing Delivery Skills in Oral Business Communication," *Bulletin of the Association for Business Communication* 43, no. 3 (September 1980), pp. 21–24.

23. Dave Clarke Mora, "Carly, Reconsidered," *Continental*, September 2003, pp. 31–33.

24. Mary Ellen Murray, "Painless Oral Presentations," *Bulletin of the Association for Business Communication* 52, no. 2 (June 1989), pp. 13–15.

25. Lee Iacocca, *Lee Iacocca Talking Straight* (New York: Bantam Books, 1988).

26. Evan Blythin and Larry A. Samovar, *Communicating Effectively on Television* (Belmont, CA: Wadsworth Publishing Co., 1985), pp. 92–96.

27. Tom Hajduk, "Communication Audit: TV/Videoconference Presentation," Communication Consulting Group, (2003), www.ccg-usa.com (v11.1) (retrieved October 2003).

Appendix

Supplemental Articles for Chapter 3—Technologically Mediated Communication

The following articles were composed by graduate business students at Sam Houston State University under the supervision of the author. They reflect the latest research on emerging technologies. Each article describes a different technology and how it is being applied in U.S. business today. The authors also look to the future and track trends in technologically mediated business communication. Guidelines for best practices relevant to each technology are presented. A list of references and topics for class discussion appear at the end of each article. They are intended to provide supplemental material for Chapter 3.

TABLE OF CONTENTS

1. TEXTING VS. E-MAILING IN BUSINESS

Anna Turri, Sam Houston State University

Text messaging, also known as Short Message Service (SMS), is quickly becoming the new way for businesspeople to communicate in the 21st century. Wikipedia defines text messaging as a service available on most digital mobile phones (and other mobile devices such as PDAs or occasionally even desktop and laptop computers). It permits the sending of short messages between mobile phones, other handheld devices, and even landline telephones.[1] Such messages are also known as text messages, or more colloquially SMSes, texts, or even txts. Young people in the U.S. seem to have adopted texting as their primary means of communicating with each other. Their typical attitude is that e-mail is old-school technology, useful only for exchanging messages with parents, grandparents, and professors. On the other hand, contemporary business professionals are being encouraged to use this channel together with e-mail. Therefore, it does not appear that e-mail will be replaced anytime soon in business and industry.

ADVANTAGES OF TEXTING

Text messaging has many advantages. The most commonly identified benefits of text messaging are its speed, access, and discretion. Texting is fast because the message you send travels instantaneously, like a live conversation in person or by telephone. By contrast, e-mail is asynchronous and not expected to be real-time. There is a lag, especially when servers accumulate e-mails before delivering them to members of the network.

Accessibility is another advantage of text messaging. An SMS can be sent to anyone, anytime, anywhere. For this reason many companies are using it to communicate with employees as they travel or to send important announcements to everyone in the company. Text messages, unlike e-mail, can be delivered directly to someone's desktop so they can receive immediate attention.[2] In fact, 83 percent of 450 CEOs and CMOs responded to a survey by stating that SMS is a key way their company sends alerts and notifications.[3] As an extension of this technology's use, managers can set up their e-mail so it will text them when something important comes in, including a summary of the message.

Finally, sending an SMS is a discreet way to get in touch with someone. Most instant messaging devices have a setting that will permit the device to vibrate when a new message hits, preventing disruptions and intrusions. One handy application is when an employee urgently needs to communicate with the boss while she or he is in a meeting. Because it is less disruptive than a phone call while remaining more "personal" than e-mail, texting is handy for dual communications.

DRAWBACKS OF TEXTING

The most commonly listed disadvantages to text messaging are its lack of security, structure, and compatibility. The potential for employee abuse is an additional concern.

First, security is a major issue with regard to text messaging. Since texting is instantaneous, it does not allow enough time for virus scanners to check completely for viruses, thus leaving computers unprotected. No matter how fast virus scanners become, they will always be able to protect against e-mails better than SMSes.[4]

Lack of structure is another disadvantage of instant messaging. Unlike e-mails, which are set up in memo format, text messages do not have a set form. Most are sent as very short messages by using a shorthand code that users must learn to decipher. For example, a synopsis of the classic novel, *Pride and Prejudice*, sent as a text message, might look like the following:

5SistrsWntngHsbnds.NwMenInTwn-Bingly&Darcy Fit&Loadd

This mysterious string of letters and symbols translates to:

Five sisters are wanting husbands. They have their sights set on two new men in town—Bingley and Darcy. They are handsome and wealthy.[5]

Here is another, less literary, message to try decoding:

#s lk gd . . . lnch@1/back l8r

The text-message generation knows it means, "The numbers look good. I'm leaving for lunch at 1:00 p.m. and I'll be back later."

This type of message can be difficult for new users to understand and write. Perhaps more importantly in business settings, a cryptic text message may lead to serious misunderstandings and costly errors.

The third major disadvantage of texting is the lack of compatibility between SMS systems. Since there is not one universal standard protocol for instant messaging, competing SMS systems cannot talk to one another.[6] For example, a message sent from AOL cannot be displayed on a device using MSN or vice versa.

Finally, managers may be reluctant to allow texting technology because they fear employees will abuse it. IM was designed for recreational "chatting," and it is easy to get involved in personal exchanges that take up valuable work time. Additionally, from a distance, an employee who is typing messages may appear to be on task. A recent study by research company Radicati Group indicated that most employees in enterprise environments use texting more for casual intra-company communication and personal messaging than for communicating with customers or business partners.[7] A flood of nonurgent or personal text messages can be distracting to busy workers, as well.

A LOOK TO THE FUTURE

After reviewing the advantages and disadvantages, a business can decide whether using SMS technology will be beneficial to them. Many companies that have already adopted this technology have been increasing their usage of this communication channel, but they are not abandoning e-mail. Instead, they are using texting in tandem with e-mail to send reminders or announcements that need to be communicated immediately.[8] For example, an employee might send an important e-mail to his boss and then send a reminder SMS, letting her know the e-mail was sent.

Results of a recent informal survey of 11 officers in east Texas banks and financial institutions demonstrate the current role of text messaging in business. The survey showed that the officers have been texting with their PDAs and cell phones for the past two years or so. However, 82 percent of the officers said that texting is not their primary form of communication at work. They use text messaging in addition to, rather than instead of, e-mail and phones. They consider texting to be most helpful for direct questions, requests, updates, and confirmations. They also agree that texting is a key tool for sending alerts.

Best practices for IM use in business settings are still evolving, but it is likely they will include the following guidelines:

- IM should not be used as a substitute for e-mail.
- IM use should be restricted to short questions or announcements that must be communicated immediately.
- Users should signal when they are "busy" or "offline" to avoid being flooded with distracting messages.
- The software should be standardized and controlled by the company's IT department, as with other business technology.
- IM should never be used for confidential communications unless encrypted.
- A company should create a clear policy for IM and disseminate it to employees. The policy must be enforceable, with stated penalties for violations.[9]

Overall it appears that business professionals will continue to increase their use of text messaging. With its many advantages, including mobility, convenience, and immediacy, more companies will use it to stay in touch with employees and bosses as they travel or when a message needs to be received quickly. Beyond convenience, this technology offers businesspeople the competitive advantages of increased productivity and efficiency. However, with the security problems and other disadvantages, it is unlikely that SMS will replace e-mail anytime soon, at least for business purposes.

Discussion Questions

1. What are some business uses of text messaging that students have observed?
2. To what extent does texting technology shape the message?

3. How can text messaging affect other forms of communication at work?
4. What are the major reasons that managers resist adoption of texting as a communication tool?

Endnotes

1. *Wikipedia,* the Free Encyclopedia, http://en.wikipedia.org/wiki/Text_messaging.htm.
2. *CIO, Executive Summaries Text Messaging,* September 8, 2003, www.cio.com/summaries/communications/messaging/index.html (retrieved January 3, 2007).
3. *Customer Relationship Management,* June 2006.
4. B. J. Gillette, "AOL, MSN, Yahoo: Instant Message vs. E-mail," *trimMail's E-mail Battles,* November 4, 2005, www.e-mailbattles.com/2005/11/04/e-mail_aacaachjgd_hf/ (retrieved January 3, 2007).
5. Lauren Barack, *School Library Journal* 52, no.1 (2006).
6. *CIO, Executive Summaries Text Messaging,* September 8, 2003, www.cio.com/summaries/communications/messaging/index.html (retrieved January 3, 2007).
7. www.instantmessagingplanet.com/enterprise/article.php/3423321. Updated April 6, 2005.
8. Deb Shinder, "Instant Messaging: Does It Have a Place in Business Networks?" Viewed online January 3, 2007 at http://www.windowsecurity.com/articles/Instant-Messaging-Business-Networks.html (retreieved January 3, 2007).
9. *Ibid.*

2. INSTANT MESSENGER COMMUNICATION IN A MULTINATIONAL CORPORATION

Stephen Hunt, Sam Houston State University

In the 1990s, software developers released a communication tool called instant messaging. This new communication method allowed users to communicate through a common instant messaging program. America Online was the first company to successfully attract a strong instant messaging customer base. The majority of AOL's customers were young and technologically savvy. These young consumers quickly made AOL IM a success.[1]

The first generation of IM consumers who flocked to these early IM programs has entered the work force. They bring with them a level of technological comfort that is changing the face of modern business communication. The following research is a combination of primary research in the oil trading industry and secondary research. This research will explore the advantages, disadvantages, future applications, and best management practices to effectively utilize instant messaging applications.

The oil trading industry regularly uses Yahoo instant messenger for daily business operations.[2] Traders use Yahoo to communicate with counterparties and brokers.[3] Operations managers use Yahoo to check the status of vessels moving around the world. A survey and several interviews were conducted to collect data regarding instant messaging use in a small international oil trading company, Mabanaft, Inc., based in Houston, Texas. Senior managers at Mabanaft authorized a survey of employees in North America, Europe, and Asia. Twenty-seven surveys were completed and returned, for a 60 percent response rate, which provided very strong data for analysis.

ADVANTAGES OF IM

Instant messaging has several unique advantages over other communication methods. International communication, message archiving, improved communication efficiency, and ease of implementation are the primary advantages of instant messaging.

Communication can be very expensive for international organizations. International phone calls are very expensive and videoconferencing hardware both is expensive and requires a fixed location. Most free instant messaging programs have conferencing features that allow team members around the world to collaborate instantly using cellular phones. They can also access these chat functions from any Internet connection in the world without IT support. Our survey results indicate that 57.7 percent of Mabanaft employees frequently use instant messaging to communicate with colleagues in other countries. Instant messaging improves international collaboration without increasing expenses.

Maintaining accurate records of communication improves employee efficiency and is beneficial during legal proceedings. Referring to transcripts of a conversation allows employees to retain and understand the intent of the conversation. During legal discovery, these archives may protect an organization from false accusations. Most free instant messaging programs have message archiving options. These archives are easy to set up and require significantly less server space than e-mail archives.[4] Archiving is especially important in oil trading because an offer and acceptance over instant messaging programs can be legally binding.[5] Instant messaging archives provide the same level of legal documentation as e-mail archives at a lower cost.

Instant messaging greatly improves communication efficiency compared to traditional electronic communication. E-mail is a one-way communication method with significant delays between the original message and follow-up questions to clarify intent. It is also possible to delete sections of the original e-mail during the reply phase. This can cause confusion between the communicating parties. Telephone communication requires all parties to process and react quickly to the ongoing conversation. This can be especially difficult for parties communicating outside their native language. Instant messaging programs allow users to immediately ask clarifying questions, converse at a comfortable pace, and also have a transcript of the conversation for review. In the early days of oil trading, all transactions were made over the phone. This required significantly more time than modern trading.[6] Instant messaging allows traders to participate in numerous negotiations at once. The archive feature allows traders to easily document their negotiations.

Finally, instant messaging programs are very easy to implement because many employees already use them. In 2004, the U.S. Air Force decided to add secure instant messaging portals to their communications network. The Air Force made this decision because military personnel were already using AOL and Yahoo IM to conduct daily military affairs.[7] Rather than ban an effective communication method, the Air Force took steps to formalize and effectively manage the grassroots movement toward IM communication.

DISADVANTAGES OF IM

Several disadvantages to instant messaging must be identified to minimize their impact. Effectively managing these disadvantages will protect your organization. Instant messaging can establish legally binding contracts, distract workers, and expose companies to legal jurisdiction in other states.

The legal elements of a contractual agreement are offer, consideration, and acceptance. E-mail or instant messenger conversations that include these elements can be legally binding even if the specific details of the deal need further negotiation. The following conversation could be considered a legal contract.[8]

> *Buyer:*   *How's it going? Hope to see you and the family on the lake Friday.*
>
> *Supplier:* *We should be there.*
>
> *Buyer:*   *Could you get me six of those new widgets by the end of the month? Got a project coming up, and the boss is pushing hard.*
>
> *Supplier:* *Those systems are pricey.*
>
> *Buyer:*   *They would make the job go a lot easier.*
>
> *Supplier:* *No problem. We've got plenty in stock, so I'll deliver them on the 20th.*
>
> *Buyer:*   *Great. See you Friday.[9]*

Any specific details not included would be negotiable, but the supplier could be forced to deliver six widgets to the buyer on the 20th. Breaching a contract can expose a company to legal liability and hurt its reputation. An oil trader once reneged on a deal that prompted a 25-year refusal to trade between the two companies.[10] Employees must be educated on safe use of electronic communication for both e-mail and instant messaging to protect the organization.

Instant messaging can also disrupt workplace productivity. Instant messaging and e-mail can be used for personal communication, thereby reducing the time spent on a task. Instant messages can easily be archived and reviewed if managers believe this is a problem in their organization. Company policies for e-mail can easily be adapted to manage instant messaging. Ignoring this easily corrected disadvantage to instant messaging can reduce company productivity.

Instant messaging can expose companies to legal jurisdiction liability in other states. In 2006, the New York Court of Appeals ruled that a Montana business could be sued in a New York court. The Montana business entered into and later breached a contract using instant messages. Conducting business over instant messenger was sufficient contact for New York courts to have jurisdiction over the Montana business. Employees using instant messaging to conduct business with outside parties must understand the legal implications.[11]

A LOOK AHEAD

Clearly, great potential exists for growth in instant messaging by businesses. Many companies are already utilizing instant messaging in their daily operations. Our survey of Mabanaft employees showed that 48.1 percent either agree or strongly agree that their preferred method of communication is instant messaging. IBM employees send an average of 6 million internal instant messages on a daily basis. In 2006, they were sending 4 million internal instant messages daily.[12] Managers cannot ignore the growth of instant messaging communication.

As the generation of consumers that made Yahoo, MSN, and AOL household names enters the work force, instant messaging usage will increase. Our research at Mabanaft showed that instant messaging accounts for over 40 percent of the daily business communication for 55.5 percent of Mabanaft employees between 20 and 30 years of age. By comparison, 35.3 percent of Mabanaft employees between 31 and 70 years of age use instant messaging for 40 percent of daily communication. This trend can be seen in other organizations around the world. Junior members of the labor force are bringing instant messaging programs to organizations around the world.

BEST PRACTICES FOR IM

It is clear that instant messaging is a growing form of organizational communication. Analysts estimate that 25 million employees currently use instant messaging without the permission of management.[13] Managers must draft policies to address instant messaging use in their organizations. Organizations should review and consider the following best practices even if they decide not to implement instant messaging.

Best Practices for Instant Messaging Communication:

- All incoming and outgoing messages should be archived.
- Instant messaging should not be used for highly sensitive communication.
- An instant messaging policy should be developed and circulated among employees, even if the company does not officially use instant messaging.
- Employees should be educated about the potential legal liability they expose the company to through instant messaging.
- Instant messaging should not be banned without serious consideration. Employees have and will continue to use it without authorization.

Billions of dollars in commodities, stocks, bonds, and commercial goods are traded every day using instant messaging technology. The strong international communication, easy message archiving, high level of efficiency, and easy implementation will lead more organizations to use instant messaging. The contract formation issues, employee distraction, and legal jurisdiction concerns associated with instant messaging can be easily managed. The productivity and cost reduction benefits of instant messaging far outweigh the potential negatives to businesses.

Discussion Questions

1. How frequently and for what purposes do you use instant messaging? Why do you prefer IMing over phone or e-mail in these situations?
2. What are the major advantages of IM for multinational corporations?
3. What are the major disadvantages of IM for multinational corporations?

Endnotes

1. Jeff Tyson and Alison Cooper, "How Instant Messaging Works," *How Stuff Works,* http://communication.howstuffworks.com/instant-messaging1.htm.
2. Kim Kyoungwha and Nesa Subrahmaniyan, "An Unlikely Trading Hub in Asia," *International Herald Tribune,* www.iht.com/articles/2005/12/01/bloomberg/sxtrades. php.
3. Anthony Reuben, "What Is It Like Being an Oil Trader?" *BBC News,* http://news.bbc. co.uk/2/hi/business/7250554.stm.
4. Nancy Flynn, *Instant Messaging Rules* (New York: AMACOM, 2004), pp. 145–55.
5. Stephen Yoch, "When 'You've Got E-mail' Means 'You've Got a Deal!'" *Felhaber, Larson Fenlon & Vogt,* www.felhaber.com/ARTICLES/e-mail.html.
6. Robert McGarvery, "Instant Messaging Comes to the Office," *Executive Travel,* www. executivetravelmagazine.com/page/Instant+Messaging+comes+to+the+office?t=a non.
7. William Jackson, "Air Force Abuzz over Instant Messaging App," *Government Computer News,* http://gcn.com/articles/2004/06/06/air-force-abuzz-over-instant-messaging-app.aspx.
8. Yoch, "When 'You've Got E-mail' Means 'You've Got a Deal!'"
9. *Ibid.*
10. Personal interview, Mabanaft employee.
11. Kenneth Rashbaum, "A Single Instant Message Can Land Your Company in a New York Court: The Deutsche Bank Case," *The Privacy and Data Security Law Journal* 10, (2006), pp. 889–96.
12. McGarvery, "Instant Messaging Comes to the Office."
13. Flynn, *Instant Messaging Rules,* p. 146.

3. PODCASTING IN CORPORATE AMERICA

Antonette Harvey, Sam Houston State University

What Is Podcasting?

Podcasting dates back to 2001 and culminated from the development of blogs. Podcasting met the consumer's desire to have downloadable audio and video that could be delivered to a portable media device. "The key common ingredients of a podcast are:

1. an audio and/or audiovisual file that is
2. archived and available on the Internet,
3. such that it is accessible by a computer automatically,
4. is downloaded, and
5. is transferable to a portable media player."[1]

What makes podcasts different from the average download file on the Internet is the publish/subscribe model, which uses feed technology, such as Really Simple Syndication (RSS) or Atom, to deliver the file content. RSS is computer code that points to a file on the Internet.

When Entergy Corporation, a utility headquartered in New Orleans, LA, was considering the use of podcasting in 2007, they consulted several sources including the "Introduction to Podcasts" provided by the Communications Executive Council, part of the Corporate Executive Board to which Entergy belongs.[2] According to the Communications Executive Council, the figure on the next page demonstrates how the podcasting process works.

Podcasts are basically digital files that can be downloaded from the Internet. Free software allows users to subscribe to regular podcast programs, automatically download them, and transfer the podcast to iPod-like devices. "According to the audience measurement service Bridge Ratings, podcast usage has exploded from 820,000 users in late 2004 to almost five million one year later."[4] Bridge predicted that by 2009, that number would be at least 45 million. If you search for the term *podcast* on Google, it will return 121 million responses.[5]

Who Uses Podcasts?

Strip away the image that podcasting is only for young people listening to music on iPods dangling from their neck and "you've got radio on steroids—high quality audio distributed via the Internet."[6] By mid-2006, more than 22 million adults in the United States owned an iPod or MP3 device. By age group, 19 percent of those aged 18–28 years old own an iPod or other MP3 player, and 14 percent of those in the 29–40 age range own an iPod.[7] Twenty-nine percent of these owners have downloaded at least one podcast, which includes approximately 6 million adults.

An Entergy employee survey conducted in 2008 indicated that more than 30 percent of responders had listened to a podcast.[8] This is up from around

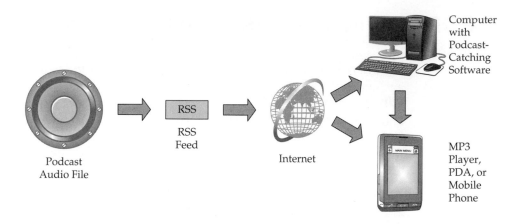

20 percent one year earlier. Therefore, it is reasonable to conclude that podcasts can be accessible and utilized across many generations, for personal as well as business purposes.

How Can Podcasts Be Used in Business?

Communication specialists use podcasting for three primary purposes: marketing, community building, and as an alternative form of employee communications.[9] Companies use podcasts to promote products and/or services, while community building focuses on providing information of interest that is intended to help the public at large. Lastly, the additional means of communicating with employees and investors through podcasts offers their audience easy and convenient tools to stay informed about the company's activities. Thus, podcasting can be a resource utilized externally or internally to an organization.

External Communication

Companies and public relations professionals can utilize podcasts to advance their position in the public eye. Companies can enhance news announcements by developing a podcast to accompany the press release, thereby taking the product expression to another level. If a company has a good speaker, the company should take advantage of their ability to communicate to customers, investors, and other podcast listeners. Companies can offer podcast seminars that allow listeners the ability to receive the message without being tied to a computer.

Alternatively, external communication may be more focused on consumers. For example, Whirlpool's "American Family" podcast in July 2005 addressed issues that impact families with diverse backgrounds in an effort to build personal relationships with consumers.[10]

Internal Communication

As we have seen, podcasting can be a powerful tool in communicating with customers. But it can be powerful as an internal communication tool as well.

Internal communication options for podcasting include the ability to provide training and other forms of employee interaction to reduce the expense of satellite conferencing and/or employee travel. The low cost and convenience attributed to podcasting makes the tool inviting to companies looking to expand their communication options.[11] Management can provide personalized messages which can be posted on intranets to allow all employees to feel they are informed. EarningsCast.com even podcasts their earnings calls.[12]

Podcasting can be used for training modules that employees must complete annually or on a routine basis. This is particularly cost effective for factual-based information sharing. The company creates one consistent message and employees have the convenience to download and complete these training modules as it fits into their schedule. This flexibility benefits both the employee and management.

In addition to information-sharing and training, managers that need to keep current on news events can benefit from the news media's move to podcast programming. National Public Radio and its member stations offer podcasts, ABC podcasts *Nightline* and *Good Morning America,* and NBC podcasts the *Nightly News* and *Meet the Press* commercial-free.[13] Managers can download and listen to these podcasts at their convenience and strategize their business accordingly.

Why Implement Podcasting?

Now that we know how podcasts can be used in the workplace, we next consider why managers should implement such technology.

In 2005, the British Broadcasting Corporation (BBC) conducted a trial using interactive media players (iMP). The BBC allowed its radio broadcasts to be downloaded to iPod-type devices, thereby allowing listeners to play the content at any time. Three programs taking part in the initial MP3 download trial were downloaded a total of 270,000 times in the first four months of the trial.[14] Further, a range of businesses, from small to large (like IBM), produce podcasts to connect with clients, customers, and even provide special event lectures.[15] During times of crisis, a podcast can be immediately uploaded to a Web site that reflects the corporate executive officer (CEO) or other official's response.[16] This allows the organization to deliver a consistent and direct message to the media in a timely fashion. Therefore, podcast technology must be considered in a company's communication portfolio.

"As a manager of internal communications, having alternate communications channels to use in support of conventional print communications, as well as online news channels, has been a driving reason for adopting podcasting," said Christopher Smith of Entergy Corporation.[17] This is particularly important as Entergy addresses the implications to the company and industry of a mature workforce and significant retirement-related turnover in the next decade. As an employer of nearly 15,000 employees, podcasting is a means by which Entergy can communicate with a geographically dispersed organization. Podcasts appear to be a more personal, immediate, and interactive communication medium with the audience.[18]

Smith indicated that the research conducted by the Communications Executive Council (CEC), as well as Entergy's own spot polls of employees and interaction with colleagues in the industry, told them that nontraditional media such as blogs, podcasts, and other channels would increasingly become necessary for reaching employees in a multigenerational workforce.[19] The CEC projections in late 2006 showed a likely acceleration in demand over the next five years.[20] The next step was to learn how to create the podcast.

How to Create Podcasts?

The equipment needed to implement podcasting at Entergy Corporation cost under $250 and as such, their corporate communications department was producing podcasts within days of inception.[21] Since mid-2007, Entergy has produced more than two dozen podcasts on a variety of topics.

Creating and distributing an audio or video podcast consists of five basic steps:

1. Write up the material intended for the podcast or plan on winging it.
2. Record the content to a digital device, such as a camera or even a cell phone.
3. Edit the podcast content on a computer to introduce voice over and/or insert music using editing software.
4. Upload the audio/video content to a Web server and create an RSS feed that points to the podcast (the feed needs to include an ID3 tag and enclosure tags that reflect the file's full address, title length, and a short description of content).[22]

The end user of the podcast will click the feed button, whereby the content will download to a user's software, such as iTunes. The user can then transfer the podcast to mobile devices as needed for portability.

Furthermore, Entergy Corporate Communications recently developed formal guidelines to help individual communicators and their teams replicate the corporation's success with podcasting. Those guidelines may also help form the best practices for using other new communications channels such as blogging, wikis, Twitter, and more.[23]

Are There Disadvantages to Podcasting?

Along with the advantages of podcasting, such as convenience and ease of use, managers must consider whether there are reasons not to implement podcasting. This section reviews three negative factors: technology, accessibility, and legal implications.

Technology

While content digital rights management (DRM) software controls can be established to limit content accessibility, managers must evaluate the distribution channel, user needs, speed of technology, and whether various content should be available for different periods of time. This can require considerable technological testing and monitoring.

Since some podcasts attract as many as 50,000 listeners, podcast directories can track user patterns.[24] This information can become a source for advertising revenue and/or spam marketing tools.

Accessibility

Podcast shortcomings within a large organization may include employees' inability to access such technology on a regular basis. Entergy employs many field workers, such as linemen, who do not spend much time at the computer, may not have computer speakers or headphones, or are not generally frequent users of iPods or other MP3 players themselves.[25] Therefore, there is a natural limit to how many employees can benefit from podcasting. Other digital media, such as wikis, blogs, online videos, and so on face such technology-usage limitations.

Legal Implications

When creating podcasts, the producer must ensure that permissions are secured for the presentation material as well as issues resolved regarding copyright ownership and registration. Managers must know whether older material used by the corporation is actually owned. If hiring a third party to develop a podcast series, an express license for the content is necessary for copyright protection. Corporations may also want to register their podcasts for additional security.[26]

Any content to be included in the podcast, whether music or otherwise, that is not expressly owned by the corporation requires copyright permission. These legal implications must be overcome to ensure that the technology does not cost the corporation considerably in the future.

Conclusion

Terry Seamons, senior vice president of Entergy Human Resources and Administration, believes that podcasting has significant potential for Entergy and other large organizations. He recently reported, "After I was interviewed for an Inside Entergy podcast, I received a number of comments from people around the company who said, in essence, 'It was really good to hear what you think personally, in your words, and not get just a written company line about the issues.'" Seamons said that the spontaneity and personal style of informal podcasts caused employees to focus on what he believes, what he is all about, and not just on a remote idea of company leadership.[27]

Podcasting provides a low-cost in-house option for creating management messages, employee engagement communications, training programs, and other content. The ability to distribute podcasts and other digital media over existing company intranets may in some cases reduce travel and physical meeting costs. More importantly, the new media helps the company prepare to meet its multigenerational workforce on their terms, and in ways that match a variety of learning and work styles. With diligence in ensuring the legal rights are retained for corporate podcasts, this communication medium may continue to increase in use by both young and old.

Consumer demand and influence are becoming more and more critical factors that cannot be ignored. Wtopnews.com Managing Editor Steve Dolge said, "We need to go where the people are instead of trying to force them where we are."[28] Podcasting cannot replace live interaction, but as technology is becoming accessible in real-time, podcasting audio and video capacity may be necessary for survival.

Discussion Questions

1. What are the advantages of podcasting implementation?
2. What are the disadvantages of podcasting in business?
3. How can podcasts be used as an internal or external tool for an organization?
4. Describe how a company can use podcasting to promote a product or service.

Endnotes

1. Colette Vogele and Elizabeth Gard, "PodCasting for Corporations and Universities: Look Before You Leap," *Journal of Internet Law* 10, no. 4 (2006), pp. 3–13.
2. Communications Executive Council (2006), www.cec.executiveboard.com (retrieved June 17, 2009).
3. *Ibid.*
4. Deborah Potter, "iPod, You Pod, We All Pod," *American Journalism Review* 28, no. 1 (2006), pp. 64–66.
5. Google, www.google.com (retrieved July 24, 2009).
6. Farrell Kramer, "Enhance Your Communications Program with Podcasting: Providing What Blogs and Press Releases Can't," *Public Relations Tactics* 13, no. 11 (2006), p. 39.
7. Vogele and Gard, "PodCasting for Corporations and Universities: Look Before You Leap."
8. Christopher Smith, Manager of Employee Communications, Entergy Services, Inc. Personal interview, June 15, 2009, Houston, Texas.
9. Communications Executive Council.
10. Vogele and Gard, "PodCasting for Corporations and Universities: Look Before You Leap."
11. Communications Executive Council.
12. Vogele and Gard, "PodCasting for Corporations and Universities: Look Before You Leap."
13. Potter.
14. Chris Forester, "People at the Top," *Communications Engineer* 3, no. 4 (2005), pp. 22–27.
15. Vogele and Gard, "PodCasting for Corporations and Universities: Look Before You Leap."
16. Eric N. Berkowitz, PhD, "The Evolution of Public Relations and the Use of the Internet: The Implications for Health Care Organizations," *Health Marketing Quarterly* 24, no. 3/4 (2007), p. 126.
17. Smith.
18. Vogele and Gard, "PodCasting for Corporations and Universities: Look Before You Leap."
19. Smith.
20. Communications Executive Council.
21. Smith.
22. Vogele and Gard, "PodCasting for Corporations and Universities: Look Before You Leap."

23. Smith.

24. Holly Beth Billington, "The Podcasting Explosion: U.S. and International Law Implications," *Intellectual Property & Technology Law Journal* 18, no. 11 (2006), pp. 1–5.

25. Smith.

26. Vogele and Gard, "PodCasting for Corporations and Universities: Look Before You Leap."

27. Terry Seamons, Senior Vice President of Human Resources and Administration, Entergy Services, Inc. Personal interview, June 17, 2009, Houston, Texas.

28. Potter.

4. BLOGS AS A BUSINESS COMMUNICATION TOOL

Matthew O'Rourke, Sam Houston State University

The use of blogs (short for Weblog) as a technological communication tool is a growing trend among Internet users today. It is estimated that 27 percent of Internet users in the United States read blogs on a regular basis.[1] The number of blogs online is estimated to be over 112 million.[2] Approximately 40,000 new blogs spring up every day.[3] However, very little academic research has focused on blogs as a business communication tool.[4] The purpose of this paper is to familiarize the audience with blogs, discuss the ways blogs can be used at your company, highlight the advantages and disadvantages of using blogs to communicate, and provide some suggestions for properly implementing blogs.

What Is a Blog?

A blog is an online journal that typically displays messages in reverse chronological order. In other words, today's message will be shown above yesterday's message on the same page. The very first blogs were online "diaries."[5] Blogs can be updated at any time from any place. Unlike most Internet pages, blogs are dynamic. An individual can easily update the information in their blog, add more information, or start a completely different train of thought.[6] Blog composition requires no knowledge of Web-programming language such as HTML.[7] Blogs are made available via Really Simple Syndication (RSS), the technology that allows blogs to reach audiences worldwide.[8]

Blogs have evolved into an online conversation of sorts. Individuals include links to other blogs or Web sites as well as other media such as video and music.[9] Many blogs allow readers to leave comments for the blog writer (blogger) that can be viewed by all readers. Blogs often provide "commentaries" on news or particular subjects. Media companies, large and small, have begun to embrace blogs as a way to report news as well as engage readers in a dialogue.[10] However, it appears that many U.S. corporations are wary to drink the blog Kool-Aid.

Following the dot-com bubble burst of the late 1990s, this should come as no surprise. Despite their wariness, corporations need to be aware that there is no "blog bubble" to burst. Most bloggers are "Average Joes" that operate with no business plan, no budget, and no sense of competition with other bloggers.[11] Blogs are inexpensive to operate and do not require a large capital investment to start. Blogs are not a "new way of conducting business" and should only be seen as an *additional* way to communicate. Blogs will not *replace* typical communication channels but can be used by corporations to increase both internal and external communication effectiveness.

Blog Usage in the Business World

Blogs should be used in the business world as an additional communication tool.[12] Blogs open up new internal and external communication channels. Although the technology is the same, the ways that blogs are used internally and externally differ.

Internal Blogging

The most common use for blogs within businesses today is as a project coordination tool. A team working on a project can use a blog to share information or provide progress updates. This information can be seen by the team members, managers that wish to "check in," or any other individuals within the company that are allowed access. Instead of spending the time to have a meeting with the team to discuss the team's progress on a project, the manager can simply take a look at the group's project blog. The benefit of blogs as a project coordination tool is amplified for teams that include members located in different geographic locations.

Blogs can also be used internally as a means of sharing information and collecting feedback from stakeholders.[13] If a company is looking for feedback from employees about a new policy, for example, they could start an internal blog about the issue. Previously, a series of meetings, reports, letters, memos, or "town-hall" gatherings may have been necessary. Blogs allow everyone to participate in the discussion at their convenience and keep a permanent record of all the thoughts, comments, and input that can be reviewed and considered at the convenience of the decision maker.

External Blogging

Blogs can be used externally to accomplish a variety of tasks. Companies can begin blogs to communicate with customers, potential customers, or even external vendors and supply chain members.[14] Communication using blogs or similar technology is viewed as more genuine, credible, and "real" compared to the rote and boring language of mission statements and press releases. Blogs are written in a conversational tone, which external stakeholders view more favorably.[15] Companies can use external blogs to obtain feedback from their customers about current or future products. Companies can use blogs to respond to criticism or crisis in the market. Companies can use blogs to gather new ideas about changes or new products that they should consider offering.[16] The sum of a customer-focused blog is that companies can use blogs to build and maintain relationships with the public, strengthening their brand and positioning in the marketplace.[17]

A second way to use external blogs to a company's advantage is by using an aggregator to track blogs.[18] An aggregator is a tool that constantly monitors the blogging world (blogosphere). Users can enter specific blog sites, authors, keywords, and other "search" criteria into an aggregator, and the aggregator will continually scan the Internet for matches to the search criteria. Aggregators are different from traditional search engines because they continually search, 24 hours a day, seven days a week, until they are told to stop. The results from aggregators are compiled on the user's computer and the user has the freedom to go back and read the blogs at their discretion.

Companies can use aggregators to get a pulse on what customers are thinking, saying, or wanting in new products. Companies can track their competition and customer feedback on competitor actions. Aggregators allow companies to gather up-to-the-minute information about what is being said about their products and/or services. By continually monitoring the market, companies will be able to respond more quickly to issues that arise.[19]

A third external use for blogs is to advertise. Many companies operate in niche markets and are constantly looking for new ways to reach their target market.[20] With over 112 million blogs online to choose from, chances are good that a blog focused on any given industry exists. Companies can capitalize on this opportunity by running banner ads on these blog sites, virtually guaranteeing that the people who come to read the blog are in their target market.

Advantages of Blogging

Blogs offer several advantages over more traditional communication channels. The first advantage is that blogs are not "frozen in time" but are constantly changing and evolving. Corporations use Web sites to communicate with consumers, but this communication can be likened to checking a book out at a library. If you were to go check out a copy of *The Call of the Wild* today, return it, and come back next week to get the same title, chances are good that you would find the exact same book. In the same sense, if you were to go to your company's Web site today and then go to the exact same Web address tomorrow, chances are good you would see the exact same thing. Blogs are different. Go to a blog today and read it. Return to the same blog tomorrow and you'll see the same information you read yesterday, but you may also find new topics, updates, and/or reader comments. This "new" Internet tracks not only the stale thoughts and messages of corporate Web sites, but also the "pulse" of what consumers are thinking—in real time.[21]

A second advantage of using blogs is that blogs are very user-friendly.[22] Blogs require no special programming knowledge. Chances are that if you can send an e-mail, you can contribute to a blog. Blogs are also cheap. Blogging software can be found for free online or users can register with a site that will host their blog at no cost. If a company wants to host their own blog, the software is not very expensive relative to the cost of maintaining a large corporate Web site and intranet. Blogs are easy to access and update. They simply require an Internet connection.

Again, the example works that if you can get online and check your e-mail, you can get online to read blogs, leave comments, or even write your own. Many blogs openly encourage reader interaction by providing a response form on the same page as the blog.

Blogs also offer companies a chance to learn of criticisms, crises, or simply share information much more quickly. In return, blogs also offer an avenue to respond to such criticisms, crises, or information quickly.[23] Previously, corporations had to rely on press releases, industry trade publications, or tedious Web site upgrades to announce new products or services. Blogs provide a means for corporations to communicate with consumers before, during, and after new products are brought to market.

A final advantage that blogs offer is that they encourage dialogue. Blogs allow individuals or corporations to gather feedback from others about any number of things. Unlike traditional media, there is very little "censorship" with blogs.[24] For example, new products are typically reviewed in trade journals or publications when they enter the market. The group responsible for the review (for example, *Car & Driver* reviewing a new Mercedes) has the "final say" about the product. The OEM or other consumers rarely have a chance to voice their opinion of the product or respond to the initial review. They can write letters to the editor, but again the publishing company has the final say about what letters are viewed by the general public. Blogs completely circumvent this entire process. Everyone now has a chance to provide feedback to anybody that is willing to "listen."

Disadvantages of Blogs

The "everyone is a publisher" mentality of the blogosphere can also be considered one of the disadvantages of blogs. Critics and/or competitors can use blogs to bash your products, gripe about your service, or even spread rumors that are untrue. Companies can "buy bloggers' support" or start "unbranded blogs of their own to promote their products."[25] While a company can certainly use this to their advantage, it is important to remember that competitors have the opportunity to do the exact same thing.

Blogs also offer some challenges in managing external relations. Corporate blogs, although maintained by individual employees, do represent the "voice of the corporation." Without proper monitoring, it is possible that the company could get a bad reputation.[26] Companies must also remember that most blog posts are permanent. There is little that companies can do after the fact to remedy situations such as releasing information in a blog that was not meant to reach the general public and/or competition.

The final disadvantage of blogs is more of a "threat" than a "disadvantage" in the sense that it can be overcome. Corporations have grown accustomed to being able to strongly shape their company message and reputation. Blogs take some of that power away from those corporations that choose to use them and give it to the readers/external users.[27] Although blogs offer an additional way to communicate with external stakeholders, they simultaneously open up a new channel for criticism. Although "censoring" those criticisms is possible, much credibility is lost in doing so.[28]

Implementing Blogs at Your Company

Blog usage will continue to grow. If your company has not entered the blogosphere yet, now may be the time to consider doing so. It is important to remember that communication via blogs is likely different than any type of communication your company is currently using. A thorough discussion of how to implement blogs at your company is beyond the scope of this appendix, but the following sections bring up some points you should be sure to cover when you decide to enter the blogosphere.

Creating Employee Blogging Guidelines

Blogs are seen as another "voice" of your company. Therefore, it is important to ensure that the voice speaking in external blogs agrees with the voice speaking in mission statements, press releases, advertisements, Web sites, and other forms of external communication. One way to ensure this continuity of voice is to create guidelines that employees must follow when writing blogs for your company. Guidelines may also help avoid legal troubles that could result from improper blog usage. The "proper" guidelines will vary from company to company, but two generic guidelines should be followed by all companies.[29]

- Require disclaimers for all employee blogs posts.
- Remove reader comments that are unrelated or include profanity or personal attacks.

Using Conversational Language

A second thing to consider when implementing guidelines is the "personal" nature of blogs. Blogs should be genuine. They should avoid the boring and mundane language of press releases, annual reports, and mission statements. Blogs should be open and honest communication that seeks response. Remember that the point of a blog is not only to share information with the public, but to also open a dialogue between the blogger and the readers.[30] If readers perceive the language to be too "stand-offish," they will not respond to corporate blogs and the company will not be able to capitalize on several of the opportunities that external blogs present.

Using RSS Syndication to Reach Larger Audiences

Companies must also ensure that their blogs are available via RSS.[31] In today's world, most blogs are automatically made available via RSS, but companies should take the extra steps to ensure that their blogs are broadcast via RSS.[32] RSS technology is what makes aggregators possible. By syndicating your blog on RSS, your company is helping your blog reach a larger audience. The use of aggregators has changed the way people search for information in blogs. In fact, with the use of an aggregator, people do not need to do any searching—the aggregator does the searching for you and brings the results to you to read on your own time. In turn, companies should also ensure they are using aggregators to monitor what is being said about their company, their competitors, their industry, and any other factors that they feel are important.[33]

Blogging for the Right Reasons

Finally, it is important that companies enter the blogosphere for the right reasons. This paper has highlighted the ways that companies can use blogs as both an internal and external communication tool. The benefits that blogs can bring to your company have also been discussed. However, that is not to say that blogs are for everyone. Companies should not begin blogging simply because their competitors are. Blogs should be used to fill a current communication gap or to strengthen communication channels that are currently in place.[34]

Conclusion

The blog "bubble" is not going to pop. Blogs have the ability to open up new avenues of communication in the business world. They have the advantages of being real-time, easy to operate, and are a great way to open up communication between groups. Blogs can be used to increase internal communication and coordination or be employed as a tool to reach external audiences and monitor the market. Blogs provide businesses with a valuable tool to add to their communication arsenal, but they must be implemented for the right reasons.

Discussion Questions

1. What are the advantages of corporate blogs for internal communication? What are the disadvantages of corporate blogs for internal communication?
2. What are the factors that a company should consider before setting up a blog for communication with customers?
3. Which target market is most likely to be responsive to a corporate blog?

Endnotes

1. S. Baker and H. Green, "Social Media Will Change Your Business," *BusinessWeek Online*, February 20, 2008, www.businessweek.com/go/blog (retrieved February 21, 2008).
2. *Wikipedia*, "Blog," http://en.wikipedia.org/wiki/Blog (retrieved February 23, 2008).
3. Baker and Green, "Social Media Will Change Your Business."
4. C. Catalano, "Megaphones to the Internet and the World: The Role of Blogs in Corporate Communication," *International Journal of Strategic Communication* 1, no. 4 (2007), pp. 247–262.
5. *Wikipedia*, "Blog."
6. S. Baker, "The Inside Story on Company Blogs," *BusinessWeek Online*, February 14, 2006, www.businessweek.com/technology/content/feb2006/tc20060214_402499.htm (retrieved February 21, 2008).
7. *Wikipedia*, "Blog."
8. Baker and Green, "Social Media Will Change Your Business."
9. *Wikipedia*, "Blog."
10. Baker and Green, "Social Media Will Change Your Business."
11. *Ibid.*

12. L. Rosencrance, "Blogs Bubble into Business," *ComputerWorld Online,* January 26, 2004, www.computerworld.com/softwaretopics/software/story/0,10801,89283,00.html.

13. Baker, "The Inside Story on Company Blogs."

14. *Ibid.*

15. P. Blackshaw and M. Nazzaro, "Consumer-Generated Media (CGM) 101: Word-of-Mouth in the Age of the Web-Fortified Consumer," Nielsen BuzzMetrics White Papers, Spring 2006, www.artsmarketing.org/marketingresources/files/Consumer-Generated percent20Media.pdf (retrieved March 8, 2008).

16. Baker and Green, "Social Media Will Change Your Business."

17. Baker, "The Inside Story on Company Blogs."

18. Baker and Green, "Social Media Will Change Your Business."

19. *Ibid.*

20. *Ibid.*

21. *Ibid.*

22. Baker, "The Inside Story on Company Blogs."

23. Catalano, "Megaphones to the Internet and the World."

24. Baker and Green, "Social Media Will Change Your Business."

25. *Ibid.*

26. Catalano, "Megaphones to the Internet and the World."

27. Baker and Green, "Social Media Will Change Your Business."

28. Baker, "The Inside Story on Company Blogs."

29. Catalano, "Megaphones to the Internet and the World."

30. *Ibid.*

31. *Ibid.*

32. *Wikipedia,* "Blogs."

33. Baker and Green, "Social Media Will Change Your Business."

34. Catalano, "Megaphones to the Internet and the World."

5. HELLO—IT'S INDIA CALLING: THE EFFECT OF OFFSHORING ON BUSINESS

Anna Turri, Sam Houston State University

Imagine that while working at your computer you consistently receive an error message from one of your programs and it always results in your computer shutting down. You are losing valuable work time so you finally decide to call your tech support hotline. The person who answers the phone is very considerate, but he has a thick accent and is hard for you to understand. Therefore, you decide to end your conversation with this individual and call again, hoping to have someone else answer the call. Once again your call is answered by someone with an accent so you ask where the tech center is located and the representative replies that all the calls are answered at a center in India. India? The response is somewhat shocking. After all, you are calling from San Diego, California, and you dialed a regular toll-free number, so how did someone in India end up answering the call?

The answer is simple: Many companies today are contracting out parts of their operations to separate vendors located in other countries. This process is known as offshoring.[1] This global type of outsourcing has come about as a result of three major economic developments: new political stability, strong educational systems, and cheaper high-bandwidth communication.[2] This last development is the result of advances in technology. Technological advances are really allowing communications to take place overseas with frequency and ease. "For the first time, satellite communication technology is allowing direct interactions between caller and customer across long distances and across national borders."[3]

But why India? India is one of the prime locations for call centers. "India call center work involves employees' providing voice-to-voice service to clients dialing toll-free numbers primarily in North America."[4] With its highly qualified work force and cheap labor, India is an ideal location for U.S. companies to offshore parts of their customer service departments. The number of foreign companies offshoring to India increased 1200 percent between 2000 and 2003, and many U.S. companies are continuing to invest in the market. For example, Dell is one of many U.S. companies that has call centers located in India and is expected to have over 15,000 employees there by 2008.[5]

Overall, offshoring has many advantages for businesses. These include reductions in cost, reallocation of internal resources, and access to a larger qualified work force. However, it also has many disadvantages, such as a loss of U.S. jobs to foreign workers, the possibility of dissatisfied customers, a decrease in quality, and problems with security and legal issues. Each of these will be looked at in detail, and some of the future trends in sourcing will be discussed.

Advantages of Offshoring

To begin with, why is everyone jumping on the offshoring bandwagon? The obvious answer is cost savings. When a company can buy a product or a service for less than the company can produce it internally, then the company can save a lot of money. Moreover, with China and India now a part of the global workplace, companies in America and Europe have access to a very large low-cost work force.[6]

Offshoring first started out affecting manufacturing jobs with the production of actual commodities overseas in places like India and China. However, now it is also affecting the service industry and white-collar workers with many middle-class jobs being transferred overseas. For example, "Processing insurance claims, selling stocks, and analyzing companies can all be done in Asia for one-third to half of the cost in the U.S. or Europe."[7] One reason these service industry jobs can now be done effectively overseas is because of the vast improvement of the Internet and the reduced costs of high-bandwidth data networks in places like India over the last few years. Now the data for jobs like processing insurance claims can be moved back and forth overseas faster and more efficiently than it has ever been done in the past. Also, this inexpensive communication via computers makes it possible for large groups of employees to be managed at almost any location.[8]

But reducing costs is not the only benefit of offshoring. In fact, the number one reason most companies gave for outsourcing overseas was so they could reallocate internal resources to more important areas.[9] For example, if companies can limit the amount of time per day employees spend on mundane tasks, then this will allow these same employees to focus on more critical aspects of their jobs. In fact, offshoring can be an important aspect of company innovation and expansion.[10]

Finally, offshoring allows U.S. companies to have more access to a qualified work force. In other areas of the world, such as India and China, strong educational networks are turning out highly educated and motivated individuals who are willing to work for less than an average American or European worker.[11] The Philippines has about 380,000 new college graduates per year and India graduates approximately 520,000 IT engineers every year.[12] These software engineers are willing to work for an average of $20,000 annually compared with U.S. software engineers, who command annual salaries of $150,000.[13] So, it is no wonder that a major New York securities firm plans to replace 800 of their software engineers with ones from India over the next three years.

Disadvantages of Offshoring

One of the most common complaints heard when offshoring is discussed is that American workers are losing their jobs to foreign workers. While this is sometimes the case, most companies assert that they are not getting rid of workers; instead, they are reallocating their work force to more essential, better paying jobs.[14] In any event, no matter what companies claim, outsourcing overseas has affected U.S. jobs, and as more companies take advantage of cheap overseas labor "the transition will not be painless and will hit the middle classes of the developed world in particular."[15] Any employee whose job does not require daily face-to-face dealings is now in danger.[16]

Another disadvantage of offshoring is the possibility of customer dissatisfaction. The company 1-800-FLOWERS recently experimented with using a call center based in India to take orders from customers. However, the firm stopped the experiment after customers complained that the representatives were hard to understand. If they had not listened and acted on these customers' complaints, the dissatisfied customers would have switched to one of their competitors.[17]

Some companies that have outsourced their work overseas have noticed that the quality of the work is not quite on par with their expectations. One possible reason is as follows:

> When people don't identify with the organization on whose behalf they're working, their performance typically suffers. . . . It's human nature: Since the name of their organization is not directly associated with the services that contractors provide, there's less motivation to make sure it's done right.[18]

This can definitely be a problem if a company hires a relatively unknown outsourcing firm and does not verify the quality of their past work.

A final problem area associated with offshoring involves security and legal concerns. If a company is sending private data such as Social Security and credit card numbers overseas, then it is out of the hands of United States law enforcement. This would make it hard to prosecute someone who uses this information for illegal purposes overseas.[19] Also, U.S. companies are taking a chance with their patents and copyrights since they might not be valid in other countries.[20] Moreover, overseas "intellectual property is in the hands of nonemployees over whom it (the company) has little control . . . loyalty is nil, and poaching and piracy are rampant."[21]

Homeshoring as an Alternative to Offshoring

Given all the disadvantages previously described, some U.S. companies have turned from offshoring to homeshoring. Homeshoring is the term given to domestic home-based phone jobs, which are projected to increase from 112,000 to 300,000 by 2010.[22] JetBlue Airways Corporation was one of the first companies to take advantage of homeshoring with 1,400 reservation agents working from the comfort of their own home. [23]

Homeshoring offers many benefits. First, it allows companies to access a large group of untapped potential workers: stay-at-home parents. These people like the flexibility the job offers, and the companies like the fact that it provides an inexpensive just-in-time work force.[24] Second, "if offshore jobs tend to offer cheaper labor, homeshoring's big advantage is that there is virtually no capital expense for offices, parking lots, cafeterias, and other employee amenities, not to mention benefits."[25] Finally, homeshoring also helps solve the problem of customer dissatisfaction from dealing with customer service representatives in other countries. With homeshoring there is less risk associated with misunderstandings due to heavy accents or problems associated with cultural disconnections.[26]

The Insourcing Trend

Another trend that seems to be occurring on a more regular basis is insourcing. Foreign companies want to increase their presence in the American market and are beginning to insource their operations to the United States. Insourcing, also known as reverse outsourcing, happens when companies from other countries like China and India establish operations in the United States or when foreign companies recruit employees from other areas of the world.[27] These insourced jobs increased from 2.5 million in 1983 to 6.5 million in 2000, and the numbers are still growing.[28]

This increase in reverse outsourcing should help calm fears that too many American jobs are being sent overseas. Since these foreign companies are now locating in the U.S., they are creating jobs and helping to increase U.S. living standards. In fact, these companies employ more than 5.4 million people in the United States and have added to the U.S. economy by increasing investments in research and development as well as physical capital. They also "typically purchase a majority of their supplies from domestic (and not foreign) firms—to the tune of 80 cents out of every dollar, or $1.26 trillion."[29]

In addition, some of the foreign companies that are not quite ready to establish offices in the U.S. are beginning to contract-out Americans to work on their projects. Indian software companies are now faced with a shortage of labor and are outsourcing some of these jobs to the U.S. and other parts of the world.[30] For example, the largest Indian phone company, Bharti Tele-Ventures, has outsourced its technical tasks to IBM in America.[31] If this shortage of workers continues, more foreign companies will begin to follow in Bharti's footsteps.

A Look to the Future

Given the facts regarding offshoring, a few things can be said about the future. First, given the lower costs for labor and production overseas, global outsourcing will continue until "rising global salaries dissipate the easy cost gains."[32] As long as costs can be reduced and the quality of products and services is not sacrificed, offshoring should continue to be used by U.S. companies. However, if problems surface with regard to quality or poor customer service, companies will have to weigh the advantages gained by lower costs against the potential loss of customers and tarnished reputation. In the end, they might find that the cost outweighs the benefits and have to move the offshored service/product back in-house.

Second, more companies will begin to move some of their offshore call centers back to the U.S. and homeshore the operations. Homeshoring appears to still reduce cost for U.S. companies and it has a better track record when it comes to customer satisfaction than overseas call centers.

Finally, with labor shortages beginning to happen in other countries like India, more foreign companies will begin insourcing to America. If this type of reverse outsourcing continues, we will be looking at "a big circle, where Indians hire Americans and other foreigners, and global Western companies hire Indians, Chinese, etc."[33]

Discussion Questions

1. Define and compare each of the following terms: outsourcing, insourcing.
2. Define and compare each of the following terms: offshoring, homeshoring.
3. What are the advantages of a company's outsourcing certain business functions, such as accounting, human resources, and customer service?
4. What are the disadvantages of a company's outsourcing certain business functions, such as accounting, human resources, and customer service?

Endnotes

1. W. J. Keehan and M. C. Green, *Global Marketing*, 5th ed. (Upper Saddle River, NJ: Pearson/Prentice Hall, 2008).
2. C. Schumer and C. Roberts, "Second Thoughts on Free Trade," *The New York Times*, January 6, 2004.
3. W. R. Poster, "Who's on the Line? Indian Call Center Agents Pose as Americans for U.S.-Outsourced Firms," *Industrial Relations* 46, no. 2 (2007), pp. 271–304.
4. M. Pal and P. Buzzanell, "The Indian Call Center Experience: A Case Study in Changing Discourses of Identity, Identification, and Career in a Global Context," *Journal of Business Communication* 45, no. 1 (2008), pp. 31–60.
5. *Ibid.*

6. L. Dobbs, "The Global Outlook on Outsourcing," January 31, 2005, www.cnn.com/2005/US/01/28/world.outsourcing (retrieved February 28, 2006).

7. P. Engardio, A. Bernstein, and M. Kripalani, "The New Global Job Shift," February 3, 2003, www.businessweek.com (retrieved February 28, 2006).

8. Schumer and Roberts, "Second Thoughts on Free Trade."

9. PR Newswire Europe, "Outsourcing Industry at a Crossroads: Annual DiamondCluster Survey Finds Customers Questioning Value," June 7, 2005, http://web.lexis-nexis.com.unx1.shsu.edu (retrieved March 31, 2006).

10. S. Fullmer, "Why to Support Global Outsourcing," www.informit.com (retrieved February 27, 2006).

11. Schumer and Roberts, "Second Thoughts on Free Trade."

12. Engardio, Bernstein, and Kripalani, "The New Global Job Shift."

13. Schumer and Roberts, "Second Thoughts on Free Trade."

14. D. Drezner, "The Outsourcing Bogeyman," *Foreign Affairs*, May/June 2004.

15. Dobbs, "The Global Outlook on Outsourcing."

16. Schumer and Roberts, "Second Thoughts on Free Trade."

17. M. Conlin, "Call Centers in the Rec Room: 'Homeshoring' Takes Off as Moms and Others Provide an Alternative to Offshoring," *BusinessWeek* 76 (January 23, 2006), http://web.lexis-nexis.com.unx1.shsu.edu (retrieved March 24, 2006).

18. J. Pfeffer, "The Hidden Cost of Outsourcing," March 1, 2006, www.cnnmoney.com (retrieved March 12, 2006).

19. Conlin, "Call Centers in the Rec Room."

20. A. Gore, "The Future of Outsourcing: September 11, 2011," October 3, 2003, www.informit.com (retrieved February 7, 2006).

21. A. Fisher, "Bringing the Jobs Home," *Fortune* 22 (March 20, 2006).

22. J. Fitzgerald, "Some Workers Show Up in PJ's; 'Homeshoring' Springing to Life," *The Boston Herald*, January 6, 2006, p. O27, http://web.lexis-nexis.com.unx1.shsu.edu (retrieved March 24, 2006).

23. Conlin, "Call Centers in the Rec Room."

24. *Ibid.*

25. K. Hall, "New Homegrown Operations Challenge Offshoring Trend," *Knight Ridder/Tribune News Service*, December 1, 2005, http://web.lexis-nexis.com.unx1.shsu.edu (retrieved March 23, 2006).

26. Conlin, "Call Centers in the Rec Room."

27. P. Keefe, "Reverse the (Outsourcing) Curse," June 2, 2006, www.informationweek.com (retrieved March 13, 2007).

28. Drezner, "The Outsourcing Bogeyman."

29. S. Swoyer, "Outsourcing in Reverse: Foreign Companies Send Jobs to the United States," October 26, 2004, www.esj.com (retrieved March 13, 2007).

30. Keefe, "Reverse the (Outsourcing) Curse."

31. E. Frauenheim, "Does 'Reverse Outsourcing' Mean Much?" January 18, 2005, http://news.com.com/2061-10788_3-5540692.html (retrieved March 13, 2007).

32. P. Engardio, M. Arndt, and D. Foust, "The Future of Outsourcing," January 30, 2006, www.businessweek.com (retrieved February 15, 2006).

33. Keefe, "Reverse the (Outsourcing) Curse."

6. LIVE CHAT IN E-COMMERCE

Anna M. Turri, Sam Houston State University

The emergence of online shopping as a retail phenomenon is undisputed. One feature that helps make online shopping seem closer to the traditional bricks-and-mortar experience is live chat. A Web site's live chat feature represents a salesperson who can provide assistance, direction, encouragement, and support for the shopper. The interaction between shopper and sales assistant is synchronous and text-based. Leigh Duncan, of KPMG Consulting, calls live chat "revolutionary" because it brings the cost of customer service down significantly and puts the retail sales rep in the home with customers while they are shopping."[1]

Benefits of Live Chat for Online Retailers

Live chat is an exploding technology that brings the Web-shopping experience closer to the real-world. Retail sites have adopted the feature because it is a low-cost simple way of communicating with customers. LivePerson, Inc., a leading provider of the software and support headquartered in New York City, has more than 4,000 client companies, including EarthLink, Hewlett-Packard, Microsoft, Verizon, Neiman Marcus, QVC, New Line Cinema, Charles Schwab, Qwest, and Sony. Their revenue for 2006 is projected to be over $32 million, and they are experiencing quarterly revenue increases of some 40 percent from the previous year.[2]

The hosted software enables companies to identify and engage online shoppers, thereby increasing sales. Reports indicate that the greatest advantage of this feature is that it increases the "conversion rate," or the likelihood that a shopper will actually buy a product. Shoe company K-Swiss, Inc., for example, reports more than double the average conversion rate when customers use live chat, since 75 percent of chats are directly related to product knowledge.[3] Live chat also allows cross-selling and up-selling. It lowers shopping cart abandonment and increases the customer's confidence to complete a purchase. According to an Andersen Consulting poll, almost 62 percent of Internet consumers said they would purchase more products online if live customer support were available.[4]

Second, live chat does not require a huge technology investment. Vendors and analysts say the cost of implementing live chat on a commercial site is low. Generally, the application can be downloaded onto a retailer's server in under an hour. Customer service representatives merely need browsers on their computers.

Third, live chat costs less than customer service phone calls and e-mails. ServiceReps.com Inc., another major provider, offers these comparisons: Depending on wait time, it can cost $15 to $35 to handle phone calls. E-mails can cost $7 to $13, with that price affected in part by the fact that reps deal with e-mails serially rather than simultaneously. Live chats are about $2 per transaction. Part of the cost analysis considers the length of time it takes to resolve customer questions. E-mails can take up to three days, while phone and chat questions are resolved immediately.[5]

Fourth, text chat is growing in consumer acceptance. Many shoppers use instant messaging and text messaging for personal and professional communication. Live chat on retail sites is merely an extension. The instant results make it superior to going offline to call the customer service center or waiting for an e-mail response to the customer's question. Sixty-three percent of U.S. online consumers reported that they had used live chat in 2005, an increase of 22 percent from 2001. In addition, 58 percent of those using chat in 2005 said they were satisfied with the results, up 13 percent from 2001.[6]

Retailers can improve the ROI of live chat by limiting its availability to certain situations, according to a new JupiterResearch report. One model, *reactive chat*, uses the feature only for complex issues and for troubleshooting. A second model, *proactive chat*, uses pop-up chat requests or chat buttons only at critical phases, such as after products have sat in shopping carts for a length of time. A third model, *automated chat*, uses live agents only to answer inquiries that automation cannot handle, reducing service costs by some 80 percent.[7]

Drawbacks of Live Chat for Online Retailers

Andrews and Haworth observed that there is little empirical evidence demonstrating the value of live chat for e-commerce.[8] They conducted a usability study of five e-commerce Web sites that offer live chat in order to evaluate customers' actual satisfaction level and purchase behavior. Their results confirm that a positive chat experience increases purchase rate. However, they identified both technical and sociability issues that are relevant to live chat's effectiveness.

Technical issues include consumer access to the chat function—that is, a shopper with a question who must search for the link/icon may become frustrated and abandon the Web site. In addition, shoppers expect to interact with an actual person during the chat and are disappointed with canned responses or inattentive interaction.[9] The software can be complex, and difficult to properly install and manage.[10] It can be poorly designed[11] or unable to handle complex problems.[12]

Sociability issues are housed in the actual interactions between shopper and customer service representative. Andrews and Haworth identified five specific problems with sociability:

- Asking for personal information that shoppers did not consider relevant
- Missing privacy statements
- Referring shoppers to a Web page instead of answering the shopper's question directly
- Impersonal, generic, cryptic, or canned responses
- Lack of politeness and etiquette, including typos, sentence fragments, using all capital letters, not saying "please" and "thank you"

Implications for Interpersonal Communication Skills

From the retailers' perspective, live chat's efficiency is paramount. Service representatives must be able to handle multiple chats at one time. Call center reps are trained for typing speed, grammar and spelling skills, and overall quality of written skills. Preformatted answers are often used to make the chat move faster.

From the shoppers' perspective, however, such efficiency factors may detract from the live chat experience. A poorly worded response negatively affects shoppers' opinions of the chat, even if the shopper receives the information they need.[13] Shoppers want to connect with the service rep and have personal conversations, sometimes about irrelevant topics such as where the rep is located. Clearly, consumers expect live chat to mirror face-to-face communication as much as possible.[14] Personalized chats can be important determinants of perceived service quality, satisfaction, and purchase behavior.

Live chat experiences show how interpersonal communication leads to interpersonal relationships, which leads to trust, which leads to purchase. For instance, when asked directly for their reasons for buying at a Web site after experiencing live chat, shoppers consistently stated five reasons for a positive buying intention:

- Overall positive experience with the Web site, including the chat
- Trust in the retailer
- Confidence in the products
- Price acceptability
- Low risk of purchase[15]

Trust, or reputation, is related to communication in concrete ways. When technical problems occur during e-commerce, trust may keep the customer pursuing a purchase rather than abandoning the effort. Conversely, poor technical performance or a poor live chat experience appears to drive away new online customers.

Discussion Questions

1. What is the function of the live chat feature in online retail sites?
2. What is the function of the telephone support/help line?
3. Compare live chat with telephone support, including the advantages and disadvantages of each for online shoppers.
4. Compare both of these support features to the clerical help offered in a bricks-and-mortar retail store. What are the advantages and disadvantages of each?
5. As a business communication consultant, what would you recommend to online retailers to improve the live chat feature?

Endnotes

1. A. M. Findlay, "Answering Questions the Instant the Online Shopper Asks Them," 2002, www.internetretailer.com/article.asp?id=6475 (retrieved September 5, 2006).

2. *Internet Retailer,* "LivePerson Reports Second Quarter Revenue Increase of 40% to $7.4 Million," 2006, www.internetretailer.com/pressReleaseDetail.asp?id=19461 (retrieved September 5, 2006).

3. A. M. Findlay, "Answering Questions the Instant the Online Shopper Asks Them."

4. *Volusion*, "Live Chat Software: Online Customer Service for Online Selling, the Commodity Becomes the Necessity," message posted July 14, 2006, to http://online-business.volusion.com/articles/live-chat-software.

5. A. M. Findlay, "Answering Questions the Instant the Online Shopper Asks Them."

6. *Internet Retailer*, "LivePerson Reports Second Quarter Revenue Increase of 40% to $7.4 Million."

7. *Ibid.*

8. D. C. Andrews and K. N. Haworth, "Online Customer Service Chat: Usability and Sociability Issues," *Journal of Internet Marketing* 2, no. 1 (2006), www.arraydev.com/commerce/jim/0203-01.htm (retrieved September 5, 2006).

9. *Ibid.*

10. C. Hodge, *Message Posted to the Netpreneur Ad-marketing Listserv*, message posted January 23, 2000, to www.netpreneur.org.

11. M. Puente, "Customer Service with a :-)," [Electronic version], *USA Today*, December 6, 2000, www.usatoday.com (retrieved September 5, 2006).

12. K. Bannan, "Chatting Up a Sale," [Electronic version], *The Wall Street Journal*, October 23, 2000, http://pqasb.pqarchiver.com/wsj/access/62807962.html?dids=62807962:62807962 (retrieved September 5, 2006).

13. D. C. Andrews and K. N. Haworth, "Online Customer Service Chat."

14. K. E. Reynolds and M. J. Arnold, "Customer Loyalty to the Salesperson and the Store: Examining Relationship Customers in an Upscale Retail Context," *The Journal of Personal Selling and Sales Management* 20, no. 2 (2000), pp. 89–98.

15. D. C. Andrews and K. N. Haworth, "Online Customer Service Chat."

7. VIDEO RÉSUMÉS

Anna Turri, Sam Houston State University

When it comes time to look for a job, the most important item to have on hand is a résumé. This one-page document gives a potential employer the chance to look over an applicant's accomplishments and make a decision on whether or not to call them in for an interview. At this interview, a potential employee gets a chance to sell themselves and let their qualities and abilities truly shine. However, some individuals are saying "Why wait for the interview? Why not let employers know what I have to offer from the start?" In order to do this, they are turning to video résumés, a brief video made by job seekers that allows them to state their qualifications and convey to the employer why they feel they are the right person for the particular job in question.[1]

This form of résumé appears to be catching on quite quickly. With digital video images becoming faster to upload and with the majority of job seekers having access to Web-cams, it seems natural that video résumés would take off.[2] In fact, on August 8, 2007, CareerTV.com launched in New York with the idea to provide the largest collection of employer videos and help potential employees make and distribute video résumés. The company could not say enough about the benefits of video résumés and how they would revolutionize companies' recruiting processes. However, by November 6, 2007, their video résumé service was being shut down with claims that there was not enough interest from employers.[3] It appears that CareerTV.com focused only on the benefits of video résumés and failed to see their shortcomings.

Advantages of Video Résumés

Video résumés have some distinct advantages over their paper counterparts. First, résumés done on video give employees a chance to better showcase their persona. According to Travis Cloyd, a co-owner of a video résumé service named Workblast.com, they "are offering the job seeker a chance to display their personality and enthusiasm, their passion for a particular industry."[4] Many job candidates feel that if given the right opportunity, they could impress the potential employer enough to secure the position. For many, the use of the video résumé is their opportunity to let their best qualities shine.

Employers also see the benefits of the video résumé. Thirty-one percent of employers who responded to a 2007 *Vault Employer Video Resume Survey* think that these types of résumés will be valuable when looking for future employees.[5] They feel that video résumés will make it easier for employers to do the following:

- Judge an applicant's professional manner and presentation.
- Get a better feel for an applicant's past job experience.
- Assess an applicant's way of speaking.
- Evaluate an applicant's potential leadership and magnetism.
- Determine whether an applicant is part of a targeted minority group.[6]

Overall, a video résumé can enable potential employees to express themselves better than they can on paper and it also allows employers to gather more information than they can discern from a traditional résumé.

Disadvantages of Video Résumés

Even though employers and potential employees alike see the many benefits of the video résumé, several drawbacks exist.

First, there is the problem of time. Traditional paper résumés usually only take seconds to scan through and distinguish the good from the bad. However, video résumés can range between one to three minutes long and for a job with many potential applicants employers do not have the time to sit and view them all.

Second, there is the problem of comparisons. Paper résumés allow employers to compare potential candidates side by side, as well as make notes and underline key points. However, since there is currently no standard format, there is no way to easily compare video résumés to each other, let alone to standard résumés.

A third problem is storage. As part of record retention requirements, employers are required to keep the résumés they receive, which obviously can result in a problem if they receive hundreds of videos for one position.[7]

Finally, there are the legal issues. According to the EEOC video résumés give potential employers a lot of information that they usually do not have access to with paper résumés and can therefore lead to "unconscious biases."[8] Years ago the U.S. prohibited the inclusion of pictures with résumés, but with video résumés there is no way to exclude the picture. Another problem according to the EEOC is "a disproportionate exclusion of applicants of color who may not have access to broadband-equipped computers or video cameras."[9] Even though computers are accessible to many people there are still those who do not have access or cannot afford to make a video résumé. Since most legal advisors do not know exactly how video résumés will be dealt with in the legal arena, their best advice is to use them only as a supplement to traditional paper résumés.

Dos and Don'ts

If a video résumé must be made, it should be constructed with the same care and attention to detail that one would give to a regular résumé. Listed below are some tips for how to make a video résumé look professional.[10]

Do	Don't
• Dress professionally	• Dress in casual clothes
• Introduce yourself	• Tell your life story
• Be concise	• Read from a script
• Be enthusiastic	• Just read your résumé
• Thank the employer for their time	• Speak too fast
• Make practice recordings	• Include information that should be excluded from traditional résumés
• Look at the video before sending it	
• Cut down on background noise	

A good example of what not to do comes from a recent graduate of Yale University who applied for a job using a video résumé, but did not follow the tips given here. Instead of keeping the video focused on his professional endeavors, it showed him lifting weights, dancing, and playing tennis. It also ran more than six minutes long instead of the preferred one to three.[11] Needless to say, the video did not land him the job and instead ended up on YouTube for the whole world to watch. Please let this example reinforce the need to keep video résumés short, clear, and professional.

Conclusion

Video résumés may help potential employees distinguish themselves from other candidates and they certainly have their benefits. They can clearly help employers better assess certain skills when compared to a paper résumé. However, they should be used with caution. Candidates using video résumés have a higher chance of accidentally disclosing inappropriate information on a video résumé than they normally would on a traditional one. They therefore have a higher chance of being discriminated against. Employers must also be aware of the potential downfalls to video résumés since they can take up a lot of the recruiters' time and cause a lot of legal headaches. If a video résumé is created, it is important to put as much time and effort as would be spent to polish a paper résumé. It is important to make the video as professional as possible and to make it relevant to the future employer. Finally, given some of their downfalls, it seems that video résumés are best used in tandem with traditional ones in order to enhance what is seen on paper, not to replace it.

Discussion Questions

1. What are the benefits of video résumés?
2. Why would an employer prefer a video résumé and why might they prefer a paper résumé?
3. Choose whether you would prefer to submit a paper or video résumé if you were applying for a job as a media coordinator in an advertising agency and give your reasons why. Would your answer be the same if you were applying for a job as an investment banker at a top investment firm? Why or why not?

Endnotes

1. A. Doyle, "Video Resumes Tips," http://jobsearch.about.com/od/videoresumes/a/videoresume.htm?p=1 (retrieved November 13, 2007).
2. R. Singh, "Time to Hit Pause on Video Resumes," *Electronic Recruiting Exchange,* February 13, 2007, www.ere.net (retrieved November 13, 2007).
3. "CareerTV to Abandon Video Resumes," November 6, 2007, www.cheezhead.com/2007/11/06/video-resumes/ (retrieved November 13, 2007).
4. B. Beard, "Video Resume Site Blasts Off," *The Arizona Republic,* April 20, 2007, www.azcentral.com (retrieved November 13, 2007).
5. K. Gurchiek, "Video Resumes Spark Curiosity, Questions," *HR Magazine,* May 2007, pp. 28–30.
6. *Ibid.*
7. J. Sullivan, "Resumes: Paper, Please," *Workforce Management* 86, no. 18 (October 22, 2007), p. 50.
8. B. Beard, "Video Resume Site Blasts Off."
9. K. Butler, "Too Much Can Go Wrong with Using Video Resumes in Hiring," *Employee Benefit News* 21, no. 13 (October 2007), p. 7.
10. "Do's/Don'ts," 2007, www.careerbuilder.com/JobSeeker/VideoResumes/DosDonts.aspx (retrieved November 13, 2007).
11. D. Ransom, "Video Resumes Are Taking Off," *The Wall Street Journal Online,* January 1, 2007, www.careerjournal.com (retrieved November 13, 2007).

8. E-RÉSUMÉS IN THE 21ST-CENTURY JOB SEARCH

Harini Vemulapati, Sam Houston State University

The résumé is most often the first point of contact that job-seekers have with potential employers. Employers use it to assess a candidate's qualifications and accomplishments and to decide whether he/she is a good fit for the job. This makes résumés excellent marketing tools that give job-seekers an opportunity to sell themselves for a position. With the growing use of technology among employers and applicants, online and electronic résumés have become very popular in today's work environment. Taleo Research, which studies management practices, found that 94 percent of the top 500 U.S. corporations solicit online résumés so their human resources departments can use software to narrow down a huge stack of candidates quickly to a manageable list of finalists.[1]

Before proceeding to a detailed discussion, it is important to differentiate between two types of online résumés.

- **Online résumé:** A résumé that individuals submit to online résumé databanks like Monster.com and Careerbuilder.com, which store résumés and make them accessible to various employers. This type of résumé can either be designed for a human reader or a computer.[2]
- **Scannable résumé (electronic résumé):** A résumé that is specifically designed to be read electronically by a company's optical character recognition (OCR) hardware and software. An OCR converts the characters from a printed page into text and stores them in the company's résumé database. This type of résumé is originally printed on paper and scanned directly into the company's database. It is designed to be read by a computer.

Electronic Résumés

In this appendix, we will focus on the type of résumés that most graduate students use in their job search—scannable or electronic résumés. All electronic résumés submitted to a company are stored in a single database that is monitored by the company's Human Resources Department. This database then facilitates the search process that managers use to evaluate the applications and is done through the usage of keywords specific to a position.

Advantages of E-Résumés

Electronic résumés have many advantages for both job-seekers and employers. First, the candidate can be considered for a greater number of openings than he or she would be if submitting only a paper résumé. Since the electronic résumés are stored in the company's database, the candidates may also be considered for future openings without having to reapply. Second, electronic résumés enable job-seekers to tailor their résumés according to the requirements of the job they are applying for, and it also allows them to include all the appropriate keywords pertaining to a position.[3] Finally, the initial screening is done by a bias-free computer rather than a potentially biased interviewer. This ensures that all applicants are given the same opportunity to land an interview.

Electronic résumés are also advantageous to recruiting employers. The first advantage is that companies do not need to scan hundreds of résumés manually because electronic résumés are stored in a database and the employer can search only for the most qualified candidates using keywords. The hiring supervisor can request a candidate with specific experience, skills, or qualifications in the database search. Also, computers can scan the databases more economically than the company personnel are able to. Second, since the scanning technology significantly reduces the time taken to screen candidates, this results in cost savings for the company since fewer personnel are necessary to process the résumés.

Disadvantages of E-Résumés

Using electronic résumés has its disadvantages, however. First, some companies do not update the status of vacant positions often. Therefore, even though a candidate submits his/her résumé to the company's database, it may never be noticed if that particular position is already filled and the candidate may still be hoping for a response from them.[4] Second, résumés that have been in a database for a long period of time may become outdated and no longer reflect a candidate's most recent qualifications. Another disadvantage of electronic résumés is that any errors in the optical scanning technology software may cause disruptions to the original content of the scanned résumé, and the manager who is reviewing that résumé may not see the content in the exact way it was submitted originally. This results in an unattractive appearance of the résumé and may cost the candidate his/her shot at the job. Finally, since the résumé search is done using keywords, any absence of a particular keyword on the applicant's résumé may hinder its possibility of appearing in the search results.

Best Practices

Because of the complexity of technologies involved in the conversion process of scannable résumés, it is very important to keep their format plain and simple. A résumé that is not formatted correctly will not appear in the keyword search process. Unlike a traditional résumé, which focuses on visual aesthetics and use of action verbs, electronic résumés should be simple and easy to read and use nouns to enhance the keyword search.

Here are some basic format guidelines for preparing scannable résumés:

- Use a simple font. The standard fonts for résumés are Times New Roman and Arial. The standard font sizes are 10 and 12.[5]
- Avoid fancy formatting like graphics, shading, headers, footers, italics, text-boxes, pictures, or tables in the résumé.[6] If you must include any of these in your résumé, it is better to have them as a separate attachment or Web page and link them to the résumé.

- Use keywords effectively.[7] To improve the number of hits on your résumé, use specific keywords for your job and industry. The most common types of keywords are:

  - **Job Titles:** Include job titles that describe the position you are applying for. Some examples are Project Manager, Quality Assurance Analyst, Financial Analyst, Credit Analyst, and Administrative Assistant.

  - **Skills and Responsibilities:** These are specific to a job. Study job postings in your field to learn what employers are looking for. Examples include proficiency in Microsoft Office, QuickBooks, leadership qualities, good communication skills, Accounts Receivable, type 90 wpm with complete accuracy, highly focused and results-oriented in supporting complex deadline-driven operations.

  - **Position and Industry Buzzwords:** Research industry trends and professional association Web sites to uncover current buzzwords that employers use and include them in your résumé. Examples include TQM, client-server, value-added, ROI, interculturalism.

  - **Education and Certifications:** Include specific educational degrees and certifications such as Master's in Business Administration, Certified Public Accountant (CPA), Six Sigma Certification.

  - **Professional Organizations and Affiliations:** List the names of all professional organizations you are a part of. Examples include the IMA (Institute of Management Accounting), SHRM (Society for Human Resource Management), AMA (American Management Association). Include student chapters that you joined on campus, too.

- Provide a keyword summary at the beginning of your résumé, immediately after the Career Objective section. List all the keywords directly related to the position for which you are applying. This will provide an opportunity to include other variations of a keyword that may not fit in the rest of the résumé.

Converting a Paper Résumé into an E-Résumé

As mentioned earlier, the most important difference between traditional paper résumés and electronic résumés is that paper résumés are designed to be read by the hiring personnel in a company. An electronic résumé is read by the OCR technology, which scans résumés for keywords and presents a manageable final list to the hiring agents. Therefore, extra care must be taken to make it simple and easy to read.

The first step in converting a paper résumé into an electronic one is to save the file as a text file in a word-processing program like MS Word. The second step is to edit this file by taking out special formatting like bold, italics, lines, and indents. Also, all bullets in the file must be replaced with asterisks.[8] Then, all font styles and sizes must be changed to standard formats. It is also important to have your name on the very first line of the résumé. If the organization has specific guidelines for formatting a résumé, follow these while preparing your résumé. After making the necessary changes, save the document with a separate name. The last step is to print the résumé on white paper using a high-quality laser printer in black ink. The résumé can be mailed or scanned and sent to the company directly.

Conclusion

Because of the impact that electronic résumés have on the job-search process, it is important that job-seekers be familiar with the design and structure of e-résumés. Also, with the increasing use of electronic technology in organizations, it is important to make résumés easily adaptable to the new environment.

Discussion Questions

1. What are the main reasons that employer companies have migrated to electronic résumé databases?
2. What are the advantages of formatting your résumé for electronic searches?
3. What are the disadvantages of formatting your résumé for electronic searches?

Endnotes

1. "The Art of the Online Résumé," May 2007, www.businessweek.com/magazine/content/07_19/b4033099.htm (retrieved December 3, 2008).
2. "'Take Five' When Applying for Jobs Online," *Associations Now* 4, no. 7 (2008), p. 90.
3. Z. K. Quible, "The Electronic Résumé: An Important New Job-Search Tool," *Journal of Education for Business* 74, no. 2 (1998), p. 79.
4. L. G. Salters, "Résumé Writing for the 21st Century," *Business & Economic Review* 48, no. 3 (2002), p. 18.
5. L. Schneider, "How to Make a Resume: Tips for Resume Formats," http://jobsearchtech.about.com/od/gettingthejob/a/HowToMakeResume.htm (retrieved December 4, 2008).
6. J. T. Chyna, "Crafting an Electronic Résumé," *Healthcare Executive* 18, no. 6 (2003), p. 44.
7. Career Development Series, Miami University, "Online Resumes," www.units.muohio.edu/careers/cds/onlineresumes.pdf (retrieved December 2008).
8. S. D. Greene and Melanie Martel, "Converting Your Resume Electronic Format," http://apps.byuh.edu/career/Documents/Search/Get%20Equipped/Resume/E-Resume%20Tip%20Sheet.pdf (retrieved December 5, 2008).

9. MONITORING IN THE WORKPLACE

Anna Turri, Sam Houston State University

Imagine that while you are at work you receive a very funny, albeit somewhat questionable, e-mail from your best friend. Knowing your co-workers will find this e-mail hilarious, you forward it to everyone and go about your day. You don't give it another thought until the next day when you are called in to your boss's office, see a copy of your e-mail on his desk, and are asked to explain yourself. How could this happen? Isn't your e-mail private?

Many employees are under the false assumption that their time spent on a computer is personal if no one is there to physically watch them. However, nothing could be further from the truth. With new advances in technology it is now possible for your boss to monitor your every move from afar. In fact, new electronic monitoring allows employers to monitor a number of employees at once and gather very detailed information about how their employees spend their time at work.[1] The key point to remember is that while working, employees should assume they are being watched at all times.

Why Companies Monitor

Companies may choose to monitor employees for many reasons. These include the following:

- Mitigating legal liability
- Reducing the misuse of company resources
- Protecting intellectual property[2]

First and foremost, companies monitor in order to prevent lawsuits. This is true because companies can be held liable for any and all communication that uses their computer systems.[3] In fact, a sexual harassment suit was brought against Chevron when an employee sent an offensive e-mail over the company system. This seemingly incidental e-mail ended up costing the company $2.2 million.[4]

Second, companies also monitor to catch employees who are misusing the company's resources. For example, employers want to know if an employee is spending valuable work time surfing the Internet, playing computer games, or planning a vacation online. A 2002 study by the Computer Security Institute states that "78 percent of polled enterprises reported employee abuse of Internet access privileges by workers, including downloading pirated software or pornography, shopping on the Internet, and inappropriate use of e-mail systems."[5] This statistic shows that a significant number of employees are spending too much time on the computer performing non-work related activities. While some personal time on the computer is inevitable, excessive amounts can hurt the company's productivity in the long run.

Third, many companies have intellectual property and trade secrets that they need to protect. Monitoring employees is one way to keep tabs on their property and make sure it is not leaked out to a competitor. All an employee would have to do is accidentally or even purposely send an e-mail to the wrong person and it could end up out of the company's control. For example, last year the FBI caught employees from Coca-Cola trying to sell trade secrets to Pepsi.[6] Luckily for Coke, the people at Pepsi went straight to Coca-Cola when they were offered the information and the FBI began an investigation. However, this case demonstrates how easy it would be for one employee to harm a company by using e-mail inappropriately. Therefore, companies hope monitoring will help protect their intellectual property and catch an employee if they do intend to pass on secret information.

TABLE 1   Monitoring Programs

WinWhatWhere Investigator	This program can run on a computer without detection and can monitor and record all computer activity.[7]
Spector Software	This program takes snapshots of your computer screen at various time intervals.[8]
Little Brother Software	This program has a cost/benefit calculator that will approximate the cost of Internet browsing done by employees.[9]
Peek and Spy	This program allows employers to "peek" in on employees' computers. Using the "peek" function will let the employee know you are watching. However, using the "spy" function will let employers secretly look in on the employees.[10]

* Information from Bupp, 2001.

How Companies Monitor

Companies now have various ways to monitor employees in the workplace. They range from programs that block access to certain Internet sites to ones that record every keystroke ever typed on your computer (even ones that have been deleted). Some of the different programs companies use, along with their descriptions, are listed in Table 1.

Secret monitoring by employers is widespread.[11] Some employers automatically send copies of every e-mail to the sender's supervisor.[12] They can also use global positioning systems on employees' badges to allow them to record workers' movements.[13] In addition, 32 percent of employers even use video surveillance to watch employees, and of these organizations 20 percent do not inform workers they are being taped.[14]

Many people wonder how this type of uninformed monitoring can legally take place, since it seems to be a huge invasion of privacy. In reality, only two states—Connecticut and Delaware—require organizations to provide employees with notification of any monitoring that goes on within the company.[15] In fact, no federal law exists requiring any type of notification, and in general employers may monitor workers and record their communications without any written notice.[16] Therefore, employers are allowed to monitor employees in any way they see fit, if they are on company time and/or are using company resources.

The Electronic Communications Privacy Act (ECPA) is the only law that provides some protection regarding the monitoring of employees' e-mail. The ECPA "prohibits attempted interception and disclosure of the content of electronic messages and extends to private communication systems operated or subscribed to by most private employers."[17] Although it seems that this law would not allow employers to use private e-mail correspondence against employees, the law provides three exceptions that benefit the employer. These exceptions are listed in Table 2.

TABLE 2   Exceptions to the ECPA

- The consent exception allows the interception of electronic communications if one party has consented.
- The ordinary course of business exception gives employers the right to intercept employee communication if it is intercepted in the ordinary course of business.
- The provider exception states that if the employer provides the communication service, they are allowed to look at and disclose the information found in e-mail communications.[18]

* Information from Elmuti and Davis, 2006.

As you can tell from the third exception, if the employer is providing the e-mail service, they have the right to look at and disclose any information they find in an employee's e-mail. This one exception really does give the employer the upper hand when it comes to any litigation brought forth by a disgruntled worker. In fact, in the past, courts have consistently ruled on the side of the employer in cases brought against companies with regard to employee monitoring.[19]

Results of Monitoring

The monitoring of individuals has enabled employers to stop problems before they happen and to reprimand workers who have disobeyed corporate policies. The New York Times, Xerox Corp., and First Union Bank have apparently terminated employees after discovering improper use of company-provided Internet.[20] A *CIO Magazine* survey stated that 90 percent of chief information officers reported they would fire an employee if they used the company e-mail to sexually harass someone else.[21] Eighty-four percent stated they would fire someone for sending pornography to co-workers, and 80 percent would fire an employee for compromising trade secrets.[22]

The 2005 Electronic Monitoring & Surveillance Survey[23] co-sponsored by the American Management Association and the ePolicy Institute showed some very interesting results. Of the 526 companies that participated in the surveys, 56 percent had disciplined an employee for the misuse of e-mail or for the private use of company e-mail.[24] Of this 56 percent, 25 percent fired the employee, 33 percent gave a formal reprimand or warning, and the remaining 45 percent gave an informal reprimand or warning.[25] Sixty-one percent of the companies responding to the survey also said they have disciplined employees for the misuse or the private use of the office Internet connections.[26] Twenty-six percent of these have actually fired the employee for this infraction, with the remaining 59 percent either giving a formal or informal reprimand.[27] On the whole, it seems that the penalties can and do result in employees losing their jobs as a result of abusing Internet technology.

A Look to the Future

Overall, it appears that the monitoring of employees will continue to increase over the next few years. As technology continues to improve and more employees start using the Internet for work, it is inevitable that employers will need to know how employees spend their time. Employees should realize that any time spent on a computer at work should focus on work-related activities. And any communications being sent or received to a work e-mail address should be considered appropriate for anyone to read. Since employers are not required to let employees know when they are monitoring, it is up to the employee to be on their best behavior and to think twice before doing something even slightly inappropriate while on the job.

Discussion Questions

1. What are the drawbacks to constantly monitoring employees?
2. How would you handle being caught using company equipment to handle personal business?
3. When would it be appropriate for an employer to fire an employee for handling personal business while at work?

Endnotes

1. H. J. Wen, D. Schwieger, and P. Gershuny, "Internet Usage Monitoring in the Workplace: Its Legal Challenges and Implementation Strategies," *Information Systems Management* 24, no. 2 (2007), pp. 185–196.
2. D. Elmuti and H. H. Davis, "Not Worth the Bad Will," *Industrial Management* 48, no. 6 (2006), pp. 26–30.
3. R. L. Wakefield, "Computer Monitoring and Surveillance," *The CPA Journal* 74, no. 7 (2004), pp. 52–55.
4. *Ibid.*
5. G. D. Nord, T. F. McCubbins, and J. H. Nord, "E-monitoring in the Workplace: Privacy, Legislation, and Surveillance Software," *Communications of the ACM* 49, no. 8 (2006), p. 74.
6. Associated Press, "Three Arrested for Allegedly Stealing, Plotting to Sell Coca-Cola Recipes," June 5, 2006, www.foxnews.com/ printer_friendly_story/0,3566,202235,00. html (retrieved July, 2, 2007).
7. N. Bupp, "Big Brother and Big Boss Are Watching You," *Working USA* 5, no. 2 (2001), pp. 69–81.
8. *Ibid.*
9. *Ibid.*
10. *Ibid.*
11. G. S. Alder, M. L. Ambrose, and T. W. Noel, "The Effect of Formal Advance Notice and Justification on Internet Monitoring Fairness: Much about Nothing?" *Journal of Leadership and Organizational Studies* 13, no. 1 (2006), pp. 93–108.
12. J. Lloyd, "Management E-mail Monitoring Brings 'Big Brother' to Mind," *The Receivables Report for America's Health Care Financial Managers* 21, no. 1 (2006), pp. 6–7.
13. A. D. Moore, "Employee Monitoring and Computer Technology: Evaluative Surveillance vs. Privacy," *Business Ethics Quarterly* 10, no. 3 (2000), pp. 697–709.
14. American Management Association, "2005 Electronic Monitoring and Surveillance Survey: Many Companies Monitoring, Recording, Videotaping—And Firing—Employees," 2005, www.amanet.org/press/amanews/ems05.htm (retrieved July 1, 2007).

15. A. M. Everett, Y. Wong, and J. Paynter, "Balancing Employee and Employer Rights: An International Comparison of E-mail Privacy in the Workplace," *Journal of Individual Employment Rights* 11, no. 4 (2004–2005), pp. 291–310.

16. C. M. DePree and R. K. Jude, "Who's Reading Your Office E-mail? Is That Legal?" *Strategic Finance* 87, no. 10 (2006), pp. 45–47.

17. Elmuti and Davis, "Not Worth the Bad Will," p. 28.

18. *Ibid.,* p. 29.

19. R. L. Wakefield, "Computer Monitoring and Surveillance," *The CPA Journal* 74, no. 7 (2004), pp. 52–55.

20. Everett, Wong, and Paynter, "Balancing Employee and Employer Rights: An International Comparison of E-mail Privacy in the Workplace."

21. *Ibid.*

22. *Ibid.*

23. American Management Association, "2005 Electronic Monitoring and Surveillance Survey: Many Companies Monitoring, Recording, Videotaping—And Firing—Employees."

24. *Ibid.*

25. *Ibid.*

26. *Ibid.*

27. *Ibid.*

10. USING E-SENSORS TO IMPROVE NONVERBAL COMMUNICATION IN BUSINESS

Matthew O'Rourke, Sam Houston State University

There is more to communication than the words that are used. A number of nonverbal communication factors have been identified but have been, until now, impossible to objectively measure. Electronic sensors capable of measuring anything from alterations in voice pitch to body language have been invented and are being used to improve the effectiveness of communication between individuals. This article will discuss the nonverbal factors of communication events, explain the ways that sensors can now measure nonverbal communication, and investigate ways that this information could be used in a business setting to improve internal and external communication.

What Is Communication?

How do we communicate? What is the most important part of communicating a message effectively? Is it the words that are used? Or is it the tone of voice or body language used by the communicator? Perhaps some sort of middle ground? The truth is that there are a number of factors in any communication event. The words used (verbal communication) are important, as are things like tone of voice, variation in pitch, body language, eye contact, proximity to the message receiver, and others (nonverbal communication). The equation that determines the effectiveness of the message can get more convoluted when more nonverbal channels of communication are used (in other words, you can monitor the body language of a person in a face-to-face conversation but not when you talk to them on the phone).

"Man is the rational animal."

—Aristotle

Philosophers have been investigating the foundation of communication for centuries. Aristotle defined "man" (humans) as the "rational animal."[1] Aristotle differentiated humans from all other animals in the kingdom by our ability to reason, and it is our ability to reason that allows us to communicate using language. Rationality allows us to create "words" that are symbolic of objects, ideas, feeling, actions, and other things, and communicate with other humans that understand the meaning of the words.[2] Without our ability to reason, there would be no way for you, the reader, to understand the words on this page. Without rationality there is no language, and without language, there is no communication, right? Aristotle would have you believe so.

Aristotle was one of the first individuals to develop a theory of communication. His theory was largely targeted for persuasion/public speaking situations. Aristotle's model consists of three parts: the speaker, the message, and the audience.[3] Aristotle believed that the speaker was active in the communication process and was responsible for developing a message that is meant to influence the audience.[4] The speaker uses his ability to reason when developing the message and, according to Aristotle, the words that are used are the key to developing a message that impacts the audience in the way that the speaker desires. In other words, Aristotle believed that words (verbal communication) *were* communication.

Is Man the Semi-Rational Animal?

Several philosophers, psychologists, and scientists over the past several centuries have challenged Aristotle's argument. Contrary to Aristotle's beliefs, we now know that words are not all that are involved in communication, although they are what most people (including Aristotle) consider to be the "focus" of any communication event.

First, it is important to remember that during Aristotle's times, the idea of evolution had yet to be introduced. Prior to the existence of Homo sapiens, animals were able to communicate with each other through other means. Grunts, postures, eye contact, and a number of other behaviors were the basis of communication for animals and continue to be today for all nonhuman animals. These animals (and early humans) were able to communicate without the use of a "formal" language, which points to another aspect of communication that is separate from the words used. We now refer to this other part of communication as "nonverbal communication."

Scientific studies focusing on nonverbal communication did not begin until many years after Aristotle's death. Today, we know that several facets of communication exist and that humans can employ multiple channels to communicate. The most obvious channel is the language: the words used to convey a message. Most of us probably ascribe to Aristotle's theory and consider this to be the most important part of interactions with others.

Nonverbal cues are also used to communicate: things like tone of voice, body language, eye contact, and so on.[5,6] Studies focusing on measuring the influence of nonverbal communication have become more and more popular in the past 50 years.

Perhaps the most famous study in the area of nonverbal communication patterns was published by Albert Mehrabian in his 1971 book, *Silent Messages*. Mehrabian proposed that there are three factors to communication:[7]

- Words (the actual words and our ability, through reason, to understand their meanings and the associated implications)
- Tone of voice
- Body language (posture, movements, eye contact, proximity of sender/receiver, and others)

Mehrabian used self-reported responses to determine if different factors played larger or smaller roles in leaving an impression on a message receiver. Mehrabian concluded that only 7 percent of a message's impact is conveyed with the actual words used. Tone of voice was reported to account for 38 percent of the message's interpretation, and body language accounted for 55 percent of the message's interpretation.[8]

Although this study did not point out the roles of the three factors in everyday communication, it did shed some empirical evidence on the idea that there is much more to communication than the words we use. Mehrabian also concluded that in cases where the verbal and nonverbal parts of the message disagree, people are more likely to give nonverbal factors more weight when developing an impression of the message.[9]

This should come as no surprise. Most people can recall instances where a person told them one thing with words but the overall impression of the message was contrary to the words used. What is surprising is the contrast between Mehrabian's conclusions and the claims of Aristotle. Aristotle proposed a theory of communication that was based largely on the words used, whereas Mehrabian's study revealed that nonverbal factors can account for a much larger piece of the pie.

Following up on studies such as Mehrabian's was complicated by the fact that nonverbal factors were, until recently, impossible to objectively measure. However, modern technology has given us the ability to objectively measure some of the nonverbal factors of communication and that knowledge has the potential to change the effectiveness of work place communication.

The Use of Electronic Sensors to Monitor Nonverbal Communication

Researchers at the Human Dynamics Group at the Massachusetts Institute of Technology (MIT) Media Lab have developed a number of electronic sensors to objectively measure nonverbal communication techniques such as tone of voice, proximity, and body language.[10] They believe that collecting data about nonverbal communication patterns can be used to help improve the communication effectiveness of individuals in a given setting (for example, in an office).

In one case, they worked with a British call center outsourcing company, Vertex Data Services, to attempt to improve the effectiveness of call center operators. The MIT group used sensors to measure the speech patterns of operators during calls with customers. The group did not measure the actual words used by the operator and only focused on variations in tone and pitch of voice as well as the amount of time that the operator spent talking versus listening to the caller.[11]

The group concluded that successful operators spend more time listening than talking and use strong fluctuations in their voice amplitude and pitch to suggest interest and responsiveness to the customer's needs. After only a few seconds of measuring these factors, the group was accurately able to predict the eventual success or failure of a call the majority of the time.[12]

The MIT group has also developed instruments capable of measuring personal movements. In a separate study, the group simulated face-to-face salary negotiations and was able to accurately predict the "winner" of the negotiation with 87 percent accuracy after only five minutes of measuring body movements and speech patterns.[13]

Factors like proximity to others and body language (movements) can also be measured and considered in the communication event. The researchers believe that these factors have effects on social communication effectiveness, such as in group or team settings.[14] Equipped with the proper amount of data, the MIT group and others could optimize the communication effectiveness within an organization. The ability to do this in a business setting could have huge implications for company success or failure.

Nonverbal Communication in Business

The ability to effectively communicate internally and externally is key to a successful business. However, communicating effectively continues to be a problem in many businesses. People working in teams often have trouble communicating, the flow of information within an organization is difficult to track, and every company can always have better customer service. The problem appears to be our continued focus on the words used to convey a message instead of considering all facets of the communication event (verbal and nonverbal factors).[15]

With today's technology, the problem of objectively measuring nonverbal communication factors is becoming obsolete, and studies being conducted today could have huge implications for strategies to improve communication effectiveness in the business world.

Using Electronic Sensors to Improve Nonverbal Business Communication

Incorporating knowledge about effective nonverbal communication patterns has the potential to radically change the effectiveness of communication in a business setting, resulting in higher performance for the business. Companies can incorporate this technology into their operations in many way, so as to improve their performance.

Hiring Decisions

Several positions within an organization are more communication intense than others. For example, a customer service representative or salesperson will do more communicating that is directly related to company success than a database administrator. Thus, if a company is able to determine that individuals that use many variations in their voice tone and pitch during conversations with customers are more successful than individuals that speak with little variations in their voice, they could use that information to target new employees that naturally speak with many variations. Alternatively, they could train the customer service representatives to use their voices more effectively. Likewise, certain communication patterns could be identified within a successful team in the company and the manager could use that information when looking for new members or replacements.

Groups and Teams

"Groupthink" is a problem that many corporations suffer from when using teams. The theory behind groupthink is that individuals often conform to the perceived "group consensus" despite their personal reservations. Sensors capable of objectively measuring nonverbal communication behaviors could potentially help prevent groupthink.[16]

E-sensors that measure nonverbal communication will raise awareness of individual nonverbal communication patterns. Perhaps one or two individuals in the team are overbearing and do not realize that their nonverbal behaviors encourage others to timidly conform instead of voicing their opinions. Monitoring the nonverbal behaviors of all team members could help prevent timid conformity.[17]

Additionally, the MIT group believes that they could eventually use sensors to select team members with complementary nonverbal communication styles such that the team is "optimized" for effectively communicating messages. Further, they believe they can create "smart environments" capable of monitoring a team's interactions and identifying nonverbal behaviors that could potentially have negative effects on communication in *real time*, allowing them to proactively identify and prevent communication breakdowns.[18]

Formal Meetings

Formal meetings can be a breeding ground for poor communication techniques. Meetings should be focused and directed at sharing relevant information with those involved. However, managers running formal meetings are often left wondering why the topics that they discussed in the previous meeting are still in question. This could be a result of meeting participants being confused as they receive incongruent verbal and nonverbal messages in the meeting. Perhaps the manager is not using enough variation in their voice or body language to convey the importance of the message. The use of electronic sensors in the meeting could show the manager what is confusing the meeting participants and could eventually lead to much more effective and efficient meetings.

Informal Communication

A large portion of communication within a business takes place in "informal" settings. Conversations at water coolers, happy hour, in the hallway, and so on are largely responsible for spreading messages throughout a company. Nonverbal communication is a part of how these messages are interpreted, and one could argue that the negative impact of poor nonverbal communication could be much greater, as the informal situation in which the communication event takes place may weaken the self-awareness of the message sender. Using sensors to monitor nonverbal communication among co-workers in informal settings and using the data to suggest ways to improve the communication would likely result in more people being on the same page. Factors such as proximity, body language, voice tone and pitch variation, and others could be measured and considered.

For example, perhaps Bob from the accounting department has a habit of standing uncomfortably close to people when he talks to them, and those people become so uncomfortable standing next to Bob that they are not able to focus on what he is saying. Wearable electronic sensors are capable of tracking how close people are to each other during communication events.[19] In this particular case, data can be collected that compare the proximity of individuals during their informal communication events. Bob will see empirical evidence that he stands the closest to others during conversations and that his messages are also the least likely to be conveyed effectively. Bob will then become aware of his proximity to others during conversations and give them more space, allowing them to relax and concentrate on what he is trying to tell them.

Monitoring the Flow of Information

Another difficulty that many companies face is the ability to monitor how information flows within the organization. With so many communication channels to choose from when passing information throughout the company (e-mail, phone calls, formal meetings, informal "water cooler talk," and so on), it should be no surprise that people in the same department often hear about important information from different sources. E-sensors can be used to monitor the way information passes from one person to another.[20]

For example, say a company executive has a meeting every Wednesday afternoon with department managers where important issues and projects are discussed. The department managers are then responsible for passing the information from the meeting to their employees. Using sensors to track the managers will allow the company to get a picture of how the information from the executive meeting is passed throughout the different departments. Perhaps they will discover that the Marketing manager (who incidentally leads a department that is commonly known within the company to be a couple steps behind) leaves the company campus immediately after the meeting every Wednesday for lunch and then returns to his department where he speaks with a couple of individuals in the department before returning to his office to return phone calls. The Marketing manager then holds a formal meeting on Thursday morning with his department where, among other things, the topics from Wednesday's executive meeting are discussed.

On the other hand, the manager of the Accounting department returns to his department immediately after the Wednesday meeting where he has a quick formal meeting with all of his employees. The manager of the Finance department returns to his office after the Wednesday meeting and sends out a bulk e-mail to all members of his department discussing important topics from the executive meeting. Armed with this kind of information, executives will quickly be able to see why members of the Accounting and Finance departments are generally "in the know" while the Marketing department is not. The company will be able to implement strategies to improve the way in which information is passed throughout the Marketing department. Additionally, the company will be able to create a "map" of the organization that shows "hot spots" of key information, which will allow employees to tap into information resources more accurately.[21]

External Service to Customers and Clients

Customer service is another area where data about nonverbal communication patterns can be used to benefit the company. The example of Vertex Data Services' use of electronic monitoring of their call center operators was given earlier. The company was able to use the information they collected from the monitoring to improve the service they provided, and their performance.

However, call centers are not the only way companies can use electronic sensors to improve their nonverbal communication. Salespeople/teams and customer service personnel (for example, receptionists at hotels) could also receive valuable information from studies like the one conducted at Vertex. Again, the goal is to improve the level of service that customers receive, resulting in more business or a better reputation for the company. For example, the following excerpt from an article about customer service in the tourism and hospitality industry speaks to the need to provide great customer service, especially when the customer is not happy. Again, nonverbal communication plays a key role.

> Following service failure, customers are desirous of getting their problems or elements of their dissatisfaction resolved as quickly as possible and, in doing so, they have certain expectations with respect to service providers' behavior. During this period of anxiety, customers are particularly vigilant to notice nonverbal cues in an attempt to discern the service provider's intentions and attitudes regarding helping them. In such situations, the display of inappropriate nonverbal cues (e.g., frowning, lack of eye contact, closed body posture, etc.) is likely to create even more negative feelings on the part of the customer . . . (p. 218).[22]

The ability to objectively measure nonverbal communication with electronic sensors and use that information to convey the most successful nonverbal message would be incredibly beneficial to an organization that regularly has employees in the aforementioned situation.

Additionally, with the emergence of a worldwide economy, more and more companies are operating on an international level. Acceptable nonverbal communication varies from culture to culture and it is possible that the use of electronic sensors can be used to train international salespeople in the most effective nonverbal communication patterns for the country that they will be working in. The result will be more sales for the company.

Finally, independent agencies (such as advertising firms) and/or individuals within a corporation who participate in B2B relationships with other professionals could benefit from the use of sensors that measure nonverbal communication. These individuals regularly meet with clients and other executives where they give presentations. The ability to learn the most effective nonverbal communication patterns (such as conveying confidence in your message) will greatly benefit these individuals as they will be able to communicate in the most effective way with their clients. This may prove especially beneficial in meetings where the news is not positive and may help maintain and/or improve relationships with their clients.

Conclusion

Humans consider verbal and nonverbal factors when interpreting a message that is communicated to them. Until recently, no objective way existed to measure and consequently optimize nonverbal communication factors. The invention of a number of electronic sensors that can measure nonverbal cues during a communication event now allows people to learn if and when their verbal and nonverbal messages are in conflict. These sensors have the ability to drastically influence the behaviors of individuals in a business setting and can be used to improve the daily operations of the business from making hiring decisions to improving customer service and monitoring the flow of information within a corporation.

Discussion Questions

1. What implications are there for today's growing preference for "rational-based" methods of communication (those that nearly eliminate nonverbal aspects, such as e-mail, text messaging, and instant messaging)?

2. What are the ethical issues surrounding the monitoring of employees' nonverbal communication in the workplace? Does it violate their right to privacy? Would you be willing to participate in similar studies/programs at your organization?

Endnotes

1. Aristotle, "Metaphysica" (W. D. Ross, Trans.) in R. McKeon, ed., *The Basic Works of Aristotle* (New York: Random House, 2001), pp. 681–926.

2. *Ibid.*

3. Aristotle, "Rhetorica" (W. Rhys Roberts, Trans.) in R. McKeon, ed., *The Basic Works of Aristotle* (New York: Random House, 2001), pp. 317–451.

4. *Ibid.*

5. Wikipedia, http://en.wikipedia.org/wiki/Nonverbal_and_Gestural_Communication (retrieved November 3, 2008).

6. A. Mehrabian, "Nonverbal Communication," *Nebraska Symposium on Motivation,* 1971, pp. 107–61, www.kaaj.com/psych/articles/NonverbalCommunication.pdf (retrieved November 3, 2008).

7. Wikipedia, http://en.wikipedia.org/wiki/Albert_Mehrabian (retrieved November 3, 2008).

8. *Ibid.*

9. *Ibid.*

10. A. Pentland, *Honest Signals: How They Shape Our World* (Boston: MIT Press, 2008).

11. M. Buchanan, "The Science of Subtle Signals," Strategy + *Business Online,* www.strategy-business.com/press/article/07307?pg=all&tid=230 (retrieved June 30, 2008).

12. *Ibid.*

13. *Ibid.*

14. *Ibid.*

15. *Ibid.*

16. *Ibid.*

17. *Ibid.*

18. *Ibid.*

19. *Ibid.*

20. *Ibid.*

21. *Ibid.*

22. D. S. Sundaram and C. Webster, "The Role of Nonverbal Communication in Service Encounters," in S. Kusluvan, ed., *Managing Employee Attitudes and Behaviors in the Tourism and Hospitality Industries,* pp. 209–21, http://books.google.com/books?hl=en&lr=&id=eQp1t_lHgzwC&oi=fnd&pg=PA209&dq=non+verbal+communication&ots=uIS16qz41p&sig=6gt1u31unOAjYAEipYS-8PjhYS0#PPA218,M1 (retrieved November 3, 2008).

Index